Lecture Notes in Computer Science 5002

Commenced Publication in 1973
Founding and Former Series Editors:
Gerhard Goos, Juris Hartmanis, and Jan van Leeuwen

Holger Giese (Ed.)

Models in Software Engineering

Workshops and Symposia at MoDELS 2007
Nashville, TN, USA, September 30 - October 5, 2007
Reports and Revised Selected Papers

 Springer

Volume Editor

Holger Giese
Hasso-Plattner-Institut
für Softwaresystemtechnik
Prof.-Dr.-Helmert-Str. 2-3
14482 Potsdam, Germany
E-mail: holger.giese@hpi.uni-potsdam.de

Library of Congress Control Number: 2008930116

CR Subject Classification (1998): D.2, D.3, I.6, K.6

LNCS Sublibrary: SL 2 – Programming and Software Engineering

ISSN 0302-9743
ISBN 978-3-540-69069-6 Springer Berlin Heidelberg New York

Springer is a part of Springer Science+Business Media

springer.com

© Springer-Verlag Berlin Heidelberg 2008

Typesetting: Camera-ready by author, data conversion by Scientific Publishing Services, Chennai, India
Printed on acid-free paper   SPIN: 12282005   06/3180   5 4 3 2 1 0

Preface

Following the tradition of previous instances of the MoDELS conference series, 11 workshops and two symposia were hosted in 2007. These satellite events complemented the main conference by providing room for important subject areas and enabling a high degree of interactivity.

The selection of the workshops was organized like in former instances of the MoDELS conference series by a Workshop Selection Committee. The following well-known experts agreed to serve on this committee:

- Gabor Karsai, Vanderbilt University, USA
- Thomas Kühne, Darmstadt University of Technology, Germany
- Jochen Küster, IBM Research Zurich, Switzerland
- Henry Muccini, University of L'Aquila, Italy
- Sebastian Uchitel, Imperial College London, UK

The workshops provided collaborative forums for particular topics. They enabled a group of participants to exchange recent and/or preliminary results, to conduct intensive discussions, or to coordinate efforts between representatives of a technical community. They served as forums for lively discussion of innovative ideas, recent progress, or practical experience on model-driven engineering for specific aspects, specific problems, or domain-specific needs.

As in previous editions, there were a Doctoral Symposium and an Educators' Symposium. The Doctoral Symposium provided specific support for PhD students to discuss their work and receive useful guidance for the completion of their dissertation research. The Educators' Symposium addressed how to educate students as well as practitioners to move from traditional thinking to an engineering approach based on models.

These satellite-event proceedings published after the conference include summaries as well as revised versions of up to two best papers from the workshops, the Doctoral Symposium, and the Educators' Symposium.

I am grateful to the members of the Selection Committee who did a great job in reviewing the workshop proposals and selecting the best workshops. In particular Thomas Kühne (member of the Selection Committee and my predecessor as Workshop Chair) was of great help to me and eased my work by generously sharing his experiences from the former year with me.

February 2008   Holger Giese

Sponsoring Institutions

 ACM Special Interest Group on Software Engineering
(www.sigsoft.org)

 IEEE Computer Society
(www.computer.org)

Table of Contents

Model Size Metrics

Model-Based Design of Trustworthy Health Information Systems

Model-Driven Engineering, Verification and Validation

Ocl4All: Modelling Systems with OCL

Models@run.time

Multi-Paradigm Modeling: Concepts and Tools

Quality in Modeling

Doctoral Symposium

Educators' Symposium

11th International Workshop on Aspect-Oriented Modeling

Jörg Kienzle[1], Jeff Gray[2], Dominik Stein[3], Walter Cazzola[4],
Omar Aldawud[5], and Tzilla Elrad[6]

[1] McGill University, Canada
[2] University of Alabama at Birmingham, USA
[3] University of Duisburg-Essen, Germany
[4] University of Milano, Italy
[5] Lucent Technologies, USA
[6] Illinois Institute of Technology, USA

joerg.kienzle@mcgill.ca, gray@cis.uab.edu,
dominik.stein@icb.uni-due.de, cazzola@dico.unimi.it,
oaldawud@lucent.com, elrad@iit.edu

Abstract. This report summarizes the results and discussions from the 11th Workshop on Aspect-Oriented Modeling (AOM). The workshop was held in conjunction with the International Conference on Model-Driven Engineering, Languages, and Systems (MODELS), which was located in Nashville, Tennessee, on September 30, 2007. Over 20 researchers and practitioners attended the workshop with various backgrounds in aspect-oriented software development and software model engineering. The workshop provided a forum for discussing the state of the art in modeling crosscutting concerns at different stages of the software development process: requirements elicitation and analysis, software architecture, detailed design, and mapping to aspect-oriented programming constructs. This workshop summary provides an overview of the accepted submissions and summarizes the results of the different discussion groups. Papers, presentation slides, and photos from the workshop are available at http://www.aspect-modeling.org/.

1 Introduction

This brief summary reports on the outcomes of the *11th International Aspect-Oriented Modeling Workshop*. The workshop took place at the Marriott Hotel in Nashville, Tennessee, on Sunday, September 30, 2007. The workshop was part of the *10th International Conference on Model Driven Engineering Languages and Systems – (MODELS 2007)*. A total of 10 position papers were submitted and reviewed by the program committee, 7 of which were accepted to the workshop. Over 20 participants attended the presentation session and took part in afternoon working group discussions. Papers, presentation slides, and further information can be found at the workshop website, which is at http://www.aspect-modeling.org/. The website also has links to the previous editions of the workshop.

The rest of this report is structured as follows: Section 2 provides a general overview of the motivation, goals, and challenges of aspect-oriented modeling.

H. Giese (Ed.): MoDELS 2007 Workshops, LNCS 5002, pp. 1–6, 2008.

Section 3 gives a summary of the papers that have been accepted to this workshop. Section 4 outlines the results of the discussion groups. Finally, section 5 concludes the report.

2 Overview to Aspect-Oriented Modeling

Aspect-orientation is a rapidly advancing technology. New and powerful aspect-oriented programming techniques are presented at many international venues every year. However, aspect-oriented software development techniques are often deeply-rooted in the "intimate essence" of a program, i.e., the syntax and structure of its code. As a consequence, developers may easily be overwhelmed with implementation details, while loosing track of the intentions and goals of the interacting (formerly crosscutting) concerns, as well as of where and how they interact. Aspect-oriented modeling has the potential to provide the necessary tool for abstracting from the essence of the problem and for taking root in the semantic nature of the interacting concerns and their interaction.

Over the last five years, much research work has been presented at the various editions of this workshop, which all aim at helping developers not to get lost in the "code space" and its associated accidental complexities. Consolidating that work, three important fields of research have emerged that are frequently and recurrently tackled by different researchers.

One major field of research is concerned with finding appropriate modeling abstractions for aspect-oriented programming language constructs, such as pointcuts, advice, introductions, stateful aspects, aspect-oriented hooks and connectors. The options are usually to define a new modeling language or modeling notation, or to extend an existing one. The goal is to provide aspect-oriented software developers with appropriate means to facilitate the analysis of their problems as well as the design of their solutions. The challenge is to find the right level of abstraction so that the invented modeling means are suitable for a variety of problems as well as for a variety of aspect-oriented implementation techniques (e.g., languages and frameworks).

Another major field of research is concerned with bringing forth the benefits of aspect-orientation to the modeling level and, thus, to model-driven development. Much work in this field of research is concerned with model transformation, model composition, and/or model weaving. One key question is to determine the similarities, differences and relationships between these terms and techniques. A frequent issue that emerges is to what extent conventional transformation techniques can be used to implement aspect-oriented model weavers. The ultimate goal is to free aspect-oriented software developers from the need of using aspect-oriented programming languages.

Yet another field for research that attained much research efforts recently is the specification of validation and verification frameworks for aspect-oriented software. Key concerns in this field include the detection of conflicts between different aspects, the confirmation whether or not aspects affect the correct points in the base application, and the disclosure of the presence of crosscutting in software. Some of the key questions are focused on the formalisms that should be used, how such formalisms can be adopted to aspect-orientation, and how its application can be facilitated for the ordinary aspect-oriented software developer.

These three core research concerns represent a non-exclusive list. Multiple researchers have addressed many other issues. Several of the papers presented at the current workshop edition fall into the second category. The workshop discussions considered all of these issues and other concerns, as noted in the next two sections.

3 Summary of Accepted Position Papers

Jon Whittle from Lancaster University, UK, presented MATA [1], an approach to aspect-oriented modeling that can be applied to any modeling language with a well-defined meta-model. MATA provides expressive composition mechanisms. The weaving in MATA is based on graph transformations, and hence any composition technique is possible. MATA also provides support for detecting some aspect interactions automatically. The MATA tool is implemented as a bridge between IBM Rational Software Modeler (RSM) and Attributed Graph Grammar System (AGG).

Frank Fleurey from IRISA/INRIA in France presented a generic approach for automatic model composition [2]. In the approach, the two models that are to be composed are first pre-processed, then merged, and finally the resulting model is post-processed. The composition is signature-based: if a signature matches, the elements are merged and recursively processed; in case there is no match, both elements are copied to the target model. He presented a reusable composition framework, in which a meta-model is extended to obtain a "composable meta-model": mergeable model elements have to define *getSignature* operations that allow the composition algorithm to match them. Special signatures have to be defined that make sense for each model element.

Hua Xiao from Queens University, Canada, presented an approach to weave business requirements into model transformations [3]. He argued that there is a gap between the business domain, the concerns of business stakeholders, and the technical domain, as considered by the developers. With their work, the authors want to help to integrate business requirements into generic design models and implementation models. BPEL (Business Process Engineering Language) is too limited to represent all requirements specified by the business analysts. The authors use AOM techniques to enhance a primary BPEL model with other concerns such as time, cost, resource usage, performance, and frequency. A weaver combines the BPEL and aspect models to yield a composed model, which is wrapped and can then be fed to a simulation engine. After the simulation, the developer can validate the successful achievement of business requirements (e.g., compare revenue and cost per request).

Stefan Van Baelen from the Katholieke Universiteit Leuven, Belgium, presented an approach that composes application models and security models [4]. He highlighted the fact that security concerns are very spread out through an application and cannot easily be isolated in an application layer. He compared the advantages and disadvantages of the classical AOP approach, the MDD approach (a security-independent application model is transformed to a security-aware application model, then mapped to an execution platform), and the AOM approach: generate a woven model, and then generate OOP code. They also support generation of CeasarJ code. Their approach allows the definition of company-wide access policies, which can be woven into many applications. At run-time, the application contacts an authorization engine to check access rights. The sample application he showed defined concepts with a UML class diagram. Access policy subjects and objects are also represented in UML class diagrams, and then "merged" or assigned to each other.

Jaime Pavlich-Mariscal from the University of Connecticut, USA, presented his position paper on how to enhance UML to model custom security aspects [5]. He first presented different access control models (RBAC, MAC and DAC), and highlighted that UML does not explicitly support any of them. Also, it is not easily possible to use capabilities of different access control models in combination. As a result, traceability of access control policies is also difficult to achieve. Their approach adds four security-specific models, which are then composed with the application model to create a security-aware model. Security features that can be modeled include: positive/negative permissions, MAC or delegation rules. Model composition is achieved by merging meta-models.

Jörg Kienzle from McGill University, Canada presented an aspect-oriented modeling approach for specifying reusable aspect models [6]. His aspect models define structure using class diagrams, and behavior using sequence diagrams. The weaver, based on existing class diagram and sequence diagram weavers, is capable of weaving aspects with other aspects or base models. In his talk, Jörg demonstrated the high degree of reusability of the aspect models by modeling the design of 8 inter-dependent aspects of the *AspectOptima* case study, an aspect framework that implements support for transactions. Based on this experience, he identified several modeling language features that seem essential to support reusable aspect modeling.

Steffen Zschaler from the University of Dresden, Germany, presented a talk entitled "Aspect-Orientation for your Language of Choice" [7]. He presented *Reuseware*, a tool based on invasive software composition that makes it possible to define fragments of models, where each fragment can define interfaces in forms of slots. Later, elements identified as anchors within one model can be bound to the slots in another model using queries based on pattern-matching expressions.

4 Overview of Discussion Topics

This section offers a summary of the most interesting and significant issues that were addressed during the discussion sessions. These issues also emerged during the questions and comments in the presentation sessions.

What are the characteristics of a good aspect modeling language? Participants in the aspect composition group considered this question and stated that a good aspect modeling language would have a rigorous semantic definition with a mixture of external and internal behavior descriptions. A question arose in the discussion regarding whether the aspect modeling language needed to be similar to the base modeling language. If the modeled concern is close to the domain, there may be benefits in having the aspect and base modeling languages similar.

Should an aspect modeling language be standardized? There was an overwhelming consensus that it is too early to have a standardized aspect modeling language. At this stage of AOM maturity, standardization may be too restrictive because no aspect language fits all concerns. An aspect modeling language that is too general may lose its usefulness. Dedicated formalisms can have specific meaning, purpose, and analysis capabilities.

What is the current status of model composition languages to address crosscutting concerns? Current model composition languages are very low-level and force a model engineer to bind too early in the life cycle. Precise bindings may be uncertain at early stages of development (e.g., there may not be clearly defined connections between early aspects and aspects in design). There is a need to model composition relationships over several abstraction levels. Some of the questions that remain to be answered include: Is a simple linear progression through the development phases too naïve? How soon should the aspect binding be realized? How to manage relationships in aspect models (e.g., new relationships appearing and old relationships disappearing)?

What modeling language features enable the creation of reusable aspect models? A reusable aspect model should not refer to any base model element directly, or prescribe a binding to a particular base model element, or depend on the existence of a specific base element. A modeling formalism supporting reuse must provide means to define reusable aspect models in a base model independent way. Mappings between the reusable aspect model and the base should be established in separate bindings. In order to create reusable aspect libraries, the modeling formalism must be able to provide a means to describe aspect specifications, as well as the contexts in which the reusable aspect can be applied. Ideally, a means for detecting conflicts among reusable aspects when they are applied to the same base model should be provided as well.

5 Concluding Remarks

The workshop continued the tradition of having a very diverse representation of participants. The authors came from nine different countries (Argentina, Belgium, Canada, France, Germany, Luxembourg, Netherlands, United Kingdom, and the United States.); likewise, the organizing and programming committees represented eleven countries (Belgium, Canada, France, Germany, Ireland, Italy, Netherlands, Portugal, Switzerland, United Kingdom, and the United States.). In addition to the geographical diversity, the AOM workshop also attracted participants with wide research interests in aspects across the entire spectrum of the development lifecycle. As a result, this provided opportunities for a variety of opinions that were well-informed from the accumulated experience of the participants.

The workshop provided a forum for presenting new ideas and discussing the state of research and practice in modeling various kinds of crosscutting concerns at different levels of abstraction. The workshop identified and discussed the impacts of aspect-oriented technologies on model engineering to provide software developers with general modeling means to express aspects and their crosscutting relationships onto other software artifacts. This workshop report is a summary of the activities for those who could not attend the workshop and provides an opportunity to gain insights to these issues, and to initiate a future research agenda in the field of aspect-oriented modeling.

Acknowledgements

We would like to thank the program committee members who have helped to assure the quality of this workshop: Mehmet Aksit (University of Twente), Aswin van den Berg (Motorola Labs), Thomas Cottenier (Illinois Institute of Technology), Sudipto Ghosh (Colorado State University), Stefan Hanenberg (University of Duisburg-Essen), Andrew Jackson (Trinity University), Jean-Marc Jézéquel (IRISA), Kim Mens (University Catholic of Louvain), Alfonso Pierantonio (University of Aquila), Awais Rashid (Lancaster University), Raghu Reddy (Rochester Institute of Technology), Ella Roubtsova (Open University, Netherlands), Bedir Tekinerdogan (University of Twenty), Markus Völter (Independent Consultant), and Jon Whittle (Lancaster University).

We also thank all submitters and workshop participants who helped to make this workshop a success.

References

[1] Whittle, J., Jayaraman, P.: MATA: A Tool for Aspect-Oriented Modeling based on Graph Transformation
[2] Fleurey, F., Baudry, B., France, R., Ghosh, S.: A Generic Approach For Automatic Model Composition
[3] Zou, Y., Xiao, H., Chan, B.: Weaving Business Requirements into Model Transformations
[4] Hovsepyan, A., Van Baelen, S., Yskout, K., Berbes, Y., Joosen, W.: Composing Application Models and Security Models: On the Value of Aspect- Oriented Technologies
[5] Pavlich-Mariscal, J., Michel, L., Demurjian, S.: Enhancing UML to Model Custom Security Aspects
[6] Klein, J., Kienzle, J.: Reusable Aspect Models
[7] Heidenreich, F., Johannes, J., Zschaler, S.: Aspect Orientation for Your Language of Choice

A Generic Approach for Automatic Model Composition

Franck Fleurey[1], Benoit Baudry[1], Robert France[2], and Sudipto Ghosh[2]

[1] IRISA/INRIA – Université de Rennes 1, Campus Universitaire de Beaulieu,
35042 Rennes, France
{bbaudry,ffleurey}@irisa.fr
[2] Colorado State University, Fort Collins, CO, USA
{france,ghosh}@cs.colostate.edu

Abstract. Analyzing and modelling a software system with separate views is a good practice to deal with complexity and maintainability. When adopting such a modular approach for modelling, it is necessary to have the ability to automatically compose models to build a global view of the system. In this paper we propose a generic framework for composition that is independent from a modelling language. We define a process for adapting this framework to particular modelling language (defined with a metamodel) and illustrate how the generic composition has been specialized for class diagrams.

1 Introduction

When using aspect-oriented modelling to build the model for a large system, the modellers identify different views. They model each view and reason about these separate models. They can also perform validation tasks on each model, for example using model checking techniques. Once all these models have been correctly built in isolation, it is necessary to compose these different models. The composed model can be used to

- check the global consistency of the system's model,
- better understand the interactions across the composed views
- analyze interactions to identify conflicts and undesirable emergent behaviours

When the models are small enough and developed by a single or a couple of designers, they can be composed manually. However, in most cases, the models are too large to be composed manually and it is necessary to develop an automatic composition operator to ensure that all the elements in the model are handled. Moreover, an automatic composition operator allows the designer to try different solutions for composition that correspond to different decision (e.g., try different orders for composition, or different solutions for one view…).

There exist several solutions to automatically compose models in different languages (class diagrams [1, 2], statecharts [3], sequence diagrams [4]…). If there is no composition operator for one modelling language, it is necessary to build a completely new operator for this language. In the future, there might be more and more domain-specific modelling language developed for model-driven development.

H. Giese (Ed.): MoDELS 2007 Workshops, LNCS 5002, pp. 7–15, 2008.
© Springer-Verlag Berlin Heidelberg 2008

In that case, we do not want to generate a new algorithm and a new environment for each language. It becomes necessary to reuse algorithmic and design knowledge from composition operators in other languages.

In this paper we propose a generic framework for automatic model composition. There are two main steps for composition: matching and merging. The matching step is specific to a modelling language. It specifies which element in the language can match and how they can match. The merge step can be defined independently from any language. The framework we propose implements a generic merge operator. It defines, how two model elements that match are merged, as well as a mechanism for conflict detection. The framework also implements a language to specify composition directives as they are defined by Reddy et al. [2] and specifies a clear interface to specify a match operator. This framework can then be specialized for a particular metamodel in order to add composition capabilities to a particular language.

In section 2 we discuss the generic framework for model composition. In section 3 we explain how this framework can be specialized to add composition capabilities to a particular metamodel and in section 4 we illustrate this specialization on an example.

2   A Generic Framework for Model Composition

This section describes the generic composition algorithm that is implemented in the generic composition framework. The composition mechanism implemented in this framework is structured in two major steps:

1   **Matching:** Identifies model elements that describe the same concepts in the different models that have to be composed.
2   **Merging:** Matched model elements are merged to create new model elements that represent an integrated view of the concepts.

The merging operator builds a new model from two models. It merges elements that match according to the matching operator and creates new elements in the target composed model. This operator is independent of a specific domain. It consists in going through the set of elements that match in both input models and if they can be merged the operator creates a new model element in the output model. If the elements can not be merged, a conflict is detected that has to be solved. This happens when elements that match based on a subset of their properties (*e.g.*, when merging two class diagrams, classes with same names match) can not be merged because of other properties that do not match (*e.g.*, if there is one concrete class and one abstract class). The whole process of conflict detection and model elements creation is generic.

The semantics of matching is domain specific. The knowledge for detecting model elements that describe the same concept is based on information dependent on the meaning of the model. Thus, the matching operation has to be specialized for each modelling language. However, in order to interact correctly with the merging operator, the matching operator has to have a clear interface.

The generic framework described in this section implements the behaviour of the merging operator and offers a precise interface for the definition of the matching operator. The framework can then be specialized by providing specific matching operators through this interface.

2.1   Generic Framework for Composition

Figure 1 describes the class diagram of the generic composition framework. It defines the interface of a matching operator for a specific metamodel and it implements the merging operator that is independent of any metamodel.

The abstract operation getSignature in MERGEABLE has to be specialized to define the algorithm for matching elements. The getSignature operation defines the signature of the model elements. This signature is compared with the signature of other model elements to check if these elements have to be merged. A default comparison is implemented in the equals operation of STRINGSIGNATURE. This operation can be specialized in other subclasses of SIGNATURE in order to compare signatures which are more complex than simple strings.

For example, two methods in a class diagram can match because they have the same name or because they have the same name and the same parameters. In the first case, the getSignature operation will return the name of the methods and the default equals is sufficient. In the second case getSignature will return the name and the list of parameters and it is necessary to redefine the equals operation.

The merge operation in class MERGEABLE implements the generic algorithm for merging two model elements. The complete algorithm is defined in [5]. If two model elements match according to their signature, this operation tries to merge them into a new model elements. The algorithm compares the values of each property of the elements to merge to detect possible conflict. If no conflict is detected the new model element is created, otherwise the conflict must be solved using composition directives.

The class CompositionContext contains the data structures and utility methods that are used by the merge operation in order to create the merged elements and keep a traceability information between the input models and the composed model.

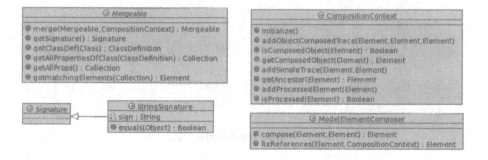

Fig. 1. Generic framework for Composition

2.2   The Composition Directives

Modellers can specify composition directives that are used during composition to force matches, disallow merges, and to override default merge rules. Two types of composition directives are currently supported in the composition metamodel:

- **Pre-Merge Directives:** These directives specify simple model modifications that are to be made before the models are merged. These changes will force or disallow element matches. These directives can specify renaming model elements, removing or adding elements.
- **Post-Merge Directives:** These directives specify simple modifications to the merged model. For example, it may be the case that a security view requires the removal of associations that are present in other views. This restriction can be specified as post-merge directives that remove these associations from the merged model.

The language for model directives is domain independent and is part of the generic composition framework. The metamodel for this language is shown Figure 2. There are two main types of directives: CREATE and CHANGE directives. CREATE directives are used to create new model elements. CHANGE directives are used to modify model elements. These directives can be used to remove an element from a namespace, set a property value associated with an element, and add an element to a namespace. A CHANGE directive is associated with a reference to the model element it modifies.

A SET directive is associated with two instances of ELEMENTREF one is the target property and the other is the new value for the property. Elements can be reference by (1) a name that is an instance of NAMEREF, (2) their literal value, or (3) a unique identifier that is an instance of IDREF.

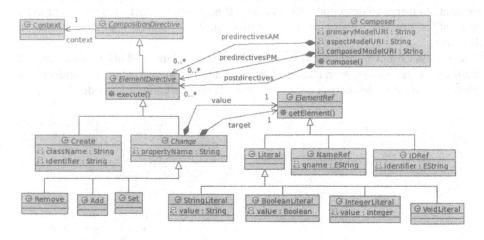

Fig. 2. The composition directives language

3 Specializing the Framework for a Particular Metamodel

This section summarizes how to specialize the generic framework to add composition capabilities to a metamodel. The framework has been defined in such a way that it can be specialized for any metamodel that conforms to EMOF. The specialization process is described in Figure 3.

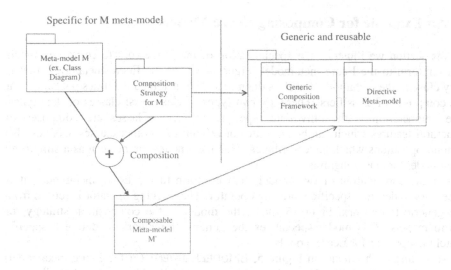

Fig. 3. Adding composition capabilities in a metamodel

To specialize the generic composition framework, for a metamodel M, it is necessary to define a *composition strategy*. This strategy specifies which elements of the metamodel can be merged. This consists in selecting the classes in the metamodel that will have composition capabilities, *i.e.*, the classes which instances will be composable in models that conform to M. The strategy defines the equality between elements, and the signature of these elements.

The composition strategy is a model with major parts: the classes of the metamodel M that are mergeable and how the signatures are computed and the classes that define comparison between signatures. The classes of M that are mergeable inherit from MERGEABLE in the strategy and they implement the getSignature operation. The other classes of the strategy specialize the SIGNATURE class of the generic framework. These subclasses specialize the equals operation that defines the equality between two model elements. We can notice that the generic framework defines a default behaviour for the equals operation. Thus, it is not mandatory to specialize the SIGNATURE class.

Once the strategy is modelled it can be composed with the metamodel M. As a result of the composition, the metamodel M is augmented with the classes and methods that are necessary to provide composition capabilities. Moreover, the resulting metamodel M' inherits form all the operations implemented in the generic framework through inheritance relationships with the MERGEABLE and SIGNATURE classes.

M' is obtained using the composition mechanism of Kermeta[1] [6]. This composition only allows adding operations and classes in a metamodel and ensures that every model that conforms to the original metamodel can be viewed as an instance of the composed metamodel. Thus the models that conform to M also conform to M' and can be composed thanks to the capabilities added in M'.

---

[1] It can be noticed that the composition operation in Kermeta is a specialization of the generic framework presented here.

4 An Example for Composing Ecore Models

In this section we illustrate the specialization of the framework to compose models that conform to the Ecore metamodel. Figure 4 shows the Ecore metamodel that is very close to the metamodel for class diagrams. The metamodel defines packages that are composed of classifiers. There are two types of classifiers: classes or data types. The enumeration is the only data type present here. Classes are composed of structural features which can be attributes or references to other classes. Classes also contain operations which have attributes. This metamodel can be seen as a simplified metamodel for class diagrams.

For the composition of two models that conform to the Ecore metamodel, it is necessary to define a specific matching operator. The merging operator is reused from the generic framework. Figure 5 shows the model of the composition strategy for Ecore models. This model specializes the generic framework to define a specific matching operator for Ecore models.

According to the model in Figure 5, EMODELELEMENT (of the Ecore metamodel) inherits from MERGEABLE (from the generic framework). This means that all model elements from Ecore have to implement the getSignature operation. However, the operation only has to be implemented three times in the case of the Ecore meta-model.

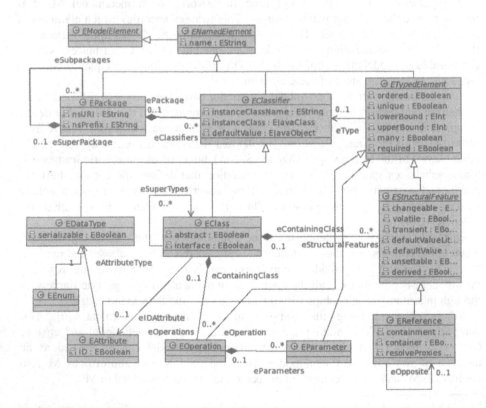

Fig. 4. The Ecore metamodel

A default signature corresponding to their name is associated with all ENAMEDELEMENT. This signature is used to match classes, data types, attributes and references. For operations and parameters specific signatures have to be defined. Two operations will match only if they have the same names, parameters that match and the same return type. Two parameters will match only if they have both the same name and the same type.

Both the generic framework presented in the previous section and its specialization for adding composition capabilities to the Ecore meta-model have been implemented in an open-source tool called Kompose [7]. Kompose was built using the Kermeta language and integrated in the Eclipse IDE as a plug-in. A complete demo of the tool

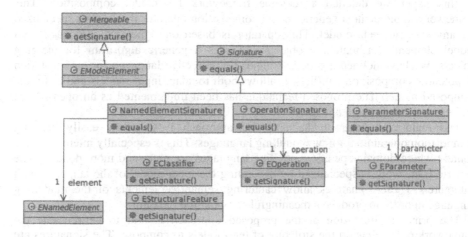

Fig. 5. The composition strategy model for Ecore

```
package ecore;

require "http://www.eclipse.org/emf/2002/Ecore"

@aspect "true"
class EModelElement inherits kompose::Mergeable {}

@aspect "true"
class ENamedElement
{
  method getSignature() : kompose::Signature is do
    var s : kompose::StringSignature init
      kompose::StringSignature.new
    s.sign := name
    result := s
  end
}
```

Fig. 6. The composition strategy model for Ecore

can be found in [7]. Figure 6 presents an excerpt of the Kermeta listing corresponding to the extension depicted in Figure 5. The first line specifies the working package and the second line imports the original Ecore meta-model. The class EMODELELEMENT is then reopened to add the inheritance relation to class MERGEABLE of Kompose and the class ENAMEDELEMENT is reopened to specify how signatures should be computed. These extensions do not break the conformance of existing Ecore models and thus allow directly composing them.

5 Conclusion

In this paper we detailed a reusable framework for model composition. This framework implements a generic model composition operator that can be specialized for any specific meta-model. This operator is based on signatures associated with model elements for matching objects and uses a generic algorithm for merging objects. We have defined a generic composition directive language for the resolution of potential composition conflicts. It allows both to adapt input models and to fix the composed model. The proposed technique has been implemented as an open-source tool using the Kermeta language.

The main advantage of the proposed approach is to allow easily defining composition operators for new modelling languages. This is especially interesting in a context where domain specific modelling languages are more and more popular. The generic framework is specialized by decorating the meta-model of the language with signatures. These signatures allow capturing semantic elements of the modelling language in order to produce a meaningful composition operator.

The principal limitation of the proposed approach is that to be reusable the framework only relies on the structure of the models to compose. The signatures are the only elements which can be used to take into account some semantics of models to compose. Our current experiments show that it is not an issue when working with structural models such as class diagrams, database schemas or components model but it becomes a clear limitation when working with modelling languages such as sequence diagrams.

To produce a meaningful composition operator for sequence diagrams, the order in which events and messages have to be composed is based on the semantics of sequence diagrams [8]. Using the current version of our composition framework, the only way to implement such a composition operator is to redefine the generic merge operation for the classes of the sequence diagram meta-model which contain properties that have to be semantically composed. For these classes there is no clear benefit from extending the generic framework as the merging algorithm has to be fully redefined.

As a future work to what is presented in this paper we are currently investigating a finer-grained redefinition mechanism that allows redefining independently the composition strategy for each property of the modelling language meta-model. This allows focusing on properties that require special semantic composition and benefit from the generic implementation for the others.

References

1. Baniassad, E., Clarke, S.: Theme: An Approach for Aspect-Oriented Analysis and Design. In: Proceedings of ICSE 2004 (Int. Conference in Software Engineering), Edinburgh, Scotland, pp. 158–167 (2004)
2. Reddy, R., Ghosh, S., France, R., Straw, G., Bieman, J.M., McEachen, N., Song, E., Georg, G.: Directives for Composing Aspect-Oriented Design Class Models. Transaction on Aspect Oriented Development 1(1), 75–105 (2006)
3. Nejati, S., Sabetzadeh, M., Chechik, M., Easterbrook, S.M., Zave, P.: Matching and Merging of Statecharts Specifications. In: Proceedings of ICSE 2007 (International Conference on Software Engineering), Minneapolis, USA, pp. 54–63 (May 2007)
4. Klein, J., Helouet, L., Jézéquel, J.-M.: Semantic-based Weaving of Scenarios. In: Proceedings of AOSD 2006 (International Conference on Aspect-Oriented Software Development), Bonn, Germany (2006)
5. Reddy, R., France, R., Ghosh, S., Fleurey, F., Baudry, B.: Model composition - a signature-based approach. In: Proceedings of Aspect Oriented Modeling (AOM) Workshop associated to MoDELS 2005. Montego Bay, Jamaica (October 2005)
6. Muller, P.-A., Fleurey, F., Jézéquel, J.-M.: Weaving executability into object-oriented meta-languages. In: Briand, L.C., Williams, C. (eds.) MoDELS 2005. LNCS, vol. 3713, pp. 264–278. Springer, Heidelberg (2005)
7. Fleurey, F.: Kompose : a generic model composition tool. 2007, http://www.kermeta.org/kompose/
8. Klein, J., Fleurey, F., Jézéquel, J.-M.: Weaving multiple aspects in sequence diagrams. Trans. on Aspect Oriented Software Development (2007)

MATA: A Tool for Aspect-Oriented Modeling Based on Graph Transformation

Jon Whittle[1] and Praveen Jayaraman[2]

[1] Dept of Computing, Lancaster University,
Bailrigg, LA1 4YW, UK
whittle@comp.lancs.ac.uk
[2] Dept. of Information and Software Engineering,
George Mason University, Fairfax VA 22030
praveenjayaraman@yahoo.com

Abstract. This paper describes MATA (Modeling Aspects Using a Transformation Approach), a UML aspect-oriented modeling tool that uses graph transformations to specify and compose aspects. Graph transformations provide a unified approach for aspect modeling. The methods presented here can be applied to any modeling language with a well-defined metamodel. This paper, however, focuses on UML class diagrams, sequence diagrams and state diagrams. MATA takes a different approach to aspect-oriented modeling since there are no explicit join points. Rather, any model element can be a join point and composition is a special case of model transformation. We illustrate MATA on structural and behavioral models for a cell phone example.

1 Introduction

Broadly speaking, there have been, to date, two approaches for modeling aspects in UML. The essence of the first approach is that two models are composed by identifying common elements and applying a generic merge algorithm. This is a symmetric form of aspect modeling and common elements are found according to some matching criteria, e.g., two classes with the same name are merged. Examples of this approach include Theme/UML [1] as well as work by France et al. [2]. The essence of the second approach is to reuse, at the modeling level, mechanisms for specifying and weaving aspects from aspect-oriented programming. There has been a significant amount of research, for example, that identifies a join point model for a modeling language and then uses the AspectJ advices of before, after, and around for weaving. Examples of this type include [3, 4].

These two kinds of approaches are not always sufficient. In the first approach, a merge algorithm based on general matching criteria will never be expressive enough to handle all model compositions. Matching by name, for example, may not work for state diagrams. Given two states with the same name, the states may need to be merged in one of a variety of ways depending on the application being modeled: (1) the two states represent the same thing, which implies making the states equal; (2) the two states represent orthogonal behaviors of the same object, which implies enclosing the states by a new orthogonal region; (3) one state is really a sub-mode of the other,

H. Giese (Ed.): MoDELS 2007 Workshops, LNCS 5002, pp. 16–27, 2008.
© Springer-Verlag Berlin Heidelberg 2008

which implies making one state a substate of the other; (4) the behaviors of the two states must be interleaved in a complex way, which implies weaving the actions and transitions in a very application-specific way to achieve the desired result.

Only the first of these can be accomplished based on merge-by-name. Furthermore, these are only four of many possible options so it is not generally sufficient to provide a number of pre-defined merge strategies.

In the second approach, specific elements are allowed to be defined as join points and others are not. For example, in state diagrams, some approaches define events as join points. Others, however, define states as join points. One could even imagine more complex join points, such as the pointcut of all orthogonal regions. (This pointcut might be used, for example, by an aspect that sequentializes parallel behaviors.) Defining only a subset of a model's elements as join points seems to be overly restrictive. In addition, limiting advices to before, after, and around is also rather restrictive since it may be desired to weave behavior in parallel, or as a sub-behavior of a behavior in the base, for example.

MATA is an aspect-oriented modeling tool that tackles these problems by viewing aspect composition as a special case of model transformation. In MATA, composition of a base and aspect model is specified by a graph rule. Given a base model, M_B, crosscut by an aspect model, M_A, a MATA composition rule merges M_A and M_B to produce a composed model M_{AB}. The graph rule, r: LHS $\rightarrow$ RHS defines a pattern on the left-hand side (LHS). This pattern captures the set of pointcuts, i.e., the points in M_B where new model elements should be added. The right-hand side (RHS) defines the new elements to be added and specifies how they should be added to M_B. MATA graph rules are defined over the concrete syntax of the modeling language. This is in contrast to almost all known approaches to model transformation which typically define transformations at the meta-level, that is, over the abstract syntax of the modeling language. The restriction to concrete syntax is important for aspect modeling because a modeler is unlikely to have enough detailed knowledge of the UML metamodel to specify transformations over abstract syntax.

MATA currently supports composition for UML class, sequence and state diagrams. In principle, however, it is easy to extend MATA to other UML models (or, indeed, other modeling languages as long as a metamodel for the language exists) because the idea of using graph rules is broadly applicable. The focus in this paper is on the MATA tool and so the presentation will be by example. Details can be found elsewhere. [5] describes MATA's expressive pointcut mechanisms for state diagrams. [6] describes an application of MATA to composition in software product lines.

2 The MATA Language

MATA considers aspect composition as a special case of graph transformation. In general, a graph consists of a set of nodes and a set of edges. A typed graph is a graph in which each node and edge belongs to a type. Types are defined in a type graph. An attributed graph is a graph in which each node and edge may be labeled with attributes where each label is a (value, type) pair giving the value of the attribute and its type. The UML metamodel can naturally be represented as a type graph. Each metaclass becomes a node in the type graph and each meta-association becomes an edge in the type graph. A UML model, therefore, can be represented as an instance of this type graph and a graph rule, defined over the type graph, will transform the UML model into another model that also conforms to the type graph (i.e., another UML model). In this way, existing graph theory can be used to transform UML models.

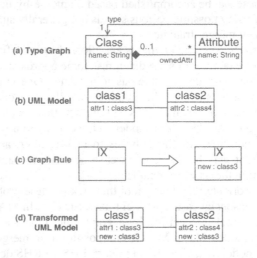

Fig. 1. Graph Rules for UML

Figure 1 illustrates these concepts, using a simple example that adds an attribute to an existing class. (a) is a type graph defining a very simple metamodel for a subset of UML class diagrams. (b) is a UML class diagram that will undergo a transformation. The result of applying the rule in (c) to this class diagram is given in (d). Note that the left-hand side (LHS) of the rule in (c) defines a pattern over which the rule applies. Variables are prefixed by 'I'. Hence, 'IX' matches any class. The right-hand side (RHS) describes elements that should be added or removed. Any element that matches a variable on the LHS and does not appear on the RHS is removed. New elements on the RHS are added. The effect of applying the rule in (c) twice is to add two new attributes since 'IX' matches against both class1 and class2.

MATA uses graph rules to define aspects. The pattern on the LHS essentially defines the pointcuts to match against. The RHS defines new model elements that should be added at these pointcuts (or it defines existing model elements that should be removed). There are two points of note about the graph rules in MATA.

Firstly, graph transformations are typically defined over the type graph. For UML models, this means that approaches such as FUJABA [7] and others define rules over UML's metaclasses. Whilst this is the most powerful approach, it is very inconvenient for a modeler because s/he must have a detailed knowledge of the UML metamodel. MATA instead represents graph rules in UML's concrete syntax, as given in the example in Figure 1(c), although minor extensions to the concrete syntax are introduced to allow for powerful pointcut expressions and variable expressions.

Secondly, it is also rather inconvenient to write graph rules using both a LHS and a RHS because elements that are unchanged must be repeated on both sides. Hence, MATA follows approaches such as VIATRA2 [8] in that the rule is given on one diagram. This is done by using a MATA profile which defines three new stereotypes:

- <<create>>, which can be applied to any model element, states that an element should be created by a graph rule.
- <<delete>>, which can be applied to any model element, states that an element should be removed by a graph rule.
- <<context>> is used with container elements to avoid elements being affected by <<create>> or <<delete>> (see below).

Figure 2 gives an example MATA graph rule to add parallel behavior in a sequence diagram. (a) is the MATA rule itself and (b) shows the application of the rule to a particular example. (a) has two parts to it—the pattern to match against and elements to add. In this case, the pattern is defined in two ways. Elements without a stereotype are matched against. In addition, any elements stereotyped as <<context>> are also matched against. This is because the semantics of <<create>> and <<delete>> are defined such that if these stereotypes apply to an element, then they also apply to all of the element's *immediate neighbors*. This is done simply to avoid having to write a <<create>> or <<delete>> stereotype for all neighbor elements. For example, in Figure 2(a), the immediate neighbors of the **par** fragment include any messages inside the fragment. Hence, <<create>> also applies to messages *r* and *s*. To avoid <<create>> being applied to *p*, it is marked with <<context>>. Therefore, the match defined in 2(a) is any pair of lifelines with a message *p* from one lifeline to the other. Note that not specifying an instance and type for a lifeline is equivalent to using two variables, $lx:lX$. The effect of applying the rule in Figure 2(a) is to introduce a new **par** fragment around all instances of message *p*, and this new fragment will have messages *r* and *s* occur in parallel with *p*.

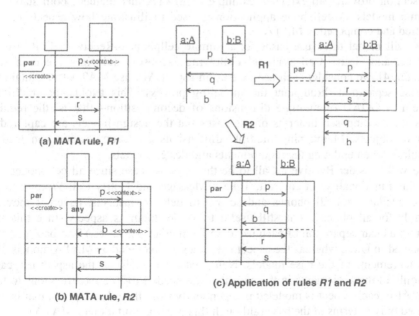

(a) MATA rule, *R1*

(b) MATA rule, *R2*

(c) Application of rules *R1* and *R2*

Fig. 2. MATA Rules

As stated earlier, the notion of immediate neighbor is used to reduce the number of elements that must be stereotyped with <<create>> or <<delete>>. This is purely a convenience for the modeler. The definition of immediate neighbor is specific to each model element. For a class, its immediate neighbors are all its associations. For a state, its immediate neighbors are its transitions and its actions. For a combined fragment in a sequence diagram, its immediate neighbors are all model elements contained inside the fragment.

Figure 2 also shows an example how sequence pointcuts can be defined in MATA. A sequence pointcut is a match against any number of consecutive model elements— for example, a sequence of messages, or a sequence of transitions. Sequence pointcuts are handled naturally since the approach is based on patterns. In the example, the MATA combined fragment **any** is used to match against a sequence of messages of unknown length. So the rule R2 in Figure 2(b) will match any two lifelines with messages p and b with any number of messages between p and b. The result of applying the rule is shown in Figure 2(c). Note how the result is different than if rule R1 is applied. For R2, the pointcut is the sequence of messages p, q, b, and so, these messages all appear in the first operand of the **par** fragment.

These examples show that expressive pointcut expressions can be naturally specified using MATA. Figure 2 only shows examples for sequence diagrams. Similar rules for state diagrams can also be specified in the current implementation of MATA.

3 Extended Example

This section provides an extended example of MATA that includes both static and dynamic models. A cellphone application is used to illustrate how aspects can be specified and composed in MATA.

We will model three use cases for a simple cellphone—Receive a Call, Take a Message, and Notify Call Waiting. Following Jacobson and Ng's use case slice approach [4], we consider each use case as an aspect. We use MATA to maintain the use case separation throughout the modeling process. This avoids the traditional problem in OOAD of multiple dimensions of decomposition—that is, the requirements are decomposed in terms of use cases but the design models are captured in terms of objects. Maintaining multiple dimensions of decomposition can lead to difficulties when updating the requirements and design models.

We will consider Receive a Call to be the base use case since all cellphones will have this functionality. In contrast, Take a Message and Notify Call Waiting might not be available for all phones and so are modeled as aspects. (Even if they are available for all phones, it is still useful to model them as aspects since this will maintain a clear separation of each use case from other use cases.) The base use case is modeled in UML whereas the aspect use cases are modeled as MATA models, that is, as increments of the base models. Note that the models for the aspect use cases refer only to those elements in the base that are needed for the modifications to take place. Also, each aspect is modeled independently from the other aspects, that is, it is modeled only in terms of the base (although this is not a limitation of MATA).

Figure 3 shows (simplified) static and dynamic models for the base use case, Receive a Call. The phone contains a ringer, a phone component, a display unit and a keypad. Upon receiving an incoming call, the phone notifies the user by displaying the caller information on the display unit and sending a ring message to the ringer. The user is allowed to either accept the call (then hang up later) or not accept (i.e., disconnect) the call.

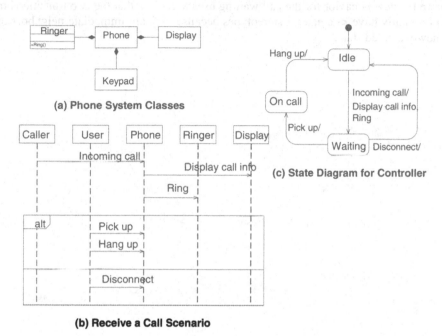

(a) Phone System Classes

(b) Receive a Call Scenario

(c) State Diagram for Controller

Fig. 3. Models for the Base Use Case

Figure 4 gives the behavior models for the two aspects, Take a Message and Notify Call Waiting. 4(a) is a sequence diagram for Take a Message. If the phone rings for a specified amount of time, the call goes to a messaging system. In MATA, this is specified by creating a new **alt** fragment since forwarding to voice mail is an alternative scenario to the case where the callee accepts the call. Note that an **any** fragment is used to match against all messages coming after Ring in the base. This is needed since once a message is taken, the user should not be able to pick up the call or disconnect it. Hence, the **alt** fragment must be wrapped around all messages in the base concerned with call pick up or disconnect.

In Figure 4(b), the aspect rule matches any two states which have a transition between them with an event named Incoming call. The effect of the aspect is to add an additional transition capturing the voicemail behavior. When this rule is applied, the two states will match against Idle and Waiting in Figure 3(c). The effect is to add a transition from Waiting back to Idle.

Figure 4(c) introduces messages for putting an incoming call on hold when a call is already underway. These new messages are only relevant when a call is taking place, that is, in between messages Pick Up and Hang Up in the base. Hence, the **loop** fragment is marked with a <<create>> stereotype and this fragment is inserted in between Pick Up and Hang Up. Note that, in this case, it would be sufficient to leave out the Hang Up message in 4(c), which, in effect, would insert the new behavior *after* Pick Up. However, we include Hang Up because there may eventually be other occurrences of Pick Up which should not be affected by the aspect.

Figure 4(d) introduces a new state, Waiting for hold prompt, into the base to capture the new behavior for the call waiting use case. Note that the two transitions in 4(d) implicitly have <<create>> stereotypes because they are immediate neighbors of the newly created state.

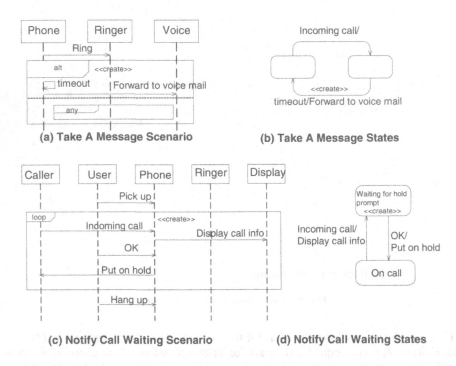

(a) Take A Message Scenario   (b) Take A Message States

(c) Notify Call Waiting Scenario   (d) Notify Call Waiting States

Fig. 4. Aspect Models for Take a Message and Notify Call Waiting

3.1 Interactions between Aspects

MATA comes with some support for automatically detecting interactions between aspects. Since aspects in MATA are graph rules, the technique of critical pair analysis (CPA) [9] can be used to detect dependencies and conflicts between rules. CPA examines rules in a pair wise fashion and declares a dependency if one rule requires a model element introduced by another rule. A conflict is declared if one rule modifies the base in such a way that another rule can no longer be applied. Conflicts and dependencies usually imply that the rules should be applied in a particular order since the result may be different depending on the order. A conflict may also mean that two rules that should both be applied cannot be, and therefore, the rules themselves should be modified. In any case, CPA provides a degree of automatic feedback to the modeler that both provides assistance in ordering rules and provides some assurance that the composition is correct.

Considering the example again, we can see that there is a dependency between the two state diagram rules for Take a Message and Notify Call Waiting. This dependency arises because Notify Call Waiting creates a transition with event Incoming Call (Figure 4(d)) whereas Take a Message matches against the event Incoming Call (Figure 4(b)). Hence, if Take a Message is applied to the base before Notify Call Waiting then any incoming call that is received during an existing call cannot be sent to voicemail. Figure 5 gives the results of composing the two aspects with the base in either order. In 5(a), Take a Message is applied to the base before Notify Call Waiting. In 5(b), it is applied after. The difference is that there is an extra transition from Waiting for hold prompt to On call in 5(b) which captures the fact that an incoming call may be sent to voice mail even when there is currently an active call taking place. The difference in the composed state diagrams arises because the rule for Notify Call Waiting introduces a new transition with event Incoming call. Hence, when the Take a Message rule is applied in 5(b), there are two transitions with event Incoming call and so the rule applies twice.

MATA detects these kinds of dependencies automatically. Ultimately, the modeler must decide which order is the correct one, but MATA can at least provide some assistance in flagging cases that must be considered more carefully. If there are no conflicts or dependencies found by CPA, then the rules can be applied in any order. CPA is particularly important when aspects are reused in a different context than originally intended since new conflicts and dependencies may then arise inadvertently.

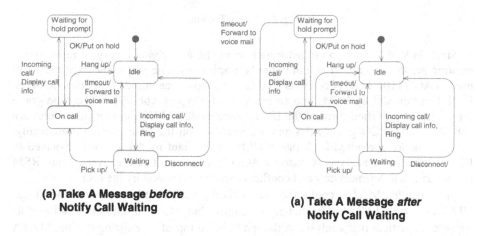

(a) Take A Message *before*
Notify Call Waiting

(a) Take A Message *after*
Notify Call Waiting

Fig. 5. Base and Aspect State Diagrams Composed

4   Tool Implementation

This section describes the implementation of MATA. MATA is designed as a vendor-independent tool but currently works on top of IBM's Rational Software Modeler (RSM). Each aspect is modeled as a package. Within this package, the class diagrams, sequence diagrams and state diagrams for the aspect are maintained. Users may select a subset of the aspects and the tool generates the composed model for all of these aspects and the base. The user may also define an ordering of aspect composition in the case that one aspect needs to be composed before another. If an ordering is not specified, the tool selects an order nondeterministically. Figure 6 illustrates this process.

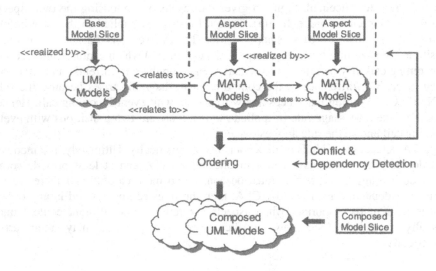

Fig. 6. MATA Tooling

Since MATA uses graph transformations as the underlying theory, it relies on an existing graph rule execution tool to apply graph rules. The graph rule execution tool used is AGG [10]. MATA converts a UML base model, captured as an instance of the UML2 metamodel by RSM, into an instance of a type graph, where the type graph represents a simplified form of the UML2 metamodel. MATA composition rules are converted into AGG graph rules and are executed on the base graph automatically. The results are converted back into a UML2 compliant model and are displayed in RSM. Critical pair analysis is done by AGG and the results are converted into RSM so that detected dependencies and conflicts can be understood by the user.

In principle, MATA could use any existing graph rule execution tool (e.g., VIATRA2 or FUJABA) as its underlying engine, but AGG was chosen because of its support for critical pair analysis. Although built on top of an existing engine, MATA provides some unique features that make it very suitable for aspect modeling and composition, namely: (1) graph rules are defined graphically using the concrete syntax of UML rather than using metaclasses; (2) MATA supports sequence pointcuts, that is, an aspect may match against a sequence of messages or a sequence of transitions. This is supported directly in the MATA rule syntax; (3) the stereotype <<context>> is unique to MATA; (4) dependencies and conflicts between aspects can be detected automatically using critical pair analysis.

5 Related Work

Most research on aspect-oriented modeling has focused on static models (e.g., [1, 2]). Some work has addressed behavioral models (e.g., [3, 11-13]). This paper is different from previous work in three key respects. Firstly, there are no explicit join points but instead composition is viewed as a special case of model transformation. Secondly, graph transformations provide a formal foundation for aspect composition. Finally, there is support for statically analyzing aspect interactions via critical pair analysis.

Related work that is closest to ours includes join point designation diagrams (JPDDs) [14]. JPDDs are similar to defining patterns using graph rules. The advantage of using graph rules is the existence of formal analysis techniques. In addition, JPDDs focus on defining join points and are not so much concerned with composition. MATA provides a full composition tool in which very expressive composition relationships can be specified. This is not possible with JPDDs.

More generally, model composition has been addressed outside of the AOSD community. In particular, [15] investigates how to merge state machines using composition relationships and category theory. This is similar in many respects to our work but has a different goal in that it addresses how to reconcile state machines produced by different development teams. Model composition is also important in feature-based approaches to software product lines.

6 Conclusion and Future Work

This paper presented a new approach for modeling and composing aspect models written in UML. Tool support for MATA is built on top of IBM's Rational Software Modeler. A prototype has been implemented and a number of case studies have been modeled with this prototype. MATA uses the graph rule execution tool AGG as a back-end for executing graph transformations and performing critical pair analysis.

There are a number of interesting avenues for further work that would build upon MATA. Firstly, base models in MATA are currently completely open, in the sense that any base model elements can be accessed by aspect models. This has shown to be absolutely essential in some application areas. In particular, for the software product line method PLUS [16], which can be handled in MATA by modeling features as aspects, models of non-kernel features can be added to models of the kernel in many and varied different ways. It would not have been possible to restrict the join point model and still allow the case studies from [16] to be modeled faithfully.

However, it may be desirable for other application areas to restrict the join point model so that only certain base model elements can be affected by an aspect. This kind of approach would potentially support improved modular reasoning for aspects. MATA could support such a technique easily as interfaces could be designed on top of the existing language. In any case, we feel that the modeler should be in control of whether or not full access is required by the aspects and it is not up to the language designer to restrict the join point model for him/her.

Another area where MATA could potentially be extended is to provide domain-specific composition operators, built on top of the existing language. A key contribution of this paper is that MATA allows all modeling languages to be handled in a uniform way. However, the current composition operators in MATA are quite low level because they are at the same level as the underlying modeling language. One could imagine defining more abstract operators, for example, in software architecture composition, that would be then mapped down to MATA's operators. This would raise the level of discourse of aspect modelers but would retain the strong benefits of the MATA foundations. Such a path should be taken with caution, however. A great deal of effort has already gone into language design for existing modeling languages and it is not completely clear that an additional layer of abstraction would be beneficial.

Along similar grounds, MATA's composition is purely syntactic currently. This means that aspect modelers define aspects based on the syntactic elements of the underlying modeling language. Whilst this is in line with current practice in modeling, it would be interesting to investigate semantics-based composition techniques, similar to those developed for aspect-oriented requirements engineering languages [17]. This would allow modelers to specify aspects in terms of semantic concepts of the domain rather than syntactic modeling elements. For example, one might wish to define the pointcut of all model elements related to access control. The techniques in [17] rely on natural language processing techniques to extract semantic content from textual requirements documents and it is not clear how such an approach could be adapted to analysis and design models. However, it is certainly an open area of research that could provide fruitful solutions to the fragile pointcut problem in aspect-oriented modeling.

Finally, we hope that the expressive composition mechanisms provided by MATA might have some consequences for aspect-oriented programming. Whilst modeling is different from programming, it seems that AOP could also benefit by more expressive pointcut languages or more expressive advices. We believe that the rich language in MATA might offer some insights as to how such languages should be developed.

References

1. Clarke, S., Baniassad, E.: Aspect-Oriented Analysis and Design: The Theme Approach. Addison Wesley, Reading (2005)
2. France, R., Ray, I., Georg, G., Ghosh, S.: Aspect-oriented approach to early design modeling. IEE Proceedings - Software 151, 173–186 (2004)
3. Cottenier, T., van den Berg, A., Elrad, T.: Motorola WEAVR: Model Weaving in a Large Industrial Context. In: Aspect-Oriented Software Development (AOSD), Vancouver, Canada (2007)
4. Jacobson, I., Ng, P.-W.: Aspect Oriented Software Development with Use Cases. Addison-Wesley Professional, Reading (2004)
5. Whittle, J., Moreira, A., Araújo, J., Rabbi, R., Jayaraman, P., Elkhodary, A.: An Expressive Aspect Composition Language for UML State Diagrams. In: Engels, G., Opdyke, B., Schmidt, D.C., Weil, F. (eds.) MODELS 2007. LNCS, vol. 4735, pp. 514–528. Springer, Heidelberg (2007)
6. Jayaraman, P., Whittle, J., Elkhodary, A., Gomaa, H.: Model Composition in Product Lines and Feature Interaction Detection using Critical Pair Analysis. In: Engels, G., Opdyke, B., Schmidt, D.C., Weil, F. (eds.) MODELS 2007. LNCS, vol. 4735, Springer, Heidelberg (2007)

7. Nickel, U., Niere, J., Zuendorf, A.: The FUJABA Environment. In: International Conference on Software Engineering, Limerick, Ireland, pp. 742–745 (2000)
8. Csertan, G., Huszerl, G., Majzik, I., Pap, Z., Pataricza, A., Varro, D.: VIATRA - visual automated transformations for formal verification and validation of UML models. In: Automated Software Engineering, 2002 (ASE), Edinburgh, UK, p. 267 (2002)
9. Heckel, R., Küster, J., Taentzer, G.: Confluence of Typed Attributed Graph Transformation Systems. In: Corradini, A., Ehrig, H., Kreowski, H.-J., Rozenberg, G. (eds.) ICGT 2002. LNCS, vol. 2505, pp. 161–176. Springer, Heidelberg (2002)
10. Taentzer, G.: AGG: A Graph Transformation Environment for Modeling and Validation of Software. In: Pfaltz, J.L., Nagl, M., Böhlen, B. (eds.) AGTIVE 2003. LNCS, vol. 3062, pp. 446–453. Springer, Heidelberg (2004)
11. Klein, J., Helouet, L., Jézéquel, J.-M.: Semantic-Based Weaving of Scenarios. In: Aspect-Oriented Software Development (AOSD), Vancouver, Canada, pp. 27–38 (2006)
12. Araújo, J., Whittle, J., Kim, D.-K.: Modeling and Composing Scenario-Based Requirements with Aspects. In: International Conference on Requirements Engineering, Kyoto, Japan, pp. 58–67 (2004)
13. Mahoney, M., Elrad, T.: Generating Code from Scenario and State Based Models to Address Crosscutting Concerns. In: Sixth International Workshop on Scenarios and State Machines (2007)
14. Stein, D., Hanenberg, S., Unland, R.: Expressing Different Conceptual Models of Join Point Selections in Aspect-Oriented Design. In: Aspect-Oriented Software Development (AOSD), Bonn, Germany, pp. 15–26 (2006)
15. Nejati, S., Sabetzadeh, M., Chechik, M., Easterbrook, S., Zave, P.: Matching and Merging of Statecharts Specifications. In: International Conference on Software Engineering, pp. 54–64 (2007)
16. Gomaa, H.: Designing Software Product Lines with UML: From Use Cases to Pattern-based Software Architectures. Addison-Wesley Object Technology Series (2005)
17. Chitchyan, R., Rashid, A., Rayson, P., Waters, R.: Semantics-Based Composition for Aspect-Oriented Requirements Engineering. In: Aspect-Oriented Software Development (AOSD), Vancouver, Canada, pp. 36–48 (2007)

4th International Workshop on Language Engineering (ATEM 2007)

Jean-Marie Favre[1], Dragan Gašević[2], Ralf Lämmel[3], and Andreas Winter[4]

[1] University of Grenoble, France
http://www-adele.imag.fr/~jmfavre
[2] Athabasca University, Canada
http://www.sfu.ca/~dgasevic/
[3] Universität Koblenz-Landau, Germany
http://homepages.cwi.nl/~ralf/
[4] Johannes Gutenberg-Universität Mainz, Germany
http://www.gupro.de/~winter/

1 ATEM Workshop Series

Following the great success of previous editions, ATEM2007 is the 4th edition of the ATEM workshop series. The first two editions were held with WCRE in 2003 and 2004, while the 3rd one was held with MoDELS 2006. ATEM has always been focused on engineering of language descriptions. In order to cover as many aspects of language descriptions important for greater success and adoption of model-driven engineering, ATEM has been evolving so as its scope:

- The first edition was about *metamodels* and *schemas*.
- The second about was *metamodels, schemas* and *grammars*.
- The third edition was about *metamodels, schemas, grammars* and *ontologies*.

Throughout the interaction with the MDE community and based on the papers submitted to and topics discussed about in the previous ATEM editions, we have decided that ATEM2007 is about language engineering. Thus, the intention of ATEM2007 is to further encourage and expand inter-disciplinary work (e.g., natural language engineering) on language descriptions that should bring many promising opportunities for the area of model-driven engineering.

If Software Engineering is "the application of a systematic, disciplined, quantifiable approach to the development, operation, and maintenance of software" [1], then **Software Language Engineering (SLE)** can be viewed as *the application of a systematic, disciplined, quantifiable approach to the development, use, and maintenance of languages in software engineering* [2]. SLE is particularly concerned with

(i) the life cycle of software languages including design, implementation, documentation, testing, deployment, evolution, recovery, and retirement;
(ii) the treatment of language descriptions as software artifacts, akin to programs, subject to tailored engineering principles and methods such as modularization, refactoring, refinement, composition, versioning, and analysis;

H. Giese (Ed.): MoDELS 2007 Workshops, LNCS 5002, pp. 28–33, 2008.
© Springer-Verlag Berlin Heidelberg 2008

(iii) programming support and engineering principles for transformations (or mappings, translations, conversions) between different software languages or different manifestations of the same software language such as those in X/O/R mapping;

(iv) the management of coupling and cohesion in software systems caused by the invasive use of languages;

(v) consistency management for the uses of languages in software systems;

(vi) language integration for interrelated uses of software languages.

ATEM 2007 aimed a providing a forum to discuss software language engineering from various perspectives to facilitate a broad knowledge of methods and techniques and enable an integrated use of these.

2 ATEM 2007 Workshop

The objective of ATEM2007 was to bring together researchers from different communities to study the use of various language descriptions and technical spaces in order to further expand frontiers of their synergetic use in model-driven engineering.

The intended audience of the workshop was researchers and practitioners using various *language descriptions* (e.g., metamodels, models, ontologies, grammars, and schemas) for forward/reverse engineering, recovery, and reengineering in model-driven software development.

2.1 Scope

The importance of *language descriptions*, which include models, schemas, grammars, and ontologies, is generally acknowledged by the model-driven engineering community, but, as yet, the study of these artifacts lacks a common umbrella. Language engineering (in the context of software engineering) promotes language descriptions to first class citizens, just like programs, data, and models based on the systematic, programmatic (e.g., rule-based) analysis and manipulation of these language descriptions. The typical ATEM paper studies *language descriptions* in the context of engineering of software systems and languages.

The language engineering view is generally consistent with MDE; it is specifically aligned with approaches for *grammar engineering, Domain Specific Language (DSL) engineering, software factories, ontology engineering, schema engineering* and others. To have a deeper focus on the language engineering perspective of MDE, ATEM2007 pays attention to the fact that language descriptions that are used in developing software systems can be defined in different ways and used to define for different software artifacts (e.g., source code, binaries, databases contents, database schemas, UML diagrams, XML files, XML schemas, software architecture descriptions, passive or active web pages, versioned repositories, configuration files, service descriptions, XML style sheets, user interfaces descriptions, RDF or OWL ontologies, natural text documents, and SQL, XQuery, RDQL queries), but still they have to be used together in integrated software development and software evolution. Thus, we need ways that enable us to take advantage of all these various language descriptions when engineering, re-engineering, recovering, and testing software systems. Since most of language descriptions have rather different technological, research and cultural origins, the synergic use is rather a complex task that requires join efforts of different communities.

2.2 Program

From 27 submitted papers, 13 papers were accepted to be presented in Nashville, TN. The papers accepted were into two main categories: full and short papers. All papers accepted as full papers showed important approaches and applications of language engineering by various techniques and led to interesting and fruitful discussions during the workshop. Short papers presented either work in process or discussed controversial issues in the field or describe interesting or thought-provoking ideas that are not yet fully developed. Out of 13 accepted papers, 5 were accepted as full papers, and 8 as short papers, which were presented into four workshop sessions based grouped around the following topics: foundations, domain-specific languages, transformations and modeling techniques, and data mapping/migration.

Besides the peer-reviewed paper presentations, the program included a panel.

2.2.1 Selected Papers

This workshop proceedings of the *ACM/IEEE 10th International Conference on Model Driven Engineering, Languages and Systems (MODELS 2007)* contains two *summarized versions of the full papers* presented at ATEM 2007:

- **A Comparison of Standard Compliant Ways to Define Domain Specific Languages** by *Ingo Weisemoeller* and *Andy Schuerr* investigates various approaches to define DSLs, focusing on architectural description languages as an example.
- **Designing Syntax Embeddings and Assimilations for Language Libraries** by *Martin Bravenboer* and *Eelco Visser* overviews the design space and research questions in language library realization, in particular, the identification of research issues for realizing an independently extensible language library framework.

2.2.2 Full Papers

The full papers, not summarized in this proceedings, include:

- **A Language Description is More than a Metamodel** by *Anneke Kleppe* proposes a framework for defining software languages by emphasizing the fact that a language's concrete syntax and semantics are as important as abstract syntax (i.e., metamodel), which currently a common misconception in model-driven engineering of languages.
- **Metamodel-based UML Notations for Domain-specific Languages** by *Achim D. Brucker* and *Juergen Doser* presents a metamodel-based approach for specifying UML notations for domain-specific modeling languages.
- **Zhi# - Programming Language Inherent Support for Ontologies** by *Alexander Paar* proposes a novel compiler framework that facilitates the cooperative usage of external type systems based on the XML Schema and OWL languages with C#.

2.2.3 Short Papers
The short papers presented at ATEM 2007 include:

- **Making Modeling Languages Fit for Model-Driven Development** by *Thomas Kühne* argues that a modeling language that aspires to be used in a model-driven development context must fulfill more requirements than traditional notations that have been primarily used for solution sketching.
- **Towards Semantic Integration of Multiple Domain-Specific Languages Using Ontological Foundations** by *Henrik Lochmann* and *Matthias Bräuer* presents an approach that facilitates the integration of domain-specific languages on a semantic level by mapping language constructs to concepts in an upper ontology.
- **Prototyping Domain-Specific Languages for Wireless Sensor Networks** by *Daniel A. Sadilek* proposes a language engineering approach that allows rapid prototyping of domain-specific languages.
- **CoCloRep: A DSL for Code Clones** by *Robert Tairas, Shih-Hsi Liu, Frederic Jouault,* and *Jeff Gray* describes an investigation into the development of CoCloRep, a domain-specific language for the representation of code clones.
- **Model-based Aspect Weaver Construction** by *Suman Roychoudhury, Frederic Jouault,* and *Jeff Gray* describes an approach that combines model engineering with program transformation techniques to construct aspect weavers for general-purpose programming languages.
- **An Algebraic Approach for Composing Model Transformations in QVT** by Claudia Pons presents a software tool supporting the algebraic formalization for composing model transformations in QVT.
- **Text-based Modeling by Hans Groenniger** by *Holger Krahn, Bernhard Rumpe, Martin Schindler,* and *Steven Voelkel* discusses the advantages of text-based modeling over commonly used graphical representations.
- **Biological Data Migration Using a Model-Driven Approach** by *Abel Gomez Llana, Jose A. Carsi, Artur Boronat, Isidro Ramos, Claudia Taeubner,* and *Silke Eckstein* shows how model-driven software development can be applied in the bioinformatics field by expressing biological data structures by means of models.

2.2.4 Proceedings
All papers presented at ATEM 2007, are published in [1] and all of them are online available at both the publisher's website and the workshop's website: http://planetmde.org/atem2007/.

2.2.5 Panel
ATEM 2007 featured a panel on *Grand Challenges in Software-Language Engineering* that involved panelist from different technical spaces to discuss the future of software language engineering: *Ralf Lämmel* (moderator), *Anneke Kleppe, Thomas Kühne, Eelco Visser, Krzysztof Czarnecki,* and *Dragan Gašević*. The panel is video recorded and the video clip of the panel is available at ATEM 2007 website: http://planetmde.org/atem2007/.

3 Beyond ATEM 2007

There are several activities planned to further stimulate the exchange of research results in *software language engineering*.

First, we decided to scale the ATEM workshop series up into a new series of conferences entitled – **International Conference on Software Language Engineering** (SLE). The steering committee of the MODELS conference series has kindly accepted our proposal to host SLE 2008 as two days long conference at *ACM/IEEE 11th International Conference on Model Driven Engineering, Languages and Systems (MODELS 2008)* that will be held in Toulouse in France in the period September 28 – October 3, 2008. The SLE 2008 conference will be organized by joining the forces with the community organizing the International Workshop on Language Descriptions, Tools and Applications (LDTA).

Second, the editorial board of *IEEE Transactions on Software Engineering* kindly accepted our proposal to organize a special issue dedicated to *Software Language Engineering* to be published in May-June Issue of 2009 [2]. This call for papers has been complied based on the discussions at ATEM 2007, and it helped us define a scope of software language engineering to be explored in the special issue

Acknowledgement

We, the organizers, thank the program committee and additional reviewers who reviewed the submissions and provided useful feedback to the authors within a very short period of time. The program committee of ATEM 2007 consisted of:

- Dave Akehurst, University of Kent at Canterbury, UK
- Colin Atkinson, University of Mannheim, Germany
- Artur Boronat, Universidad Politecnica de Valencia, Spain
- Charles Consel, INRIA, Bordeaux, France
- Jim Cordy, Queen's University, Canada
- Krzysztof Czarnecki, University of Waterloo, Canada
- Juan De Lara, Universidad Autonoma de Madrid, Spain
- Arie Van Deursen, Delft University of Technology, The Netherlands
- Stephane Ducasse, University of Savoie, France
- Gregor Engels, University of Paderborn, Germany
- Mike Godfrey, University of Waterloo, Canada
- Martin Gogolla, University of Bremen, Germany
- Jeff Gray, University of Alabama at Birmingham, USA
- Reiko Heckel, University of Leicester, UK
- Frederic Jouault, INRIA/UAB, France/USA
- Gabor Karsai, Vanderbilt University, USA
- Elisa F. Kendall, Sandpiper Software, USA
- Pierre-Alain Muller, University of Mulhouse, France
- Richard Paige, University of York, UK
- Jeff Z. Pan, University of Aberdeen, UK

- Juergen Rilling, Concordia University, Canada
- Steffen Staab, University of Koblenz, Germany
- Juha-Pekka Tolvanen, Metacase, Finland
- Laurence Tratt, King's College, London, UK
- Daniel Varro, Budapest University, Hungry
- Chris Verhoef, Vrije University Amsterdam, The Netherlands
- Eelco Visser, Delft University of Technology, The Netherlands
- Joost Visser, Software Improvement Group, The Netherlands
- Jos Warmer, The Netherlands
- René Witte, University of Karlsruhe, Germany
  The additional reviewers of ATEM 2007 are:
- Dimitrios Kolovos, University of York, UK
- Mirco Kuhlmann, University of Bremen, Germany
- Robert Tairas, University of Alabama at Birmingham, USA
- Pieter van der Spek, Vrije Universiteit, The Netherlands
- Vadim Zaytsev, Vrije Universiteit, The Netherlands

We thank our authors for their papers and interesting talks, and the participants for intensive and valuable discussions. Our thanks also go to the MODELS 2007 organizers of for accepting ATEM 2007 as part of the conference program. We also thank our supporters, who helped in advertising and organizing ATEM 2007:

- planetmde.org, the community web portal on model-driven engineering;
- SRE, the German GI special interest group on software reengineering;
- RIMEL, the French special interest group on Reverse Engineering, Maintenance and Software Evolution.

References

1. IEEE Standard Glossary of Software Engineering Terminology (IEEE Std 610.12-1990), Institute IEEE, Los Alamitos, CA (1990), http://ieeexplore.ieee.org/iel1/2238/4148/00159342.pdf?tp=&arnumber=159342&isnumber=4148
2. Call-for-Papers: Special Issue on Software Language Engineering. IEEE Transactions on Software Engineering 33(12), 891 (2007), http://www.computer.org/portal/cms_docs_transactions/transactions/tse/CFP/389.pdf
3. Favre, J.M., Gašević, D., Lämmel, R., Winter, A. (eds.): Proceedings of the 4th International Workshop on Software Language Engineering (ateM 2007), Technical Report, Informatik Bericht 4/2007, Johannes Gutenberg-Universität Mainz (2007), http://www.informatik.uni-mainz.de/867.php

Designing Syntax Embeddings and Assimilations
for Language Libraries

Martin Bravenboer and Eelco Visser

Software Engineering Research Group, Delft University of Technology,
The Netherlands
martin.bravenboer@gmail.com, visser@acm.org

Abstract. *Language libraries* extend regular libraries with domain-specific notation. More precisely, a language library is a combination of a domain-specific
language *embedded* in the general-purpose host language, a regular library implementing the underlying functionality, and an *assimilation* transformation that
maps embedded DSL fragments to host language code. While the basic architecture for realizing language libraries is the same for all applications, there are
many design choices to be made in the design of a particular combination of library, guest language syntax, host language, and assimilation. In this paper, we
give an overview of the design space for syntax embeddings and assimilations for
the realization of language libraries.

1 Introduction

Software libraries provide reusable data structures and functionality through the built-
in abstraction facilities of a programming language. While functionally complete, the
interface through regular function or method calls is often not appropriate for efficiently and understandably expressing programs in the domain of the library. *Language libraries* extend regular libraries with domain-specific notation. More precisely, a
language library is a combination of a domain-specific language *embedded* in a general-
purpose host language, a regular library for the underlying functionality, and an *assimilation* transformation that maps embedded DSL fragments to host language code.

In recent years case studies of language libraries have been conducted for a number of host languages and types of applications, including concrete object syntax for
meta-programming [3,24], embedding of domain-specific languages in general purpose
languages (MetaBorg) [11,6], and syntax embeddings for preventing injection attacks
(StringBorg) [7]. While there is a common architecture underlying all these language
libraries, there are many design choices to be made in filling in the parameters to the
architecture. For example, a recent innovation is type-based disambiguation of syntax
embeddings [26,10], which uses the type system of the host language to disambiguate
quoted code fragments, thus allowing a more lightweight syntax.

In this paper, we present an overview of the design space for syntax embeddings and
assimilations for the realization of language libraries. The contribution of this paper is
an overview of the state-of-the-art, providing insight in the design space, and research
questions in language library realization, in particular, the identification of research
issues for realizing an independently extensible language library framework. In the next

H. Giese (Ed.): MoDELS 2007 Workshops, LNCS 5002, pp. 34–46, 2008.

section we give an overview of the various types of applications of language libraries illustrated with examples. In the remaining sections we discuss technical considerations and trade-offs in the realization of language libraries.

2 Applications of Language Libraries

In this section we consider different types of applications, which are characterized by the target of assimilation. We distinguish four types of language libraries; libraries for transformation, generation, string generation, and DSL embedding. We consider each of these categories in turn and show typical examples. Figure 1 gives an overview of some libraries that we have realized.

Transformation of structured data is typically used for program transformation, but also for transformation of other structured data, such as XML documents. Direct manipulation of the structures through their API can lead to tedious coding in which the natural structures are hard to recognize. Syntax embeddings can be used to provide concrete syntax for patterns used to match and construct code fragments [24]. The target of assimilation in these applications is an API for analysing and constructing abstract syntax trees. For example, consider the following Stratego rewrite rule that defines the desugaring of the sum construct in terms of a for loop with an auxiliary (fresh) variable:

		host language			
guest lang.		Stratego	Java	Perl	PHP
Stratego		T			
Tiger		T			
ATerm		T	T		
C		G(T)			
Java		G(T)	G		
XML		G(T)	G		
SQL			S	S	S
Shell			S	S	S
XPath			S	S	S
Swul			D		
Regex			D		

Fig. 1. Examples of realized embeddings with host languages in columns and embedded languages in rows. The letters indicate the type of embedding with G = generation, T = transformation, S = string generation, D = DSL embedding.

```
DefSum :
  I[ sum x = e1 to e2 ( e3 ) ]I ->
  I[ let var y := 0
       in (for x := e1 to e2
               do y := y + e3); y end ]I
  where y := <newname> x
```

The terms between I[and]I are quotations of Tiger code patterns that are used both to pattern match *and* to compose code. For example, the left-hand side I[sum x = e1 to e2 (e3)]I of the rewrite rule is assimilated to the term pattern Sum(Id(x), e1, e2, e3), where x, e1, e2, and e3 are *meta-variables*, i.e. variables that match subterms when the rule is applied. (newname is used to create a fresh variable in order to avoid accidental capture of free variables.)

A similar idea can be used with Java as host language. While Stratego natively supports terms for representing abstract syntax trees, Java requires such structures to be defined using objects. A syntax embedding of terms in Java (JavaATerm) can be used to make analysis and construction of term structures in Java programs easier. For example, the following is a code fragment from a transformation from an ATerm representation of bytecode files to a BCEL representation of bytecode:

```
private void addInstructions(ATerm code) {
  ATerm optlocals = null, optstack = null;
```

```
ATerm is = null, excs = null;
match code with
  Code(MaxStack(optstack), MaxLocals(optlocals)
  , Instructions([...] and is)
  , ExceptionTable([...] and excs)
  , Attributes(_));
```

The embedding provides (among other things) concrete syntax for term patterns and the match <expr> with <term> construct, which is assimilated to statements that implement the matching by analyzing the ATerm argument against the declared pattern.

An important requirement for the use of syntax embeddings in transformations is that the structure of the quoted pattern coincides with the structure of the program to which it is applied. This does not hold in scenarios where the abstract syntax tree of a program is heavily analyzed, modified, and/or attributed before being transformed. For example, abstract syntax trees for C and Java require static semantic analysis before they can be properly transformed.

Code generation involves the composition of programs from templates based on input such as a DSL program or user input. Construction of large pieces of code using string concatenation is tedious and error-prone. Templates are not checked statically for well-formedness and meta characters need to be escaped. Furthermore, a textual representation does not allow further processing. Use of an API provides a structured representation, but is not suitable for encoding (large) templates. Syntax embeddings allow encoding templates in the concrete syntax of the language, but at the same time producing structured code. Embedded code fragments are assimilated to API calls for *constructing* structured data (such as ASTs). The API does not need to support *transformation* of patterns derived from concrete syntax. For example, the back-end of the Stratego compiler uses rules such as

```
TranslateStrat(|S,F) :
  |[ s1 < s2 + s3 ]| ->
  stm|[ { ATerm ~id:x = t;
          ~stm:<translate-strat(|Next,F')>s1
          ~stm:<translate-strat(|S,F)>s2
          ~id:F' : t = ~id:x;
          ~stm:<translate-strat(|S,F)>s3 } ]|
  where x := <new>; F' := <new>
```

to implement schemes for translating Stratego to C. In this example *two* languages are embedded in the host language; the left-hand side of the rule is a Stratego code fragment, while the right-hand side is a C code fragment. The right-hand side template uses recursive calls to generate code for the subterms of the left-hand side pattern. The results are integrated by *anti-quotations* such as ~stm:t and ~id:t that convert a Stratego term into the right syntactic sort. Note that quotations and antiquotations are *tagged* with syntactic sorts such as stm|[and ~id:, this is necessary to avoid ambiguities in parsing.

The same technique is used for other host languages. For example, the following fragment shows a Java method generating Java code represented using the Eclipse JDT.

```
public CompilationUnit run(ClassDescriptor cd) {
  CompilationUnit result = |[
```

```
   import java.util.*;
   public class #[ cd.getName() ] {
     #[ attributes(cd) ]
   }
 ]|;
 return result;
}
```

Note that unlike in the Stratego case, the (anti)quotations are not tagged; this information can be deduced from the types of the host language (e.g., `CompilationUnit`)[10].

String generation is commonly used in libraries supporting domain-specific languages such as XML, XPath, regular expressions, and SQL to provide an interface that uses character strings to communicate programs in these language. For example, a method `execQuery` from an SQL library might take a string containing an SQL query as argument, such as

```
execQuery("SELECT * FROM Users where username = \'" + name + "\'");
```

Insertion of run-time data (e.g., user input) is done by composing queries using string concatenation from constant parts and dynamic parts provided by variables. The approach suffers from a number of problems. First, strings are not statically guaranteed to be well-formed, which may lead to run-time errors. Second the approach requires escaping of meta-symbols (such as the quotes in the example above), which can lead to tedious and obfuscated code. Worst of all, the approach leads to software that is prone to *injection attacks*, where ill-formed user input may lead to breakdown or security compromises. For example, insertion of the string ' OR 1=1-- in the query above would lead to dumping a list of all users.

These problems can be avoided by using syntax embeddings instead of string concatenation [7]. By quoting a query, as in the following code fragment

```
SQL.QueryExpr q = <| SELECT * FROM Users WHERE username = $str{arg} |>;
execQuery(q);
```

the query is syntactically checked at compile-time, no spurious escaping is needed, and insertion of run-time data is guaranteed to be properly escaped to avoid injection attacks. Embedded queries are assimilated to calls to methods in a *syntax API*, which provides for each production in the syntax definition a corresponding method. This ensures that well-formedness of queries is verified by the type system of the host language.

Domain-specific language (DSL) embedding is concerned with providing better notation for programming in a certain domain, and are typically designed around an existing library. The DSL abstracts over normal usage of the library, and assimilation is to sequences of library calls. For example, JavaRegExp is a DSL built on top of the Java regular expression library. In the first place it provides a syntax for quoting regular expressions without spurious escaping, similar to the string generation examples above. Building on this basic embedding, JavaRegExp provides a DSL for defining and combining string rewrite rules in Java. For example, the following code fragment defines several string rewrite rules for escaping HTML special characters, their composition with a choice operator <+, and the application of the rules to the contents of a string in variable `input`:

```
regex amp = [/ & /] -> [/ &amp; /];
regex lt  = [/ < /] -> [/ &lt;  /];
regex gt  = [/ > /] -> [/ &gt;  /];
regex escape = amp <+ lt <+ gt;
input ~= all(escape);
```

Another example in this category is JavaSwul, an embedding in Java of a dedicated language for creating Swing user-inteface widgets, following the hierarchical structure of the class hierarchy of Swing [11,6].

3   Syntax Embedding and Assimilation

Language libraries are realized by means of *syntax embeddings and assimilations* as illustrated by the architecture diagram in Figure 2. An implementation typically consists of four components, *i.e.* a parser, typechecker, assimilator, and pretty-printer. Together these components transform programs in the extended language to programs in the host language only. Each of the components is parameterized with data that are specific for the syntax embedding at hand. The *parser* is parameterized with the syntax of the extended

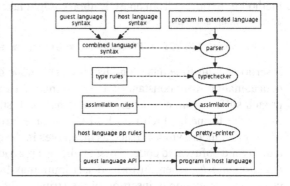

Fig. 2. Components for syntax embedding and assimilation. Solid arrows denote data-flow, dashed arrows parameters of tools in the chain.

language. This requires syntax definitions for the *host language* and the *guest language*, and a definition of how guest language fragments are inserted in host language programs. The parser converts a textual representation of a program in the combined language to a tree structure that is suitable for further processing. *Type rules* extend the *typechecker* of the host language to check extended programs. This component is optional. Having an extensible typechecker avoids type error messages expressed in terms of assimilated programs. The *assimilator* transforms embedded guest language fragments to an implementation in the host language. The assimilator is parameterized with a set of *assimilation rules* that define the translation schemes for the guest language. For certain applications the assimilation rules may be generic in the guest language. A *pretty-printer* converts the tree structure produced by the assimilator to text, which can be fed to a host language compiler or interpreter. Pretty-printing can be avoided if transformations are expressed directly on parse trees, rather than abstract syntax trees. Another option is not to produce a textual representation of the assimilated program at all, but instead link assimilation into the host language compiler. This is done for example in Stratego, where assimilation of concrete object syntax is built into the compiler [24]. Finally, the assimilator may generate code that makes calls to an *API corresponding to the guest language* (the 'run-time system' for the embedding).

3.1 Syntax Embedding

A syntax embedding is an extension of the syntax of the host language with the syntax of a guest language. Such an extension is achieved by an extension of the grammar of the host language, which introduces the language constructs of the guest language at specific places in the host language. To illustrate the basic principles of syntax embeddings, we use an embedding of SQL in PHP using SDF [23], a

```
module TinySQL exports
lexical syntax
    [A-Za-z]+ -> Id                                     1
    [A-Za-z0-9\ \"\-\;] -> Char
    "\'" ("\'\'" | Char)* "\'" -> CharString            2
context-free syntax
    "SELECT" Id* "FROM" Id Where?-> Query               3
    "WHERE" Expr -> Where                               4
    Expr "=" Expr -> Expr {left}                         5
    CharString -> Expr
    Id -> Expr
```

Fig. 3. Syntax definition for a tiny subset of SQL

modular syntax definition formalism for defining the lexical as well as context-free syntax of language in a single formalism. Figure 3 shows the syntax definition for a tiny subset of SQL, the guest language of this example. We omit the syntax definition of the host language. The module TinySQL defines the lexical and context-free syntax of a stylized subset of SQL in reversed EBNF notation, namely simple queries [3] with where clauses [4], equivalence expressions [5], identifiers [1] and character strings with escaped quotes [2].

The syntax of TinySQL is embedded in PHP by creating a new SDF module (Figure 4) that imports the syntax definitions of PHP as well as TinySQL [6]

```
module SQL-in-PHP imports PHP TinySQL  6 exports
context-free syntax
    "<|"      Query[SQL] "|>" -> Expr[PHP]              7
    "${"      Expr[PHP]  "}"  -> Expr[SQL]              8
    "$str{"   Expr[PHP]  "}"  -> CharString[SQL]        9
```

Fig. 4. Embedding of syntax for SQL in syntax for Java

and defines how the languages are combined, *i.e.* where TinySQL can be used in PHP and vice versa. The productions of this module use *parameterized non-terminals, e.g.* Expr[PHP] and Expr[SQL], which are used to indicate the language of the non-terminal. The first production [7] of SQL-in-PHP defines the *quotation* of SQL queries, i.e. that they can be used as PHP expressions between the quotation tokens <| and |>. The second [8] and third [9] productions define the *anti-quotations* of this embedding, which allow an SQL expression or character string to be constructed by an arbitrary PHP expression. In this way, queries can be composed dynamically. From this combined syntax definition a parser is generated, which is used to parse PHP programs that use the SQL syntax extension. After that, the resulting parse tree or abstract syntax tree is transformed to a plain PHP program by an assimilation.

3.2 Assimilation

The assimilation phase provides the actual implementation of the embedded syntax of the domain-specific language. In this phase the embedded language constructs are removed from the source program by a translation to the host language, using any necessary translation scheme. The implementation of the assimilation phase largely depends on the application for which the embedded language is intended. The complexity of the implementation depends on the particular combination of the embedded language and the host language. The design of the assimilation is influenced by the requirements to make embeddings (a) easy to understand, (b) composable, and (c) analyzable.

Assimilation rules are the basic transformation steps of the assimilation that have a pattern of guest code at their left-hand side and produce a pattern of host code at their right-hand side. In our examples the assimilation rules are implemented in the Stratego program transformation language. Figure 5 illustrates two assimilation rules for the embedding of Java in Java. The first rule [10] assimilates an array type by generating invocations of the Eclipse JDT API for the representation of Java programs in Java. The second rule [11] assimi-

```
Assimilate : [10]
  ArrayType(type) -> e[ _ast.newArrayType(e) ]
  where e := <Assimilate> type

Assimilate : [11]
  Field(e,y) -> [
    {| FieldAccess x = _ast.newFieldAccess() ;
       x.setExpression(e1); x.setName(e2);
     | x |}
  ]
  where <newname> "expr" => x;
    [e1,e2] := <map(Assimilate)> [e,y]

Assimilate = [12]
  ?AntiQuote(<assimilate-strat>)

assimilate-strat = [13]
  alltd(?Quote(<Assimilate>))
```

Fig. 5. Assimilation of Java in Java

lates a field access by creating a FieldAccess object and invoking some methods on it for initialization. The assimilation rules are applied by an *assimilation strategy* [13], which traverses the program and applies the rules where necessary. Most assimilation strategies have the same structure: they traverse the program topdown and apply the assimilation rules if a quotation is found. If an anti-quotation is found [12], then assimilation is stopped and the assimilation strategy is invoked recursively.

4   Design Issues

There are many variation points in the realization of syntax embedding and assimilation for a language library. In this section we give an overview of the main issues. An in depth discussion of the issues and the range of solutions and their relative advantages and disadvantages is beyond the scope of this paper.

4.1   Syntax Embedding

The grammar formalism that is used for defining the syntax embeddings should allow **modular extension of grammars**. A modular grammar formalism implies support for the **full class of context-free grammars**, since that is the only class that is closed under composition. In particular, grammar classes such as LL and LR, which are supported by conventional parser generators are not adequate. Similarly, the lexical syntax is usually defined using a collection of regular expressions. However, the class of regular grammars is also not closed under composition. Solutions to **composition of lexical syntax** that are used in practice are: (1) Ignoring the problem, which entails that the lexical syntax of host and guest language are merged, e.g. keywords of one become keywords of the other. Used in Bali, from the pioneering AHEAD/JTS tool set [3] (see [11] for a discussion). (2) Use lexical states to distinghuish the context in which a program fragment should be interpreted. In language libraries for program generation such as Meta-AspectJ [26] and JavaJava [10] with explicit quotation symbols this is a possible solution (3) Control the state of the lexical analyzer from the parser. While this a major complication of the interface between the scanner and the parser and seems to be rather unpopular in practice, it has recently been applied in the Silver extensible compiler system [22]. (4) Let the scanner produce all possible interpretations of tokens. This is only possible if the token boundaries of the host and guest languages are exactly the same, which is often not the case. (5) Integrate lexical syntax and context-free syntax in the same formalism as is realized in the syntax definition formalism SDF, which implemented by using scannerless parsing This means that a separate lexical analysis phase is omitted and the parser operates directly on the individual characters of a source file. This is the only solution that can gracefully deal with combinations of languages.

Requiring support for the full class of context-free grammars reduces the number of **parsing algorithms** that can be used. Currently, the best studied algorithms for parsing possibly ambiguous context-free grammars are generalized-LR [21,18] and Earley [12] parsing. Scannerless parsing [19], which is an important feature for syntax embedding, has been integrated with generalized-LR in the implementation of SDF [23]. Known issues with (S)GLR are the poor quality of error messages and the absence of error recovery. Packrat parsing [13] is another candidate for parsing syntax embeddings. Packrat parsers are used to parse languages defined by *parsing expression grammars*, which are closed under composition, intersection and complement. Scannerless packrat parsers are available and have been shown to perform very well [14] compared to current GLR parser implementations. Unfortunately, packrat parsers are not able to produce all possible alternatives for ambiguities.

When the basic requirements for modularly combining grammars are met, there are additional **modularity features** a grammar formalism should have to support syntax embeddings. A notion of namespaces is needed to manage the scope of definitions in grammars to be combined. The host and guest language grammar may use the same non-terminal, which will become a single syntactic category when combined. To keep such non-terminals separated and to control exactly which non-terminals are identified, a namespace or renaming mechanism is necessary. A related issue is that the set of identifiers that should be considered as reserved keywords depends on the context. For example, `class` is a keyword in Java, but not in SQL. Also the rules for layout (whitespace and comments) are different depending on the context. For example, `//` is a comment symbol in Java, but an operator in XPath. In a declarative syntax definition of AspectJ [8], the notion of **grammar mixins** was introduced to deal with these issues (except for modular layout). The parameterized sorts and modules of SDF, along with a mixin generator, were used to implement grammar mixins. A proper language design for grammar mixins is needed.

In code and string generation, **quotations and anti-quotations** are often highly ambiguous if the quotations of the various guest non-terminals all use the same syntax. There are three solutions to this problem. (1) The number of quotations can be restricted. For example, if the embedding allows the quotation of a list of statements as well as a single one, then a quotation of a single statement will always be ambiguous. In some applications, having only a quotation for the list of statements might be sufficient. (2) The quotations and anti-quotations can be explicitly tagged with their syntactic type, basically introducing different quotation symbols for every quotable non-terminal. This solves the ambiguity problem, but the user now needs to know when and how to use these tags. Furthermore, the tags obfuscate the code and often feel redundant to the user. In some cases explicit tagging can be made less unattractive by using keywords from the guest language. For example, the anti-quotation of an optional where clause of an SQL query can be tagged using WHERE?, which looks like the keyword WHERE from SQL.

```
"WHERE" "?" "${" E "}" -> Where⟦SQLCtx⟧?
```

(3) The ambiguities can be preserved by parsing the ambiguous source file to a parse forest. The ambiguity can then be dealt with at a later phase (for instance, by leveraging the type system of the host language [10]), or can even be ignored if the exact representation is irrelevant. For the user this is by far the most attractive solution, since the embedding is not restricted and no knowledge about the ambiguities is required.

Having a single extension of a host language available is useful, but many applications require **multiple extensions** to be available in a single source file. For example, in web applications, the main application domain of StringBorg, XML, SQL, Javascript, and Shell, are often used together. Extensions should preferably not be deployed as closed extensions of the host language, but rather as separate plugins that can be selected by the user and combined *on the fly* by the system. This requires **independent extensibility** of the host language, that is truly modular implementations of language libraries.

4.2 Assimilation

The **scope** of a transformation [25] indicates the parts of the source and target program that are involved in the transformation. Scope has a major impact on the complexity of assimilations. We distinguish the following types of scopes. (1) *Local-to-local* assimilations map guest code fragments directly to host code fragments, which are at the exact same place in the abstract syntax tree as the original guest code. Local-to-local rules are easy to implement, since the rules are all independent and do not influence the assimilation strategy. (2) *Local-to-global* assimilations do not just locally replace guest code fragments, but in other places in the abstract syntax tree as well. These assimilations are typically needed when fragments to be generated cannot be expressed locally. For example, executing statements, declaring new methods, or introducing import declarations. (3) *Global-to-local* assimilations need context information from the original program for a local assimilation, such as the current package, class, method, or even type information. (4) *Global-to-global* assimilations need context information from the source program and also produce global host code. Dynamic rewrite rules [9] are typically used to implement context-sensitive transformations, that is all but those with local-to-local scope.

To avoid name capture, assimilation rules should be **hygienic**, that is, generated names should all be unique. This can be achieved easily with a gensym-like mechanism that guarantees generation of unique names.

If the embedding is part of a family of embeddings that all implement a similar assimilation, the assimilation may be **generic** in the guest language. For example, the representation of object programs in Stratego is directly based on the syntax definition of the object language, thus the transformation from the guest code to Stratego is implemented generically [24]. In some cases the assimilation can even largely be *host language* independent [7].

If the host language can be typechecked statically, then it is useful to **typecheck before assimilation**, to keep the error reports as close to the original source as possible. This requires extension of the typechecker of the host language with type rules for the guest language.

5   Related Work

Syntax Embedding. Macro systems usually restrict the syntax that can be introduced. For an extensive review of the relationship to JSE [1], Maya [2], Metafront [5], JTS [3], and camlp4 [20] we refer to [11] and [10]. There are a number of parser generators that could be applied for the parsing of syntax embeddings. Harmonia's Blender [4] and Cardelli's extensible syntax have been discussed in detail in [11]. Packrat parsing [13,14] has been discussed in Section 4.1. The Polyglot parser generator [17] supports modular adaptation of LR-grammars, which has been discussed in [7].

Furthermore, there is a wide range of applications that apply a form of syntax embedding. In these particular applications (Template-Haskell, MetaOCaml, Meta-AspectJ, SafeGen, etc.) the parsing problem is often reduced because the host language is embedded in itself or development time for parsing this combination of languages is acceptable. Hence, no general method for language libraries is required, though they could profit from such a facility. Recently, support for quoting expressions has been introduced in C#. C# does not introduce a syntax for quotation, but infers quotations from the type of variables and parameters. One of the main purposes of this facility is to use C# expressions to express query expressions, *e.g.* SQL, without introducing syntax (see also [7]).

Assimilation. Macro systems usually only allow a straightforward local-to-local mapping from the introduced syntax to the host language. Our assimilation rules and strategies allow local-to-global and global-to-local transformations, which is somewhat related to the desire for macros to reach out and touch somewhere [15], one of the ideas leading to AspectJ. Macro systems that allow context-free grammars as macro arguments often provide more advanced facilities for transformations. For example, Metafront [5] associates transformations to all productions and additionally guarantees termination of the transformation.

Open Compilers.   Open compilers such as Polyglot [17] are not designed to facilitate DSL embedding in particular. Instead, they are designed for the introduction of new language features that invade the language, such as new types, optimizations, concurrency features, etc. The requirements for a system that supports the implementation of syntax embedding and assimilation by non-compiler experts are rather different. More experience with extensions is needed to give definite answers on the requirements.

Methodology.   In [16] the authors state that work is needed on DSL development methodologies, since the use of a DSL can provide major benefits, but the development of DSLs often raises many questions without clear answers or resources on the right decisions to make. Though our work chooses a particular approach to DSL development, our analysis of the design space in this area contributes to the discussion on methodologies. Also, a major focus of our work is to make the implementation of extensions as easy as possible by not imposing technical constraints on the syntax embedding and assimilation.

Domain-Specific Embedded Languages.   The term domain-specific embedded (or internal) language (DSEL/EDSL) is often used for a DSL defined within the host language, that is, without syntactically extending the host language. DSELs are popular in languages that have a flexible syntax, such as Haskell (user-definable infix operators) and Ruby. In the case of Ruby, there is extensive support for introspection, intercession, code generation, evaluation and bindings, which reduces the need for interpreting the DSL. The heavy use of run-time code generation is largely cultural (since similar functionality is available in languages such as Perl and Python) and due to seemingly irrelevant details, such as multi-line string literals. Considering the syntax, the main disadvantages of embedded domain-specific language approaches is that the syntax cannot be clearly defined separately, but has to be crafted carefully, based on the constraints imposed by the host language.

Acknowledgments.   This research was supported by NWO/JACQUARD projects 638.001.201, *TraCE: Transparent Configuration Environments*, and 638.001.610, *MoDSE: Model-Driven Software Evolution*.

References

1. Bachrach, J., Playford, K.: The Java syntactic extender (JSE). In: Object-Oriented Programming, Systems, Languages, and Applications (OOPSLA 2001), pp. 31–42. ACM, New York (2001)
2. Baker, J., Hsieh, W.: Maya: multiple-dispatch syntax extension in java. In: Programming Language Design and Implementation (PLDI 2002), pp. 270–281. ACM, New York (2002)
3. Batory, D., Lofaso, B., Smaragdakis, Y.: JTS: tools for implementing domain-specific languages. In: International Conference on Software Reuse (ICSR 1998), pp. 143–153. IEEE, Los Alamitos (1998)

4. Begel, A., Graham, S.L.: Language analysis and tools for input stream ambiguities. In: Language Descriptions, Tools and Applications (LDTA 2004). ENTCS, Elsevier, Amsterdam (April 2004)
5. Brabrand, C., Vanggaard, M., Schwartzbach, M.I.: The metafront system: Extensible parsing and transformation. In: Language Descriptions, Tools and Applications (LDTA 2003), ACM, New York (April 2003)
6. Bravenboer, M., de Groot, R., Visser, E.: MetaBorg in action: Examples of domain-specific language embedding and assimilation using Stratego/XT. In: Lämmel, R., Saraiva, J., Visser, J. (eds.) GTTSE 2005. LNCS, vol. 4143, pp. 297–311. Springer, Heidelberg (2006)
7. Bravenboer, M., Dolstra, E., Visser, E.: Preventing injection attacks with syntax embeddings. A host and guest language independent approach. In: Lawall, J. (ed.) Generative Programming and Component Engineering (GPCE 2007), pp. 3–12. ACM, New York (October 2007)
8. Bravenboer, M., Tanter, E., Visser, E.: Declarative, formal, and extensible syntax definition for AspectJ. A case for scannerless generalized-LR parsing. In: Object-Oriented Programing, Systems, Languages, and Applications (OOPSLA 2006), ACM, New York (October 2006)
9. Bravenboer, M., van Dam, A., Olmos, K., Visser, E.: Program transformation with scoped dynamic rewrite rules. Fundamenta Informaticae 69(1–2), 123–178 (2006)
10. Bravenboer, M., Vermaas, R., Vinju, J.J., Visser, E.: Generalized type-based disambiguation of meta programs with concrete object syntax. In: Glück, R., Lowry, M. (eds.) GPCE 2005. LNCS, vol. 3676, pp. 157–172. Springer, Heidelberg (2005)
11. Bravenboer, M., Visser, E.: Concrete syntax for objects. Domain-specific language embedding and assimilation without restrictions. In: Object-Oriented Programing, Systems, Languages, and Applications (OOPSLA 2004), pp. 365–383. ACM, New York (October 2004)
12. Earley, J.: An efficient context-free parsing algorithm. Communications of the ACM 13(2), 94–102 (1970)
13. Ford, B.: Packrat parsing: simple, powerful, lazy, linear time, functional pearl. In: International Conference on Functional Programming (ICFP 2002), pp. 36–47. ACM, New York (2002)
14. Grimm, R.: Better extensibility through modular syntax. In: Cook, W.R. (ed.) Programming Language Design and Implementation (PLDI 2006), ACM, New York (June 2006)
15. Kiczales, G., Lamping, J.: L.H.R., Jr., Ruf, E.: Macros that reach out and touch somewhere. Technical report, Xerox Corporation (December 1991)
16. Mernik, M., Heering, J., Sloane, A.M.: When and how to develop domain-specific languages. ACM Computing Surveys 37(4), 316–344 (2005)
17. Nystrom, N., Clarkson, M.R., Myers, A.C.: Polyglot: An extensible compiler framework for Java. In: Hedin, G. (ed.) CC 2003 and ETAPS 2003. LNCS, vol. 2622, pp. 138–152. Springer, Heidelberg (2003)
18. Rekers, J.: Parser Generation for Interactive Environments. PhD thesis, University of Amsterdam (1992)
19. Salomon, D.J., Cormack, G.V.: Scannerless NSLR(1) parsing of programming languages. ACM SIGPLAN Notices 24(7), 170–178 (1989); In: PLDI 1989 (1989)
20. de Rauglaudre, D.: Camlp4 reference manual (September 2003)
21. Tomita, M.: Efficient Parsing for Natural Languages. A Fast Algorithm for Practical Systems. Kluwer Academic Publishers, Dordrecht (1985)
22. Van Wyk, E., Schwerdfeger, A.: Context-aware scanning for parsing extensible languages. In: Lawall, J. (ed.) Generative Programming and Component Engineering (GPCE 2007), pp. 63–72. ACM, New York (October 2007)
23. Visser, E.: Syntax Definition for Language Prototyping. PhD thesis, University of Amsterdam (September 1997)

24. Visser, E.: Meta-programming with concrete object syntax. In: Batory, D., Consel, C., Taha, W. (eds.) GPCE 2002. LNCS, vol. 2487, pp. 299–315. Springer, Heidelberg (2002)
25. van Wijngaarden, J., Visser, E.: Program transformation mechanics. a classification of mechanisms for program transformation with a survey of existing transformation systems. Technical Report UU-CS-2003-048, Institute of Information and Computing Sciences, Utrecht University (May 2003)
26. Zook, D., Huang, S.S., Smaragdakis, Y.: Generating AspectJ programs with Meta-AspectJ. In: Karsai, G., Visser, E. (eds.) GPCE 2004. LNCS, vol. 3286, pp. 1–19. Springer, Heidelberg (2004)

A Comparison of Standard Compliant Ways to Define Domain Specific Languages

Ingo Weisemöller and Andy Schürr

Real-Time Systems Lab
Technische Universität Darmstadt
D-64283 Darmstadt, Germany
{weisemoeller,schuerr}@es.tu-darmstadt.de
http://www.es.tu-darmstadt.de/

Abstract. Domain specific languages are of increasing importance for today's software development processes. Their area of application ranges from process modeling over architecture description and system design to behavioral specification and simulation. There are numerous approaches for the definition and implementation of DSLs. Among others, the OMG offers UML profiles as a lightweight extension of a predefined multipurpose language and MOF as a metamodeling language, which can be used to define DSLs from scratch. This contribution investigates various approaches to define DSLs, focusing on architectural description languages as an example. Besides the usage of UML profiles and the definition of an entirely new language with MOF, the adaption of the UML based on a metamodel extension is also considered. As a consequence of the shortcomings depicted for the different approaches, we suggest to combine UML profiles and metamodeling in order to compensate their weaknesses and take advantage of their benefits.

1 Introduction

Nowadays the usage of domain specific languages (DSLs) is of growing importance in software development processes. Languages like BPMN [13], ACME [5] or MATLAB/Simulink [19] offer support for various phases of the software development process. Most of them are built up from scratch, often by means of a proprietary metamodeling language. As a matter of fact this results in high efforts, when building tools based on these languages. The Object Management Group (OMG) has, therefore, introduced profiles as a mechanism to describe lightweight extensions of the Unified Modeling Language [16,17] (UML) as well as the Meta Object Facility [14] (MOF) as a meta modeling language to provide standard methods for the definition of domain specific languages.

From the coexistence of different standards for the definition of DSLs arises the question for which languages UML profiles are appropriate and in which cases we need to define a heavyweight extension or specify a new metamodel. On the one hand, UML is wide spread and well known, and commercial tool support is available at least for editing UML diagrams. Constraints on the models can

H. Giese (Ed.): MoDELS 2007 Workshops, LNCS 5002, pp. 47–58, 2008.

be defined in the Object Constraint Language [15] (OCL), for which support is currently available in some research projects [3] and in a few commercial tools. On the other hand, customized languages do not only offer potentially greater expressive power than profiles, and allow the usage of domain specific modeling elements. Their users also benefit from the availability of code generators, which results in lower efforts to build analysis tools and editors with a customized concrete syntax. Besides that, a customized language may be smaller and easier to learn than is UML.

The following sections deal with various approaches to define a DSL for software architectures and architecture families. As we primarily address users of UML, we focus on profiles and MOF as metamodeling techniques. Indeed we accept to run the risk of omitting the advantages of other languages, but this makes it much easier to bring together the benefits of metamodeling and profiles, since we already have MOF-QVT [11] as a standard for model-to-model transformations, which we want to use to combine profiles and metamodeling in the future. Altogether, we distinguish between three approaches of metamodeling:

- The description of a lightweight extension of the UML by using profiles and the equivalent extension of the UML metamodel. (Section 3)
- Using inheritance to extend the UML metamodel fragment that deals with components, thus introducing subclasses of the metaclasses defined in the UML 2.1 specification. (Section 4)
- The specification of a metamodel for MVC architectures in MOF. (Section 5)

For each approach we will consider the models and the metamodel of both the MVC design pattern and the architecture of the "Java Pet Store" (cf. section 2). We will then survey each approach with respect to the clarity of the corresponding metamodels and their semantics, usability for modelers and metamodelers, ease of defining constraints, and tool support.

2 Running Example

Each approach to define DSLs will be discussed based on the example of a language for software architectures. In particular, we will focus on the formal description of architectural guidelines and how to provide tool support for the automated checking of these guidelines. As an example for a concrete software architecture the Java Pet Store 1.1 web application, Sun's sample application for J2EE technology, will be used. It has been designed according to the Model View Controller (MVC) design pattern, and a detailed textual description of the architectural concepts [20] is available. Thus we have sufficient information about its architectural concerns without being biased due to the usage of a certain modeling language. Figure 1 shows an excerpt from the architecture in a notation based on UML component diagrams.

The basic idea of the MVC design pattern is to decouple a system into three areas of responsibility, each of which is improved in terms of extensibility, maintainability and replacability. We want to ensure architectures preserve this separation of concerns by demanding that each component of a system may only

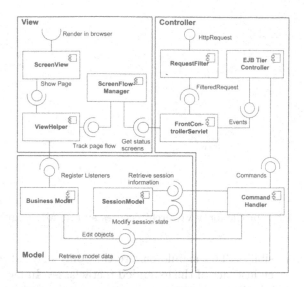

Fig. 1. Simplified architecture model of the Java Pet Store

provide interfaces of the same area of responsibility as the component. Additionally, we will distinguish between *critical*, *stable*, and *unstable* components, and define whether the usage of a component is *strict*, in which case the used component must be at least as stable as the one that uses it.

3 Using UML Profiles

Profiles have been introduced by the OMG to allow users to adapt the UML to their personal needs. According to the UML Superstructure specification [17], profiles are not supposed to extend the UML metamodel. Thus they are conceptually interchangeable between tools, using XMI [12] as data format, though this results in technical difficulties in practice, because most commercial tools do not completely comply to the standard. However, although the specification states that the UML metamodel is not extended by profiles, it describes metamodels that are equivalent to a given profile. There has been a considerable amount of publications on the modeling of architectural styles with UML profiles before, most of which deal with UML 1.x (cf. section 6).

A sample profile for the distinction between model, view or controller elements is shown on the left side of figure 2. To keep the example small, the separation into the three areas of responsibility is limited to Interfaces and Components. The right side of the same figure shows an extension of the UML metamodel that is equivalent to the profile according to the UML Superstructure specification [17].

For the specification of the desired stability of a Component we introduce the stereotype Importance, which provides an attribute of the Stability enumeration type. An abstract stereotype Responsibility that generalizes the three stereotypes Model, View, and Controller has been defined for the decoupling of the system

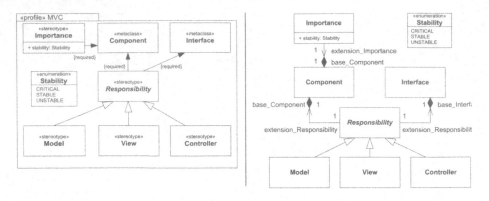

Fig. 2. A UML profile for MVC architectures and its MOF equivalent

into areas of responsibility. This should ensure that only one of the stereotypes can be applied to each instance of the extended metaclasses. In fact this depends on the mapping of inheritance between stereotypes to the metamodel. It relies on the creation of an extension_Responsibility link each time a substereotype is applied. This is what commercial tools like Enterprise Architect in fact pretend to do, but the UML specification does not clarify how to handle inheritance of stereotypes. Therefore, the creation of associations for the concrete classes with properties base_Interface, base_Component, extension_model, extension_View and extension_Controller must also be taken into consideration. If these associations are marked as subsets of the one shown in the figure, the application of only one stereotype would be ensured for the above reason. If a tool behaves different in this point, this may force the user to introduce appropriate constraints and make model interchange by means of XMI difficult or even impossible.

Figure 3 shows a small example of inheritance between an abstract and a concrete stereotype (A) and possible mappings to an equivalent MOF model (B–C). It must be pointed out that none of them can be applied by a tool directly, since this cannot modify its own metamodel at runtime. Instead, appropriate behavior must be ensured by other means, but the implementation is left up to the tool

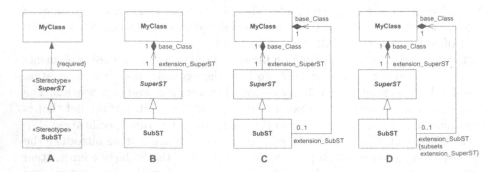

Fig. 3. Generalization of stereotypes (A) and mappings to a MOF model (B–D)

developers. Getting back to the figure, we see that Mapping B is the one applied in figure 2, introducing a single association in the MOF model. This ensures exactly one subtype of SuperST (only SubST is available in the example) is applied to each instance of MyClass. Mapping C introduces an additional association between each substereotype and the extended class, but this association does not subset the one between the superclass and the extended class. If the superclass is abstract and the stereotype is required (as in the example), there are three possible ways to reflect the application of SubST to a MyClass instance. The first one is to set only the extension_SuperST property, in which case the other association is useless. The second way is to set only the extension_SubST property, which results in a violation of the 1 multiplicity of the extension_SuperST association end, though we would expect this to result in a valid model. The third possibility is to create two links (one for each association), which will result in a violation of the 1 multiplicity of the extension_SuperST association end in case multiple substereotypes are applied to an element. The mapping shown in figure 3 D is only affected by the latter problem, since the application of an instance of SubST to an instance of MyClass results in a link in both associations due to the subsets property of the extension_SubST association end.

For the remainder of this section we will assume that the extension of classes by stereotypes is mapped to the metamodel as shown in figures 2 and 3 B. Based on this, the following constraint can be added to Responsibility to ensure that all Interfaces and their providing Components are of the same responsibility:

```
context Component inv: self.provided->forAll(i |
   i.extension_Responsibility.getMetaClass() =
   self.extension_Responsibility.getMetaClass())
```

As you will have noticed, the provided property and getMetaClass() method are not defined in our profile, but are available from the UML metamodel respectively the MOF reflection. Moreover we want to specify whether a Usage relation between Components is strict, i.e. whether it may point from a component of a certain level of stability to a less stable one. Therefore, we introduce a stereotype Strict, which extends the Usage metaclass, and attach this constraint to it:

```
context Usage inv: Stability.ownedLiteral->indexOf(
    self.client.extension_Importance.stability)
 >= Stability.ownedLiteral->indexOf(
    self.supplier.extension_Importance.stability)
```

Finally, let us look at the appliance of this profile to the concrete architecture (figure 4). We will restrict this to the EJB Tier Controller, since the effect on other components is basically the same. The concrete syntax for our extended metamodel is defined by the UML specification. A minor issue is the presentation of the stability tag in a note, where an additional attribute for the EJB Tier Controller would be preferable.

Altogether, modeling of architectural styles based on UML profiles is quite an extensive approach. It requires an OCL expression for the rather simple constraint on relationships between components and interfaces. All constraints are

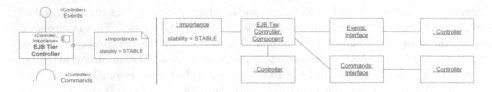

Fig. 4. The UML profile applied to the architecture and an equivalent object diagram

rather complicated since we have to navigate between stereotypes and the extended classes, and there are some ambiguities concerning inheritance between stereotypes. The advantage of UML profiles, besides reusability of the UML metamodel, is the variety of existing tools we can use to describe architectures now. Support for UML profiles is provided by a series of commercial products, though not all of them do support UML 2 yet. These tools allow the definition of profiles as well as their appliance to a model, thus being usable as an editor not only for UML, but also for DSLs defined by means of UML profiles. Unfortunately, the validation of OCL constraints does not work properly in general.

4   Extending the UML Metamodel

This section addresses heavyweight extensions of the UML by means of a MOF tool. This differs from the approach described in section 3, for which a UML tool supporting profiles is sufficient. Unfortunately, the definition of a metamodel *extension* is not that easy. If the creation, deletion and modification of arbitrary elements was allowed, it might be "extended" to any other metamodel. To our knowledge there is no generally accepted definition of a metamodel extension. However, the OMG suggests to use the package merge concept from the UML Infrastructure [16, pp 162ff] for this. Therefore, we limit extensions of a metamodel to the merge of an arbitrary package into the outermost package of the original metamodel.

Based on this, one obvious way to distinguish between interfaces provided by model, view and controller components is to introduce subclasses for Component and Interface from the UML metamodel. Unfortunately, we cannot make existing metaclasses abstract to ensure only the subclasses are instantiated. This is due to the definition of package merge: "For all matching classifier elements: if both matching elements are abstract, the resulting element is abstract, otherwise, the resulting element is non-abstract", which implies that a non-abstract UML metaclass remains non-abstract in our extended metamodel. Therefore, we have to attach the constraints shown in figure 5 to Component and Interface to ensure no instances of them can be created. The new subclasses do not necessarily have additional attributes, but they allow us to redefine associations and introduce constraints for our needs to describe MVC architectures.

As with UML profiles, we will try to express that an interface of a specific type must be provided by a component of the same type. Therefore, we introduce an association between each subclass of Component and the corresponding subclass

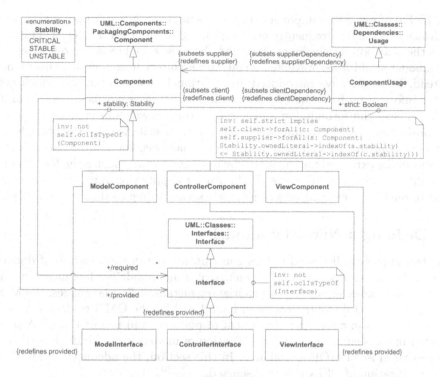

Fig. 5. Excerpt from the UML metamodel extended by subclasses

of Interface, which redefines the association between the superclasses as shown in figure 5. We can also define several categories of stability in an enumeration and add a new attribute of this type to a subclass of Component. Additionally, we introduce a subclass ComponentUsage of the Usage relation from the UML metamodel and add the attribute strict to it. The association ends between this class and Component redefine those from the UML metamodel. Thus all usages of components must be properly modeled by an instance of the new ComponentUsage class. The following constraint ensures a component does not depend on a less stable one if the strict attribute is set:

```
inv: self.strict implies self.client->forAll(c: Component|
  self.supplier->forAll(s: Component|
  Stability.ownedLiteral->indexOf(s.stability)
  <= Stability.ownedLiteral->indexOf(c.stability)))
```

Each component and interface in a model must now be represented by an instance of one of the new subclasses instead of Component and Interface from the original UML metamodel. The association refinements and the constraints make sure components provide only interfaces of appropriate types and do not strictly depend on less stable components. The concrete architecture will basically look the same as the one shown in Figure 1, except that a concrete syntax for the new subclasses and relation needs to be introduced.

The FrontController component from our sample architecture provides a view interface which offers frequently used pages, e.g. login or error screens. This violates the association refinements specified above, so a tool based on our extended metamodel would have prevented a software architect from creating this model. Instead, he might have introduced an additional view component, which gets status information from the FrontController and creates status screens from it.

As we see, the formulation and check of some basic constraints can be accomplished in an UML metamodel extended by inheritance. On the other hand, elements from the original metamodel which have become unnecessary are still present in the extended metamodel. The most serious problem is the loss of compatibility to existing UML tools. So, in order to apply this approach, one would have to modify an existing or write a new tool according to the new metamodel.

5   Defining a New Metamodel

The last approach discussed in this contribution is the specification of domain specific languages from scratch by means of a metamodeling language. In contrast to an increasing number of proprietary metamodeling languages, the Meta Object Facility [14] (MOF) has been introduced by the OMG to describe models of metadata in a format independent of platform and manufacturer. A small number of tools supporting the specification of models using MOF [1] or its less expressive subset EMOF is available. In this section, the adequacy of MOF for the specification of DSLs will be discussed.

Figure 6 shows a simple metamodel to distinguish between model, view and controller components or interfaces. It is similar to the extended UML metamodel discussed in section 4, but there are some differences due to the fact that we did not start with a predefined metamodel: First of all, the subsystems of

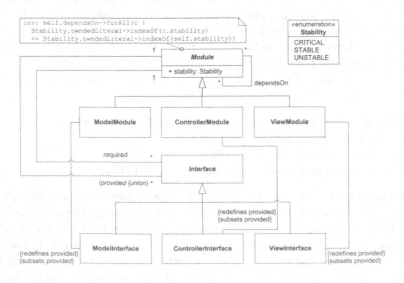

Fig. 6. A MOF model for the MVC design pattern

an architecture are no longer referred as components, but as **Modules**. When building a metamodel from scratch, arbitrary names can be given to the model elements, which allows the usage of identifiers specific to the users organisation for instance. Second, the superclasses **Module** and **Interface** can be abstract classes, so we do not have to define a constraint to ensure they cannot be instantiated. Third, the **provided** property of a **Module** is the derived union of its subsets (which may be determined by a different derivation rule in turn), instead of the derivation rule taken over from the UML into our extended metamodel.

Fig. 7. An excerpt from the architecture model of the Pet Store

Since we have not introduced any notation, an excerpt from the architecture of our sample application is shown as an object diagram in figure 7. To be able to build a graphical editor for DSLs, a concrete syntax needs to be defined; frameworks for building editors and tools based on MOF or EMOF models are currently being developed by several organisations, e.g. [10]. The figure shows the coupling of the model and the view subsystem, which is realized by the registerListeners interface. Due to the usage of this interface the **viewHelper** module depends on **businessModel**, which requires the **businessModel** to be at least as stable as the **viewHelper**. The corresponding constraint from the metamodel is fulfilled in the example, so this is a valid model.

As we have seen, the most important advantage of building a new metamodel are the extensive possibilities to adapt it to our needs and preferences. The association concepts of MOF provide a more precise and convenient way to specify relationships. Besides that, the elements can be defined in a way that makes the OCL constraints more compact than in UML profiles. Basic support for MOF based metamodeling is available as well as support for building tools on top of these metamodels. Nevertheless, building tools is still a complex and extensive task. Moreover, the introduction of a new language may require more practice than the extension of UML by means of profiles, which requires neither an entirely new concrete syntax nor new tools for the introduction of domain specific modeling elements.

6   Related Work

Several publications address the definition of DSLs, many of which deal with extensions of the UML or the specification of a new DSL by means of MOF.

Dong and Yang suggest to use UML profiles to describe architectural styles in [4], but they focus on the visualization of patterns in system design rather than consistency checking, though a few examples of constraints are given.

A publication of Henderson-Sellers and Gonzalez-Perez [7] investigates the differences between stereotypes in UML 1 and UML 2 and points out some issues about their specification from a set theoretical point of view. However, it contains some serious flaws. For instance, the authors state that "the Stereotype metaclass in UML 2.0 is a subtype of Class, so only classes can be stereotyped", where the first has nothing to do with the latter (and it should be mentioned that "classes" in this sense are more than classes in class diagrams), or they point out the "inability of stereotypes to express behavior", although this does obviously not hold for stereotypes which extend behavioral constructs.

The authors of [6] use a framework for model-to-model transformations to map domain specific languages to UML. As discussed in the previous sections of this contribution, they state that code generation and automated model analysis usually come along with the introduction of DSLs, whereas UML is primarily used as a target language for the visualization of models. However, their approach does not make use of UML profiles yet, but is focused on basic UML instead.

Besides these scientific projects there are a few commercial, proprietary meta-case-tools available [8], which in general lack interoperability, because they do not comply to a standard meta modeling language, and modularization concepts.

7   Conclusions

Our comparison of various approaches to define domain specific languages has shown the benefits and drawbacks of UML profiles and metamodeling. Profiles are supported by current CASE tools, but the concepts to refine associations are rather weak in comparison to those of a metamodeling language. They also suffer from a lack of flexibility, which makes the specification of constraints for consistency and integrity checking more complicated than necessary. In addition to these issues, there are some uncertainties about how to map profiles to an equivalent metamodel. Domain specific languages built up from scratch or as a heavyweight extension of the UML are better suited for these purposes, but they require high effort on tool building to be really usable for model editing.

Table 1. Overview of approaches to specify DSLs

	UML profiles	UML extension	New Metamodel
Expressive power	-	+	+
Flexibility	-	o	+
Clarity of semantics	-	+	+
Simple constraints	-	o	+
Model Notation	-	-	+
Tool support	+	-	-

8 Future Work

From the benefits and drawbacks of the approaches discussed in the previous sections follows the desire to combine the advantages of UML profiles and meta-modeling. More precisely, a way to define DSLs and make them usable without building entirely new tools is required. For this purpose, we suggest to define a mapping from a limited set of domain specific languages to UML profiles and vice versa, which will make the use of commercial CASE tools as editors possible, but enable us to revert to the possibilities provided by metamodeling tools for integrity and consistency checking of the models. For the definition of a DSL and adaption of existing tools to this language we want to perform the following steps as shown in figure 8:

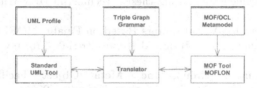

Fig. 8. Combination of UML profiles and metamodel based technologies

1. The abstract syntax of a DSL is defined in a MOF-compliant metamodeling tool like MOFLON [1]. OCL constraints may be used to define static semantics of models described in the DSL.
2. A UML Profile is used to define the concrete syntax of the new language with constructs similar or identical to those used by UML.
3. An implementation of QVT based on Triple Graph Grammars [9,18] is used to translate the stereotyped UML model into an instance of the metamodel and vice versa.

The combination of UML profiles and metamodel based technologies is supposed to be a systematic replacement for extensive usage of profiles [2], reducing the effort of implementations to ensure the proper use of such profiles.

References

1. Amelunxen, C., Königs, A., Rötschke, T., Schürr, A.: MOFLON: A Standard-Compliant Metamodeling Framework with Graph Transformations. In: Rensink, A., Warmer, J. (eds.) ECMDA-FA 2006. LNCS, vol. 4066, pp. 361–375. Springer, Heidelberg (2006)
2. Basin, D., Doser, J., Lodderstedt, T.: Model driven security for process-oriented systems. In: SACMAT 2003: Proceedings of the eighth ACM symposium on Access control models and technologies, pp. 100–109. ACM Press, New York (2003)
3. Chiorean, D., Demuth, B., Gogolla, M., Warmer, J.: OCL for (Meta-)Models in Multiple Application Domains. In: Kühne, T. (ed.) MoDELS 2006. LNCS, vol. 4364, pp. 152–158. Springer, Heidelberg (2007)

4. Dong, J., Yang, S.: Visualizing design patterns with a uml profile (2003)
5. Garlan, D., Monroe, R.T., Wile, D.: Acme: Architectural description of component-based systems. In: Leavens, G.T., Sitaraman, M. (eds.) Foundations of Component-Based Systems, pp. 47–68. Cambridge University Press, Cambridge (2000)
6. Graaf, B., van Deursen, A.: Visualisation of Domain-Specific Modelling Languages Using UML. In: ECBS 2007: Proceedings of the 14th Annual IEEE International Conference and Workshops on the Engineering of Computer-Based Systems, Washington, DC, USA, pp. 586–595. IEEE Computer Society, Los Alamitos (2007)
7. Henderson-Sellers, B., Gonzalez-Perez, C.: Uses and abuses of the stereotype mechanism in uml 1.x and 2.0. In: Nierstrasz, O., Whittle, J., Harel, D., Reggio, G. (eds.) MoDELS 2006. LNCS, vol. 4199, pp. 16–26. Springer, Heidelberg (2006)
8. Isazadeh, H., Lamb, D.A.: CASE Environments and MetaCASE Tools. Technical report, Queen's University School of Computing (1997)
9. Königs, A.: Model Integration and Transformation – A Triple Graph Grammar-based QVT Implementation. PhD thesis, Technische Universität Darmstadt (to appear, 2007)
10. Minas, M.: Generating Visual Editors Based on Fujaba/MOFLON and DiaMeta. In: Proc. 4th Fujaba Days, Technical Report tr-ri-06-275, pp. 35–42, University Paderborn (2006)
11. Object Management Group, Inc. Meta Object Facility (MOF) 2.0 Query/View/Transformation Specification (November 2005), http://www.omg.org/cgi-bin/apps/doc?ptc/05-11-01.pdf
12. Object Management Group, Inc. MOF 2.0/XMI Mapping Specification, v2.1 (September 2005), http://www.omg.org/cgi-bin/apps/doc?formal/05-09-01.pdf
13. Object Management Group, Inc. Business Process Modeling Notation Specification (February 2006), http://www.omg.org/cgi-bin/apps/doc?dtc/06-02-01.pdf
14. Object Management Group, Inc. Meta Object Facility (MOF) Core Specification (January 2006), http://www.omg.org/cgi-bin/apps/doc?formal/06-01-01.pdf
15. Object Management Group, Inc. Object Constraint Language (May 2006), http://www.omg.org/cgi-bin/apps/doc?formal/06-05-01.pdf
16. Object Management Group, Inc. Unified Modeling Language: Infrastructure (February 2007), http://www.omg.org/cgi-bin/apps/doc?formal/07-02-06.pdf
17. Object Management Group, Inc. Unified Modeling Language: Superstructure (February 2007), http://www.omg.org/cgi-bin/apps/doc?formal/07-02-05.pdf
18. Schürr, A.: Specification of Graph Translators with Triple Graph Grammars. In: Mayr, E.W., Schmidt, G., Tinhofer, G. (eds.) WG 1994. LNCS, vol. 903, pp. 151–163. Springer, Heidelberg (1995)
19. Simulink - simulation and model-based design (1994–2007), http://www.mathworks.com/products/simulink/
20. Sun Microsystems, Inc. Java pet store architectural overview (2001), http://java.sun.com/blueprints/code/jps11/archoverview.html

Third International Workshop on Model Driven Development of Advanced User Interfaces

Andreas Pleuß[1], Jan Van den Bergh[2], Stefan Sauer[3], Daniel Görlich[4],
and Heinrich Hußmann[1]

[1] University of Munich, Germany
{Andreas.Pleuss,Heinrich.Hussmann}@ifi.lmu.de
[2] Hasselt University, Belgium
Jan.VandenBergh@uhasselt.be
[3] University of Paderborn, Germany
sauer@upb.de
[4] University of Kaiserslautern, Germany
goerlich@mv.uni-kl.de

Abstract. The workshop *Model Driven Development of Advanced User Interfaces (MDDAUI)* aims at integrating results from the area of human-computer interaction and user interface modeling with the concepts of model-driven engineering. This paper provides a summary on the third edition of MDDAUI held as part of the MoDELS 2007 conference in Nashville, USA. In particular, it presents the results of the two group discussions of the workshop.

1 Workshop Topic

The user interface of an application is often one of the core factors determining its success. While model-based user interface development is an important line of research in the human-computer-interaction (respectively human-machine-interaction) community, model-driven application development is an important area in the software engineering community. This workshop aims at integrating the knowledge from both domains, leading to a model-driven development of user interfaces. Thereby, the focus of the workshop is on advanced user interfaces corresponding to the current state-of-the-art in human-computer-interaction, such as multimedia or context-sensitive user interfaces or multimodal interaction techniques.

The workshop builds up on the results of the previous editions in 2005 [1] and 2006 [2]. While the first two editions mainly provided an overview of the topic, the current edition aims at addressing more advanced topics in this area, including usability of the approaches, their integration with informal techniques like visual design and prototyping, and a better utilization of concepts from model-driven engineering, e.g., more flexible transformations leading to better adapted user interfaces. The research area is still evolving as new user interface technologies and paradigms are coming along and model-driven technologies are becoming more mature.

H. Giese (Ed.): MoDELS 2007 Workshops, LNCS 5002, pp. 59–64, 2008.

2   Submissions, Participants, and Program

Interested participants were invited to submit a paper of four pages length in double-column format. We mainly asked for technical papers presenting concrete solutions that consider the concepts of model-driven engineering, e.g., specified in terms of a concrete metamodel. We received fourteen submissions and accepted nine of them as the result of an intensive peer-review process by the programme committee. Five papers were selected to be presented as long presentations and four for short presentations at the workshop. Workshop participants basically came from two different groups: Some were frequent participants of the MoDELS conference who have a strong background in model-driven development while others were mainly based in the area of human-computer interaction (or human-machine interaction).

The workshop took one day during the MoDELS conference. In the morning sessions all accepted papers were presented; according to the foregoing selection process either in a long presentation or a short presentation. After each talk there was some discussion and in addition there was time for additional discussion and general questions at the end of each session. In the afternoon the topics for group discussions were selected and participants joined one of the two discussion groups. The detailed program can be found on the workshop Web page [4]. Official proceedings including all accepted papers are available electronically [3].

3   Workshop Discussions

After paper presentations two discussion groups were formed around the following topics:

- Usability of Model-Driven UI Development for the Developers
- Combination of Modeling Techniques

At the end of the workshop, both groups presented their discussion results which are summarized in the following.

3.1   Usability of Model-Driven UI Development for the Developers

A core issue in user interface development is usability: The user interfaces resulting from a user interface development process must be usable, and the development process should ensure usability as much as possible. In addition, the development tools and methods itself should be usable as well. This, in turn, will improve the usability of the developed user interfaces. The discussion summarized here focuses on the usability of a model-driven user interface development process.

A specific characteristic of user interface development is the participation of different experts, like graphic designers, interaction designers, and programmers. The integration of these experts is one of the main benefits models can provide in user interface development. The discussion group aimed at further specifying the role of models in user interface development. Finally, the following statement was found adequate:

Models shall act as a kind of bridge between input from various people involved in UI development (end users, domain experts, UI developers, management people, etc.) to integrate all this knowledge and to transfer it into the software engineering process.

Participants agreed that currently no modeling language completely satisfies in covering all aspects of all the different experts. Moreover, it was considered likely that a "universal" language of this kind, covering all possible situations and projects, will be too complex to be used in practice. An attractive solution may come from domain-specific user interface modeling languages (DSUL) and corresponding tools. It was mentioned that the required meta-tools for this approach are not easy to handle, and probably the definition of a DSUL for a specific project, company or domain may be expert work or a consultancy task.

In order to actually be accepted by user interface developers, such a modeling approach has to offer significant practical advantages. From the comparison with other technologies, which were around for some time before having been embraced by the developer community (code version management, IDEs), it becomes clear that a successful tool must leverage reuse of previous work. Things to be reused in the user interface context are, among others: patterns, anti-patterns, usability heuristics, usability metrics, interface components, etc. In particular, reuse here includes knowledge about the usability of user interfaces.

Furthermore, it has to be taken into account that the people who will actually work with a modeling tool are quite heterogeneous, as mentioned above. Each of these user groups will have a specific view on a model. So for instance, end users and domain experts can be involved best if the tool comprises a facility to carry out prototyping experiments or to incorporate the results of such experiments. For modeling experts, tools for creating abstractions from actual interaction sequences will be most important. For user interface developers, the tool shall provide detailed technical information; maybe even on code level. In order to keep all these views consistent under modifications in various views, techniques like those known as "round-trip engineering" from CASE tools are desirable.

3.2   Combination of Modeling Techniques

In model-driven user interface development, a large spectrum of different approaches exists. Although there are many commonalities between these approaches, they are often isolated from each other. However, there is variability between them because of their distinguished focus or the particular application domain. For example, some of them support context-sensitive user interfaces, collaborative applications, mixed interactive systems, multimedia user interfaces, etc.

This discussion aims at a better understanding of the relationships between the different models and concepts in user interface modeling. The resulting benefits can be in first place a better general understanding. In longer terms, it might also be possible—considering the concepts of model-driven engineering— to provide operations on the different metamodels in user interface development to support a seamless spectrum of user interfaces to be developed. For example, a user interface can be multimedia *and* context-sensitive. In the ideal case, modeling support for such a user interface can be provided by reusing and combining modeling concepts (metamodels) for these two aspects. The combination of metamodels probably has to be performed manually, but a general overview on the landscape of existing modeling concepts can strongly help the modeling experts to identify and reuse the required concepts. It should be mentioned that basically it would also be possible to construct an overall metamodel for user interface development which already covers all possible aspects of user interfaces, but in practice this would be a very hard and error-prone task.

In the discussion we identified the following issues as the starting point:

- Identify relevant dimensions to structure the models.
- Identify relationships between user interface models.
- Identify relationships from user interface models to other kinds of models (of the software engineering domain) in application development.

Initially, two dimensions were identified to be most relevant for structuring the user interface metamodels:

Semantic aspects: The aspects of the user interface represented by a specific metamodel; i.e., the kind of information in the model. Examples are the user tasks to be supported by a user interface or its dynamic behavior. A specific aspect of the user interface can be represented by different modeling concepts, i.e., different metamodels. For example, the user tasks can be represented by *ConcurTaskTrees*, or *MAD*. *Discourse Models* do not directly represent user tasks but can (partially) replace task models as they also specify the purpose of the user interface but on a different level of abstraction. The dialogue or interaction to be performed by the user interface can be specified for example using *Statecharts* or *Petri Nets*.

Level of abstraction: The level of abstraction on which a metamodel represents the respective aspects of the system. Usually, the level of abstraction is related to the position of the model within the development process: In early stages the user interface will be modeled in a more abstract way while models specifying the final implementation must be very concrete. However, the concrete temporal order of models within a development process depends on the chosen process. In particular, it might be possible that some very concrete information is already available at an early stage of the development. In this case, it can be useful to be able to specify it immediately.

Figure 1 provides a first attempt to arrange some typical user interface models within these two dimensions. Two kinds of relationships are specified:

Contributes to: A (meta-)model contributes to another (meta-)model, i.e., the target model is created based on information from the foregoing model. In particular, this can mean that the target model is derived by a transformation from the source model. For example, the *Abstract Presentation* and the *Dialogue* are usually created based on a *Task* model.

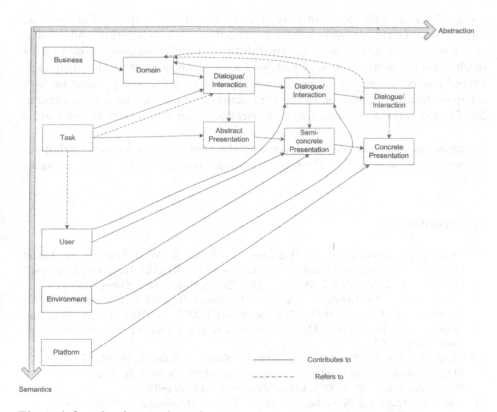

Fig. 1. A first sketch towards a schema structuring common metamodels in user interface modeling and their relations

Refers to: If a model refers to another, existing model, this means that some model elements in the former model contain references to model elements specified in another, the latter model. For example, the *Dialogue* usually refers to the *Domain* model as for example interactive user interface elements usually trigger some operations from domain classes.

The models in the presented schema basically can be applied to the development of any kind of user interface. Some domains require models for additional information, e.g.:

— user interfaces for mixed interactive systems require specification of physical objects,
— user interfaces for multimedia applications require specification of media objects.

4   Conclusion

The area of model driven engineering is continuously evolving and, as the workshop discussions show, the area of user interface modeling can directly profit from these advances. This does not only concern better tool support but also the foundations. Currently, well-defined metamodels allow comparing and reusing user interface modeling concepts. Tunability of transformations can be used as mechanism to ensure the usability of developed user interfaces. In the future, advanced concepts of model driven engineering, like model weaving, might be used for more flexible integration of different concepts for advanced user interfaces, like for user interfaces supporting collaboration, multimedia, *and* mixed-reality.

Acknowledgements. We thank the workshop participants for their high quality contributions as well as the program committee members for their valuable reviews.

References

[1] Pleuß, A., Van den Bergh, J., Hußmann, H., Sauer, S.: Workshop Report: Model Driven Development of Advanced User Interfaces (MDDAUI). In: Bruel, J.-M. (ed.) MoDELS 2005. LNCS, vol. 3844, pp. 182–190. Springer, Heidelberg (2006)

[2] Pleuß, A., Van den Bergh, J., Hußmann, H., Sauer, S., Bödcher, A.: Model Driven Development of Advanced User Interfaces (MDDAUI) - MDDAUI 2006 Workshop Report. In: Kühne, T. (ed.) MoDELS 2006. LNCS, vol. 4364, pp. 100–104. Springer, Heidelberg (2007)

[3] Pleuß, A., Van den Bergh, J., Hußmann, H., Sauer, S., Görlich, D.: MDDAUI 2007 – Model Driven Development of Advanced User Interfaces 2007. In: CEUR Workshop Proceedings, vol. 297 (2007), http://ceur-ws.org/Vol-297

[4] Third International Workshop on Model Driven Development of Advanced User Interfaces (MDDAUI 2007) (2007), Workshop Web page, http://planetmde.org/mddaui2007/

Domain-Specific Methods and Tools
for the Design of Advanced Interactive Techniques

Guillaume Gauffre, Emmanuel Dubois, and Remi Bastide

IRIT – University of Toulouse
118, route de Narbonne
31062 Toulouse Cedex 9, France
{gauffre,emmanuel.dubois,bastide}@irit.fr

Abstract. Novel interactive systems such as Augmented Reality are promising tools considering the possibilities they offer, but no real development methods exist at the moment to help designers in their work. We present in this paper a design method for tightly coupling early interaction design choices and software design solutions. Based on an existing model used for abstract UI design, our work introduces a second model dedicated to the software UI specification and the model-based process used to derive one from the other. To achieve this, we present here a framework based on domain-specific models and transformations to link them and thus support the development process.

Keywords: Mixed Interactive Systems, Model-Driven Engineering, Domain-Specific Languages, Metamodeling, Model Transformations, Design Process.

1 Introduction

In the past 10 years, a new HCI trend has emerged: traditional "Window, Icon, Menu, Pointing device" interfaces tend to be replaced by new forms of interaction that involve physical artifacts, easily manipulated by users. Augmented Reality systems, for example, are interactive systems in which the realization of a physical task is enriched by the presence of digital data and/or services. Tangible User Interfaces and ubiquitous systems are other forms of interactive systems which merge physical and digital worlds. Because they deal with similar concepts and techniques, we group these approaches under the single term: Mixed Interactive Systems (MIS). To support the development of such systems, MIS frameworks have been developed and adopt bottom-up or top-down approaches. Each of them brings consequent advances at different levels of abstraction of the design [7], but interlacing them remains difficult to accomplish, thus limiting the coverage of the development process.

As the use of MIS increases, enhancing the robustness, efficiency and quality of these systems is required. In this sense, elaborating a convenient development process becomes necessary. To cover the different steps of such a process, our approach promotes the results gathered in the early design phases and bridges the gap between the abstraction levels of these results and the implementation. To do so, we articulate

H. Giese (Ed.): MoDELS 2007 Workshops, LNCS 5002, pp. 65–76, 2008.
© Springer-Verlag Berlin Heidelberg 2008

models to progress along the development process and adopt an MDE approach, thus introducing a Domain-Specific Language [1] for MIS.

2 MIS Engineering Framework

Common processes for HCI development include four phases: requirements gathering, design, implementation and evaluation. Figure 1 presents how our tools cover the first three phases.

Following interviews and observations, task modeling is one of the major tools used to support the requirements gathering. Task models are used to characterize the sequence of sub-tasks with their type (i.e., user's activities, system's activities or interactive activities), the domain objects involved and the events triggered, and to structure these sub-tasks in a hierarchical form corresponding to the global system task.

The design phase can be decomposed into two separate steps: UI design and the related software specification. The former step is concerned with user interaction aspects. It may be linked to requirements gathering by combining users' observation, brainstorming or focus-groups to collect user needs, and an interaction model to organize them according to the specificities of MIS [4]: domain objects description, user abilities, physical and digital artifacts, forms of interaction. During the latter step, design aspects related to the software architecture are considered, using a model dedicated to the description of MIS architectures.

The next step is the implementation of the system by using component-based platforms improving flexibility and adaptability.

Finally an evaluation can be carried out in different ways such as user experiments or ergonomic inspection.

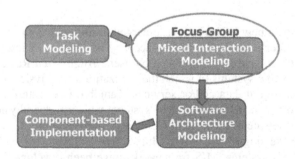

Fig. 1. MIS domain-specific process

At each step, a set of existing models, notations and tools exists: task model in the requirements gathering, dialog and interaction models in the UI design, software architecture and system objects models in the software specification. In this context, rather than modifying the different models involved in order to articulate their usage, we describe a DSL to support this process. Indeed, the current state of the design approach is consistent with two major aspects that are well addressed by an MDE approach:

- Multiple models are required in each phase of the development process and one role of MDE is to "promote models to primary artifacts that drive the whole development process" [1]. MDE will facilitate their articulation and permit the elicitation of coherence rules.
- The MIS domain, with regards to its applications in our every day life, produces emergent systems. Elaborating methods for developing them requires to evaluate the adequacy of models and to support their evolution when required. The MIS domain is in a phase of empiricism and begins to develop theories; MDE will be a powerful support of this evolution.

3   Two Domain-Specific Models

The core of the MIS Domain-Specific Language is based on two models:

- ASUR [4], a model which describes the user's interaction with a Mixed Interactive System. It can be used by itself or as mentioned before, in combination with a focus-group.
- ASUR-IL [4], a complementary model that have been introduced to cover the description of the software decomposition and structure. Its aim is to prepare the implementation step by producing a coherent architecture, promoting the forms of interaction chosen in a technological perspective.

After an overview of the ASUR metamodel in the next section, we present the ASUR-IL metamodel to enable the collaboration of our two domain-specific models.

3.1   ASUR Overview

For a given task, the role of ASUR is to support the description of the physical and digital entities that make up a mixed interactive system and the boundaries among them. ASUR components are *adapters* (A_{In}, A_{Out}) that bridge the gap between both digital and physical worlds, digital tools (S_{Tool}) or concepts (S_{Info}, S_{Object}), the *user* (U) and physical artifacts that are used as tools (R_{Tool}) or objects of the task (R_{Object}).

Components can be interconnected by several kinds of relationships. The most important one, *data exchange*, is used to describe the kind of data that is transmitted. In the physical part, the relationships represent the information channels between components, and in the digital part the way the system treats them. The *representation* link is used to express the fact that two components are two representations (one digital and one physical) of the same concept: this link is characterized in terms of behavior and rendering. Finally, *real associations* express the physical proximity of two physical components and *triggers* represent an action of one component on another. On the basis of previous works in the domain, design-significant aspects have been identified and added to the model as objects attributes: ASUR characteristics improve the specification of components (*perception/action sense, location*, etc.) and relationships (*type of language, point of view, dimension, etc.*). By analyzing the characteristics of each element, the model supports the predictive analysis of two properties: continuity and compatibility of interactions.

To illustrate ASUR (Figure 2), let us consider a system for 3D object modeling. This system offers, among other features, a dedicated physical artifact for translating, scaling and rotating the 3D object during its edition. This tool embeds a marker for video-based detection of its position and a pressure sensor for switching between each mode (translation, scale and rotation). The physical tool is modeled in ASUR as an R_{Tool}, manipulated by the user. The 3D object is the main digital concept of the task and is modeled as an S_{Object}. The second digital concept is the interaction mode and is typed as an S_{Tool}. Two *adapters* for input (A_{In}) collect data (marker detection and pressure sensor) to control each digital concept. These are in turn connected to one A_{Out} for visual output: the mode is rendered as textual data and the 3D object in a 3D scene.

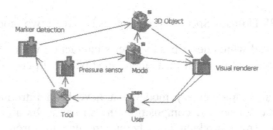

Fig. 2. ASUR model of the 3D object modeler example

3.2 ASUR-Implementation Layer: Towards the Implementation Phase

For each ASUR model, i.e. a given mixed interactive task, an ASUR-IL model is associated. The main contribution of this model is to identify the software components and relationships required to implement this specific task. Only the components involved in the interaction part of the system are described. The description of functional parts of the system is out of ASUR-IL scope. This model is also the frontier between Platform Independent Model (PIM) and Platform-Specific Model (PSM): it describes the software components involved in the task and their communications, the next step being the transfer to a PSM where each ASUR-IL component will be associated to existing software component or new ones.

An ASUR-IL model is an assembly of components which contains two kinds of sub-assemblies: *adapters* and *entities*. Each of them is related to ASUR components (ASUR *adapters* → ASUR-IL *adapters*, ASUR *system* components → ASUR-IL *entities*). Each sub-assembly regroups several components with specific roles in the architecture (*devices, APIs, models, controllers, and views*). ASUR-IL *adapters* for input or output, corresponds to the *adapters* in the ASUR model and group *devices* and software libraries (*APIs*), used to connect physical and digital worlds. *Devices* are used to capture/render data from/to the physical world. They can translate physical phenomenon into digital data and vice versa. *APIs* permit to combine several computing facilities to obtain required data: for example, ARToolKit is a specific toolkit for Augmented Reality, which grabs a video frame and produces 3D coordinates of the recognized markers. Therefore *adapters* compose the system part which is likely to be reused: a software implementation of an *adapter* can either exist and satisfy the

ASUR modeling, or be developed on the basis of a combination of existing *devices* and *APIs*.

ASUR-IL *entities* are the other kind of sub-assemblies that make up an ASUR-IL model. They correspond to the digital concepts that are involved during interaction and which are identified in ASUR as S_{Tool}, S_{Object} or S_{Info}. They are triplets of three ASUR-IL components called *models*, *views* and *controllers*, inspired by the MVC decomposition [8]. *Controllers* interpret the physical phenomena and translate data from *adapters* into commands on *model* parts. *Models* are the entry point to the functional core. They are an abstraction of it, enabling the dialog with the application core. Finally, *views* are in charge of the computation required to reflect the state of each digital concept on each output *adapter* connected.

Finally, the relationships named *data flows* connect each component by using the interfaces *port*. The correctness of the *data flow* between two components is ensured by the value given to the attribute *data type* of each *port*.

The ASUR-IL model (Figure 3) that describes the 3D object modeler cited in the previous section is composed of 13 components. A first *adapter* collects the pressure level on the tool using only one *device* component. A second one produces a 4x4 matrix for position and orientation of a marker, captured by a camcorder *device* and computed by the ARToolKit *API*. The last adapter is in charge of rendering the digital concepts, using a screen *device* connected to a window *API*. To render each concept, two *API* components are added: a text field and a 3D canvas.

The two ASUR-IL *entities* follow the MVC decomposition. For example, the 3D object is composed of one *model* which contains the object's characteristics (position, size, etc.). One *controller* transforms a 4x4 matrix into a scale/rotation/translation factor. Finally, one *view* is in charge of inserting the object into the 3D scene by using 3D primitives. The second *entity*, the interaction mode, follows the same decomposition: one *model* containing the three states, one *controller* to convert one level of pressure into one of these three values and a *view* to express the current mode as a string of characters.

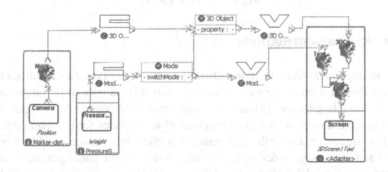

Fig. 3. ASUR-IL model of the 3D object modeler example

3.3 MIS Design Support

ASUR has its own editor: GuideMe [6]. It is a graphical editor which can export diagrams as XML files. After its metamodel was defined [3], a second version of the editor was developed using EMF to separate graphical editing from model manipulation. As mentioned above, ASUR and ASUR-IL are two models required at different steps of a MIS design process. Other models could also be required such as task models for requirements gathering or system models for functional core specification. To support the integration of our two models and further evolution, we adopt an MDE approach and choose to instrument it with tools from the Eclipse Modeling Project (EMP [5]). This enables the creation of dedicated tools for each model with EMF, GMF, and others. Therefore each model can be edited using the corresponding plug-ins in Eclipse (cf. Figure 4).

Using these tools, the designer can manipulate the two models easily. The main challenge is now to link them by model transformations to rapidly observe the consequences of modifying the description of the interactive situation modeled with ASUR on the software architecture described with ASUR-IL. The next section presents the transformation between ASUR and ASUR-IL and finally introduces the transformation between ASUR-IL and a software component model: WComp [2].

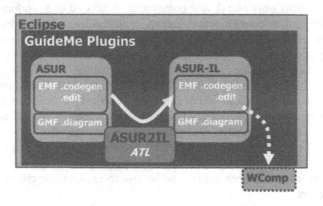

Fig. 4. Tools integration

4 Domain Transformations

In order to implement domain transformations, the Atlas Transformation Language (ATL) was chosen. One of the main reasons is that ATL is now fully integrated with the Eclipse Modeling Project [5] and so ensures complete coherence between the different tools. ATL also provides some precious characteristics for the manipulation of our models: transformation rule inheritance (as class inheritance in object-oriented language) and three ways to define a rule: using a declarative paradigm, an imperative or a mixed one. A model-2-text engine (JET) is also used to produce the PSM for the WComp platform, from the PIM ASUR-IL. The metamodel of the software component model WComp is currently only expressed as code in the platform itself. Thus at the moment, only platform-specific code generation is supported in the framework.

4.1   ASUR2ASUR-IL: Software Modeling Initialization

The goal of this transformation is to prepare the construction of a component-based architecture. ASUR identifies several digital concepts and describes their roles in the interaction: this is the left-hand side of the transformation. On the right-hand side, ASUR-IL is in charge of describing the different kinds of software components involved in the interactive part of the system, with adequate *ports* and *data flows* between them. Practically, the principles of the correspondence between these two parts are well-known, but verbally or textually expressed and not formalized. With ATL, these rules are expressed using a transformation specification language and thanks to the transformation engine, are applied on the models.

Each ATL rule follows roughly the same behavior: the type of each ASUR component plus the characteristics of the relationships between them are identified, and the satisfying rules are applied. It consists, for example, in creating for each ASUR *adapter*, an ASUR-IL *adapter* (Figure 5-1) that contains one default *device* and some *APIs* that account for the kind of interaction modalities described in the ASUR model. The rules include imperative code to interconnect components (Figure 5-3) and to factorize common processes. When ASUR digital components are transposed into ASUR-IL (Figure 5-2), they potentially trigger the creation of multiple *views* and *controllers* after *models* have been created: one *controller* per modality used to interact on the digital component, one *view* per modality used to reflect its state.

This transformation is the starting point of the software architecture design. From the characterization of a mixed interactive situation with ASUR, it produces the basis of the software architecture. It offers to rapidly design the software components structure of a concrete system before starting its implementation. This combination supports the designers during design phases, by linking abstract UI design and software UI specification. Following the transformation, designers can extend the specification

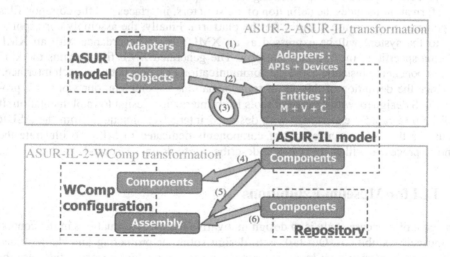

Fig. 5. Specific transformations of MIS process

by additional design decisions, such as the instantiation of other *APIs* or *devices* considering some technical limitations.

Based on this software specification, the next step is defining a platform-specific model of the system. We present in the next section another transformation process to support this final transition.

4.2 ASUR-IL2WComp: Platform-Specific Model Definition

Assuming, that during ASUR-IL editing the designers carefully identified each component of the system, they now must be transposed to the platform model. The currently chosen platform is WComp [2] which is dedicated to rapid prototyping of wearable and ubiquitous interactive systems. Considering these purposes, this platform allows the creation of assemblies of components with a small granularity and the runtime adaptation to the platform context (i.e., low battery level, devices disconnected, etc.). Its flexibility and its simplicity are the major reasons that motivated its use.

The definition of this transformation is on-going work using the model-2-text engine of EMF: JET. It will build the bridge from the PIM (ASUR-IL) to the PSM (an assembly of WComp components), with two goals:

- Creation of software components. It consists in:
  - describing the data manipulated and the associated interfaces (Figure 5-4),
  - identifying an existing software component in a repository (Figure 5-6) that contains previously developed components or standard *APIs* and *devices*,

- Management of the assembly of components (Figure 5-5) to establish the connections between each component in accordance with the ASUR-IL model.

The code required for implementing new components that will be generated by the transformation includes the definition of constructors, interfaces and the common files to generate ready-to-use libraries for the platform. Finally, the assembly corresponding to the system will be expressed as an XML file, in accordance with an XML schema specific to the WComp platform. The generated XML file contains the kind of components to instantiate and the communication channels between each interface.

Once the definition of this set of transformations is complete, our work will provide MIS designers with a range of tools from interaction design to implementation. It will help to rapidly experiment with designed interactive situations from the ASUR results to the WComp assembly of components dedicated to MIS. To illustrate the kind of process it will create, we next describe our tools on a case study.

5   TUI for Museum Exhibitions

The goal of this case study is to design innovative interactive situations in the context of museum exhibitions. Our task is to design solutions promoting knowledge transmission and entertainment in a science museum for particular themes: in this case the evolution of species. By using this approach, we can rapidly experiment with advanced interaction and adapt them to other themes by reusing components.

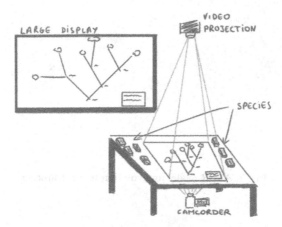

Fig. 6. Schema of the mixed interactive system

The current project aims at proposing visitors to discover species evolution by elaborating an evolution tree based on phylogenetic criteria. Adopting MIS in that context offers the opportunity to keep the visitors away from technologies as much as possible, by letting them manipulate physical objects: visitors thus remain focused on the content and are not impressed or afraid of the use of technologies such as mouse, keyboard, complex 3D devices, etc. Using MIS also increases the visitor's experience by adding digital rendering (video, 3D, sound, etc.). To elaborate the evolution tree, the user manipulates physical representations of species (a frog, a crocodile, etc.) to add them to the tree which is rendered by video on the interactive space with related phylogenetic criteria (Figure 6).

The first solution (Figure 7) uses marker-based detection to capture tangible objects (species) and visual rendering to report the data. These two facets of the interaction are described by three *adapters* on the ASUR model. The first one, marker-detection, is able to determine the position and orientation of each physical component representing species. The second one is capable of visually rendering the state of each digital component of the system. Another *adapter* for output is used for displaying the evolution tree to the rest of the audience using a large display. When describing with ASUR the task of inserting a species in the tree, an ASUR *system* component is identified to depict the digital object that includes the characteristics of the selected species. A second *system* component is required to depict the digital information related to the hierarchical classification of the species: this is a second digital concept manipulated in this task. These two digital concepts are thus connected to the three ASUR *adapters*: these relationships express the fact that information captured by the *adapter* for input (the camcorder) will affect the two digital concepts and that these two digital concepts are also affecting the *adapters* for output (namely the video-projection and the large-display).

Figure 8 shows the ASUR-IL model resulting from the asur2asur-il transformation. Each *adapter* has been translated into an ASUR-IL *adapter*, combining a default *device* connected to one *API* component which will be used to adapt the data emitted or needed by each device. In this case, the localization of each physical object

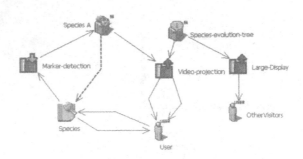

Fig. 7. ASUR model for evolution-tree construction

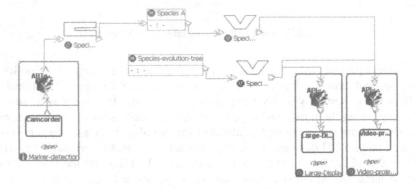

Fig. 8. Asur2asur-IL transformation result

representing one species will be made using a camcorder, producing a picture used by the *API* ARToolkit to obtain the 3-dimensional coordinates.

For each ASUR digital component, an ASUR-IL entity is created with the correct amount of *controllers* and *views* depending on the number of modalities used during the interaction. In this case, only one *controller* and one *view* are necessary for the interaction with the species, and only one *view* is used to render the evolution tree (same modality on each *adapter*: video-projection and large-display). The core behavior of each digital concept will be implemented in the *model* components, and the interaction with them will be coded into *controllers* for input and *views* for output.

To illustrate the dependencies between the two models, we focus on the case where the system also provides vocal feedback when selecting a species. This way, the user gets a description of the selected species. It results (Figure 9) in the addition of an A_{Out} in the ASUR model, an *adapter* for output corresponding to Voice synthesis, and its translation to the ASUR-IL model. The transformation will produce another *view* component for the species because of the two modalities used.

Once the architecture is designed, the next step is to use the ASUR-IL model for the implementation of the system on the WComp platform, a .NET platform using C# code. This transformation will generate component skeletons, such as interfaces, constructors and parameters, to be loadable into the platform. This is the behavior for

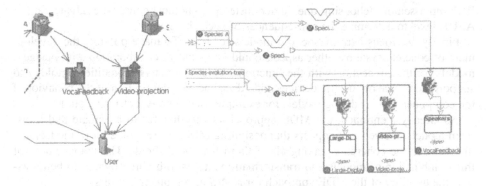

Fig. 9. Model evolution

novel components. The other choice is to specify a component that has already been developed and is described in a repository. Following this step of choosing or generating components, an XML file will be generated containing the assembly description of the system, used by WComp to run it. In the example, the components for AR-Toolkit *API* and camera *device* but also the frame component based on the *device* for video-projection, have been yet developed. Finally only *entities* and PiccoloCanvas components must have to be developed on the platform WComp.

6 Conclusion and Future Work

This work is a step toward the definition and instrumentation of a design process for Mixed Interactive Systems. This process will permit us to increment on the designed solution until obtaining a convenient degree of usability. The advances presented here, ASUR-IL model and related transformations, offer rapid navigation between the abstract design of innovative interaction techniques, expressed with ASUR, their concrete specification, expressed in ASUR-IL, and the final realization corresponding to their implementation by a WComp assembly. The Domain-Specific Language developed is an efficient tool for promoting the characteristics issued from the user-centered design into the crucial phase of implementation. As this approach uses models as primary artifacts, thanks to the MDE tools, each level of abstraction defined in the development process embeds properties standing for the usability of the interactive system.

The ASUR model defines some properties related to the quality of the interaction between a user and a mixed environment. Our goal is to integrate them throughout the entire process, to finally evaluate their evolution during each cycle of the process. Further work will aim at identifying additional properties, relevant at the software design level (ASUR-IL) such as computing time or hardware constraints, and structuring their impacts on the remaining design steps of our process. It will increase the ability to evaluate the quality of each interactive situation.

Another perspective is to study the feasibility of reverse transformations between each step and their impact on the higher levels of abstraction. A modification of a

WComp assembly (choosing one device instead of another) could be evaluated at the ASUR level to determine the consequences of such choices.

Finally, we focus here on specific models for MIS. To make possible the development of concrete systems, other aspects could be included: collaboration with business models for the connection with the functional core, interactive modalities ontology to support the choice of specific devices and APIs, and also description of the behavior of the components using dialog models for example (State charts, Petri nets, etc.).

As already mentioned, the MDE approach is very helpful to articulate and transform models. However, it appears that designing MIS may rely on a lot of models and maintaining the coherence among all of them may be difficult. The management of this combination of models and transformations needs to be investigated to better assess the usability of the MDE approach for a MIS development process.

References

[1] Bézivin, J., Jouault, F., Kurtev, I., Valduriez, P.: Model-based DSL frameworks. In: 21st ACM SIGPLAN conference on Object-oriented programming systems, languages, and applications, Portland, USA, pp. 602–616 (2006)
[2] Cheung, D.F.W., Tigli, J.Y., Lavirotte, S., Riveill, M.: WComp: a Multi-Design Approach for Prototyping Applications using Heterogeneous Resources. In: Proceedings of the 17th IEEE International Workshop on Rapid System Prototyping, Chania, Crete, pp. 119–125 (2006)
[3] Dupuy-Chessa, S., Dubois, E.: Requirements and Impacts of Model Driven Engineering on Mixed Systems Design. In: Gérard, S., Favre, J.-M., et Xavier Blanc, P.-A.M. (eds.) Proceedings of the conference IDM 2005, Paris, France, pp. 43–54 (2005)
[4] Dubois, E., Gauffre, G., Bach, C., Salembier, P.: Participatory Design Meets Mixed Reality Design Models. In: Conference Proceedings of Computer Assisted Design of User Interface (CADUI 2006), Bucarest, Romania. Information Systems Series, pp. 71–84. Springer, Heidelberg (2006)
[5] Eclipse modeling Project, http://www.eclipse.org/modeling/
[6] GuideMe, http://liihs.irit.fr/guideme
[7] Hampshire, A., Seichter, H., Grasset, R., Bilinghurst, M.: Augmented Reality Authoring: Generic Context from Programmer to Designer. In: Proceedings of the 20th conference CHISIG of Australia, OZCHI 2006, pp. 409–412. ACM Press, Sydney, Australia (2006)
[8] Krasner, G.E., Pope, T.: A cookbook for using the Model-View-Controller User Interface Paradigm in Smalltalk-80. The Journal of Object Oriented Programming, 26–49 (1988)

Transforming Discourse Models to Structural User Interface Models

Sevan Kavaldjian, Cristian Bogdan, Jürgen Falb, and Hermann Kaindl

Institute of Computer Technology
Vienna University of Technology, Vienna, Austria
{kavaldjian,bogdan,falb,kaindl}@ict.tuwien.ac.at

Abstract. User-interface design is still a time consuming and expensive task to do, but recent advances allow generating them from interaction design models. We present a model-driven approach for generating user interfaces out of interaction design models. Our interaction design models are discourse models, more precisely models of classes of dialogues. They are based on theories of human communication and should, therefore, be more understandable to humans than programs implementing user interfaces. Our discourse models also contain enough semantics to transform them automatically into user interfaces for multiple devices and modalities. This paper presents a two-step transformation approach with an intermediate user interface model. By showing specific transformation rules, we concentrate on a major part of the first step, transforming discourse models to structural user interface models.

1 Introduction

In previous work [7], we have already been able to automatically generate usable user interfaces (UIs), even for multiple devices and for real-world applications. We generated such UIs from models, but since these models included finite-state machinery they were more in the spirit of abstract UIs (abstracting from the interaction modality) rather than high-level interaction design.

More recently, in the OntoUCP[1] project, we wanted to work with models that are more understandable to humans and possibly more easily to build. Therefore, we studied several theories of human communication from various fields. Based on insights from some of these theories, we focus on high-level specifications of discourse in the form of models. These models specify discourse in the sense of dialogues, where monologues are embedded and connected. According to the reference framework [3], these discourse models are located at the "task and concepts" level.

From our previous work, we inherit the use of *communicative acts* (and references to domain knowledge). Communicative acts are derived from Speech

[1] OntoUCP (A Unified Communication Platform both for Machine-Machine and Human-Machine Interaction based on Ontologies), partially funded by the FIT-IT Program of the Austrian FFG as project number 809254/9312. We also acknowledge the (financial) support of the PSE division of Siemens AG Österreich.

H. Giese (Ed.): MoDELS 2007 Workshops, LNCS 5002, pp. 77–88, 2008.

Act Theory [13] and express intentions in the sense of desired effects on the environment.

By integrating communicative acts with some results from *Rhetorical Structure Theory* (RST) [10] and *Conversation Analysis* [9], we developed a new discourse metamodel [1,5]. The metamodel defines what the discourse models should look like in our approach.

So, we strive for high-level modeling of discourse, including dialogues. Such a discourse model is inspired by human communication and serves as an interaction design for a traditional information system. Currently we do not support the generation of UIs with direct manipulation.

From such an interaction design, user interfaces for several devices are to be generated automatically. Since we knew already how to generate them from a kind of abstract UI model, we strived for generating UI models from our new interaction design models. In general, this involves partitioning of a given discourse tree, which is described in [1].

The remainder of this paper is organized in the following manner. First, we explain our model-driven transformation approach on the basis of self-defined metamodels. Then we focus on concrete transformation rules for mapping a discourse model to a structural UI model. Finally, we briefly discuss our approach as compared to related work.

2   Overall Approach

Our approach to fully automated UI generation is a two-step process. Model-to-model and model-to-code transformations are necessary to transform a discourse model to structural UI models, and further to multiple UIs for diverse platforms. In the following, we present the first step (see Figure 1) and explain the input (discourse model), the output (structural UI models) and the transformation rules for the model-to-model transformations.

Our discourse models use a self-defined Domain Specific Language (DSL) for specifying the classes of possible dialogues or interactions between the human and the machine. The abstract syntax of the DSL is based on the conceptual

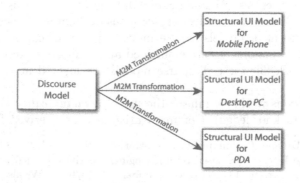

Fig. 1. The model-to-model transformation step

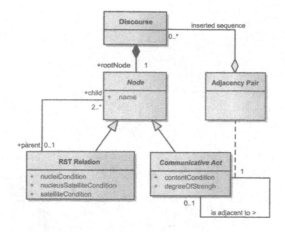

Fig. 2. Conceptual discourse metamodel

metamodel shown in Figure 2, which illustrates the concepts used. Every discourse is composed of a tree, where leaf nodes are *Communicative Acts* and inner nodes are *Rhetorical Relations* based on RST. The UML class diagram shown in Figure 2 is not as restrictive as our interpretation, since it would allow the creation of more general kinds of graphs than tree structures. The association class *Adjacency Pair* is needed to model Inserted Sequences.

The Communicative Acts are used to model the intention of a communication and refer to elements of the domain of discourse. Figure 3 shows a selection of the most important Communicative Acts used in our approach. Two corresponding Communicative Acts, like *Offer* and *Accept*, form a sequence, which is called *Adjacency Pair*. The Adjacency Pairs build up the dialogue structure.

The Rhetorical Relations are used to connect Communicative Acts or, again, Rhetorical Relations with each other. They represent the dependencies between single interactions of dialogues. Examples for Rhetorical Relations are *Condition*, *Joint* and *Background*. The *Condition* relation is used to model dependencies between adjacency pairs in the way that one branch (*satellite*) has to be executed and its Boolean expression fulfilled before the other (*nucleus*) can start. The *Joint* Relation is used to group Communicative Acts of the same type. No presentation order is presumed. The *Background* Relation is used to express that the *satellite* branch contains background information related to the *nucleus* branch.

Figure 4a shows a small part of an online shop discourse model, which we use as a running example throughout the paper. The example describes an interaction between the user and the online shop with the purpose of demanding the customer to select one product category and supporting her with background information to ease her choice. The *nucleus* branch *N* of the *Background* relation conveys the main interaction sequence. The online shop system *offers* a list of *product categories* to the user. The user *accepts* one of them. During the offering process the *satellite* branch *S* provides background information about

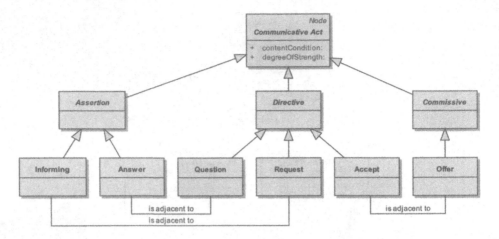

Fig. 3. Selection of communicative act taxonomy

the product categories to the user. This part of an online shop discourse model gets transformed to the structural UI model shown in Figure 4b by applying the rules *Light Background*, *Adjacency Pair*, *Offer-Accept* and *Informing* to the corresponding discourse model elements in the listed order. Details on each rule are described in section 3.

The structural UI model is basically a tree representing the UI structure independently of any toolkit (e.g., Web, Java Swing, etc.). It is not completely independent of the target device, however, since the device's real-estate is taken into account for building up the UI structure. Still, our structural user interface model is completely independent of the considered UI toolkit. This tree structure will be transformed to a toolkit-specific (final) UI. The concepts used in such a structural UI model are specified in the structural UI metamodel shown

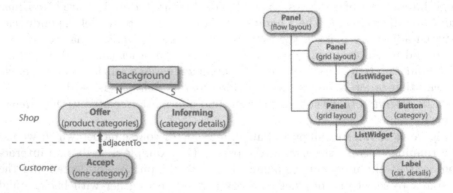

(a) Subtree of an online shop discourse.   (b) Resulting structural UI model.

Fig. 4. Online shop example showing a part of its discourse (a) and the resulting structural UI model (b) of its model-to-model transformation

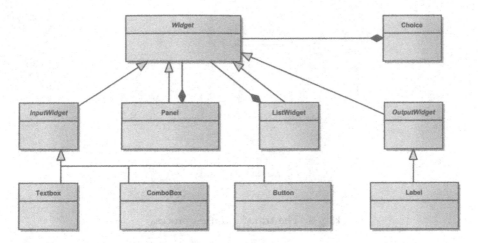

Fig. 5. Part of conceptual metamodel of structural UI models

conceptually in Figure 5. It only shows the parts that are important to our running example. The most important concept of the metamodel is the *Widget* class. It is specialized into four functional categories: *OutputWidgets*, *InputWidgets*, *ListWidgets* and *Panels*. The *OutputWidgets* present information to the user in different ways like text and images and the *InputWidgets* gather information from the user. Nevertheless, *InputWidgets* also convey information to the user like defaults, current values and type and quantity of required information.

The main issue that we address in this paper is how to transfer models as exemplified in Figure 4a to structural user interface models at the abstract widget level as in Figure 4b. In particular, it means a transformation from a mainly declarative model of a discourse to the toolkit-independent structure of a user interface.

The general principle behind our approach is that the structural UI model is made up of "presentation" units that are made visible when the logic of the interaction with the user so requires. Once this principle is established, our problem can be specified as follows:

– Given a discourse tree with communicative acts as leafs, generate the possible set of presentation units, and the transitions between these presentation units. Since each presentation unit has to be a coherent discourse itself, it corresponds to a subtree of the overall discourse tree. As such, we call this problem *the discourse tree partitioning problem*. This problem and a solution to it is described in [1].
– Given a presentation unit as a discourse subtree, generate a structural UI model based on heuristic rules. Since this effectively "pre-renders" a discourse tree into a structural UI model, we call this problem *the pre-rendering problem*.

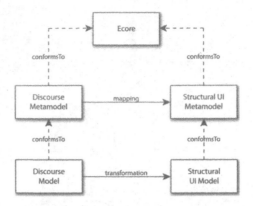

Fig. 6. The transformation process

In the structural UI model, a complete tree or subtree with a *Panel* as its root element represents a presentation unit. Hence, a complete structural UI model can, in general, be a forest consisting of possibly several trees. Trees in the structural UI model that are alternatives, i.e., trees on the same level resulting from discourse partitioning or Joint relations, will be linked in the structural UI model via a Choice element as shown in the metamodel in Figure 5. The Choice element is used to specify alternative presentation units, which can be used to fill in the same space. Our example in Figure 4a represents exactly one presentation unit that corresponds to the tree shown in Figure 4b.

Figure 6 illustrates that the transformation of one presentation unit is fulfilled by mapping elements of the discourse metamodel to elements of the structural UI metamodel. Both metamodels are based on the Ecore[2] meta-metamodel. Transformation languages like ATL[3] (ATLAS Transformation Language) or MOLA[4] (MOdel transformation LAnguage), which is used in this paper to graphically specify the transformation rules, support this transformation approach. At the same time a state machine is generated from the discourse model which controls the sending and receiving of Communicative Acts. This latter generation is beyond the scope of this paper, however.

3 Pre-rendering Rules for Transforming to a Structural UI Model

After having introduced the general transformation principles, we concentrate on the pre-rendering problem and introduce concrete rules for mapping a discourse model to a structural UI model. They are specific to certain structural patterns

---

[2] Essential MOF like core meta model of the Eclipse Modeling Framework
  (http://www.eclipse.org/emf/)
[3] http://www.eclipse.org/m2m/atl/
[4] http://mola.mii.lu.lv/

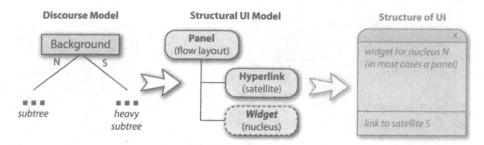

Fig. 7. Heavy Background Rule

occurring in the discourse models. We have found many such patterns during our modeling experience, and we continue to find new ones. Due to limited space, we only exemplify five rules which we believe illustrate the principle.

Heavy Background Rule: Figure 7 shows a rule for a "Heavy Background" relation, which associates a nucleus subtree with a "large" satellite subtree, i.e. a subtree that has a large number of nodes compared to the nucleus subtree and can lead to clutter if rendered in its entirety. The "nuclear" part is rendered directly since, as per the definition of RST nucleus, it is the most important part to convey, but if there is no space for its background information, the background information is rendered in a separate presentation unit. A link to the latter is presented together with the "nuclear" part, so an appropriate widget for a link (e.g., hyperlink, button) will be generated by the transformation process. Also, the action of the respective button can be generated to activate the separate presentation unit corresponding to the background.

Light Background Rule: Figure 8 shows another rule specific to the Background RST relation. The satellite is rendered on the right side of the presentation unit, while the nucleus occupies the left area, as an "aside". In accordance to the rule above, the "most nuclear part" takes the interface space that is of highest surface and most central to the user focus. Following this principle further, the layout management of the presentation unit will always give precedence to the "nuclear" side, e.g., when the window is resized by the user. This rule is used in our example to generate the basic tree structure of Figure 4b, i.e., this rules generates the root panel and places the transformation results of the pre-rendering of the nucleus and satellite subtrees next to each other by a flow layout manager. The Light Background Rule can also be localized (adapted), e.g., for cultures that write from right to left, where it may be more suitable to place the satellite at the left side. A system-wise style configuration can also render light backgrounds to the top and to the left, like it is, e.g., customary when the concrete user interface will be an HTML page. However, even there the space allocation and re-allocation in case of resizing will prioritize the nuclear part.

Figure 9 illustrates the formalized Light Background Rule in MOLA, composed of the following elements. The outer bold rectangle symbolizes a *for-each* loop. The rounded rectangle inside represents the actual rule that will be repeated for

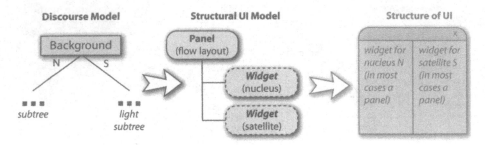

Fig. 8. Light Background Rule

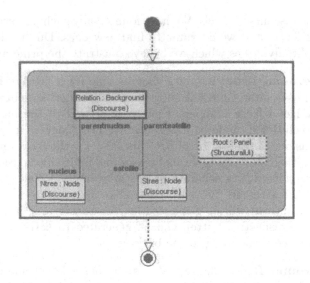

Fig. 9. Light Background Rule

each matched element. The small boxes inside the rule represent different kinds of classes, depending on their borderline style. When the thickness of the border line is regular, they represent a "normal" class. A bold border lined box represents a loop variable. A dashed lined box border represents a class that will be created by the transformation rule. The small black circle represents the starting point of the rule. The double rounded circle represents the end point of the rule. In particular, the Light Background rule iterates over all Background RST relations. Whenever a Background relation connects a nucleus tree and a satellite tree, the rule matches. In this case, a root *Panel* element of the structural UI model is generated. Next the execution is handed over to the rule responsible for the nucleus and subsequently to the rule transforming the satellite. Both rules get the panel as a parameter, so that they can add their results to the panel.

Adjacency Pair Rule: Each adjacency pair is transformed to a *Panel* element of the structural UI model containing widgets according to the related commu-

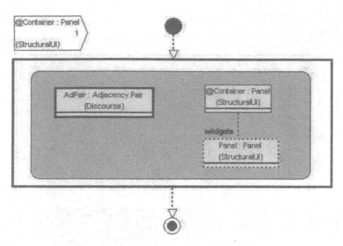

Fig. 10. Adjacency Pair Rule

nicative acts. In our example, the first panel on the second level in Figure 4b results from the application of the Adjacency Pair Rule to the Offer-Accept adjacency pair.

Figure 10 illustrates the formalized Adjacency Pair Rule in MOLA. It iterates over all Adjacency Pairs of the Discourse Model and creates a *Panel* element each. It also creates an association to the parent panel which the rule gets as a parameter. In our example, the Adjacency Pair Rule adds the created panel to the root panel of Figure 4b.

Offer-Accept Rule: Each *Offer-Accept* adjacency pair is transformed either to a *Button* or to a *ListWidget* element containing *Buttons*, depending on the cardinality of the content offered. Because our example online shop can offer more than one product category, the *ListWidget* element is needed to model an undefined number of categories. Since the acceptance of an *Offer* requires a user action, a *Button* element is embedded in the *ListWidget* in Figure 4b. As a result, the subtree of the *ListWidget* is repeated according to the actual number of product categories in the final UI.

Figure 11 illustrates the formalized Offer-Accept Rule in MOLA. It iterates over all *Offers* that are associated with an *Accept* via an *Adjacency Pair*. The parameter container of type panel represents the parent panel and allows the rule to add the generated widgets to the panel. Depending on the type of the communicative act's content, one of two alternative rules is selected. If the content is a kind of List (consisting of more than one element) a *ListWidget* and a *Button* are generated. In all other cases only a *Button* is generated in the structural UI model.

Informing Rule: Each *Informing* communicative act is transformed either to a *Label* element or to a *ListWidget* element containing a *Label* element, depending on the cardinality of the content. This rule assumes that the information will be

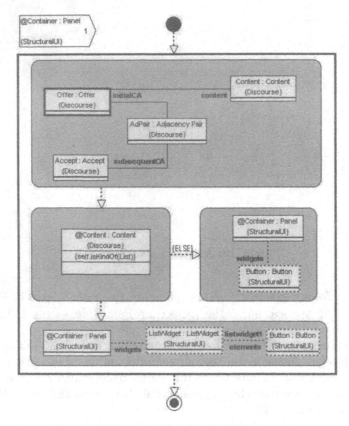

Fig. 11. Offer-Accept Rule

forwarded in textual form, otherwise, e.g., a *PictureBox* or *AudioPlayer* element
will be used. In the online shop example, information is conveyed for each product
category and, therefore, a *ListWidget* containing *Label*s is generated.

If a communicative act is not part of an adjacency pair, as it is the case with
the Informing in Figure 4a, a *Panel* element is also created as a container for
the communicative act.

More detailed information about the automatic generation that is used as a
basis for this approach can be found in [6,7].

4 Related Work

Model-based UI design methods developed and published in the nineties including OVID [12], and Idiom [14] focus on creating different kinds of models,
like user's conceptual models, task models and interaction models. Unlike our
approach, which is *model-driven*, all the mentioned approaches above are *model-
based*. That is, they allow expressing an interactive system by task, concept

and/or abstract models in a first step and use them in an informal process or in a sequence of systematic steps to construct a user interface.

In contrast, UI Frameworks like XUL[5] (XML User Interface Language) are able to generate UIs automatically but they rely on UI models at the abstract widget level, which is on a lower level than our discourse models.

An advanced approach to specifying multi-device user interfaces based on task models instead of discourse models is presented in [11]. Its basic approach is to start modeling tasks and to generate user interfaces for diverse devices according to specific device characteristics. In contrast to our approach, some of the transformations between models are done semi-automatically or manually. A major difference between task models and our discourse models is that task models express richer temporal dependencies whereas our discourse models specify causal dependencies, too. The semantic mapping of task models to dialog models based on UML State Machines is explained in [4]. A similar approach is used to generate the UI behavior from our discourse models.

Florins *et al.* describe in [8] transformation rules for pagination of UIs on different levels. Partitioning our discourse models into presentation units in the first transformation step provides important guidance for pagination [1].

Botterweck shows in [2] a model-driven approach that starts on the abstract UI level, but contains rich procedural UI descriptions together with UI elements. Thus, it requires UI modeling as well as dialogue modeling.

5   Conclusion

In this paper, we present a new approach to generating structural user interface models by applying model-driven transformations to discourse models. Our discourse models are derived from results of human communication theories, cognitive science and sociology and are used for specifying interaction design of human-computer interaction of information systems. Thus, they contain additional metainformation, like the intention of an interaction, which allows us to define sophisticated pre-rendering rules to transform the discourse models to structural UI models. Our transformation takes already device constraints into account to generate a UI structure well suited for the target device, but the resulting UI models are still independent of UI toolkits. Taking this together with our previous work on automatically generating UIs from abstract models, this paves the way for automatic generation of UIs from our new interaction design models.

References

1. Bogdan, C., Falb, J., Kaindl, H., Kavaldjian, S., Popp, R., Horacek, H., Arnautovic, E., Szep, A.: Generating an abstract user interface from a discourse model inspired by human communication. In: Proceedings of the 41th Annual Hawaii International Conference on System Sciences (HICSS-41), Piscataway, NJ, USA, IEEE Computer Society Press, Los Alamitos (2008)

---

[5] http://www.mozilla.org/projects/xul/

2. Botterweck, G.: A model-driven approach to the engineering of multiple user interfaces. In: Nierstrasz, O., Whittle, J., Harel, D., Reggio, G. (eds.) MoDELS 2006. LNCS, vol. 4199, Springer, Heidelberg (2006)
3. Calvary, G., Coutaz, J., Thevenin, D., Limbourg, Q., Bouillon, L., Vanderdonckt, J.: A unifying reference framework for multi-target user interfaces. Interacting With Computers 15/3, 289–308 (2003)
4. den Bergh, J.V., Coninx, K.: From task to dialog model in the UML. In: Winckler, M., Johnson, H., Palanque, P. (eds.) TAMODIA 2007. LNCS, vol. 4849, pp. 98–111. Springer, Heidelberg (2007)
5. Falb, J., Kaindl, H., Horacek, H., Bogdan, C., Popp, R., Arnautovic, E.: A discourse model for interaction design based on theories of human communication. In: CHI 2006 extended abstracts on Human factors in computing systems CHI 2006 (2006)
6. Falb, J., Popp, R., Röck, T., Jelinek, H., Arnautovic, E., Kaindl, H.: Using communicative acts in interaction design specifications for automated synthesis of user interfaces. In: Proceedings of the 21th IEEE/ACM International Conference on Automated Software Engineering (ASE 2006), Piscataway, NJ, USA, pp. 261–264. IEEE Computer Society Press, Los Alamitos (2006)
7. Falb, J., Popp, R., Röck, T., Jelinek, H., Arnautovic, E., Kaindl, H.: Fully-automatic generation of user interfaces for multiple devices from a high-level model based on communicative acts. In: Proceedings of the 40th Annual Hawaii International Conference on System Sciences (HICSS-40), Piscataway, NJ, USA, January 2007, IEEE Computer Society Press, Los Alamitos (2007)
8. Florins, M., Simarro, F.M., Vanderdonckt, J., Michotte, B., Michotto, B.: Splitting rules for graceful degradation of user interfaces. In: AVI 2006: Proceedings of the working conference on Advanced visual interfaces, pp. 59–66. ACM Press, New York (2006)
9. Luff, P., Gilbert, N., Frohlich, D.: Computers and Conversation. Academic Press, London (1990)
10. Mann, W.C., Thompson, S.: Rhetorical Structure Theory: Toward a functional theory of text organization. In: Text, pp. 243–281 (1988)
11. Mori, G., Paterno, F., Santoro, C.: Design and development of multidevice user interfaces through multiple logical descriptions. IEEE Transactions on Software Engineering 30(8), 507–520 (2004)
12. Roberts, D., Berry, D., Isensee, S., Mullaly, J.: Developing software using OVID. IEEE Software 14(4), 51–57 (1997)
13. Searle, J.R.: Speech Acts: An Essay in the Philosophy of Language. Cambridge University Press, Cambridge (1969)
14. van Harmelen, M.: Object oriented modelling and specification for user interface design. In: Interactive Systems: Design, Specification and Verification (1994)

Second International Workshop on Model Size Metrics

Michel Chaudron[1,2] and Christian F.J. Lange[1]

[1] Technische Universiteit Eindhoven, PO Box 513, 5600 MB Eindhoven, The Netherlands
[2] Leiden Institute of Advanced Computer Science, Leiden University, The Netherlands
m.r.v.chaudron@tue.nl, c.f.j.lange@tue.nl

Abstract. This paper reports on the Model Size Metrics (MSM) workshop held as satellite event of the MODELS 2007 conference. The focus of the workshop is to develop metrics for use in model-centric software development. As a starting point for discussion we focused on size. The workshop aim was to bring together researchers in this area, share experiences and discuss future directions. This paper summarizes the presentations that were given and the highlights of the discussion that followed and summarizes open issues for future work.

Keywords: Models, Metrics, Size, Model-driven architecture (MDA), UML.

1 Introduction

A standardized method for determining sizing concepts for software models that allows the effective base lining and comparison of model concepts is a crucial need within the MODELS community. Such metrics enable the effective estimation and quality management of model development. Additionally measuring the model size is important to provide context information for empirical studies using models.

One of the most commonly used measures of source code program size is the source lines of code (SLOC) metric. However, the concept of lines of code does not readily apply to modeling languages such as UML and SDL. Furthermore, software models are heterogeneous in nature (consisting of several different types of diagrams), can exist at varying levels of abstraction and can be created using different modeling styles. As a result, researchers face many challenges when trying to define the size of a software model. The first workshop on this topic was held in 2006 [1].

1.1 Presentations

The workshop received eight submissions. From these submissions four papers were selected for presentation at the workshop. The workshop was attended by a mix of practitioners and researchers. During the workshop ample time was spent on discussions. The papers presented are listed below. Out of these four, two papers were selected for inclusion in these proceedings (papers no. 2 and no. 3).

H. Giese (Ed.): MoDELS 2007 Workshops, LNCS 5002, pp. 89–92, 2008.

1. *Counts count* by M. Monperrus, J. Champeau, B. Hoeltzener (ENSIETA, Brest, France)
2. *Measuring the Level of Abstraction and Detail of Models in the context of MDD* by Jens von Pilgrim (FernUniversität in Hagen, Germany)
3. *On the Relation between Class Count and Modelling Effort* by Ariadi Nugruho (Leiden University, Netherlands), Christian Lange (Technische Universiteit Eindhoven, Netherlands)
4. *Effort distribution in model based development* by Werner Heijstek (Leiden University, Netherlands) and Michel Chaudron (Technische Universiteit Eindhoven and Leiden University, Netherlands)

The first paper was presented by Monperrus. He argued that basic count metrics, such as 'number of classes', are undervalued in current research on metrics for models. He proposed several arguments in support of this statement:

- Count metrics are needed for defining more complex metrics
- More elaborate metrics do not necessarily guarantee better results
- Count metrics are adopted in industrial practice
- Counting is a fully fledged modeling goal

The paper goes on to discuss what types of entities of a model should be counted and lists several requirements for the definition and automation of measures for counting.

The second presentation was by Von Pilgrim who discussed his approach for measuring 'level of abstraction' and 'level of detail' in order to assess efficiency of transformation chains in model-driven development. The notion of efficiency that is proposed is the amount of work that is needed for updating the models if the platform changes. Von Pilgrim bases his approach on "General Model Theory" by Stachowiak [2] and works towards defining a syntactic size and a semantic size of a model. The ratio between these is an indicator for the level of abstraction. Even though the approach cannot provide absolute numbers on level of abstraction, it is possible to use these metrics for relative comparison of models.

The third presentation, by Lange, explored the existence of a relation between the number of classes as a size measure of a model and the effort required for constructing a model. The data is based on two controlled experiments: in both experiments M.Sc.-level students are asked to design a UML model of a system given a description of the requirements. The first finding is that there is a large variation in the size of the models that is produced by different students for the same system. The second finding is that no significant correlation was found between the size of a model and the effort spent on constructing the model. This suggests that the number of classes is not a good predictor for the amount of effort needed for constructing a model. The differing number of classes may be explained by the following factors:

- Models may be used for different purposes like understanding what needs to be built, or detailed description for the implementation. For such different purposes, designers target different levels of abstraction, completeness and detail.
- Different designers have different styles in modeling: some focus on representing the required functionality, others on the architectural structure.

- Disproportion: Complex parts of a system are described in more detail than 'easy' parts.
- Experience: Experienced engineers create models with more classes than novice engineers.

The fourth paper, presented by Chaudron, discussed the ratio of effort spent on modeling compared to the effort spent on other disciplined in RUP-based software development projects. Also, it studied the distribution of effort over the RUP disciplines over time. This presentation included graphs that were based on around 20 RUP-based projects. One finding that was considered surprising given the prominent role of UML in RUP projects was that only a small amount of time was spent on modeling. Another finding was that the trend in the 'RUP Humps' picture is quite realistic, but in practice effort distribution has much more spikes.

Summarizing, the workshop raised more questions than answers. This indicates that this is an emerging field with opportunities for research and empirical studies.

There will not be one universal notion of size in model-based development. The large variation in uses and purposes of models requires that more context information (such as constraints, assumptions) need to be taken into account when defining size measures for models. One particular factor that was identified in the discussions was to relate size to the level of abstraction of a model. This raises the issue of how to characterize the level of abstraction of a model.

Another parameter that was considered to be of influence on the size of the model is the target level of quality. This may influence completeness of the model. Based on the experience of the workshop participants, the choice of what to model and what not to model is influenced by factors such as domain knowledge, complexity of subsystem, criticality/risk of subsystem. In general, such factors should be taken into account when investigating how model-size is related to other quantities such as requirements size and implementation size, as well as for quality and productivity measurement.

2 Issues Identified for Future Work and Future Workshops

We list some of the issues identified in the workshop as directions of collaboration and future work:

- How to measure the level of abstraction of models
- Empirical studies in general and in particular: Case studies on the use of model size metrics (measurement of size throughout development, size measurement in estimation; metrics driven process improvement)
- One of the main difficulties in empirical studies remains obtaining access to industrial UML models and related data such as associated implementation, effort, defects. Hence collecting and sharing of UML models and case study data.
- One suggestion to ease the sharing of data was to develop an 'anonymization tool' that transforms names of entities in a model such that the model can not be traced back to the organization from which it originates. However, in order to allow interesting analyses of a model it would be desirable that such an anonymization tool would maintain some properties of names of entities such as:

- names of patterns
- identical subterms in the names of different entities
- characteristical metrics properties

It was observed that no UML models have been found in the open source community.

2.1 Future Workshops

The workshop ended with a discussion on the future of MSM. There was consensus that the scope of the workshop should be broadened, such that it would also include some context that would give a purpose for interpreting metrics, such as: Economics of Modeling, Estimation and Measurement.

References

1. Weil, F., Neczwid, A.: Summary of the 2006 Model Size Metrics Workshop. In: Kühne, T. (ed.) MoDELS 2006. LNCS, vol. 4364, pp. 205–210. Springer, Heidelberg (2007)
2. Stachowiak, H.: Allemeine Modelltheorie. Springer, Wien (1973)

On the Relation between Class-Count and Modeling Effort

Ariadi Nugroho[1] and Christian F.J. Lange[2]

[1] LIACS – Leiden University, Niels Bohrweg 1, 2333 CA Leiden, The Netherlands
[2] Technische Universiteit Eindhoven, P.O. Box 513, 5600 MB Eindhoven,
The Netherlands
anugroho@liacs.nl, c.f.j.lange@tue.nl
http://www.liacs.nl/~anugroho
http://www.tue.nl/~clange

Abstract. The knowledge of size of models can be very useful to perform many kinds of estimations such as effort, cost, and productivity in software development. However, to the best of our knowledge there is no universally accepted model size measure available to date. In this paper we investigate the usefulness of class-count as a size measure of models (represented with the UML). Using empirical data collected from two student experiments we validate this measure by assessing its correlation with effort spent in modeling. The results show that merely using class-count might not provide sufficient and accurate estimation of modeling effort. Furthermore, we identify some factors that hinder class-count as a good estimate of modeling effort.

Keywords: UML, Model Size, Modeling Effort, Experiment.

1 Introduction

The size of a system has long been considered as an important attribute for measurement practice in software engineering. The most popular size measure of a system might be the SLOC (Source Lines of Code) that is still used in many measurement activities nowadays. By knowing the size of a system software engineers or project managers can calculate many other attributes related to the system or project such as productivity. As an example, a programmer's productivity can be measured from the number of lines of code he writes per day. However, the SLOC measure has been criticized as a measure of productivity, because it encourages a verbose style of programming. Another interesting use of size measure is its application to determine modules' or components' error proneness. For instance, some believed that there is an optimal size of a system's modules or components – the 'Goldilocks Conjecture'. It is believed that when a module's or a component's size is below or above the optimal size it will be more prone to error [1]. Although many computer scientists object to this hypothesis, yet this shows how size measure is very easy to use – and misused – in measurement practices.

H. Giese (Ed.): MoDELS 2007 Workshops, LNCS 5002, pp. 93–104, 2008.

With the emergence of model-driven software development, measurements are no longer solely applied to source code. As a model of a system is generally expected to be realized in the actual system, measuring the models of a system might give important information about some attributes of the actual system. This non-conventional measurement approach has the advantage of better prediction, prevention, and control over the quality of the system since the early stages of software development.

In the UML, class diagrams are used to depict the static structure of a system. In describing the dynamic behaviors of the system, each class will be represented by one or more instantiations that interact with instantiations of other classes in sequence diagrams or collaboration diagrams. The main motivation of using class-count as an estimate of modeling effort lies in the assumption that there is a relation between the way the structure and the behaviour of a system are modelled. Hence, we presume that this will subsequently influence the effort required in the modeling activity.

Additionally, the choice of using class-count as a measure was also due to the frequent usage of class diagrams in practice. A recent survey reported in [2] revealed that class diagram, use case diagram, and sequence diagram were ranked as the three mostly used UML diagram types. Having these factors in mind, in this paper we explore the usefulness of class-count as an estimate of modeling effort. In a controlled experiment with students we investigated the relation between class-count and the effort spent in modeling.

This paper is organized as follows. In Section 2 we provide some related work in this research area. Section 3 describes the experiments and how they were conducted. In Section 4 we discuss the results of the experiments and finally conclusions and future work are provided in Section 5.

2   Related Work

Effort estimation is an important activity in software development projects. The ability to estimate the effort required in developing a system will help project managers to plan, monitor, and assess the productivity of a software development process. However, effort estimation is no simple task. When it comes to accurate effort estimations, experience shows that even an average of 32% estimation error rate can be considered outstanding [3]. Furthermore, the use of Function Points in [3] to solve estimation problems in fact resulted in an average of 100% estimation error rate.

Most methods of effort estimation require an estimate of the size of software systems [4], which imply that accurately estimating the size of a system is extremely important. In this respect, many studies have been done to develop size estimates of software. Many of the previous studies on software size estimation were mainly based on the notion of Function Points (FPs) [5]. In [4] and [6] the size estimation of object-oriented systems was performed by mapping some object-oriented concepts into function point concepts. From this mapping an estimation of the system size is then calculated. Other similar approaches can be seen in [7] and [8].

More recent work on system size estimation can be found in [9]. An approach called Class Point approach was proposed to estimate system-level size. The Class Point approach combines OO measures, which take into account specific aspects of each class such as complexity.

This work is different from the above-mentioned studies in that we focus on size estimate of software models (as represented with UML). Furthermore, we limit our attention to class-count in UML models and investigate its relation with the effort spent in modeling. In this paper we also underline some important issues with respect to the use of class-count as a basis of model size measurements.

3 Empirical Data

The empirical data used in this paper originates from student experiments conducted at the TU/e (Technische Universiteit Eindhoven). The recent experiment, hereafter referred to as Experiment A, involved 12 post-master students who have sufficient knowledge and experience in system specification and design. Of the 12 participants, seven participants had one or two UML courses in the past and five participants hold UML certifications. Nevertheless, only two students have industrial experience with UML. Although the participants seem to have moderate industrial experience with UML, their knowledge and current education/training focus have made them eligible for participating in the experiment.

In Experiment A we asked the participants to develop a UML model of a Car Navigation System based on a written requirement specification. This requirement specification was high level and was given on one page of A4 (the materials can be found in [10]). Given this requirement specification, each participant was given four hours to create a UML model of the system using Rational Rose RealTime 7. Hence, the delivered models are based on the same set of requirements and the same amount of effort was spent during their creation. We are interested to find out whether the size in terms of class-count is similar for these models, given that the we controlled the aforementioned context factors. The results and the analysis are discussed in Section 4.

In addition to the main findings obtained from Experiment A, we also provide supporting findings from a student experiment discussed in [11] – hereafter referred to as Experiment B. The experiment was quite similar in that it also asked 35 teams of three master students (in total 106 students participated) to develop UML models based on certain requirements. Experiment B was originally conducted to investigate the influence of modeling conventions on (syntactic) model quality and modeling effort. To this aim three treatments were applied in creating the UML models, namely: no modeling conventions, with modeling conventions, and tool-supported modeling conventions. In this experiment we use the delivered models for analyzing the relationship between modeling effort and size. The experiment materials are available in [12].

4   Is There a Correlation between Class-Count and Modeling Effort?

In this section we discuss whether there is a correlation between class-count and the effort spent in modeling. However, we must note a few points with regard to the resulting classes in Experiment A and B. First, we found that the resulting classes are in a high level of abstraction. The classes represent key abstractions of the system and they are technology-independent — as such we found no framework classes being modeled. Second, the level of abstraction used also implies that the models are non-executable. We should keep these as a context in understanding the findings discussed in the rest of this paper.

4.1   Class-Count Varies Across Models

The result from Experiment A, as shown in Figure 1, shows that in the given time limit (4 hours) the participants delivered models with a varying size. The class-count varied from 7 up to 23. We can also see that most of the models created have between 11 and 16 classes. There were two participants that created seven classes and only one participant that created 23 classes. The median of the class-count is 13.

The variability of the class-count reveals that although the same requirements, time, and tool were provided to the participants, the resulting models were quite varied in size. One explanation behind this result might be that there are other confounding factors that influence class-count – thus requirement, time, and tool support may only explain the variability of class-count to some degree. In the next section we explore whether there is a correlation between class-count and modeling effort.

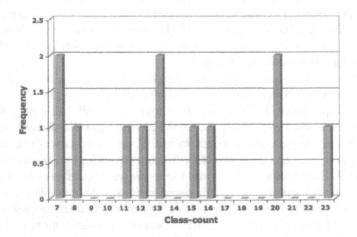

Fig. 1. Frequency distribution of class-count across models

4.2   No Significant Correlation Is Found

To clarify the result discussed previously, we perform a correlation analysis between class-count and the effort spent in modeling from the data set of Experiment B. However, since in the experiment there were treatments applied to three groups of the participants, we first had to make sure that the treatments had no effects on the variables we want to assess – that is, class-count and the time spent on modeling. To this aim we performed independent t-tests for the two variables amongst the three different groups. The result confirmed that one of the treatments, i.e., tool-supported modeling conventions, had significant effects on the time spent on modeling. Thus we must exclude the teams that received this treatment before continuing with the correlation analysis. Additionally, we omitted two influential outliers from the data, which might affect the results of the analysis.

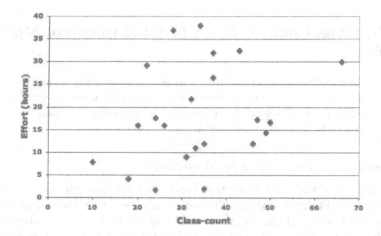

Fig. 2. Scatter plot showing the relation between class-count and effort in modeling

The scatter plot in Figure 2 shows the correlation between class-count and the time spent in modeling (in person hours). It shows that the data points are relatively dispersed, which might indicate the absence of significant trend between both variables.

Since the assumption of normality in the data is rejected, we performed Spearman correlation analysis between class-count and modeling effort. The result of the analysis is shown in Table 1.

The spearman's correlation coefficient in Table 1 shows that there's no significant correlation between Class-count and the effort spent in modeling. As suggested in [13], with 22 participants a significant correlation at $p < 0.05$ is obtained when the correlation coefficient equals to 0.422.

The correlation analysis has revealed that there is no significant correlation between class-count in a model and the effort spent in creating the model. To get the explanations of this phenomenon, we performed deeper analysis on the

Table 1. Spearman correlation coefficient between class-count and the effort spent in modeling

	Effort(hours)
Class-count	.302
Significance (2-tailed)	.171

UML models (especially the class diagrams). The result of the analysis has led us to believe that the main explanation of the absence of significant correlation between class-count and modeling effort is because class-count is not an accurate measure of model size. In particular this is due to the fact that many factors can influence class-count in a model. In the following section we discuss those factors further.

5 Why Class-Count Is Not a Good Estimate of Modeling Effort?

The main finding discussed in the previous section has shown that there is no significant correlation between the number of classes in a model and the effort spent in modeling. In this section we discuss the phenomenon based on deeper analysis of the data from Experiment A.

5.1 Designer's Approaches in Modeling

Deeper analysis of the class diagrams reveals that the participants' approaches in modeling might have strong influence on the resulting class diagrams. By analyzing the number of classes, attributes, and methods we can categorize the models into three categories, namely: 1) functionality-driven; 2) architecture-driven; and 3) a combination of both. The characteristics of these categories are described as follows.

- The participants with the functionality-driven approach tend to focus on the required functionality in creating classes. This type of participants generally creates only a few classes, but with complete role and functionality assigned to the classes (i.e., in terms of class attributes and methods). As a result, the classes are low in number, but have many attributes and methods defined.
- The participants with the architecture-driven approach tend to focus on architectural considerations in developing classes. The structure of the classes is given high importance to gain some benefits such as reusability and maintainability. Participants with this type of interest generally do not specify all class functionality explicitly. Thus, the number of class attributes and class operations created are relatively low.
- The participants that have both concerns in mind tend to focus on both functionality and architectural aspects of the classes. As a result, the number of classes, class attributes, and class operations are generally high.

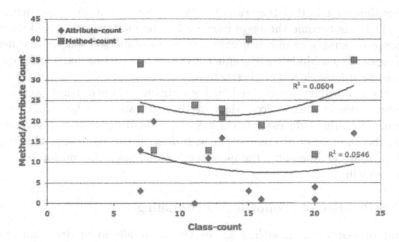

Fig. 3. Scatter plot showing the relation of class-count with method-count and attribute-count

The above points show that designers may have different approaches in modeling classes. In this respect, we have witnessed that different approaches tend to result in different number of classes, attributes, and methods in the models.

The scatter plot in Figure 3 visualizes the relation of class-count with method-count and attribute-count of UML models in Experiment A. The diamonds and squares represent attribute-count and method-count, respectively. The upper regression line fits the method-count data points while the regression line underneath fits the attribute-count. We can see that the results, although not statistically significant (with these data points, class-count only contributes six percent and five percent to the variability of method-count and attribute-count respectively) support the trend we have discussed previously. Nevertheless, this is an indication that class-count in models may vary depending on the designer's approach in modeling.

5.2   The Level of Abstraction Used in Modeling

The level of abstraction in modeling is generally related to the distance of the created models from the actual implementation. Models with a high level of abstraction only specify a system in a ballpark view. In this level of abstraction many details are omitted because they might not be relevant to the main concerns in the current level of abstraction. On the other hand, models with a low level of abstraction have a very close similarity to the intended implementation. As a consequence model with low level of abstraction are generally large and very detailed. Nevertheless, depending on the situation designers can apply more than one level of abstraction in their models.

The notion of level of abstraction in modeling as discussed above adds to the difficulty in using class-count as a size measure. As we have mentioned above, designers can use different levels of abstraction in modeling the same system –

not to mention the fact that they can also switch from one level of abstraction to another. This has become the main hurdle of using class-count as a measure of size because we simply cannot compare attributes of models that have different levels of abstraction. Models with higher levels of abstraction have fewer classes than those with lower levels of abstraction.

From the class diagrams created in Experiment A we did not see the use of different levels of abstraction. Most of the diagrams can be categorized as analysis models – they address only the key elements of the system. Nevertheless, although the same level of abstraction was used in the modeling, the level of detail used may be different – the next section discusses this notion of level of detail in modeling.

5.3   The Practice of Proportion in Modeling

We define proportion in modeling as the use of details in models that is proportional to certain aspects of a system such as complexity or importance of components. When designers model a system regardless of this consideration they generally tend to model all parts of a system at an equal level of detail – hence being disproportionate in modeling. However, practices in the industry reveal that this has seldom been the case [14]. Figure 4 shows how the drive of being simplistic, the drive of being comprehensive, and time constraint influence designer's decisions in modeling.

We have learnt from a case study conducted in the industry that designers generally try to develop models as simple as possible [15]. In order to keep the model simple, designers must make decisions concerning which parts of the system need to be modeled or which parts of the system need greater details. When simplicity is opted, designers will generally focus on modeling system components that are important or complex. For these types of components more detail might be applicable. However, the readers of the models (e.g., programmer, client, etc.) might request more comprehensive models. Thus, in the end designers must take into account all these factors so that models with appropriate level of detail can be delivered.

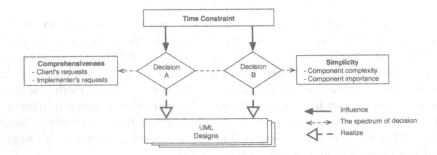

Fig. 4. The factors behind proportion in modeling

It must be clear at this point that the notion of proportion in modeling also hinders the validity of class-count as a measure of model size. The main argument is that class-count does not take into account the properties of each class such as attributes and operations, which reflect the level of detail used in modeling the classes. Hence, although two models with 100 classes are identical in terms of class-count, they might require different effort in the modeling process because they have different levels of detail. The data presented in Figure 5 illustrates the situation. We took a sample of 12 class diagrams created in Experiment B, which have class-count ranging from 30 to 38. Although the class-counts are quite similar, the class attributes and methods can be quite varied in number. This phenomenon can also be observed from the result of Experiment A as presented in Figure 3. However, please also note that here we do not see the trend as discussed previously in Section 5.1, which might due to the fact that there was no time-limit applied in Experiment B.

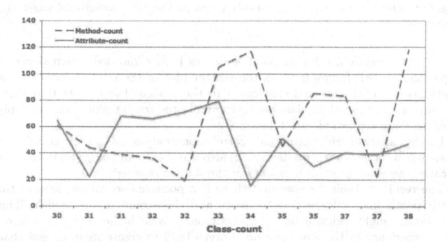

Fig. 5. Method-count and attribute-count amongst models with similar class-count

5.4 Designer's Knowledge and Experience

We investigated whether the participant's expertise affects class-count in the models. To this aim we perform another correlation analysis between the participants' knowledge background and experiences. We use the data obtained from the participant characterization questionnaire in Experiment A. In the questionnaire we asked a couple of multiple-answer questions related to participants' knowledge and experience in the following areas:

- Object oriented design
- Object-oriented programming
- UML
- Different UML diagram types (i.e., use case, class, and sequence diagram)

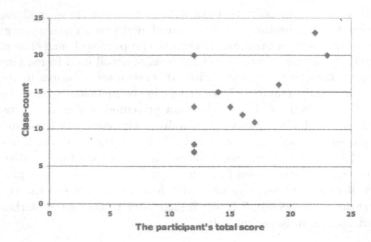

Fig. 6. Scatter plot showing the relation between participant's background scores and class-count

For each question, a higher point indicates higher knowledge/experience in a particular area. Figure 6 shows the scatter plot of the relation between the participants' total score and class-count in the models. Please note that there are only 11, instead of 12, data points shown in the scatter plot. This is simply because there are two identical data points.

Further analysis with spearman's correlation analysis reveals the correlation as shown in Table 2. Please note that we also use spearman's correlation analysis because the assumption of normality of the data is rejected.

The result in Table 2 shows that there is a positive correlation between the participant's knowledge/experience score and class-count in the models. This correlation might indicate that the participants with higher scores of knowledge/experience in the aforementioned areas tend to create more classes than those with lower scores. This result actually raises another interesting question: why do the participants with better knowledge/experience tend to produce more classes? Is it because the knowledge and experience make them more productive? Or is it because the knowledge and experience make them aware of some 'best practices' in modeling, which result in better structured class diagrams (often also means more classes)? Answering these questions would require further analysis of the UML models and is beyond the scope of this paper.

Table 2. Spearman correlation coefficient between participant's knowledge/experience and class-count

	Participant background score
Class-count	.580*
Significance	.048

* indicates correlation significant at 0.05 level (2-tailed)

Please also note that the productivity of an individual participant can be influenced by many factors including knowledge and experience in modeling. In this respect, we assumed that the influence of other factors might not be significant, hence we did not take further measures to control other factors that might have influence on individual productivity in modeling.

6 Conclusions and Future Directions

In this paper we investigated the relation between the number of classes (class-count) in models and the effort (time) spent in modeling. The analysis of empirical data leads to the conclusion that there is no significant relation between class-count in models and the effort spent in modeling. We conclude that the main reason behind this is because class-count is not a good measure of model size, which is mainly due to the fact that different factors have influence on class-count in a model. In this respect we identified the following influential factors:

- Designers' approaches in modeling
- The level of abstraction used in modeling
- The practice of proportion in modeling
- Designer's knowledge and experience

Additionally, from an analysis of the class diagrams we found an interesting observation with respect to designers' approaches in modeling. We identified the following approaches: 1) Architecture-driven; 2) Functionality-driven; 3) An approach that put emphasis on both architectural and functional aspects. These approaches seemed to have influence not only on class-count in the models, but also on the number of class attributes and methods.

Based on the exploratory observations of this study, we propose directions for future work to provide a better understanding of measuring model size. Future work should address the relation between the structural view and other views. Additionally, the factors that potentially influence the model size that were identified in this paper should be addressed in more specific studies.

Acknowledgments

This work is accomplished under the Finesse project which is funded by the STW (Stichting Technische Wetenschappen), the Netherlands. We also like to thank the students of TU/e who have participated in the experiments.

References

1. Emam, K.E., Benlarbi, S., Goel, N., Melo, W., Lounis, H., Rai, S.N.: The optimal class size for object-oriented software. IEEE Trans. Softw. Eng. 28(5), 494–509 (2002)
2. Dobing, B., Parsons, J.: How UML is used. Communications of the ACM 49(5), 109–113 (2006)

3. Vicinanza, S.S., Mukhopadhyay, T., Prietula, M.J.: Software-effort estimation: An exploratory study of expert performance. Information Systems Research 2(4), 243–262 (1991)
4. Caldiera, G., Antoniol, G., Fiutem, R., Lokan, C.: Definition and experimental evaluation of function points for object-oriented systems. In: METRICS 1998: Proceedings of the 5th International Symposium on Software Metrics, Washington, DC, USA, p. 167. IEEE Computer Society, Los Alamitos (1998)
5. Albrecht, A.: Measuring application development productivity. In: Press, I.B.M. (ed.) IBM Application Development Symp., October 1979, pp. 83–92 (1979)
6. Fetcke, T., Abran, A., Nguyen, T.H.: Mapping the OO-Jacobson approach into function point analysis. In: TOOLS 1997: Proceedings of the Tools-23: Technology of Object-Oriented Languages and Systems, Washington, DC, USA, p. 192. IEEE Computer Society, Los Alamitos (1997)
7. Whitmire, S.A.: An introduction to 3D function points. Softw. Dev. 3(4), 43–53 (1995)
8. Minkiewicz, A.: Measuring object oriented software with predictive object points. In: Applications in Software Measurements (ASM 1997) (1997)
9. Costagliola, G., Ferrucci, F., Tortora, G., Vitiello, G.: Class point: an approach for the size estimation of object-oriented systems. Software Engineering, IEEE Transactions 31(1), 52–74 (2005)
10. Nugroho, A.: Experiment materials, http://www.liacs.nl/~anugroho
11. Lange, C.F.J., DuBois, B., Chaudron, M.R.V., Demeyer, S.: An experimental investigation of uml modeling conventions. In: Nierstrasz, O., Whittle, J., Harel, D., Reggio, G. (eds.) MoDELS 2006. LNCS, vol. 4199, pp. 27–41. Springer, Heidelberg (2006)
12. Lange, C.F.J.: Experiment replication package, http://www.tue.nl/~clange
13. T.C.U. of Hongkong: Minimum significant correlation coefficient r for a sample size, Hongkong, http://department.obg.cuhk.edu.hk/researchsupport
14. Lange, C.F.J., Chaudron, M.R.V., Muskens, J.: In practice: UML software architecture and design description. IEEE Softw. 23(2), 40–46 (2006)
15. Nugroho, A., Chaudron, M.R.V.: Managing the quality of uml models in practice. In: Rech, J., Bunse, C. (eds.) Model-Driven Software Development: Integrating Quality Assurance, Idea Group Inc. (to appear, 2008)

Measuring the Level of Abstraction and Detail of Models in the Context of MDD

Jens von Pilgrim

FernUniversität in Hagen, 58084 Hagen, Germany
Jens.vonPilgrim@FernUni-Hagen.de

Abstract. In model driven development (MDD), models are transformed automatically into other models. This leads to transformation chains. The goal of MDD is to set up efficient transformation chains, i.e. adding semantics first and platform detail later. When the platform is changed, only the later, platform specific models have to be replaced. This paper constructs metrics for measuring and comparing the models obtained through transformations in MDD processes, in order to help to set up the more efficient transformation chains.

1 Introduction

In model driven development (MDD), models are transformed automatically into other models and code. This leads to transformation chains, in which the models are connected via transformations. Usually, abstract (and platform independent) models are used to define the system's semantics. These abstract models are then transformed automatically to more concrete (and platform specific) models, in which platform detail is added as required. Finally, code is generated from these concrete models. If the platform is changed, only platform specific models have to be redefined while the first, more abstract models can be reused. This leads to a higher productivity compared to manual coding if the transformation chain is configured well. That is, we have to ensure that semantics is added first and platform detail later.

As suggested by the Goal Question Metrics approach (GQM, [1]), we define a goal.

Goal: Set up or improve an efficient transformation chain. Here "efficient" means that semantics is defined in early, abstract models, while platform detail is added later in more concrete, platform specific models.

Figure 1 illustrates this goal. The figure is taken from [4] and slightly modified. The whole issue is also discussed in [6] which also contains a very similar figure [6, p. 32]. The arrows labeled "manually" and "automatically" are introduced in section 3. [1]

---

[1] Unlike the figures in [4,6] the y axis is reversed in order to visualize the raised level of abstraction.

H. Giese (Ed.): MoDELS 2007 Workshops, LNCS 5002, pp. 105–114, 2008.
© Springer-Verlag Berlin Heidelberg 2008

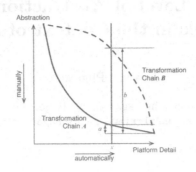

Fig. 1. Transformation chains, adapted from [4]

The figure shows two transformation chains (A and B). The x axis indicates the platform detail (in [4], the term "metamodel" is used), the y axis the abstraction. That is, abstract and platform independent models are located top left, while concrete and platform specific models are located bottom right. If the platform is changed (indicated with the vertical line at x, i.e. models at the right side of this line have to be ported to a new platform), we can observe that transformation chain A is more efficient than chain B, since in case of chain A only a very small amount of semantics has to be added (a), while in case of chain B much more semantics has to be added again (b). The goal is to define transformation chains such as A. We can now pose some questions in order to refine the goal. This paper tries to develop metrics for answering the following questions.

Questions
Is a model M_1 more abstract than model M_2? Does model M_1 contain more platform details than model M_2? Do we define most of the semantics in early models? Where do we define most of the platform detail?

This paper is organized as follows. In the next section, we will introduce different definitions of model. We then develop metrics in order to answer our questions in section 3. Section 4 proposes an additional transformation before actually measuring a model, which is implicitly used in section 5 which presents a sample to illustrate the calculation of the proposed metrics. Section 6 describes related work, followed by the conclusion and directions for future work in the last section.

2   Model Definitions

What is a model? Models can be defined as mathematical structures. Since this definition is too general to work with, models are defined here as graphs $G = (V, E)$ with vertices V and edges E or labeled graphs $G = (V, E, l)$ with labels l. In MDD, these graphs have to be valid according to a meta model, that is the elements of the graph are associated to elements of the meta model. A formal definition of models as graphs according to meta models can be found in [2].

In his "General Model Theory"[8] Stachowiak defines models using three features:

Mapping feature: A model is always a model of some original, in which the original can be a model itself.

Reduction feature: A model does not reflect all attributes of the original.

Pragmatic feature: Models are assigned to an original by some subject (human or machine).

While defining a model as a graph specifies the syntax of the model, Stachowiak's features define the semantics. We combine both definitions by introducing an *interpretation* working on "attributes". We use the term "attribute" here in a very abstract way, they are defined as pure semantics here. But, semantics cannot be expressed without symbols. So we use the *interpretation* to express attributes by elements of the graph.

Definition 1. Attributes and Graphs of a Model
An interpretation $I : V \cup E \rightarrow A$ of a model is a mapping of vertices V and edges E to attributes A, such that for all attributes $\alpha \in A$

$$V_\alpha \cup E_\alpha \rightarrow \alpha,$$
$$(V_\alpha \cup E_\alpha)\backslash\{x\} \nrightarrow \alpha \quad \forall x \in V_\alpha \cup E_\alpha$$

in which $V_\alpha \subseteq V, E_\alpha \subseteq E$.
In the following, for a model M_k we write A_k to refer to its attributes.

Definition 1 maps minimal subsets of nodes and vertices to attributes, that is no element of $V_\alpha \cup E_\alpha$ must be removed.

The "original" in Stachowiak's first feature can be a model itself. In a transformation chain, this feature is transitive, i.e. if M_1 is a model of M_2, and M_2 is a model of M_3, then M_1 is also a model of M_3. Eventually all models of a transformation chain are models of the system under construction. How does a subject assign a model to an original – in MDD this is done by automatic transformations. Stachowiak introduces a function called "icostructural image". This function maps subsets of the orignal attributes to subsets of the model attributes.[2]

3   Metrics

For answering our questions, we are interested in abstraction and (platform) detail. The first metric we define here is the semantic size of a model. We define

---

[2] Since we defined attributes differently to Stachowiak, here this assignment is a function mapping graph elements to attributes; still a subject has to interpret a model, that is define subsets of the graph elements representing an attribute.

this metric simply as the cardinality of the attribute set. While the graph reflects certain properties defined by the metamodel, attributes were defined as "pure" semantics. For example an UML association between two classes requires the two classes, the association, and – this is usually not visible in diagrams – several properties "gluing" these parts together. This "structural glue" is not present in the attribute set. We will use this first metric as an indicator for the abstraction level of a model.

Definition 2. *[Semantic Size of a Model] The semantic size of a model M is defined here as the number of its attributes A, i.e.*

$$sem(M) = |A|$$

For $sem(M_1)$ we also write sem_1 or $|A_1|$.

The second metric defined is simply the size of the graph. Since the graph contains the "structural glue", we not only count the semantics when counting the nodes and edges of a graph, but the (platform) detail, too. We use this second metric for measuring the platform detail of a model.

Definition 3. *[Size of a Model] The size of a model M is defined here as the sum of the vertices of the model graph, its edges and the graph itself. That is*

$$size(M) = |V| + |E| + 1$$

in which V and E are the vertices and edges of the graph of the model. For $size(M_1)$ we also write $size_1$.

We add 1 to the number of vertices and edges in order to count the graph itself. Besides, we use this formula later as a denominator in a fraction and this way we avoid division by zero problems.

In a first approach we state that a model M_1 is more abstract than a model M_2, if it omits more attributes, i.e. if it defines less attributes. We can also say that a model M_1 contains less platform detail than a model M_2, if it contains less "structural glue", i.e. if less graph elements represent the attributes expressed by the model. It is almost impossible to actually define the attributes, at least it requires additional effort. In order to develop a metric, we need to use the data present in the models and the transformation chain.

So we have a closer look at transformations. A model transformation transforms a model M_1 into a model M_2. We expect a transformation to preserve semantics. In [10], Steimann proposes the following consideration: An automatic transformation preserves semantics or it adds semantics.[3] If it adds semantics, it must do this randomly, since otherwise adding new semantics would be based on information found in the model which leads to preserving semantics. Usually we do not want a transformation to add semantics randomly, thus we assume here that a transformation preserves semantics. According to figure 1 this means

---

[3] The case of reducing semantics should not be considered here.

that a transformation can "move" a model only horizontal; semantics can only be added manually. This is indicated by the two arrows in figure 1.

As a matter of fact, a completely different point of view can be taken, too. We can also state that it is the transformation which adds semantics, and a model itself does not contain any semantics (this position can be found for example in [9]). If we take this position, which is of course reasonable, we can only measure syntactical properties of a model without a transformation.

How can we solve this issue? The answer is already given here by definition 1. An "interpretation" is a special kind of transformation, and it is used here as an transformation mapping syntactical elements to semantics. Then, a transformation in a transformation chain cannot add semantics. Figure 2 illustrates this process using a commutative diagram. It shows a transformation chain (with models M_1 to M_n) and their interpretations.

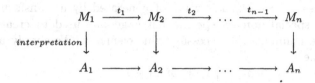

Fig. 2. Transformation and Interpretation

It is important to note that "attributes" and the attribute sets A cannot be defined explicitly. They are used here as a theoretical construct for distinguishing between platform and the semantics.

We now use a simple transformation chain for the following considerations. To distinguish between automatic transformations and manual editing, we write "$\rightarrow$" for transformation and "$\rightsquigarrow$" for manual enrichment. Let a model M_1 be automatically transformed into a model M_2. According to the first model definition, the models are graphs, i.e. $G_1 = (V_1, E_1)$ and $G_2 = (V_2, E_2)$. But these models also represents attribute sets A_1 and A_2. If model M_1 is automatically transformed to model M_2, no additional attributes could have been added by the transformation. If the transformation preserves semantics (what we assume here), after the transformation $A_1 = A_2$ must be true. During the development process, model M_2 is enriched manually, i.c. $M_2 \rightsquigarrow M_2'$ with $A_2' = A_2 \cup A_{man} = A_1 \cup A_{man}$ (A_{man} are the attributes added manually). In a transformation chain, both models are expected to be models of the same system (or original). But M_1 is also a model of M_2. That is, the manually added attributes A_{man} are omitted in M_1.

The following table summarizes the transformation chain and the terms defined above:

M_1	$\rightarrow$	M_2	$\rightsquigarrow$		M_2'
A_1		$A_1 = A_2$	A_{man}		$A_2' = A_1 \cup A_{man}$
$sem_1 = |A_1|$		$sem_2 = sem_1$	sem_{man}		$sem_2' = sem_1 + sem_{man}$
$size_1$		$size_2$		$|V_{man}| + |E_{man}|$	$size_2' = size_2 + |V_{man}| + |E_{man}|$

Because of definition 1 we know that the elements of the graph and the attributes are somehow related. Even if we cannot define the interpretation mappings exactly, we can calculate how many elements of the graph are average needed to represent a single attribute, or vice versa, how much semantics is stored in a single graph element. We call this the "ratio of abstraction and detail":

Definition 4. *[Ratio of Abstraction and Detail] The ratio of abstraction and detail of a model M is defined here as the semantic size of a model divided by its size. That is*

$$rad(M) = \frac{sem(M)}{size(m)} = \frac{|A|}{|V| + |E| + 1}$$

While we can measure the size of the models (as defined above), we cannot measure the semantic size nor the platform detail. In a transformation chain $M_1 \rightarrow M_2 \rightsquigarrow M_2' \rightarrow \ldots \rightsquigarrow M_n'$, M_1 was not generated by a transformation. We assume that a special domain specific language was used to create that model, and thus we minimize the necessary glue elements. We simply assume $|A_1| = |V_1| + |E_1|$, i.e.

$$sem_1 = |A_1| = size_1 - 1 \tag{1}$$

We further assume that the ratio of abstraction and detail of a model is constant during manual enrichment. That is, the language used to formulate a model (i.e. its metamodel), determinates this ratio, and since we do not change the metamodel, the ratio is expected to stay constant. Thus we can say

$$rad(M_2) = rad(M_2') \Rightarrow \frac{|A_1|}{size_2} = \frac{|A_2'|}{size_2'} \tag{2}$$

That is, we can calculate the semantic size of M_2, i.e. the number of its attributes, by solving (2) for $|A_2'|$:

$$sem_2' = |A_2'| = \frac{|A_1|size_2'}{size_2} \tag{3}$$

We can apply equation 3 for all manually edited models $M_i', i > 1$ in our transformation chain. All automatically created models $M_i, i > 1$ are expected to have the same semantics as their source models. Thus, we can approximate the semantic size of all models in the transformation chain.

4   Measuring as a Transformation Chain

In the example in section 5, we will count the vertices and edges as illustrated in the diagrams. That is, when we count the vertices of a class diagram, we simply count the number of drawn rectangles. Of course, class models are much more complicated according to the UML meta model. While we use this simplification here for keeping the example simple, the "simplification" itself can be used for real models, too.

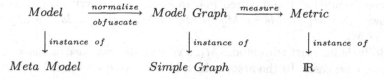

Fig. 3. Measuring as transformation chain

In terms of MDD, "measuring" can interpreted as a transformation chain. Figure 3 illustrates a sample transformation chain for measuring a model.

The transformation chain is drawn from left to right: First, a model is transformed into a graph here. This is the simplification step, which is in general optional, of course. Then the model, here the simplified graph of the model, is measured. The result is a metric which is usually a number, often normalized to the interval $[0 \ldots 1]$, that is the "meta model" of the metric is $\mathbb{R}$.

The first transformation introduced here can be used for two purposes. Firstly it can be used for simplifying and normalizing a model as it is implicitly done in the next section. Secondly it can be used for obfuscating a model but still perform metrics on it.

5   Example

We will demonstrate the metrics developed above using a well-known transformation chain. In [3,7] use case models are transformed to class models during the analysis. The resulting class models are also known as robustness diagrams, using the stereotypes boundary, control, and entity. We use a similar approach in the example here.

Figure 4 shows two transformation chains $C_1 : M_1 \rightarrow M_2 \rightarrow M_3$ and $C_2 : M_1 \rightarrow M_2^* \rightarrow M_3$. The light elements (of the models M_2, M_2^*, and M_3) were created automatically by transformations, the bold elements (of the models M_2', $M_2^{*'}$, and M_3') indicate manually added elements. If we distinguish between trans-

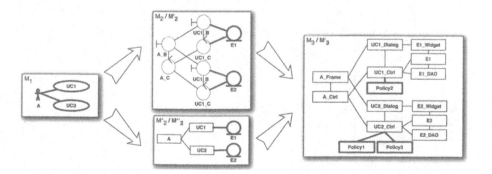

Fig. 4. Transforming use cases models to class models

formed (symbol $\rightarrow$) and edited ($\rightsquigarrow$) models, we can write the model chains as follows: $C_1 : M_1 \rightarrow M_2 \rightsquigarrow M_2' \rightarrow M_3 \rightsquigarrow M_3'$ and $C_2 : M_1 \rightarrow M_2^* \rightsquigarrow M_2^{*'} \rightarrow M_3 \rightsquigarrow M_3'$.

Both chains start with model M_1, a very simple use case model with one actor and two use cases. In the first chain, a boundary-control pair is created for each actor and use case (M_2). In the second chain, a single class is created for each actor and use case (M_2^*). Finally, M_3 is created, that is some GUI components are created and each component is managed by a controller. While the user has to define all elements in M_1, in M_2 and M_2^* only the entity classes are to be attached to the appropriate classes. In M_3 some policy classes are added to the controllers.

We now evaluate which transformation chain is more efficient according to our goal stated in the introduction. We do this by measuring *sem* and *size* of each model. We start with transformation chain C_1. The following table lists the steps we take in order to measure this chain:

Model	Description	Result
M_1	count 3 vertices and 2 edges (def. 3)	$size_1 = 6$
M_1	calculate semantic size (eq. 1)	$sem_1 = 5$
M_2	count 6 vertices and 7 edges (def. 3)	$size_2 = 14$
M_2	M_2 is automatically transformed from M_1	$sem_2 = 5$
M_2'	count 8 vertices and 11 edges (def. 3)	$size_2' = 20$
M_2'	calculate semantic size (eq. 3)	$sem_2' = 5 * 20/14 = 7.14$
...	...	...

All other models in this chain and chain C_2 are measured this way. Figure 5 shows the result of this measurement, the y-Axis is reversed for visualizing the level of abstraction.

The dark lines connect the manually enriched models $M_1 - M_2' - M_3'$ and $M_1 - M_2^{*'} - M_3'$, the light lines the complete transformation chain. We can easily see that the second transformation chain C_2 (dotted line) is more efficient than

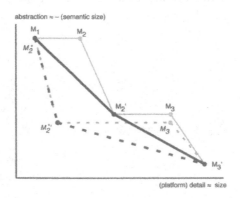

Fig. 5. Visualized and measured sample transformation chains

C_1 (solid line). So, according to our goal, we might choose C_2 when setting up the development process.

6 Related Work

In [5] Lange proposed several dimensions for measuring the size of a model. Both metrics defined here can be identified as absolute sizes. The ratio between these two sizes is a relative size because we can interpret the attributes of a model as a new model, thus the ratio is a ratio of two absolut sizes. It would be an interesting approach to replace the size metric used here with a more functional one, such as function or object points as suggested by Lange.

Stachowiak also develops certain metrics in [8] based on "abundant" and "preteriated" attributes and other terms developed in his general modeling theory. Abundant attributes are attributes of the model but not of the original, preteriated attributes are attributes of the original but not of the model. While Stachowiak's features of a model are often found in computer science literature, his whole (and formalized) model theory is mostly ignored.

7 Conclusion and Future Work

In this paper we presented two metrics to measure the size and semantic size of a model. These metrics answer questions about the abstraction level and platform detail of models in order to solve the goal of setting up efficient transformation chains. The measurement shows that even if it is not possible to explicitly count or retrieve the semantic content of a model, it is still possible to compare several models. The metrics were demonstrated using a simple example and we were actually able to measure and visualize a MDD process and compare different processes.

We still have to evaluate our metrics in greater projects with more transformations. In "longer" transformation chains comparing two chains might not be as easy as in the simple example used here and we have to develop further efficiency criteria, e.g. by measuring the area below the transformation chain graphs[4]. We are also developing a tool and a meta model to implement the first transformation as described in section 4. We try to use a parametrized transformation for mapping a model to a weighted graph which then can be used for measuring.

References

1. Basili, V., Caldiera, G., Rombach, D.: Goal question metric approach. In: Encyclopedia of Software Engineering, pp. 528–532. Wiley & Sons, Chichester (1994)
2. Bézivin, J., Bouzitouna, S., Fabro, M.D.D., Gervais, M.-P., Jouault, F., Kolovos, D., Kurtev, I., Paige, R.F.: A canonical scheme for model composition. In: Paige, R.F., Gervais, M.-P., Kolovos, D.S. (eds.) ECMDA-FA 2006. LNCS, vol. 4066, pp. 346–360. Springer, Heidelberg (2006)

---

[4] I thank Friedrich Steimann for this idea.

3. Jacobson, I.: Object-Oriented Software Engineering: A Use Case Driven Approach. ACM press, Addison-Wesley Professional (1992)
4. Koch, T., Uhl, A., Weise, D.: Model Driven Architecture. OMG Document ormsc/02-09-04 (November 2001)
5. Lange, C.F.J.: Model size matters. In: Kühne, T. (ed.) MoDELS 2006. LNCS, vol. 4364, pp. 211–216. Springer, Heidelberg (2007)
6. Mellor, S.J., Scott, K., Uhl, A., Weise, D.: MDA Distilled. Principles of Model-Driven Architecture. Object Technology Series. Addison-Wesley, Boston a.o. (2004)
7. Rosenberg, D., Scott, K.: Use Case Driven Object Modeling with UML. A Practical Approach. Object Technology Series. Addison-Wesley, Reading (1999)
8. Stachowiak, H.: Allemeine Modelltheorie. Springer, Wien (1973)
9. Stahl, T., Völter, M.: Modellgetriebene Softwareentwicklung. Dpunkt Verlag (2005)
10. Steimann, F.: Uml-A oder warum die Wissenschaft ihre eigene einheitliche Modellierungssprache haben sollte. In: Modellierung 2004, Proceedings. LNCS (2004)

First International Workshop on the Model-Based Design of Trustworthy Health Information Systems

Ákos Lédeczi[1], Ruth Breu[2], Bradley Malin[3], and Janos Sztipanovits[1]

[1] Institute for Software Integrated Systems, Vanderbilt University,
Nashville, TN, USA
{akos.ledeczi,janos.sztipanovits}@vanderbilt.edu
[2] Research Group Quality Engineering, University of Innsbruck,
Innsbruck, Austria
ruth.breu@uibk.ac.at
[3] Department of Biomedical Informatics, Vanderbilt University
Nashville, TN, USA
b.malin@vanderbilt.edu

Abstract. The objective of the MOTHIS workshop was to discuss model-based methods for the design of Health Information Systems (HIS) offering a revolutionary new way for the interaction between medical patients and Health Care Providers. Although healthcare, like other information-intensive industries, has developed and deployed standards-based, secure information infrastructures it is still dependent upon paper records and fragmented, error-prone approaches to service delivery. The primary concern is that security and privacy need to be organically integrated into HIS architectures. The workshop brought together computer scientists, medical experts, and legal policy experts to discuss research results in the development and application of model-based methods for representing, analyzing and integrating, architectures, privacy and security policies, computer security mechanisms, web authentication, and human factors engineering.

1 Introduction

The first International Workshop on the Model-Based Design of Trustworthy Health Information Systems (MOTHIS) was held in conjunction with the 10th ACM/IEEE International Conference on Model Driven Engineering Languages and Systems (MoDELS'07) in Nashville, Tennessee on September 30th, 2007. The objective of MOTHIS was to discuss model-based methods for the design of Health Information Systems (HIS) offering a revolutionary new way for the interaction between medical patients and health care providers. Many information-intensive industries have developed and deployed standards-based, secure IT infrastructures. In contrast, the healthcare industry remains, for the most part, dependent on paper records and fragmented, error-prone approaches to service

H. Giese (Ed.): MoDELS 2007 Workshops, LNCS 5002, pp. 115–117, 2008.

delivery. One of the main concerns is that security and privacy need to be organically integrated into HIS architectures. In the United States, there are various state and federal laws governing the protection of health information. In particular, the Privacy and Security Rules of the Health Insurance Portability and Accountability Act (HIPAA) sets a national baseline that requires all health care organizations to implement protections at physical, technical, and administrative levels to monitor and document access to identifiable health information. HIPAA also provides patients the right to access their medical records, request corrections to those records, and request a log of disclosures of their personal health information. The optimal design of HIS that protects patient confidentiality and respect the rights of health care providers is an unresolved challenge. The protection of patient rights and health information is a global problem and, thus, similar privacy and security regulations have been adopted in various countries around the world. MOTHIS intended to foster innovation and international cooperation to attack these challenge.

Approximately thirty people attended MOTHIS from industry and academia. In addition to two regular sessions, a keynote address and an industry session comprised the program. For the detailed program and the online proceedings, visit http://mothis.isis.vanderbilt.edu.

2   Workshop Summary

Professor Daniel Masys, the Chair of the Department of Biomedical Informatics at the Vanderbilt University Medical Center delivered the keynote address, in which he presented his vision for informatics of 21st century health care. He identified key elements of a future scenario, including: 1) enabling patients to contribute to their online health records; 2) providing patients with access to large volumes of health-related information online, which is tailored to their health status; 3) facilitating health care providers to act as coaches and consultants to their patients; 4) personalizing medical diagnoses and treatments to a patient's genomic and metabolic variations; and 5) deploying agile evidence-based care with automated, patient-specific alerts. The enabling technologies required to implement this vision are only partially available at the present time. While ubiquitous (mostly wireless) telecommunications are widely accessible, other components are lagging. These include web portals as secure bi-directional conduits for communication and documentation of care, clinical decision support systems via automated event monitors, and reliable voice recognition.

The industry session was comprised of two talks. First, Tyrone Grandison and John Davis from the IBM Almaden Research Center presented their work on the impact of industry constraints on model-driven data disclosure controls. They argued that healthcare data disclosure models have been created with the goal of meeting specific standard properties or principles, such as confidentiality, integrity, availability, limited disclosure, limited retention, and limited use. However, it is often the case that these models need to be augmented with domain-specific factors at design time. They proposed a set of constraints that could be considered when designing security and privacy models.

In the second industry talk, Peter Miller, the director of the Vanderbilt HealthTech Laboratory presented a novel approach to help manage clinical workflows. He described a tool to derive customized and individualized clinical patient care plans from evidence-based clinical guidelines/protocols. He demonstrated how they designed a model-based approach that could be easily retargeted by building on a powerful existing technology base. The tool will allow clinicians both to create and customize a plan and to monitor the execution of the plan. The model-based approach permits the use of simulation to test that complex protocols are correctly formulated and do not contain clinically undesirable paths.

The regular workshop papers covered a wide range of topics. Alam et al. presented work on modeling and enforcing advanced access control policies. As one of the best papers, a revised version follows this summary. Similarly, the manuscript of Christov et al., also included in this volume, summarizes their experiences in defining and analyzing medical processes.

In current Patient Care Reports (ePCR) systems, software components are developed without taking into account the specifics for different categories of patients or information needs of different emergency management agencies resulting in extensive alteration of user interfaces, business objects and the data layer. Shenvi et al. presented a domain-specific modeling approach to generating context-specific ePCRs automatically.

Mathe et al. introduced a model-based design technique to rapidly develop, simulate, and deploy HIS prototypes. Their design environment allows architects to create formal system models and, from these, automatically generate executable code on top of a Service Oriented Architecture framework.

Agreiter et al. proposed a practicable and efficient solution for leveraging operating system-level and application-level security mechanisms to realize security-critical applications and services for mobile applications in healthcare scenarios.

Kaviani et al. used model-driven engineering to develop service-oriented HISs. The approach relies on a modeling technique based on Web rules and enables the representation of business processes and policies in a unified framework. The system supports the development of tools for a formal analysis of existing services and their policies by using rule-based reasoning engines.

Finally, Lopez et al. argued that the introduction of HISs often requires the reengineering of the business processes used to deliver care. The authors proposed a notion of equivalence over secure business processes based on the notion of goal-equivalence. To this end, they presented a reasoning method for passing from a modeling language that captures the functional, security and trust requirements of HISs and their operational environments, to business processes specifications and vice versa.

Rigorously Defining and Analyzing Medical Processes: An Experience Report

Stefan Christov[1], Bin Chen[1], George S. Avrunin[1], Lori A. Clarke[1],
Leon J. Osterweil[1], David Brown[2], Lucinda Cassells[2], and Wilson Mertens[2]

[1] Laboratory for Advanced Software Engineering Research (LASER)
University of Massachusetts at Amherst, Amherst, MA 01003
{christov,chenbin,avrunin,clarke,ljo}@cs.umass.edu
[2] D'Amour Center for Cancer Care, 3350 Main Street, Springfield, MA 01199
{david.brown,lucy.cassells,wilson.mertens}@bhs.org

Abstract. This paper describes our experiences in defining the processes associated with preparing and administrating chemotherapy and then using those process definitions as the basis for analyses aimed at finding and correcting defects. The work is a collaboration between medical professionals from a major regional cancer center and computer science researchers. The work uses the Little-JIL language to create precise process definitions, the PROPEL system to specify precise process requirements, and the FLAVERS system to verify that the process definitions adhere to the requirement specifications. The paper describes how these technologies were applied to successfully identify defects in the chemotherapy process. Although this work is still ongoing, early experiences suggest that this approach can help reduce medical errors and improve patient safety. The work has also helped us to learn about the desiderata for process definition and analysis technologies, both of which are expected to be broadly applicable to other domains.

1 Introduction: The Problem and Our Proposed Approach

Medical errors cause approximately 98,000 patient deaths each year [1] in the United States. US Institute of Medicine (IOM) reports have suggested that the delivery of healthcare must fundamentally change to address medical errors (e.g., see [1, 2]). In particular, these studies suggest that many serious medical errors result from *system* rather than individual failures, leading the IOM to advocate the development of healthcare systems that directly address patient safety. In particular, the IOM report states, "what is most disturbing is the absence of real progress... in information technology to improve clinical *processes* [italics ours]" ([3], pg. 3). Thus, we have begun to investigate the application of software engineering process definition and analysis research to help reduce errors and improve safety in medical processes. In this paper, we use the term "guideline" (or "process/care guideline") to refer to an informal, mostly natural language, description of a medical process. And, we use the term

H. Giese (Ed.): MoDELS 2007 Workshops, LNCS 5002, pp. 118–131, 2008.

"process definition" to refer to a precise description of a process that is created using a formal language with rigorously-defined semantics.

Our preliminary research (e.g., [4]) showed that many current medical processes are described only at a high-level of generality and are often not defined completely and precisely. Because of this, healthcare providers can find themselves in situations that are not directly addressed by the processes they learned, and thus they may be unsure whether their actions conform to recommended care guidelines. In addition, aspects of current process descriptions are frequently vague, ambiguous, or inconsistent, allowing different providers to have different understandings of their specifics. Such descriptions may lead workers to believe they are following recommended guidelines when, in fact, their care has deviated, increasing the possibility of error.

In the work described here, software engineering researchers and medical experts developed precise, rigorous definitions of medical processes that capture both the standard and exceptional situations that can arise. The process definitions also capture the inherent concurrency and multi-tasking undertaken by busy healthcare providers, as well as details of the use of resources to perform the processes. Our investigations have indicated that there are somewhat different goals for defining and analyzing processes in different areas of medical practice, thus suggesting applying somewhat different approaches. For example, blood transfusion is primarily concerned with identification issues and emergency care is focused on improved patient flow.

In chemotherapy there seems to be an overriding concern for the identification and removal of process defects that create hazards to patient health and safety. These concerns suggest the value of at least two complementary engineering approaches, namely fault tree analysis and finite-state verification, each applied to a precise definition of safety-critical processes. Analysis of fault trees promises to indicate serious ramifications of incorrect performance of process steps [5, 6], while finite-state verification (c.g., [7, 8]) promises to identify sequences of tasks that, even if performed perfectly, could lead to safety violations [9]. In this initial work, we focused on the latter. This paper describes efforts to evaluate the effectiveness of defining medical processes using a rigorously defined language, formally encoding the requirements for that process, carrying out finite-state verification of the processes to detect defects, and then improving the processes by defect removal. In the next section we present the Little-JIL process definition language and provide examples of how it was used to define a chemotherapy process. Section 3 describes our experiences, and Section 4 overviews related work. Section 5 suggests some future research directions.

2 An Example: Chemotherapy Preparation and Administration

Chemotherapy is the use of chemical substances to treat disease. In its modern-day use, it refers primarily to the administration of cytotoxic drugs to treat cancer. Chemotherapy medications are typically highly toxic, and thus it is of overriding importance to be sure that the right patient receives the right medications in the right dosages at the right times. To assure this, elaborate processes are carried out that integrate the efforts of such diverse medical personnel as doctors, nurses, pharmacists, and clerical workers. Chemotherapy processes aim to speed the flow of treatment, while assuring that errors do not occur. Checks are in place to guard against committing such errors. Preliminary examination of these processes suggested that they are large and complex, and their growing complexity makes it increasingly difficult to be sure they provide sufficient protection against the commission of errors.

Our work began by defining some example chemotherapy processes. Earlier work in defining processes in such other domains as software development, scientific data processing [10], and e-government [11] suggested that a powerful process definition language would be needed. We chose to use the Little-JIL process definition language because our previous experience suggested that semantic features of this language were likely to be effective in defining processes in the chemotherapy domain.

2.1 Principal Features of Little-JIL

Little-JIL [12, 13] was originally developed to define software development processes. A Little-JIL process definition has three components, an *artifact collection*, a *resource repository*, and a *coordination specification*. The artifact collection contains the items that are the products of the process. The resource repository specifies the agents and capabilities that support performing the activities. The coordination specification ties these together, specifying which agents and supplementary capabilities perform which activities on which artifacts at which time(s).

A Little-JIL coordination specification has a visual representation, but is precisely defined (using finite-state automata), which makes it amenable to definitive analyses. Among the features of Little-JIL that distinguish it from most process languages are its 1) use of abstraction to support scalability and clarity, 2) use of scoping to make step parameterization clear, 3) facilities for specifying parallelism, 4) capabilities for dealing with exceptional conditions, and 5) clarity in specifying iteration.

A Little-JIL coordination specification consists of hierarchically decomposed steps, where a step represents a task to be done by an assigned agent. Figure 1 shows the iconic representation of a single step with some of its features. Each step has a name and a set of badges to represent control flow among its substeps, its *interface* (specifying its input/output artifacts and the resources it requires), the exceptions it handles, etc. A step with no substeps is a *leaf step*. It represents an activity performed by an agent, without any process guidance. A full description of Little-JIL is provided in [13]. Below we present some Little-JIL features, focusing on those used in the example presented in this paper.

Resources and Agents—Each Little-JIL step interface (iconically represented by the filled circle above the step name) specifies the types of resources required to support execution of the step. Some examples of resources are infusion suites and medical records. Each step has one specially designated resource, called its *agent*, which is assigned responsibility for the performance of the step. Little-JIL agents may be humans, groups of humans or automated devices.

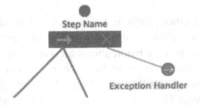

Fig. 1. A Little-JIL step icon

Substep Decomposition—Little-JIL steps may be decomposed into two kinds of substeps, *ordinary substeps* and *exception handlers*. Ordinary substeps define how each step is executed and connected to its parent through edges annotated by specifications of the artifacts that flow between parent and substep. *Exception handlers* define how exceptions thrown by the step's descendants are handled.

Step sequencing—A non-leaf step has a *sequencing badge* (an icon on the left of the step bar; e.g., the right arrow in Figure 1) that defines the order of substep execution. Little-JIL has four step kinds. The example depicted in Figure 2 uses two, the *sequential step* (right arrow), indicating that substeps execute from left to right and the *parallel step* (equal sign), indicating that substeps execute in any (possibly interleaved) order, although the order may be constrained by such factors as the lack of needed resources.

Channels—*Channels* are named entities that act like buffers, directly connecting specifically identified source step(s) with specifically identified destination step(s). This construct helps define how streaming data is handled and can also be used to synchronize concurrently executing steps.

Exception Handling—A Little-JIL step can throw an exception when some aspect of step execution fails. This triggers execution of a matching *exception handler* defined at an ancestor of the step throwing the exception. Figure 2 shows an exception handler *consider alternative treatment* (connected to the X in the root step bar), which is triggered when one of the children of the root step throws a matching exception.

2.2 An Example Using Little-JIL to Define a Chemotherapy Process

Figures 2 and 3 are diagrams that depict part of a Little-JIL definition of a chemotherapy process. Figure 2 is the top-level diagram of the process and thus represents it at a high level of abstraction. The entire Little-JIL process definition has more than 250 steps and thus cannot be shown in its entirety here. Elicitation of the

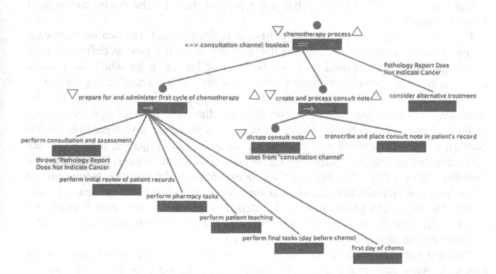

Fig. 2. A coordination diagram of Little-JIL chemotherapy process

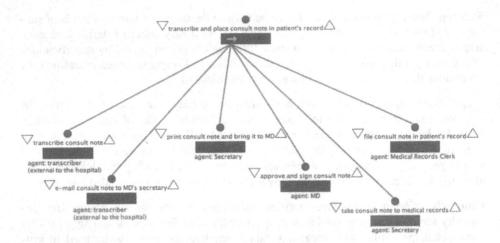

Fig. 3. The task decomposition of transcribe and place consult note in patient's record

process required two semesters of weekly meetings between process developers and medical professionals. Most of the time there were two graduate students (and at least one faculty member) meeting with two or three medical professionals. The medical professionals comprised different combinations of two physicians, one pharmacist, three nurses, and a medical assistant. The part of the process definition that is depicted here is concise but representative of many interesting issues that arise in defining and analyzing the full process.

Note that the diagrams in this paper do not include all the information needed for a complete Little-JIL process definition. A diagram is created using the Little-JIL visual editor, which allows the developer to suppress visualization of process details for the sake of clarity. Thus, Figures 2 and 3 do not display full details of the resources and artifacts declarations in each step but just represent them by the circle icon located above the step bar.

Figure 2 indicates that the process definition is decomposed into two substeps executing in parallel (note the equal sign in the step bar). In the full process definition, each substep is further decomposed down to the level of leaf steps for which the process definer is unable to provide, or uninterested in providing, process detail and guidance.

Figure 2 also shows that the root step *chemotherapy process* has a substep *consider alternative treatment* that acts as an exception handler (note the "X" sign on the *chemotherapy process* step bar to which the step *consider alternative treatment* is connected). In the step *perform consultation and assessment* in Figure 2, the doctor may determine that the patient's pathology report does not indicate cancer. In this case, the *Pathology Report Does Not Indicate Cancer* exception is thrown (the decomposition of the *perform consultation and assessment* step is not shown due to space limitations). The exception propagates up the step decomposition tree until it reaches a matching handler. Thus, control is transferred to the exception handler step *consider alternative treatment* and appropriate action is taken.

The first substep, *prepare for and administer first cycle of chemotherapy*, of the root step *chemotherapy process* is decomposed into six substeps to be executed in sequence (note the arrow pointing to the right in the step bar). The six substeps of *prepare for and administer first cycle of chemotherapy* are the major stages of the chemotherapy process. Although the agent assignments are not given in this diagram, *perform consultation and assessment* is done by a Medical Doctor (MD); *perform initial review of patient records* by a Practice Registered Nurse (RN) and a Triage Medical Assistant; *perform pharmacy task* by a Pharmacist; *perform patient teaching* by a Nurse Practitioner; *perform final tasks (day before chemo)* by a Pharmacist and a Clinic RN; and *the first day of chemo* is done again by a Pharmacist and a Clinic RN.

While step sequencing specifications provide strong control over the order of step execution, Little-JIL also enables specification of flexibility in execution sequencing through such constructs as a channel. In this example, a channel is used to specify that an MD cannot dictate the consult note before evaluating the patient's condition. But, since the consult note is primarily used for billing and legal purposes and does not directly affect the patient's treatment, the doctor may choose to dictate the consult note right after evaluating the patient or later, while the tasks in *prepare for and administer first cycle of chemotherapy* are already underway. This step sequencing flexibility is captured precisely by the coordination diagram in Figure 2, which shows that the *dictate consult note* step can potentially execute in parallel with the step *prepare for and administer first cycle of chemotherapy*. At the same time, the "consultation channel" imposes the additional restriction that the MD cannot dictate the consult note before evaluating the patient's condition – the step *dictate consult note* takes a parameter from the "consultation channel" (declared at the root step so that it is visible, hence usable, by all of its descendants) and thus cannot start until *perform patient consultation* (not shown for lack of space), which is a substep of *perform consultation and assessment,* completes and writes a parameter to the "consultation channel.

Figure 3 decomposes the substep *transcribe and place consult note in patient's record* of the root step *chemo process.* Note that the process depicted by the diagram in Figure 3 provides further details of the handling of the consult note. Figure 2 specifies that *transcribe and place consult note in patient's record* is the second substep of the sequential step *create and process consult note.* This, means that *transcribe and place consult note in patient's record* cannot start until the step *dictate consult note* has completed. This sequencing mechanism is a faithful representation of the real world situation. In this process, the doctor dictates the consult note on the phone. The doctor's message is recorded and triggers the tasks of the transcriber, who is external to the clinic. The transcriber listens to the message, transcribes the consult note, emails it to the doctor's secretary and so on.

Another interesting aspect of the diagram in Figure 3 is the diverse set of agents that execute the steps – Transcriber, Secretary, Medical Doctor, and Medical Records Clerk. Thus, the timely manner in which the step *transcribe and place consult note in patient's record* is performed depends on the availability of all those agents. In a later section, we will see that the time of completion of the *transcribe and place consult note in patient's record* step relative to the time of completion of other steps in the process is important for satisfying some of the properties of the process.

2.3   Using PROPEL and FLAVERS Analysis to Look for Process Defects

In this section, we present a short, simplified example of the application of finite-state verification to the chemotherapy process definition. Finite-state verification techniques algorithmically check all possible paths through a model of a system to determine whether any execution of the system can violate a specified system property. In the work described here, we have used the FLAVERS [8] finite-state verifier, although other tools (e.g., [14]) could have been used. Our model of the system is an annotated control flow graph derived from the Little-JIL process definition. For our purposes, a property is a specification of the requirements for some aspect of the behavior of the system. Thus, the property is a specification against which a system is to be verified. For example, a property might state that a certain event cannot occur until after some other event occurs. Our work focuses on developing such properties with the help of domain experts (chemotherapy medical professionals in this example), eliciting a process definition from domain experts, and finally comparing the process definition against the properties. If a property is violated, we change the process (assuming the property is correctly specified) and verify the modified process against the property. We iterate the above procedure until the process satisfies the property and thus the process is improved.

In our analysis, properties are encoded as finite-state automata (FSA) and represent constraints on the sequences of events that could occur during executions of the process. The FSA in Figure 4 represents the property "Before Chemotherapy Can Be Administered to a Patient, that Patient's Consult Note Needs to Be Put in that Patient's Record." The events in this property are *put consult note in patient's record* and *administer chemo*. The event *put consult note in patient's record* is bound to the step *file consult note in patient's record* in Figure 3. The event *administer chemo* is bound to the step *administer chemo drug* which is a part of the subprocess decomposition of the step *first day of chemo* in Figure 2.

At the start of execution of the process, the automaton in Figure 4 is assumed to be in its start state *q0* (indicated by the triangle to the left of state *q0*). Execution of *put consult note in patient's record* causes the FSA to transition from state *q0* to state *q1*.

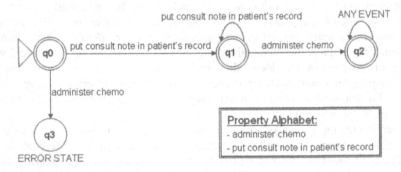

Fig. 4. An FSA corresponding to the chemotherapy property "Before Chemotherapy Can Be Administered to a Patient, that Patient's Consult Note Needs to Be Put in that Patient's Record." A transition labeled with ANY EVENT means that the transition is taken if any event from the alphabet of the FSA occurs. The ERROR STATE is a trap state, i.e. it is a non-accepting state, such that once the automaton enters that state, it remains in it regardless of what other events occur.

Then if *administer chemo* is encountered during execution of the process, the FSA transitions from state *q1* to state *q2*. The state *q2* is an accepting state (indicated by a doubled circle). Thus, *put consult note in patient's record* followed by *administer chemo* is a valid sequence of events in the chemotherapy process. On the other hand, if *administer chemo* occurs before *put consult note in patient's record* (the transition from state *q0* to state *q3* in the FSA shown in Figure 4), the automaton ends up in an *ERROR* state (*q3*) indicating that this causes the property to be violated. Also note that if *consult note is put in patient's record* does not occur at all, then the automaton will remain in its start state *q0*, which is also an accepting state thus indicating that the property is satisfied.

In our project, automata such as the one in Figure 4, were generated by the PROPEL (PROPerty ELucidator) system [15, 16]. PROPEL facilitates the elucidation of properties by providing three different representations of a property—a question tree view, a disciplined English view, and a finite-state automaton view—and assuring that the three views automatically remain synchronized with each other. The different views aim to bridge the gap between the natural language in which the properties are elicited from domain experts and the rigorous, but usually not trivial to specify correctly, mathematical formalism of the finite-state automaton used by the verification tool FLAVERS. Each view also explicitly indicates subtle choices that need to be made and questions that need to be answered in order to specify a property, such as whether certain events must always occur or whether other events can occur multiple times. For the example chemotherapy process, there are dozens of important safety and legal properties to be verified. Our experiments indicate that PROPEL is adept at supporting the definition of such properties.

Having defined the process in Little-JIL and created the property automaton using PROPEL, we then used the finite-state verifier FLAVERS to check whether the process satisfies the property on all possible paths of execution. If it does not, i.e. if a process execution can drive the property automaton to a non-accepting state, then FLAVERS reports the violation and produces a trace of the process execution that leads to the property violation. The verification example in this paper may appear relatively straightforward, given the simple property, but we note that it entails considerable challenges. The fact that the root step *chemotherapy process* is parallel requires that FLAVERS explore all possible execution interleavings of the substeps, creating a very large space of alternatives to be explored. The use of channels further complicates the verification. The fact that the chemotherapy process is of a significant size (more than 250 steps) makes the verification state space very large. FLAVERS employs optimization techniques and thus can usually cope with the verification of properties of processes whose size is similar to that of this chemotherapy process.

In fact, FLAVERS reported that this chemotherapy process example can violate the property presented in Figure 4, and it produced a trace of a valid execution of the process where *administer chemo drug* occurs before *file consult note in patient's record* completes. Although a channel imposes some synchronization between the parallel activities in the process, the verifier detected that concurrent execution can allow at least one execution sequence that leads to a property violation. Thus, this result identified a process defect, but it also raises an interesting question about whether legal and privacy issues (such as the requirement that a consult note must be in the patient's chart before administration of chemotherapy) may have received much less attention than medical safety issues and thus may not be fully addressed by standard medical processes.

3 Experience and Evaluation

Working with the chemotherapy process suggests that our approach can lead to improvements in the processes. We were able to identify process defects and raise issues resulting in defect elimination. The medical professionals involved in the project have found benefit in this work. They are even considering using the formal process definition as the basis for training documents and guidelines for medical staff.

The very task of eliciting details from the medical professionals about the chemotherapy process and capturing those details formally in Little-JIL lead to the discovery of many of the problematic aspects in the process. One of the first observations after interviewing several different medical professionals was that the terminology used for the chemotherapy process guidelines contained some inconsistencies. For example, words like "verify", "confirm", "check", "match", and "consistent" were used loosely. The same word used at different times or in different contexts often had different meanings, even when used by the same individual. Since many of the critical errors that may occur in a process like chemotherapy may arise from neglecting small details (e.g. not checking to see if the patient height or weight measurements on which the chemotherapy dose is based are sufficiently up-to-date), we had to develop a precise naming template that disambiguated the use of different terms. Thus, our experience suggests that the effort of defining and analyzing complex medical processes can benefit if some kind of ontological structure of the domain knowledge is present.

We also found that process guidelines usually contain adequate details when describing common, standard scenarios. However, process guidelines did not provide enough details, or often any details, for handling many non-typical cases. For example, there were places in the process where an agent confirms the correctness of some information and, if the confirmation succeeds, the agent continues on with the rest of the defined tasks. However, if the confirmation fails, then in many cases the process lacked specific instructions detailing how the agent should proceed. In some cases, we noted that different agents were handling the exception differently depending on personal style, level of experience, and the individual approach of other medical professionals involved in the recovery from the failure. While modeling the process with Little-JIL, the rich exception handling semantics of the language forced us to think about exceptional scenarios and ask specific questions about the exact process to be executed following the throwing of an exception, the agents involved in resolving that exception, and the place in the process to which control gets transferred once the exception has been handled. Questions like "What do you do when the check you make fails?" and "Which task do you proceed with and which tasks do you need to redo when you have resolved the problem?" typically triggered discussions among the medical professionals that resulted in more complete and rigorous specification of how to deal with these exceptional cases, thus improving the process overall.

The resource and artifact modeling capabilities of Little-JIL also led to interesting questions during the interviewing stage that exposed some deficiencies in the process. For example, the chemotherapy process relies heavily on a paper copy of a treatment plan, which is an artifact created at the earlier stages of the process and then verified independently and signed by medical professionals. However, doctors enter changes to a treatment plan electronically, which sometimes leads to inconsistencies between the current electronic version and the paper copy that circulates among the medical professionals. The artifact model of Little-JIL and the need to precisely describe and distinguish between paper and electronic records led to the discovery of such issues.

The expressive power of Little-JIL proved to be useful for the definition of the process in the chemotherapy case study. The powerful exception handling mechanisms in the language enabled the process definition to reflect the real world process more accurately. The capabilities the language provides for modeling resources (both agent and non-agent) and artifacts were an important part of the specification of the process. The synchronization mechanism and channel support for specifying direct communication between steps was also useful in this process definition. Hierarchy and abstraction were beneficial in helping to keep down the size of the chemotherapy process and the many different levels of abstraction at which it was defined.

The graphical notations in Little-JIL facilitated the communication of computer science concepts to the medical professionals. We usually tried to present the process to the medical professionals in textual, natural language form, but we were often asked to show the Little-JIL diagrams as they provide clearer understandings. Although we believe that it is most likely that the Little-JIL definitions will be written by computer scientists or medical informatics specialists, our experiences suggest that medical professionals, with a little training, can become comfortable reading Little-JIL process definitions.

The task of interviewing domain experts and specifying precisely the high level goals and requirements that the medical process needs to meet, proved to be beneficial. We worked on identifying properties at a higher level of abstraction, a level at which the property's events are not tightly coupled to concrete steps in the process definition, but rather are used to capture universal safety and legal goals that need to be satisfied no matter how the process is implemented. This approach introduced a different perspective and helped medical professionals view the process in a new light. Instead of focusing only on "what is being done", the process was approached by asking questions like "Why is this done?" and "What goal is met by this sequence of steps?" Such types of questions also helped expose deficiencies in the process and triggered discussions about how to address them. While considering the motivation behind parts of the process and the objectives that certain sequences of steps are trying to achieve, the medical professionals often identified steps that were either misplaced or missing from the process guidelines. Thus, property elicitation itself played an important role in enhancing the process.

PROPEL was of great value in facilitating the correct specification of properties. Previous experience indicated that specifying a property in a mathematical formalism, like a finite-state automaton or a temporal logic, is often not trivial and subtleties are often not captured easily or correctly. For example, consider the requirement that if patient height and weight data (used to determine correct dosage) are "stale" (i.e. the measurements are not recent enough), then height and weight must be remeasured before administration of chemotherapy. A correct formal specification of this must address such issues as whether the data can become stale several times and, if so, whether a single remeasurement is sufficient, whether the data always becomes stale, whether remeasurement is necessary if chemotherapy is not administered for some reason, etc. In addition to the finite-state automaton view of a property, PROPEL provides a natural language template, where users select phrases, and a question tree view that explicitly asks questions, like the ones above. All three of these views are equivalent and assist the user in capturing the subtleties of the property.

So far our efforts have focused on capturing the chemotherapy process in Little-JIL and specifying properties using PROPEL. Our initial use of FLAVERS focused on verifying relatively simple properties, and most of them were satisfied. In most of the cases when the verifier detected a violation, it was due to an omission or error in the process definition or property specification. However, the example in the previous section shows that our verification approach could identify real violations and pinpoint weaknesses in the process. We expect that when we begin to analyze more complicated properties over larger processes that hide potential concurrency, our approach will lead to the discovery of more defects in the process.

We note that as the size of the process under verification increases, so does the state space that needs to be explored. Large processes, like the chemotherapy one, with inherent parallelism and complex exception handling specifications, stress the importance of utilizing verifiers that scale well. At this point, our work indicates that the performance of the FLAVERS system seems to be capable of acceptable scaling. For example, the verification of the property presented in Fig. 4 took less than ten seconds of computing time running on a standard desktop computer.

4 Related Work

There has been some recent work using process definition and analysis to improve medical processes. For example, the Protocure II project [17] has goals that are quite similar to ours in that medical protocols are formally specified and verified. As part of that project, a protocol for jaundice and its properties were modeled in the Asbru language [18]. The protocol that was analyzed consists of 40 plans (where the plans seem to be similar to Little-JIL steps), whereas the chemotherapy process that we analyzed consists of over 250 steps. The Little-JIL process definition supports more detailed representation of the process, including support for exceptions and complex agent interactions. The Protocure researchers also encountered ambiguous use of medical terms, incomplete information, and inconsistencies that may support different conclusions. In another study that was also part of the Protocure II project [19], the Asbru model of the jaundice protocol and its properties were verified using the SMV model checker.

Noumeir has also pursued similar goals, but using a notation like UML to define processes [20]. Others (e.g., [21]), view medical processes as workflows and use a workflow-like language to define processes and drive their execution. But, we note that these projects seem to place less emphasis on analysis.

There have been other approaches to improving medical safety as well, but much of the emphasis of this work has been targeted towards quality control measures [22], error reporting systems [23], and process automation in laboratory settings [24], such as those where blood products are prepared for administration. In other work, Bayesian belief networks have been used as the basis for discrete event simulations of medical scenarios and to guide treatment planning (e.g., [25]).

Many languages and diagrammatic notations have been used to define processes. Some incorporated use of a procedural language [26]. Others used rules [27] and modified Petri Nets [28] to define processes. More recently, the workflow [29] and electronic commerce [30] communities are pursuing similar research. None of these approaches, however, seem able to support process definitions that are both clear and precise enough. Main failings of these approaches include inadequate specification of exception handling, weak facilities for controlling concurrency, lack of resource management, and inadequate specification of artifact flows.

There has also been considerable work on the analysis of code and models of systems. Finite-state verification, or model checking (e.g., [7], [8], [14]), approaches construct a finite model that represents all possible executions of the system and then analyze that model algorithmically to detect executions that violate a particular property specified by the analyst. A major concern of these techniques is controlling the size of the state-space model, while maintaining analytic precision. Our team has analyzed and evaluated various finite-state verification approaches [31], and developed verifiers such as FLAVERS [8] and INCA [32]. Our work seems to be among the first that has applied FSV approaches to process definitions [9].

5 Conclusion

The finite-state verification approach presented in this paper supports checking whether or not a process satisfies certain properties, but it assumes that all agents involved in the process perform their tasks without errors. However, human errors do occur in medical processes and thus complementary forms of analysis are also useful. Thus, for example, we have used a blood transfusion process definition as the basis for the automatic generation of a fault tree representation of this process and have used the fault tree to identify single points of failure in the process, thereby reducing its vulnerability to failure [6]. Similarly, our studies of delays in a hospital Emergency Department (ED) have underscored the potential for resource management to improve efficiency in the ED's processes [33]. In response, we are developing technologies to create discrete event simulations from process definitions in order to support reasoning about how to improve efficiency through better resource management.

In conclusion, we observe that this work has shown considerable promise and has suggested extensions in several directions. We propose to pursue further research in this domain. We expect that this research will provide further insights into how process definition and analysis technology can help improve the safety and efficiency of the processes in this critical domain.

Acknowledgments

This research was funded by the US National Science Foundation under Award No. CCF-0427071 and by the U. S. Department of Defense/Army Research Office under Awards No. DAAD19-03-1-0133 and DAAD19-01-1-0564. The U.S. Government is authorized to reproduce and distribute reprints for Governmental purposes notwithstanding any copyright annotation thereon. The views and conclusions contained herein are those of the authors and should not be interpreted as necessarily representing the official policies or endorsements, either expressed or implied, of the U.S. NSF, U. S. DOD/Army Research Office, or the U.S. Government.

The authors gratefully acknowledge the work of Sandy Wise, Barbara Lerner, and Aaron Cass, who made major contributions to the development of Little-JIL, to Rachel Cobleigh and Irene Ros, who helped elicit the chemotherapy process and properties, and to many members of the staff of the D'Amour Center for Cancer Care, who graciously donated their time and expertise.

References

1. Kohn, L.T., Corrigan, J.M., Donaldson, M.S. (eds.): To Err is Human: Building a Safer Health System. National Academies Press, Washington (1999)
2. Reid, P.P., Compton, W.D., Grossman, J.H., Fanjiang, G. (eds.): Building a Better Delivery System: A New Engineering/Healthcare Partnership. National Academies Press, Washington (2005)
3. Institute of Medicine: Crossing the Quality Chasm: A New Health System for the 21st Century. National Academies Press, Washington (2001)
4. Henneman, E.H., Cobleigh, R.L., Frederick, K., Katz-Bassett, E., Avrunin, G.A., Clarke, L.A., Osterweil, L.J., Andrzejewski, C., Merrigan, K., Henneman, P.L.: Increasing Patient Safety and Efficiency in Transfusion Therapy Using Formal Process Definitions. Transfusion Medicine Reviews 21, 49–57 (2007)
5. Burgmeier, J.: Failure Mode and Effect Analysis: An Application in Reducing Risk in Blood Transfusion. Quality Improvement 28, 331–339 (2002)
6. Chen, B., Avrunin, G.S., Clarke, L.A., Osterweil, L.J.: Automatic Fault Tree Derivation from Little-JIL Process Definitions. In: Wang, Q., Pfahl, D., Raffo, D.M., Wernick, P. (eds.) SPW 2006 and ProSim 2006. LNCS, vol. 3966, pp. 150–158. Springer, Heidelberg (2006)
7. Clarke, E.M.J., Grumberg, O., Peled, D.: Model Checking. MIT Press, Cambridge (2000)
8. Dwyer, M.B., Clarke, L.A., Cobleigh, J.M., Naumovich, G.: Flow Analysis for Verifying Properties of Concurrent Software Systems. ACM Trans. on Software Engineering and Methodology 13(4), 359–430 (2004)
9. Cobleigh, J.M., Clarke, L.A., Osterweil, L.J.: Verifying Properties of Process Definitions. In: ACM SIGSOFT Intl. Symp. on Software Testing & Analysis, pp. 96–101. ACM Press, Portland, OR (2000)
10. Boose, E.R., Ellison, A.M., Osterweil, L.J., Clarke, L., Podorozhny, R., Hadley, J.L., Wise, A., Foster, D.R.: Ensuring Reliable Datasets for Environmental Models and Forecasts. Ecological Informatics, ECONINF84 2(3), 237–247 (2007)
11. Schweik, C.M., Osterweil, L.J., Sondheimer, N., Thomas, C.: Analyzing Processes for E-Government Development: The Emergence of Process Modeling Languages. Journal of E-Government 1(4), 63–89 (2004)
12. Cass, A.G., Lerner, B.S., McCall, E.K., et al.: Little-JIL/Juliette: A Process Definition Language and Interpreter. In: ACM/IEEE 20th Intl Conf. on Software Engineering, Limerick, Ireland, pp. 754–758 (2000)
13. Wise, A.: Little-JIL 1.5 Language Report. Lab. for Advanced Software Engineering Research (LASER), Dept. of Comp. Sci, UMass, Amherst (2006)
14. Holzmann, G.J.: The SPIN Model Checker. Addison-Wesley, Reading (2004)

15. Smith, R.L., Avrunin, G.S., Clarke, L.A., Osterweil, L.J.: PROPEL: An Approach To Supporting Property Elucidation. In: ACM/IEEE 24th Intl. Conf. on Software Engineering, Orlando, FL, pp. 11–21 (2002)
16. Cobleigh, R.L., Avrunin, G.S., Clarke, L.A.: User Guidance for Creating Precise and Accessible Property Specifications. In: 14th ACM SIGSOFT Symp. on the Foundations of Software Engineering, Portland, OR, pp. 208–218 (2006)
17. Protocure II (2006), http://www.protocure.org
18. ten Teije, A., Marcos, M., Balser, M., van Croonenborg, J., Duelli, C., van Harmelen, F., Lucas, P., Miksch, S., Reif, W., Rosenbrand, K., Seyfang, A.: Improving Medical Protocols by Formal Methods. Artificial Intelligence in Medicine 36(3), 193–209 (2006)
19. Baumler, S., Balser, M., Dunets, A., Reif, W., Schmitt, J.: Verification of Medical Guidelines by Model Checking – A Case Study. In: Valmari, A. (ed.) SPIN 2006. LNCS, vol. 3925, pp. 219–233. Springer, Heidelberg (2006)
20. Noumeir, R.: Radiology Interpretation Process Modeling. Journal of Biomedical Informatics 39(2), 103–114 (2006)
21. Ruffolo, M., Curio, R., Gallucci, L.: Process Management in Health Care: A System for Preventing Risks and Medical Errors. Business Process Mgmt, 334–343 (2005)
22. Voak, D., Chapman, J.F., Phillips, P.: Quality of Transfusion Practice Beyond the Blood Transfusion Laboratory is Essential to Prevent ABO-incompatible Death. Transfusion Medicine 10, 95–96 (2000)
23. Battles, J.B., Kaplan, H.S., van der Schaaf, T.W., Shea, C.E.: The Attributes of Medical Event Reporting Systems for Transfusion Medicine. Arch Pathology Laboratory Medicine 122, 231–238 (1998)
24. Galel, S.A., Richards, C.A.: Practical Approaches to Improve Laboratory Performance and Transfusion Safety. Am. J. Clinical Pathology 107(Suppl. 1), S43–S49 (1997)
25. van der Gaag, L.C., Renooji, S., Witteman, C.L.M., Aleman, B.M.P., Taal, B.G.: Probabilities for a Probabilistic Network: A Case-Study in Oesophageal Cancer. Artificial Intelligence in Medicine 25(2), 123–148 (2002)
26. Sutton, S.M.J., Heimbigner, D.M., Osterweil, L.J.: APPL/A: A Language for Software-Process Programming. ACM Trans. on Software Engineering and Methodology 4(3), 221–286 (1995)
27. Ben-Shaul, I.Z., Kaiser, G.: A Paradigm for Decentralized Process Modeling and its Realization in the Oz Environment. In: ACM/IEEE 16th Intl. Conf. on Software Engineering, pp. 179–188 (1994)
28. Bandinelli, S., Fuggetta, A., Ghezzi, C.: Process Model Evolution in the SPADE Environment. ACM/IEEE 15th Trans. on Software Engineering 19(12) (1993)
29. Paul, S., Park, E., Chaar, J.: RainMan: A Workflow System for the Internet. In: Usenix Symposium on Internet Technologies and Systems (1997)
30. Grosof, B., Labrou, Y., Chan, H.Y.: A Declarative Approach to Business Rules in Contracts: Courteous Logic Programs in XML. In: ACM Conf. on Electronic Commerce, Denver, CO, pp. 68–77 (1999)
31. Avrunin, G.S., Corbett, J.C., Dwyer, M.B.: Benchmarking Finite-State Verifiers. Software Tools for Technology Transfer 2, 317–320 (2000)
32. Corbett, J.C., Avrunin, G.S.: Using Integer Programming to Verify General Safety and Liveness Properties. Formal Methods in System Design 6, 97–123 (1995)
33. Raunak, M.S., Osterweil, L.J.: Effective Resource Allocation for Process Simulation: A Position Paper. In: 6th Intl. Workshop on Software Process Simulation and Modeling, St. Louis, MO (2005)

Modeling and Enforcing Advanced Access Control Policies in Healthcare Systems with SECTET

Michael Hafner, Mukhtiar Memon, and Muhammad Alam

University of Innsbruck, Austria
{m.hafner,mukhtiar.memon,masoom.alam}@uibk.ac.at

Abstract. This contribution gives an overview of various access control strategies in use in healthcare scenarios and shows how a variety of policies can be modeled based on a single security policy model for usage control, UCON. The core of this contribution consists of the specialization of the SECTET-Framework for Model Driven Security for complex healthcare scenarios based on UCON. The resulting Domain Architecture comprises a Domain Specific Language for the modeling of policies with advanced security requirements, a target architecture for the enforcement of these policies and model-to-code transformations.

1 Introduction

The Electronic Health Record (EHR) stands for a concept aiming at the digital integration of healthcare information currently scattered over paper-based archives, databases and healthcare systems distributed accross multiple security domains. As a matter of fact, the status-quo comes at great costs to national economies, paired with an unsatisfactory level of service quality, possibly even leading to fatal errors resulting in erroneous treatment or wrong medication (e.g., [22,28,15]).

Trying to systematically resolve these system-inherent weaknesses, a growing number of countries are working towards the realization of national EHR systems (e.g., [15,12]). By now, leveraging the popularity of standards related to web services – based on the paradigm on Services Oriented Architectures – these inititiatives have set the implementation of powerful infrastructures supporting inter-operability for transorganizational healthcare services (e.g., [11]) at the top of their agenda.

Problem Statement. In a fully digitized world, patients will be concerned about retaining legal rights over their medical records. Organizations processing patient records will have to account for the preservation of data security and privacy. Although these responsibilities are codified in an impressive array of directives (e.g., HIPAA [26], EU Directive [31], PIPEDA [27]), an information-intensive industry delivering security-critical healthcare services needs to put a special emphasis on security concerns [6,3]. By now security requirements are dealt with cryptographic primitives (e.g., encryption, digital signatures) and architectural solutions (e.g., firewalls etc.). Confidentiality to patient data is enforced through access control mechanisms[33]. However, actual security concerns in healthcare scenarios go way beyond merely guaranteeing data confidentiality. A broader notion of security would have to address issues related to usage control

H. Giese (Ed.): MoDELS 2007 Workshops, LNCS 5002, pp. 132–144, 2008.

(e.g., number of times a user is allowed to view a document), issues of particular importance to the healthcare industry (e.g., rights delegation, emergency access [34]), and would have to account for legal concerns (e.g., 4-Eyes-Principle [38,37]).

Contribution. Research has started in several areas (e.g., privacy [14], distributed access [4], trust management [40] and identity management [8]). However, the treatment of domain specific security aspects in healthcare is still in its infancy. This contribution explores advanced security requirements in healthcare systems and proposes a high level policy modeling approach based on UCON – a security model unifying a broad array of security concepts like Discretionary, Mandatory and Role Based Access Control, as well as Trust and Digital Rights Management [13]. The conceptual solution for policy modeling is realized with SECTET – a framework for Model Driven Security [9]. We propose an extension to the SECTET-Framework towards a *Domain Architecture* comprising a *Domain Specific Language* for modeling the security-critical healthcare scenarios, a *Target Architecture* for the enforcement of security requirements and model-to-code transformations.

Organization. Section 2 gives an overview of the state-of-the-art of research and reference implementations related to access control in healthcare scenarios. Section 3 introduces the three building blocks of the SECTET – Domain Architecture. In Section 4 we propose extensions to the SECTET - Framework with motivating scenarios. We conclude with a sketch of our research agenda in Section 5.

2   Access Control in Healthcare

2.1   State-of-the-Art

We first analyze the capabilities of of different access control paradigms and discuss their applicability to healthcare scenarios. Comprehensive analyses can be found in [21]. We then motivate our choice of the UCON Model – the conceptual underpinning of our modeling approach.

Discretionary Access Control (DAC). In DAC based systems, users are considered to be the owners of the resources. This enables them to grant access rights to other users [21]. This notion of *Resource Ownership* makes the DAC model unsuitable for exclusive use in healthcare systems as the medical data is created by users of various collaborating partners and none of those can claim ownership of the data.

Mandatory Access Control (MAC). In MAC based systems, users and their rights are administered by a central authority. Security labels are assigned to data elements at very fine-granular levels, thereby expressing their security sensitivity. They can be used to realize *User Managed Access Control* [7] with shifting some of the controls to the user by requiring the user's consent for data access. However, inter-organizational healthcare scenarios involve many actors accessing resources scattered over multiple domains and the centralized administration in MAC is incompatible with SOA-based Systems which advocate loose coupling with decentralized control.

Role Based Access Control (RBAC). Users in RBAC [32] systems are assigned *Roles*, holding *Permissions*, specifying access rights to *Objects*. The basic RBAC model can not meet the dynamic security requirements necessitating runtime checks of mutable attributes (e.g., a principal may access a document only between 9.00 a.m. to 5.00 p.m.). Although RBAC was extended to cope with dynamic behavior based on contextual constraints (e.g., time, location, purpose etc. [20]), the shortcomings of RBAC are twofold. Firstly, the model lacks expressiveness with respect to dynamically changing subject attributes (e.g., the physician gets unrestricted access to the affected patient's medical data in the context of emergency). Secondly, it does not cater for the notion of continuity in access control (e.g., facilitating revocation of access rights once granted).

Usage Control (UCON). UCON is a comprehensive policy model for usage control. It extends traditional access control models in two respects [30]. 1. *Continuity of access decision* means that the decision to access an object is not only verified before but also during access and may result in the revocation of permissions, whenever conditions are not met. Policy conditions in UCON consist of subject, object and system attributes. 2. *Mutability of attributes* refers to subject, system or object attributes changing as side-effects of resource access. This may additionally result in a change in ongoing or subsequent access decisions.

Policy statements in UCON consist of *authorizations*, *obligations* and *conditions* (cf. Figure 1). Authorizations refer to predicates based on subject or object attributes. Obligation actions are directives to a subject to perform additional actions before or during an access. Whereas the predicates based on environment attributes such as system time, device type etc. are categorized as Conditions. Authorizations, o*B*ligations and Conditions are collectively referred to as the building blocks of UCON$_{ABC}$. UCON conditions can be used to express static constraints (e.g., duration, purpose) as well as dynamic constraints (e.g., number of times to access a resource, location-dependent access).

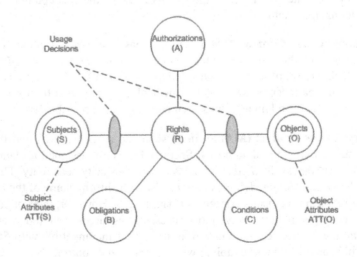

Fig. 1. Elements of the UCON Policy Model

2.2 Advanced Use Cases in Healthcare

Advanced healthcare scenarios impose complex security requirements. In this section we introduce some of them, thereby motivating our development for an elaborate policy model. Some of these use cases already stand as candidates for near future integration into "Integrating the Healthcare Enterprise (IHE)"-projects [1], whereas others represent more an educated guess based on discussions with experts on what the healthcare industry may be needing in a couple of years.

Dynamic Access Control. In many healthcare scenarios, permissions to execute healthcare services cannot be assigned statically. Instead, these are associated with a set of *Dynamic Constraints*. Such constraints refer to subject, system or object attributes and are evaluated at runtime. An example of such dynamic constraints in healthcare is the status of physician: *"A physician can modify any medical record for which she is designated as primary physician"*.

Delegation of Rights (DR). DR allows a user to delegate her rights to other legitimate users of the system in specific situations with defined limitations. For example, in patient referral, the primary physician delegates her rights to the specialist. In other scenarios the patient himself can grant access to the specialist using the delegated rights of the primary physician[23]. DR may be further restricted: the rights of the delegatee may depend on additional information such as her legal status, credentials, purpose and duration etc.

Break-Glass Policy (BGP). BGP is an authorization scheme granting access in case of emergency. An attending physician needs to bypass routine access control restrictions to guarantee timely treatment without any delay due to administrative or technical complexities (e.g., [34,20]).

4-Eyes-Principle. The *4-Eyes-Principle* is a form of *Multiple Authorization*. It requires two users with a common interest to enter the system simultaneously. This principle supports monitoring of the data access, e.g., when one user accesses data the other user monitors it (e.g., [37]). In healthcare scenarios, the 4-Eyes-Principle requires the patient to be present when a physician accesses her records. The physician's access is logged during the visit by some trusted *Proxy Service*. Enforcement of the 4-Eyes-Principle is usually performed indirectly and supported with storing the access record into logging database for future auditing. Logging and auditing capabilities permit the patient to set her privacy preferences based on access history and identify any potential abuse.

Usage Control (UC). UC is an extension of access control because it does not only control the data access but also how the accessed data may or may not be used or distributed afterwards. In a healthcare scenario a usage requirement could state that *"Access to a medical record is allowed for 5 times only and should last for at most 48 hours, after its first access"*.

3   SECTET - A Domain Architecture for Model Driven Security

SECTET is a framework for Model Driven Security which supports the design, implementation and management of secure inter-organizational workflows in a peer-to-peer environment (i.e. without central control) based on the paradigm of Service Oriented Architectures. Due to its genericity, the SECTET-Framework covers a large set of component-based applications from domains such as e-government, e-health, e-educa-tion etc. Various case studies from healthcare and e-government provided the opportunity to apply the framework in real life scenarios [2,5,9,10,19]. Security critical inter-organiza-tional workflows are modelled using a *Domain Specific Language*. Models are transformed into executable artefacts configuring a web services based *Target Architecture*. We subsequently briefly describe the three building blocks of the framework.

3.1   The SECTET-Domain Specific Language (DSL)

The SECTET- DSL is based on UML 2.0 and aims at the integration of security requirements into models of inter-organizational workflows at a level of abstraction appropriate to bridge the gap between domain experts and business analysts on one side and software architects on the other side. Security requirements are modelled at the design level and integrated as security patterns into the business requirement models. The basic SECTET modeling approach is based on two orthogonal views: the *Interface View* and the *Workflow View*. The models of the *Workflow View* depict the message exchange protocol between the cooperating partners with a focus on security requirements such as confidentiality, integrity and non-repudiation [9]. In the models of the *Interface View*, each partner is modeled as a node offering services with a given data type and access control requirements. The models are rendered with the help of SECTET-DSL [17] which consists of two sub languages: SECTET-UML and SECTET-PL.

SECTET-UML is a UML profile for modeling security-critical inter-organizational workflows. In its current state the framework supports the basic security requirements (Confidentiality, Integrity, and Non-repudiation), dynamic access constraints, rights delegation and Qualified Signature [16]. Dynamic access constraints are modeled with SECTET-PL – a predicative language in OCL style [35,25].

3.2   Target Architecture (TA)

The TA represents the runtime environment for the local, executable workflows and their back-end services at partner nodes [18]. The *Global Workflow* is considered as a virtual workflow emerging from the composition of all *Local Workflows*. The TA is based on the data-flow model of XACML [39]. Its components implement a set of XML- and web services technologies and standards. We differentiate between service and security components (cf. Fig. 2).

Service Components.   A workflow engine (3), based on an XML-based workflow Language like BPEL, orchestrates the sequence of local web services (6) as specified in the Local Workflow Model. The engine bundles the services to a composition that may be offered as a service of its own.

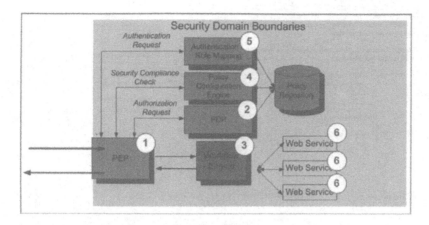

Fig. 2. Target Architecture at Peer Nodes

Security Components. The workflow engine (3) and the web services (6) in the back-end are wrapped by security components (1), (2), (4), and (5). The policy enforcement point (PEP) (1) is the single point of entry into the domain and is responsible for implementing requirements related to message security and non-repudiation with external world. It checks signatures and decrypts incoming requests or responses, and signs outgoing requests or responses and encrypts them as specified in the global workflow model. For details of security components and interactions refer to [18].

3.3   Model Transformation and Code Generation

Model transformation has two purposes (for an in-depth account on MOF-QVT based transformation in the SECTET-framework, please refer to [17]). 1. *Mapping Global to Local Workflows*. Those parts of the Global Workflow Model that correspond to interfaces that local process nodes should implement are translated into stubs of executable process code (BPEL-, WSDL-, and XSD-files). 2. *Generation of Security Artefacts*. The security requirements in the models are translated into executable XACML 3.0 artefacts configuring the policy decision point in the Target Architecture at every peer node. We extend XACML with functions to cope with security specific semantics of the SECTET-Security Policies (e.g., `subject.map()` cf. Sec. 4.2).

4   Extending the SECTET-Domain Architecture

4.1   SECTET-DSL – Sample Healthcare Policy

In this Section, we discuss the SECTET-Domain Architecture extensions and then model a sample healthcare security policy (cf. Sec. 4.1)for the the advanced requirements (Sec. 4.2) and present the DSL's structure (Sec. 4.3).

Healthcare Policy Model. Figure 3 shows an example healthcare security policy. The modeling of such a policy is supported by the framework after including the extensions

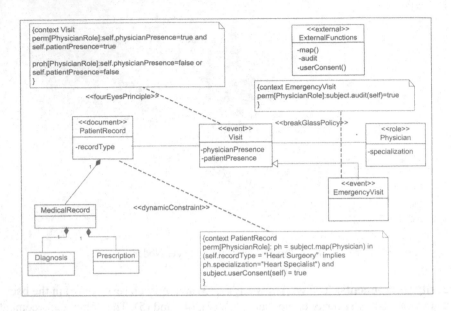

Fig. 3. UML Profile for Sample Healthcare Policy

at the three levels of the Domain Architecture. Subsequently we describe the policy's main security concepts.

Subjects. The entity Physician stereotyped <<role>>, indicates its type as defined in the SECTET- *Role Model*. The model defines roles and hierarchies such as Physician, Nurse, Pharmacist etc. (Nr. 1 in Figure 4)

Objects. The entity PatientRecord stereotyped as <<document>> indicates the element is taken from the SECTET- *Document-Model* (Nr. 2 in Figure 4). The stereotypes <<document>> and <<role>> are SECTET references to the UCON concepts of *subject* and *object* respectively. The relation is defined at the metamodel level (as described in Sec. 4.3).

Setting the Context. The entity Visit in Figure 3 is stereotyped <<event>>. This means that the role Physician can access the resource PatientRecord during an event of Visit. The policy model connects the entity PatientRecord with the entity Physician through the entity Visit of metatype Event as defined in the SECTET- *Event Model* (Nr. 3 in Figure 4).

Specifying Dynamic Constraints. Example dynamic constraints are captured in boxes in Figure 3. They are specified using SECTET-PL, according to the following structure:

> **context** Entity E
>
> **perm**[$role_i$] : $pcondExp_i$
>
> ...
>
> **proh**[$role_j$] : $ncondExp_j$
>
> ...;

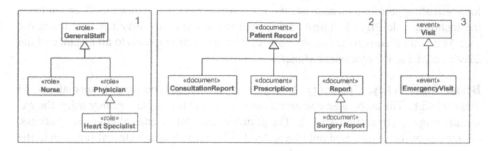

Fig. 4. Sub-models of the SECTET Interface View

The permit rule **perm**$[role_i]$: $pcondExp_i$ describes the condition $pcondExp_i$ under which role $role_i$ is permitted to access entity E, and is evaluated before an access. The prohibit rule **proh**$[role_j]$: $ncondExp_j$ describes the condition $ncondExp_j$ under which role $role_j$ is prohibited to access entity E. The prohibition rules correspond to the UCON concept of access decision continuity. The rules are repeatedly verified during an access session, which means that, if conditions defined within the prohibitions are true, the corresponding access is revoked.

4.2 Advanced Use Cases Modelled in HealthcareDSL

Referring to the sample policy model in Figure 3, this section shows how advanced security policies based on UCON are modelled with SECTET.

4-Eyes-Principle. The 4-Eyes-Principle is formalized through a constraint referring attributes of the entity Visit. The permit rule stipulates the presence of both the physician and the patient. The prohibition makes sure that, in absence of either role, the corresponding access right is revoked – even during an ongoing session though initially granted. The constraints attached to the entity PatientRecord states that user consent is needed for access. This is realized by calling the external function userConsent. We note that a patient can give conditional consent as well, which may incorporate the attributes of the physician and/or usage control requirements.

Dynamic Access Control. The constraint attached to the entity PatientRecord specifies that the subject designation should be of type HeartSpecialist, if the medical record is of type HeartSurgery.

The special construct subject.map maps the caller's identity to a specific role. This function – stereotyped <<external>> – is an example of an extension to the XACML language supported by the TA at runtime. This stereotype indicates a technical instruction and is not to be transformed to an XML schema resulting in an executable policy. It refers to the security infrastructure and instructs it to verify a certain relationship between the caller of the web service and a particular element of the policy model (e.g., map). The *identification variables* (e.g. subject) associated with these external functions distinguish different types of callers, e.g., subject.map(T) allows the connection of the calling actor with her internal representation to the business logic enabling permissions such as *"the actor has access to her own data"*. In our case, the technical role `PhysicianRole` is mapped to the entity `Physician` using the `subject.map` construct. The variable reference ph corresponds to an instance of the `Physician` in the *Document Model*.

Break Glass Policy. The entity `EmergencyVisit` of type `Event` specializes the class `Visit`. The associated constraint formalizes the break glass policy using the external obligation operation `audit`. The policy states that, in case of emergency access, all actions of the requester should be audited. The `audit` is an external function in the form of an obligation and returns a Boolean value.

Rights Delegation. A physician referring a patient to the specialist delegates her rights to access the patient's record. This is modeled with the stereotype `<<delegation OfRights>>`. The patient's `Visit` is the main event in the healthcare system, where the physician accesses the data. `Event` is a meta-concept and `Visit` is an instance of the `Event`. `Visit` is specialized on the basis of the context. For example, if the context is `Emergency`, then the instance is `EmergencyVisit`. The Access to data is logged with the `Log` entity for any Audit/Accountability in the future.

4.3   The Structure of the SECTET-DSL

We extend the DSL by integrating UCON-concepts at the meta-model level. UCON-elements such as subject and object are related to elements from SECTET-models (e.g., Document-, Role-, Access-Model).

Conceptual Framework. We base our conceptual understanding of the problem on the definition of three related *Domains*: the *Problem Domain*, the *Security Domain* and the *Application Domain*. The *Problem Domain* is specifically defined by the architectural structure of the application context. Very often a healthcare application differs from a typical e-tendering, e-commerce or e-government scenario by exhibiting a set of specific architecural patterns. For example, we noticed that most scenarios in e-government were defined in terms of documents flowing from one security-domain to the next without central co-ordination. The original SECTET-framework – designed to mainly support scenarios from e-government – accordingly supported solutions for a *Problem Domain* defined as "security-critical inter-organizational workflows". However, in healthcare, specifically in IHE-based scenarios, the problem revolves more around modeling distributed patient records and related security issues. This requires some adaptation of the original SECTET-Framework.

The *Problem Domain* relates an *Application Domain* – here defined as *Distributed Healthcare Systems* – to a *Security Domain* capturing industry specific concerns about security as *Security Policies* (e.g., emergency access, 4-eyes-principle and patient privacy). *Security Policies* in turn are realized by a specific *Security Model* – which in our case is UCON. *The Security Domain* defines security concerns through abstract *Security Requirements* which are enforced by concrete *Security Policies* (Figure 5). *The Application Domain* introduces the specific application context to which Security Policies refer (Figure 5).

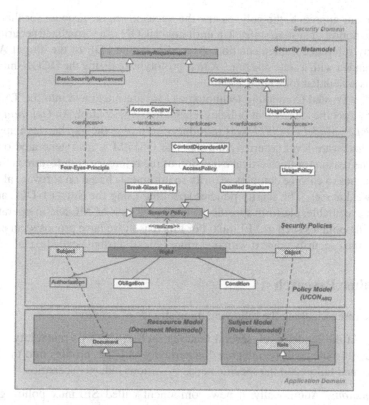

Fig. 5. Security Domain Relating Security Requirements to Policies and Security Models

The Metamodels. The SECTET-Domain Model in Figure 5 uses the MOF framework for the integration of business requirements with access requirements at the meta-level. Taking the pattern of 4-Eyes-Principle as an example, we can see that it realizes a policy for Access Control- in the context of one or more healthcare scenarios – modeled as specialization of an RBAC Policy and includes an EventRef. The latter is associated to a UCON Right and conditionally refers to one or more of the three UCON concepts, Authorization, Obligation, and Condition. In our case, referring back to the sample policy in Figure 3, Authorization, Obligation, and Condition are specified with the help of OCL-style expressions using SECTET-PL. Elements of other metamodels are referenced through proxy classes, thereby linking them semantically. For example, RoleRef references a LocalRole from the Role Metamodel, DocRef references a DocumentRecord from the Document Metamodel, and EventRef references an Event from the Event Metamodel.

4.4 SECTET–Target Architecture Extension

In order to support advanced security policies based on UCON, the SECTET TA is extended in two respects.

Firstly, XACML 3.0 [39] – the standard for the generated configuration files – needs substantial extension to support the concept of access decision continuity as defined in

UCON. In our approach, the policies and the decision engine account for that by supporting the notion of system states. Up until now UCON is a formalized security model lacking any reference implementation. Accordingly, the PDP of the Target Architecture is extended with a state machine. A first prototype realizing the UCON-model with XACML is scheduled for March 2008.

Secondly, Trusted Computing technologies [36] are integrated into the TA in order to enforce a specific category of policies related to usage control. An *Operating System Specific Policy Model (OSSPM)* was introduced to bridge the gap between application level and hardware level security controls. The OSSPM is also generated out of the models. The reason for this vertical extension of the reference architecture is that existing approaches to enforce complex security requirements based on software alone have inherent weaknesses. The seurity policies specified using the SECTET-DSL are transformed to executable, platform specific policies such as XACML and to operating systems specific policies such as SELinux. For this reason we have proposed an extension to the SELinux security context with one more type of attribute called profile [24].

5   Further Research

We pursue research along the following three strands of activity:

Modeling. At the model level, several features such as UCON's mutability of subject and object attributes will be integrated generically as UML profiles into the SECTET framework and tailored to the specific needs of various industry scenarios.

Transformations. Additionally, a new component called SELinux policy generator added to SECTET-Framework will be implemented with OpenArchitectureWare's XPAND language [29].

Target Architecture. The Architecture is extended along the two dimensions: horizontally by additional architectural components enforcing security and vertically by leveraging security primitives of the operating system (e.g., SELinux) and hardware layer (e.g., Trusted Computing).

References

1. Integrating the Healthcare Enterprise (2007), http://www.ihe.net/
2. Alam, M., Hafner, M., Breu, R.: Modeling Authorization in an SOA based Application Scenario. In: IASTED Conference on Software Engineering, pp. 79–84 (2006)
3. Anderson, R.: Security Engineering: A Guide to Building Dependable Distributed Systems. John Wiley & Sons, Inc., New York (2001)
4. Blobel, B.: Trustworthiness in Distr. Electr. Healthcare Records-Basis for Shared Care. In: ACSAC 2001: Proc. of the 17th Annual Comp. Sec. App. Conf., Washington, DC, USA, p. 433. IEEE Comp. Soc., Los Alamitos (2001)
5. Breu, R., Breu, M., Hafner, M., Nowak, A.: Web Service Engineering - Advancing a New Software Engineering Discipline. In: Lowe, D.G., Gaedke, M. (eds.) ICWE 2005. LNCS, vol. 3579, pp. 8–18. Springer, Heidelberg (2005)
6. Chanabhai, P., Holt, A.: Consumers are Ready to Accept the Trans. to Online and Electr. Rec. if They Can be Assured of the Sec. Measures. Medscape Gen. Medicine 9(1) (2007)

7. Chinaei, A.H., Tompa, F.: User-managed access control for health care systems. In: Secure Data Management, pp. 63–72 (2005)
8. Gomi, H., et al.: A Delegation Framew. for Fed. Identity Management. In: DIM 2005: Proc. of the 2005 Workshop on Dig. Identity Man, ACM Press, New York (2005)
9. Hafner, M., et al.: Sectet: An Extensible Framework for the Realization of Secure Inter-Organizational Workflows. Journal of Internet Research 16(5) (2006)
10. Breu, R., et al.: Model Driven Security for Inter-organizational Workflows in e-Government. In: Böhlen, M.H., Gamper, J., Polasek, W., Wimmer, M.A. (eds.) TCGOV 2005. LNCS (LNAI), vol. 3416, pp. 122–133. Springer, Heidelberg (2005)
11. Vogl, R., et al.: Architecture for a distributed national electronic health record in Austria. In: Proc. EuroPACS 2006: The 24th International EuroPACS Conference, pp. 67–77 (2006)
12. Schabetsberger, T., et al.: From a Paper-based Transmission of Discharge Summaries to Electronic Communication in Health Care Regions. Int. Journal of Medical Informatics 75, 3-4, 209–215 (2006)
13. Zhang, X., et al.: Formal model and policy specification of usage control. ACM Trans. Inf. Syst. Secur. 8(4), 351–387 (2005)
14. Gritzalis, S.: Enhancing Privacy and Data Protection in Electronic Medical Environments. Journal of Medical Systems 28(6), 535–547 (2004)
15. Gunter, T., Terry, N.: The Emergence of Nat. Electr. Health Record Arch. in the U.S. and Australia: Models, Costs, and Questions. Journal of Med. Internet Research 7(1):3 (2005)
16. Hafner, M., Agreiter, B., Breu, R., Nowak, A.: Sectet an extensible framework for the realization of secure inter-organizational workflows. Journal of Internet Research 16(5) (2006)
17. Hafner, M., Alam, M., Breu, R.: Towards a MOF/QVT-Based Domain Architecture for Model Driven Security. In: Nierstrasz, O., Whittle, J., Harel, D., Reggio, G. (eds.) MoDELS 2006. LNCS, vol. 4199, pp. 275–290. Springer, Heidelberg (2006)
18. Hafner, M., Breu, R., Breu, M.: A security architecture for inter-organizational workflows: Putting security standards for web services together. ICEIS (3), 128–135 (2005)
19. Hafner, M., Breu, M., Breu, R., Nowak, A.: Modelling Inter-organizational Workflow Security in a Peer-to-Peer Environment. In: ICWS 2005: Proceedings of the IEEE International Conference on Web Services (ICWS 2005), Washington, DC, USA, pp. 533–540. IEEE Computer Society, Los Alamitos (2005)
20. Hu, J., Weaver, A.: Dynamic, context-aware access control for distributed healthcare applications (August 2004), http://www.cs.virginia.edu/papers/
21. Hu, V., Ferraiolo, D., Kuhn, D.: Assessment of access control systems. Technical Report NISTIR 7316, National Inst. of Standards and Technology, US Department of Commerce (September 2006)
22. Kohn, L., Corrigan, J., Donaldson, M.: To Err is Human: Building a Safer Health System. National Academy Press, Washington DC (2000)
23. Li, M., Poovendran, R.: Enabling Distributed Addition of Secure Access to Patient's Records in A Tele-Referring Group. In: IEEE-EMBS 2005: Proceedings of the 27th IEEE EMBS Annual International Conference, pp. 308–317. IEEE, Los Alamitos (2005)
24. Alam, M., Hafner, M., Seifert, J.P., Zhang, X.: Extending SELinux Policy Model and Enforcement Architecture for Trusted Platforms Paradigms. In: Annual SELinux Symposium (2007), http://selinux-symposium.org/2007/agenda.php
25. Alam, M., Breu, R., Hafner, M.: Modeling Permissions in a (U/X)ML World. In: IEEE ARES (2006), ISBN: 0-7695-2567-9
26. United States Department of Health & Human Services. Health insurance portability and accountability act of 1996, http://aspe.hhs.gov/admnsimp/pl104191.htm
27. Office of the Privacy Commissioner of Canada. Personal information protection and electronic documents act (pipeda), http://laws.justice.gc.ca/en/P-8.6/

28. Committee on Quality of Health Care in America. Inst. of Medicine. In: Crossing the Quality Chasm: A New Health System for the 21st Century, Nat. Acad. Press, Washington DC (2001)
29. OpenArchitectureWare XPAND Language available at,
    http://www.eclipse.org/gmt/oaw/doc/r20_xPandReference.pdf
30. Park, J., Sandhu, R.: The UCON ABC Usage Control Model. ACM Transactions on Information and Systems Security 7, 128–174 (2004)
31. Europ. Parliament. Directive 95-46-ec of the europ. parl. and of the counc. of 24 october 1995 on the p protection of individuals with regard to the processing of personal data and on the free movement of such data (1995),
    http://www.cdt.org/privacy/eudirective/EU_Directive_.html
32. Role Based Access Control (RBAC) avialable at, csrc.nist.gov/rbac/
33. Schabetsberger, T.: Reference Implementation of a Shared Electr. Health Record Using Med. Data Grids with an RBAC Based Security Model. In: Proc. of the 2nd AGRID Symp. in conj. with 6th Austrian-Hungarian Workshop on Distributed and Parallel Syst. (2007)
34. Joint NEMA/COCIR/JIRA Sec. and Priv. Committee. Break-Glass – An Approach to Granting Emergency Access to Healthcare Systems,
    http://www.nema.org/prod/med/security/
35. SECTETPL : A Predicative Language for the Specification of Access Rights available at,
    http://qe-informatik.uibk.ac.at/~muhammad/
    TechnicalReportSECTETPL.pdf
36. Pearson, S.: Trusted Computing Platforms: TCPA Technology in Context. Prentice Hall PTR, Upper Saddle River (2002)
37. Straub, T.: Usability Challenges of PKI (2005)
38. Vogt, G.: Multiple Authorization – A Model and Arch. for Increased, Practical Security. In: Proc. of the IFIP/IEEE 8th Int. Symp. on Integrated Network Management (IM 2003), Colorado Springs, USA, March 2003, pp. 109–112. IFIP/IEEE, Kluwer Academic Publishers (2003)
39. Xacml v3.0 administration policy working draft 05 (December 2005), http://www.oasis-open.org/committees/documents.php?wg_abbrev=xacml
40. Yao, W.: Trust Management for Widely Distributed Systems. PhD thesis, University of Cambridge (2003)

4th International Workshop on Model Driven Engineering, Verification, and Validation: Integrating Verification and Validation in MDE

Benoit Baudry[1], Alain Faivre[2], Sudipto Ghosh[3], and Alexander Pretschner[4]

[1] IRISA/ INRIA, France
bbaudry@irisa.fr
[2] CEA-List, France
Alain.FAIVRE@cea.fr
[3] Colorado State University, USA
ghosh@cs.colostate.edu
[4] ETH Zurich, Switzerland
pretscha@inf.ethz.ch

1 Introduction

Model Driven Engineering (MDE) approaches extensively use models and automatic model transformations to handle complex software development. A plethora of software artifacts, tools, environments and modeling languages need to be developed to make MDE a reality. Consequently, there is a crucial need for effective V&V techniques in the context of MDE. Moreover, the novelty of MDE gives rise to questions concerning its impact on traditional V&V techniques, and how they can leverage this new paradigm.

The aim of the workshop on model-driven engineering, verification and validation was to offer a forum for researchers and practitioners who are developing new approaches to V&V in the context of MDE. Several interesting questions crosscut V&V and MDE, such as:

- Is the model resulting from a transformation correct with respect to the expected safety, security, time, and structural constraints?
- Is the result of a transformation really what the user intended?
- Does the implementation, which is generated after several model transformations, conform to the initial requirements?
- What models can be used for validation or verification?

This workshop solicited papers related to the following topics:

- Application of MDE to validation and verification.
- V&V techniques for MDE activities, such as refinement, abstraction, structuring, model transformations, and code generation.
- V&V at the model level: techniques for validating models or generating test cases from models. These include reviews, checking adherence with modeling guidelines, simulation, model-checking, and model-based testing.

H. Giese (Ed.): MoDELS 2007 Workshops, LNCS 5002, pp. 145–150, 2008.
© Springer-Verlag Berlin Heidelberg 2008

- Impact analysis of model changes on validation: Changes in a model can impact the results of previous validation activities.
- Automation and tool support for V&V in MDE.
- Case studies and experience reports.

The workshop had three parts, a keynote address, presentation of position papers, and a discussion among the workshop attendees. In this report, Section 2 presents summaries of the keynote address and the eight papers selected for presentations. Section 3 presents a summary of the discussion. Section 4 concludes the report.

2 Presentations

2.1 Keynote Address — Betty H. C. Cheng

The keynote address was on "Modeling and Formally Analyzing Dynamically Adaptive Software" and focussed on analysis techniques for safe adaptations. Modeling adaptive systems requires understanding the requirements and validating requirements in a real setting. This can be challenging because of unanticipated or difficult to obtain environmental conditions that trigger the adaptations. Adaptive systems are typically developed in an iterative fashion. There can be conflicting adaptations, especially when there are multiple adaptations to be performed. Trade-off analysis needs to be performed to select from multiple and often conflicting adaptations. More research needs to be done on adaptation patterns that can be reused in multiple adaptive systems. The use of aspect-oriented techniques is proposed to handle concurrent adaptations. Validation and testing of adaptive systems becomes challenging because a number of new issues need to be addressed, such as (1) simulating environmental and system requirements for adaptation, and (2) the differences and variety in mechanisms used to perform adaptation.

2.2 Paper Summaries

The program committee selected eight papers out of 23 submissions. The papers were grouped into two categories:

- Model-based testing
- Validation in MDE

Model-based testing

[1] Model-Based Testing of the ERTMS System with SysML and MARTE — Souha Kamoun and Pierre Boulet: Powerful test specification methodologies are needed to ensure efficient functional verification of safety critical systems such as the European Railway Traffic Management System (ERTMS). ERTMS is a complex railway signaling system featuring hundreds of functional requirements. The paper presents a model-based test generation technique for ERTMS. The

technique uses Systems Modeling Language (SysML) as the modeling language, which is extended with annotations from the UML profile, Modeling and Analysis of RealTime and Embedded systems (MARTE) for efficient modeling and the verification of timeliness and probabilistic behavior of ERTMS.

The paper proposes a technique to capture textual requirements by a formal model and the automatic generation of test scenarios. The requirements diagram captures the textual specifications and the activity diagram serves as the test model. Test scenarios are specified by sequence diagrams which result from the transformation of activity diagrams. The automation of the test generation process provides several benefits to the testers in terms of the time saved and lowered costs.

[2] *Novel Approach to Model-Based Acceptance Testing — Ruth Breu, Joanna Chimiak-Opoka, and Chris Lenz:* This paper presents an approach to creating model-based acceptance tests. The authors claim that a framework for executable acceptance tests like Fit/Fitnesse provides valuable concepts for specifying tests at the business level but does not exploit the potential given by the information contained in the requirements specification. The paper presents basic concepts, meta-models and a running example of an executable test framework which specifies tests in the language of the requirements specification and thus paves the way for a formal relationship between acceptance tests and the requirements specification. The approach separates the dynamic and static aspects of the tests in a rigorous manner.

[3] *Automatic Test Generation from Coupled UML Models using Input Partitions — Stephan Weißleder and Bernd-Holger Schlingloff:* Partitions of input ranges for boundary testing are automatically derived from coupled models consisting of UML state machines, class diagrams, and OCL expressions. The paper presents a test generation algorithm and its implementation, and a case study that compares the implementation to Rhapsody's ATG.

[4] *Automatic Generation of Test-Cases Using Model Checking for SL/SF Models — Ambar A. Gadkari, Swarup Mohalik, K.C. Shashidhar, Anand Yeolekar, J. Suresh, and S. Ramesh:* This paper describes the authors' experience in test generation using model checking for the Simulink/Stateflow (SL/SF) models of two automotive controller examples. Model checking based test generation is non-trivial since the SL/SF models need to be first translated into a formal language to serve as an input for the model checker tool. Moreover, to handle the size and complexities of industrial designs, the translation must make use of various abstractions, yet preserve the semantics of the original model relevant for test generation. The paper presents an outline of the scheme used for translating the SL/SF models into a formal language called SAL. Preliminary results indicate that model checking based test generation in conjunction with suitable model abstractions can yield better results in terms of coverage and efficiency of test cases as compared to the conventional approaches based on simulation and random data generation.

Validation in MDE

[5] Analysis of Model Transformations via Alloy — Kyriakos Anastasakis, Behzad Bordbar, and Jochen M. Küster: A model transformation automates the translation of models between a source and a target language. To analyze model transformations, the authors consider a model transformation specification to be a special kind of model allowing it to be subjected to existing model analysis techniques. The paper presents a systematic method of representing declarative model transformations in a formalism called Alloy. The Alloy analyzer is used to conduct a fully automated analysis of a model transformation specification represented in Alloy. The approach is illustrated with the help of an example model transformation occurring in business process modeling.

[6] Using MDE for Generic Comparison of Views — Bas Graaf and Arie van Deursen: The paper investigates the application of technologies for model driven engineering to check the conformance of two software models. This involves model-based comparison and visualization of the results. To generalize the approach, reflection, metamodel generalization, and higher-order transformations are used. The approach is applied to investigate the extent to which the implementation of an academic example system does not violate the constraints defined by its architectural specification.

[7] Data Verification using Model-Driven Architecture — M. Price, S. Demurjian, H. Sen, M. Saleem, and S. Berhe: Model Driven Architecture (MDA) promotes a process that separates platform-independent abstractions from software-specific implementations, allowing an abstraction to be reused for multiple implementations. As part of designing a submarine, data requirements of various applications need to be reconciled in an integrated design and manufacturing process. As a result, there is a critical need to verify data artifacts that share a common abstraction basis while differing in forms (alternate measurement systems), document structures (documents conforming to different schemas), and orders (XML schemas with similar content and alternate arrangements). A data verification framework is proposed to semi-automate the comparison of data from specific implementations that (1) employs UML as an independent abstraction from which an Excel XML template is generated as a common format, (2) utilizes XSLT/XQuery to translate application-specific data into Excel XML instances to create spreadsheets from this common abstraction, and (3) reconciles the resulting instances by executing a differencing script on the generated Excel XML instances to compare/contrast the data from specific implementations as viewed from the UML abstraction.

[8] Putting Performance Engineering into Model-Driven Engineering: Model-Driven Performance Engineering — Mathias Fritzsche and Jendrik Johannes: Late identification of performance problems can lead to significant additional development costs. Therefore, it is necessary to address performance in several development phases by performing a performance engineering process. The

paper presents a process that combines MDE and performance engineering called Model-Driven Performance Engineering (MDPE). The paper also presents the authors' preliminary experiences with MDPE.

3   Discussion

The workshop participants discussed several V&V challenges. Currently many techniques are being proposed for MDE and they are all generally in their infancy. Standardizing MDE techniques may make it easier to address V&V challenges in MDE.

There is a need for creating modeling languages with formal semantics because they would lend themselves to different types of analyses. However, there was also a view that if models become too formal, developers will tend not to use them. Restrictive languages like Domain Specific Modeling Languages (DSMLs) may make it easier to use formal techniques.

From the paper presentations, it was clear that more and more research is focussed on using software requirements for test case generation. Three out of four papers on model-based testing (1, 2 and 4) highlighted that one major remaining challenge for model-based test generation is how to take requirements into account. Although many test generation approaches focus on design models, it is also important to consider higher level models, such as requirements models, for automatic test generation. First, this allows validating the conformance between the system under test and the initial requirements. Second, this allows updating the test cases when requirements change during design, development, or maintenance.

Testing model transformations is a challenging area. The first challenge that was discussed was how to specify a transformation. Currently it is not clear how a model transformation can or should be specified. The authors of paper 5 proposed a solution based on a declarative version of the transformation in Alloy, which allows them to perform a number of verification tasks on the specification. However, in most cases, the declarative transformation itself is executable and is used as the transformation. Thus, in those cases, there is no abstraction that can be used as a specification for verification or test generation.

The second challenge that was discussed was the evolution of transformations. Model transformations are developed with the intent to be reused in several projects. However, in most cases they are reused with slight modifications. These changes can correspond to changes in the metamodels and to changes in the targeted platform. Thus, the transformation remains the same for the most part except a few details that must be validated before the transformation can be performed. Thus, regression testing and efficient test selection becomes an important challenge for model transformation testing. It is not clear today if existing regression test selection techniques can be used or adapted for testing model transformations.

4 Conclusions

In summary, this workshop, the fourth in a successful series, has highlighted both the prominent role and future challenges of V&V in model-driven engineering. On the problem side, not too surprisingly, model transformations, one corner-stone of model-driven engineering, require special attention in terms of V&V approaches. On the solution side, as witnessed by as many as one half of the accepted contributions, model-based testing appears as a particularly promising technology that offers many fascinating avenues of research. The breadth of sub-missions indicates that the field of V&V in model-driven engineering is a highly active field for researchers and practitioners.

We would like to thank all the program committee members, reviewers, and participants for a successful workshop. We look forward to the next workshop, to take place in March 2008.

Deriving Input Partitions from UML Models for Automatic Test Generation

Stephan Weißleder and Bernd-Holger Schlingloff

Humboldt-Universität zu Berlin, 12489, Germany
{weissled,hs}@informatik.hu-berlin.de

Abstract. In this paper, we deal with model-based automatic test generation. We show how to use UML state machines, UML class diagrams, and OCL expressions to automatically derive partitions of input parameter value ranges for boundary testing. We present a test generation algorithm and describe an implementation of this algorithm. Finally, we discuss our approach and compare it to commercial tools.

1 Introduction

Modeling languages like the Unified Modeling language (UML) [7] are widely used for system development. They are supported by many tools, some of which also provide model-based automatic generation of test suites [10,22,25]. This is advantageous compared to conventional test suite generation because the automation increases the efficiency of the test generation process.

We argue that the current approaches neglect the generation of input partitions. Therefore, we present an approach that is focused on the generation of input partitions from UML state machines and UML class diagrams. It derives test input value partitions from expressions of both diagrams, e.g. transition guards or pre-/postconditions of the Object Constraint language (OCL) [6]. The corresponding test suite is focused on detecting errors that result from differences between constraints in the model and constraints in the system under test (SUT).

The quality of test suites created with partition testing and boundary testing depends on satisfied coverage criteria and on the adequate selection of partition boundaries. Usually, the latter is done manually. Therefore, the boundary selection is error-prone and there is a high probability that the test effectiveness is low. In contrast to manual selection of input value boundaries, we derive them automatically from OCL expressions of system models. We statically analyze the interdependence of OCL expressions within the system model and transform the model into a transition tree and investigate the tree's paths. We demonstrate our approach by the example of a sorting-machine. Compared to other approaches, the contribution of this paper is a method to generate test cases by evaluating OCL expressions in postconditions, which are not restricted to equations.

The paper is organized as follows. Sections 2 and 3 contain preliminaries for this paper and the used example system models. Section 4 contains the intermediate transition tree. The test generation approach is described in Section 5. Sections 6 to 8 contain evaluation, related work, and summary.

H. Giese (Ed.): MoDELS 2007 Workshops, LNCS 5002, pp. 151–163, 2008.

2   Preliminaries

In this section, we introduce the running example of a sorting machine and describe the use of partition testing and boundary testing.

2.1   Example: The Sorting-Machine

Here, we briefly introduce our reoccuring example of a sorting-machine. The context of this machine is a post office where incoming items are wrapped up. Due to this packing, the original width of the object is doubled by foam plus two extra size units for each side of a plastic box ($m\_width = (object.width + 2) * 2$). The height is handled likewise. If wrapped-up items violate the necessary sizes for the standard shipping container, extra containers are needed. Our sorting-machine's task is to sort incoming items depending on the size after their wrapping so that they fit into given transport containers.

Fig. 1 shows the state machine and class diagram of such a sorting-machine. The sorting is fragmented into the postcondition of *recognize()* and in the guard conditions of the outgoing transitions of state *object recognized*.

2.2   Partition Testing and Boundary Testing

Partition testing and boundary testing are well-known testing techniques and are often used together: partitioning test input parameters into value domains is a prerequisite of focussing tests on the corresponding domain boundaries. As examples for partition testing we consider control systems for nuclear reactors, Geo-information systems, or sorting machines. In such cases, the exact values of boundaries (sticks in reactors, global position of elements, measures of objects) are important. The corresponding test cases have to contain values that check even small violations of the derived test input parameter boundary values. We deal with the automatic test generation for such kind of applications.

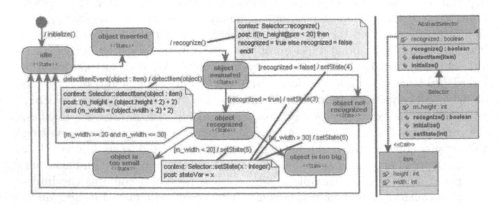

Fig. 1. State machine and class diagram for a sorting-machine

3   The UML Models: Class Diagram and State Machine

Our test generation approach uses UML class diagrams, UML state machines, and OCL to generate test code. A formalization of UML and OCL has been given in [6,7]. Subsequently, we recall the definitions that are most important for our purpose. For an example, consider the sorting-machine given in Fig. 1.

Class Diagram. A class diagram $cd = (CLS, REL)$ consists of classes CLS and relations REL between classes. The right part of Fig. 1 shows boxes depicting classes and arrows depicting relations between them. A class $c \in CLS$ contains a set of attributes AT and a set of operations OP: $c = (AT, OP)$. Each operation $op \in OP$ has an optional precondition $op.pre$ and an optional postcondition $op.post$. The condition $op.pre$ must be met before the op's execution, $op.post$ defines the condition that is met after op's execution.

State Machine. A state machine sm contains a set of regions REG, which in turn contain a set of vertices $VERT$ and a set of transitions TRS: $sm = (REG)$, $REG = (VERT, TRS)$. On the left side of Fig. 1, arrows denote transitions, which connect vertices. Each vertex $v \in VERT$ may possess a name $v.sn$, a set of incoming transitions $v.INC$, a set of outgoing transitions $v.OUT$, and an invariant $v.inv$. Each transition $t \in TRS$ has a source vertex $t.sv \in VERT$, a target vertex $t.tv \in VERT$, an event $t.ev$, a guard $t.guard$, and an effect $t.ef$. We interpret events ev solely as call events, since in most object-oriented languages events are realized by operation calls. A *guard* is a Boolean expression without side-effects. The effect ef is of type *Behavior* - in our approach, an operation call of the associated class (see Fig. 1). The example in Fig. 1 does not comprise parallelism and, therefore, contains just one region.

Conditions. The conditions $COND$ are Boolean OCL expressions contained in state machines or class diagrams. They consist of basic predicates like arithmetic conditions, which are connected by Boolean operators. The elements of the predicates are used to navigate along association relations between classes. In Fig. 1, the folded boxes contain OCL expressions. The attached lines show their assignment to effects of transitions. Furthermore, OCL provides expressions on operation calls and collections. To check the test result, OCL expressions are evaluated at run time with respect to the created objects and attributes.

Coupled Models. As shown in Fig. 1, we use models consisting of a pair of state machine and class diagram. We call such pairs *coupled models*. They are connected by references from transitions to operation calls. The constraints of both models are evaluated together. Navigation along inheritance relations helps reusing state machines. According to Liskov's substitution principle [15], properties of a class also hold for its subclasses. State machines are behavioral properties of a class. Thus, they can be reused in the subclass of a class (this time referencing the operations and the attached OCL expressions of the subclass).

4   Test Case Tree

In this section, we define a finite tree for test case generation. It contains all necessary information to derive test sequences and test input boundary values. It simplifies the evaluation because all constraints are ordered according to control flow information. This approach also allows to use another source model if an appropriate model transformation is defined.

A **Test Case Tree** tct consists of nodes NOD and directed arcs ARC: $tct = (NOD, ARC)$. Some nodes reference a state in the state machine. They are called anchor nodes $ANOD$. Furthermore, each $n \in tct.NOD$ references incoming arcs $n.IN$, outgoing arcs $n.OUT$, and contains parameter ranges $n.RANGE$: $n = (IN, OUT, RANGE)$. $n.RANGE$ maps each input event parameter used on the path from the root to n to a range of values. Each combination of representatives of these value ranges applied to the current input event sequence parameters results in reaching n. We focus on the boundary values. The tree's root is a node $sroot \in tct.ANOD$ with $sroot.IN = \emptyset$. For all other states $as \in NOD$ it holds that $|as.IN| = 1$. All leaves l are elements of $ANOD$ and satisfy $l.OUT = \emptyset$. The arcs of the tree $arc \in tct.ARC$ possess a precondition $arc.pre \in COND$ (default: $true$), a postcondition $arc.post \in COND$ (default: $true$), and an event $arc.ev$ parameterized with instances of primitive or abstract data types.

An example for the general structure of a test case tree is shown in Fig. 2. The tree contains seven nodes connected by arcs. Each arc contains a transition event, a transition guard, an operation's precondition, or its postcondition. Each path leads from $sroot$ to a leaf. All nodes on a path are ordered. So, $m \in tct.ARC$ is a **preceding arc** of arc $n \in tct.ARC$ iff n can be reached from m and $n \neq m$.

Each **Test Case** corresponds to a path from $sroot$ to a leaf $l \in ANOD$. The input for a test case is a parameterized operation call sequence corresponding to the event sequence of the selected path and one representative of each input parameter range $l.RANGE$. Expected and actual system behavior are compared by evaluating the conditions along the path from $sroot$ to l.

Each test case has to satisfy all expressions along its corresponding path. Each arc of the tree contains just one expression. This allows to form the disjunctive normal form (DNF) of the contained expressions and split up the containing arc into several arcs corresponding to the resulting conjunctions. Since this replaces all complex Boolean expressions with conjunctions, the evaluation of all expressions of one path is simplified. We describe the generation algorithm of $l.RANGE$ in *Step 2* of section 5.2.

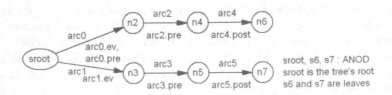

Fig. 2. General structure of a test case tree

5 Test Generation

This section describes the test generation algorithm. First, a coupled model is transformed into a test case tree. Then, test input partitions are derived by categorizing and transforming OCL expressions of the tree. Afterwards, the algorithm generates concrete test input values from these partitions.

5.1 Classification of Variables in OCL Expressions

In this section, we present a classification of OCL expressions, which is partially similar to the one used in the Leirios methodology [14]. Predicates in LTG/UML are either *active* or *passive*: Only active predicates can alter the value of attributes, the passive ones can only read. Leirios claims that their tool LTG/UML [24] can evaluate OCL expressions like pre-/postconditions or transition guards. They use an operational interpretation of equations in OCL postconditions. In contrast, our approach is not restricted to equations but can also evaluate inequations. In future work, we will aim at evaluating more complex operations on collections in OCL postconditions. Additionally, Leirios defines new interpretations for OCL constraints. For instance, in active contexts of a postcondition the mere equation $X = Y$ is interpreted as an assignment of the value of Y to X, which can lead to confusions. The OCL specification [6] does not provide such an interpretation. A corresponding assignment would be $X = Y@pre$. In our approach, we stick to the OCL specification without additional interpretations. To recognize the variables that can change and those that can not, we provide a classification of the variables in OCL expressions.

Since we focus on the values of input variables, our classification differs from the one of Leirios: our atomic classification units are variables *var*. They are part of an atomic predicate, which is in turn the *context predicate* of *var*. Each predicate consists of variables, relations between them, and operations on them. We classify the system model's variables (attributes, input parameters, or constants) and introduce *dependent* and *independent* variables. As in LTG/UML, we assume that variables not stated in postconditions are unchanged.

Subsequently, we define kinds of variables and their mutual relations.

Definition 1 (Independent and Dependent Variables). *An* independent variable *is either an event input parameter or a constant class attribute. Its value is constant. A* dependent variable *is a non-constant class attribute.*

We state that a variable *var* is active or passive depending on *var*'s context predicate. If the context predicate of *var* is a postcondition and no @*pre* is attached to *var* then the value of *var* can be changed - it is active. In all other cases, the value of *var* can not be changed - *var* is passive. Fig. 3 shows the corresponding classification.

Using Definition 1, we are able to describe the dependency between the OCL expressions along a given path. If an arc $a \in tct.ARC$ contains a condition consisting amongst others of a variable *var*, then a is said to contain *var*.

Expression Kind	Dependent Variable	Independent Variable
Postcondition (without @pre)	active	passive
Postcondition (with @pre)	passive	passive
Any other kind	passive	passive

Fig. 3. Active and passive variables

Definition 2 (Next Preceding Arc). *Assume, an arc* a1 ∈ *tct.ARC contains a dependent passive variable* var*. Then, the* next preceding arc a2 ∈ *tct.ARC of* a1 *w.r.t.* var *is* a1*'s preceding arc that is closest to* a1 *and contains* var *as an active variable. The value of the active variable* var *at the next preceding arc corresponds to the value of* var *at* a1*.*

Definition 3 (Defined Variables). *Independent variables are defined. Active variables are defined if all remaining variables contained in its context predicate are defined. Each dependent passive variable* depvar *contained in a condition* cond ∈ *COND used in an arc* a2 ∈ *tct.ARC is defined iff the next preceding arc* a1 ∈ *tct.ARC of* a2 *w.r.t.* depvar *exists and the corresponding active variable is defined.*

A condition cond *used in an arc* a2 *is defined iff each variable in* cond *is defined. The set consisting of* cond *and all conditions of all next preceding arcs w.r.t. each dependent variable along the path from the root to* a2 *is the* defined condition set *of* cond*.*

These definitions exclude the existence of two active variables in one atomic condition. Obviously, variables can be defined in atomic conditions connected by conjunctions, respectively. Consequently, the presented definitions are applicable to conjunctions. All conditions in DNF are only connected by conjunctions. Hence, expressing OCL conditions in DNF is necessary for their evaluation.

Theorem 1 (Reducible Variables). *In a defined condition set of a condition, each included dependent variable can be reduced to independent variables.*

Proof. A variable *var* is defined iff *var*'s context predicate of the next preceding arc *nparc* w.r.t. *var* contains only passive defined variables besides the corresponding active variable *var*. These variables are dependent or independent. Since all variables are defined (Definition 3), such defined variables *initvar* can only be dependent as long as there is a next preceding arc w.r.t. *initvar*. Otherwise, *initvar*'s context predicate in *nparc* contains only independent variables. Each outgoing arc *oarc* ∈ *sroot.OUT* has no next preceding arc, because *sroot.IN* = ∅. Consequently, *oarc* contains no dependent passive initialized variables. Since all paths are of finite length, all dependent variables of an defined condition set depend directly or indirectly on independent variables.   □

For instance, in a postcondition $X > X@pre + Z@pre$, the values of X and $X@pre$ are different if $Z@pre \geq 0$. Roughly speaking, we consider X and $X@pre$ as different variables with different values. X is initialized iff $X@pre$ and $Z@pre$ are also initialized, which in turn depends on their next preceding arcs. In the following, we assume that all variables are initialized.

5.2   Creating the Test Case Tree

The presented algorithm is similar to existing transformation approaches presented in [2]. Within each step of the transformation, the algorithm evaluates the OCL expressions of the test case tree *tct*. We split up the transformation in two steps: the creation of the test case tree *tct* in *Step 1* and the creation of input value partitions in *Step 2*.

Step 1. The algorithm starts at the root *sroot* of *tct* and at the state *S1* after the initial pseudostate of the state machine (see Fig. 4). For each $t \in S1.OUT$, we insert a node *n1* into *tct.NOD* and an arc *arc1* into *tct.ARC*, so that $arc1 \in sroot.OUT$ and $arc1 \in n1.IN$. The triggering event of *t* and *t*'s guard are attached to *arc1*: $arc1.ev = t.ev$; $arc1.pre = t.guard$. Subsequently, we insert the new node *n2* and the state *s* into *tct.ST* and add the arcs *arc2* and *arc3* into *tct.ARC*, so that $arc2 \in n1.OUT$, $arc2 \in n2.IN$, $arc3 \in n2.OUT$, and $arc3 \in s.IN$. The conditions of *t*'s effect *t.ef* are assigned to *arc2* and *arc3*: $arc2.pre = t.ef.pre$ and $arc3.post = t.ef.post$. We copy $sroot.RANGE$ to $n1.RANGE, n2.RANGE$, and $s.RANGE$ and let *s* refer to *t*'s target vertex *t.tv*.

Subsequently, we transform the added expressions into DNF and split up the test case tree corresponding to the resulting conjunctions (see Fig. 5). This is reasonable because a path selection is similar to a disjunction. Dealing just with conjunctions simplifies the evaluation process, because we do not have to consider dependencies between expressions like in conditioned constraints. For instance, in *if (A) then B else C endif* we have to evaluate the value of *A* before knowing whether to consider *B* or *C*. Fig. 4 shows the creation process for one transition. It terminates if the transformed transitions form a circle. Although this process seems to be similar to simple unfolding, the test case tree makes the test generation algorithm in Step 2 independent of UML. It could be reused for other formalisms.

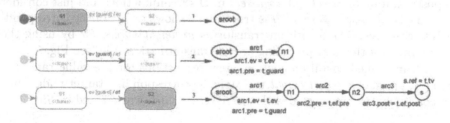

Fig. 4. Creation of the test case tree for one transition of the coupled model

Fig. 5. Exemplary transforming an expression in DNF and adapting the test case tree

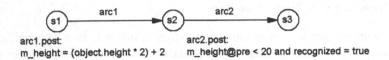

Fig. 6. Part of the test case tree for the sorting machine

Step	Conditions as transformation rules	Evaluated condition
1		m_height@pre < 20
2	m_height = (object.height * 2) + 2	
3		(object.height * 2) + 2 < 20
4		object.height < 9

Fig. 7. Stepwise transformation of the evaluated condition

Step 2. In this step, we evaluate the expressions of each $arc \in tct.ARC$ that was just inserted into the test case tree. Starting from arc's condition $cond$, we compute the initialized condition set of $cond$. We use this condition set to transform the condition $cond$ until it just contains independent variables. The postconditions of $cond$'s initialized condition set are used as the corresponding transformation rules.

The test generation process identifies the active variables in these postconditions. The values of active variables depend on the values of passive ones. Consequently, the conditions on dependent variables can be expressed as conditions on independent variables (see Fig. 3). This results in partitions of the value ranges of input parameters.

In the example in Fig. 1, we consider a short path from *idle* via *object inserted* to *object evaluated*. We insert the postcondition of *Selector::recognize()* and evaluate it using the postcondition of *Selector::detectItem()*. We split up the postcondition of *Selector::recognize()* in DNF conjunctions and just consider the case that $m\_height@pre < 20$ is true. Fig. 6 shows a part of the corresponding test case tree. The algorithm transforms $m\_height@pre < 20$ by using the postcondition of the next preceding arc as transformation rule (see Fig. 7).

The transformed condition contains new restrictions for the value ranges of the input parameter *object.height* to reach the corresponding target node. Such new conditions are intersected with $n.RANGE$, which was created in *Step 1*.

Creating the Test Cases. To create test cases from the test case tree tct, we iterate over all leaf nodes $l \in tct.ANOD$. For each leaf l, we create a test input sequence corresponding to a path from tct's root to l and parameterize each event with representatives of the value range $l.RANGE$. We use the boundary testing method [19] to select these representatives: e.g., boundary values, next inner values, and random values from within the value range. The result is a test suite that satisfies boundary-based coverage criteria [13]. Expected and actual system behavior are compared by evaluating all conditions available along the path. The resulting test cases comprise just the deducible input partitions of the variables in our system model (see *completeness* in [23]).

6 Evaluation of ParTeG

The described algorithm is implemented in the prototype *ParTeG* (Partition Test Generator) [18]. This tool is capable of handling arithmetic and Boolean operations within OCL expressions. The SUT is on the level of source code. In the current version, the generated test code is a JUnit test suite.

We use the example in Fig. 1 to compare ParTeG with Rhapsody's ATG and Leirios' Test Designer, which are popular tools in the field of automated test generation. We compare all generated test suites via mutation analysis. For that, we first define mutation operators to inject errors in the SUT. After that, we compare the generated test suites of all tools by the amount of killed mutants. At the end of this section, we discuss advantages and limitations of ParTeG.

Mutation Operators. Since we use mutation testing to compare the generated test suites, the selection of the mutation operators is critical for the quality of the comparison. We put emphasis on the recognition of changes to the OCL expressions. Consequently, our mutation operators change such expressions in the SUT. We define two mutation operators that exchange relation symbols ($\leq$ for $<$ and $\geq$ for $>$) respectively shift the boundaries of the conditions by small values like 2 or 6. We combine both mutation operators and receive 24 distinct, identifiable mutants (3 inequations with 9 mutants each: 4 for shifting boundaries, 5 for also changing the relation symbol; 3 mutants overall are not distinguishable from the original). For instance, mutating the inequation $m\_height@pre < 20$ results in the mutated conditions of the SUT that are shown in Fig. 8.

Comparison to Commercial Tools. We modeled the example of Fig. 1 in Rhapsody's ATG, in Leirios' Test Designer, and in ParTeG. The latter two support all OCL expressions needed for this example. Since ATG is restricted to the domain of C++ and does not support pre-/postconditions of OCL, we added all expressions as implementation code to the model.

Rhapsody's ATG generated 4 loop-free test cases that cover all transitions but killed only 10 out of 24 mutants (see Fig. 9). Leirios Test Designer also generated 4 loop-free test cases that cover all transitions and killed 10 of 24 mutants. Interestingly, both sets of killed mutants differ from each other.

Mutation Operators	No relation change	Exchange $\leq$ for $<$
-6	m_height@pre < 14	m_height@pre $\leq$ 14
-2	m_height@pre < 18	m_height@pre $\leq$ 18
+-0	original	m_height@pre $\leq$ 20
+2	m_height@pre < 22	m_height@pre $\leq$ 22
+6	m_height@pre < 26	m_height@pre $\leq$ 26

Fig. 8. Mutated conditions in the SUT

Tool	Generated Test Cases	Indentified Mutants
Rhapsody ATG	4	10 / 24
Leirios Test Designer	4	10 / 24
ParTeG	5	24 / 24

Fig. 9. Results of the comparison

ParTeG's implementation can generate test suites that satisfy different test criteria like *State Coverage* [24] and *Multi-Dimensional* [12]. With minimal configuration, ParTeG created 5 loop-free test cases overall that killed all 24 mutants. Manual inspection showed that the generated test suite contains no redundant test cases. For this example, ParTeG killed all mutants with the minimum number of loop-free test cases. Higher effectiveness could be reached by, e.g., concatenating all test cases.

Discussion. The above result shows the prospective strengths of our approach. Furthermore, there are many interesting points to discuss. For instance, the effect of a triggered transition can trigger other transitions. Since all events of state machines are handled in a pool, the triggered event can simply be added to this pool. Furthermore, the relative completeness of pre-/postconditions strongly influences the quality of the generated test suite. As any other model-based approach, our apporoach can only transform expressions into input value partitions if the model comprises the corresponding dependencies. Another important aspect is the effectiveness of our approach. The selected coverage criterion plays an important role for the overall costs: satisfying All-One-Loop-Paths is definitely more costly than satisfying All-States. Furthermore, it seems reasonable to combine boundary-based coverage criteria with transition-based coverage criteria. The size of the modeled systems is another important aspect. Until now, we have not performed larger case studies. The generation of test suites that satisfy criteria like All-One-Loop-Paths for state machines with many parallel regions can exceed the available memory. On the one hand, this might be a problem of ParTeG's memory management. However, for future versions of ParTeG we are planning further improvements. On the other hand, this seems to be a problem related to the selected coverage criterion: we are currently investigating the impact of the coverage criterion on the size and fault detection capabilities of the test suite. Since there is no proof that coverage criteria have an impact on the number of identified faults, the effect of coverage criteria needs to be examined.

7   Related Work

References to model-based testing and partition testing can be found in [1,2,24]. Hierons et al. [9] use conditioned slicing to check given input partitions. Dai et al. [5] use partition testing and rely on the user to provide input partitions. Our approach differs in that we create input partitions instead of relying on predefined ones. Legeard, Peureux and Utting [13] develop a method for automated boundary testing from the textual languages Z and B based on set-oriented constraint technology. They execute all operations with all input boundary values on each reachable boundary state. In contrast, our approach uses the languages UML and OCL. It is based on transformations instead of constraint solving.

OCL is object of many studies [17,26]. It can be used for contract-based design, for which Traon [23] also defines vigilance and diagnosibility but does not use it for test case generation. Hamie et al. [8] consider OCL in the context of state machines and classes. Our approach analyzes OCL expressions to automatically generate test input value partitions.

Formalisms from outside the UML (e.g., extended finite state machines [3,4]) also support automatic test generation but are not designed for object-oriented systems. Offutt and Abdurazik [16] generate test cases from state machines. However, they focus on single transitions and random source state initialization paths. Sokenou [20] alters the initialization by using sequence diagrams. Furthermore, she translates OCL constraints of the model into Java code to use them as a test oracle. Our algorithm deviates in that we also evaluate OCL constraints and use them to derive test input value partitions.

To derive test cases, we create an intermediate control-flow tree: the test case tree. In [11], Kansomkeat and Rivepiboon introduce a Test Flow Graph generated from a UML statechart diagram. Their generated test suites satisfy state coverage and transition coverage. In contrast, our tree also contains conditions from class diagrams; the nodes contain input value boundaries. This allows to generate test suites that also satisfy boundary-based coverage criteria.

Many commercial tools support testing. The Conformiq Test Generator [25] supports parallelism and concurrency in UML state machines but input values are created manually. The algorithm of the tool AETG [21] also depends on user-defined values and boundaries. In contrast, we derive input partitions automatically. The tool Rhapsody ATG [22] is based on UML state machines. It generates and executes test cases with respect to coverage criteria like MC/DC. The tool LTG/UML [24] from Leirios [14] evaluates OCL expressions to generate test cases. It interprets equations in postconditions as assignments, which allows to perform a symbolic execution of the model. In contrast to that, our approach is not restricted to active equations but can also evaluate active inequations in OCL postconditions. In future work, we also aim at evaluating more complex active OCL expressions in OCL postconditions. To our knowledge, no commercial tool creates test cases by explicitly deriving input partitions from conditions.

8   Conclusion and Future Work

In this paper, we used UML state machines and class diagrams to derive test input partitions automatically. We pointed out the importance of partition testing when dealing with numeric data, named application fields, and showed the potential of our approach with a prototype. In the future, we will evaluate a broader range of constraints in OCL postconditions, and we will use our method in the domain of Geo-information systems. We will also examine the satisfied coverage criteria of the generated test suite and, if necessary, define new ones.

Acknowledgements. This work was supported by grants from the DFG (German Research Foundation, research training group METRIK).

References

1. Beizer, B.: Software Testing Techniques. John Wiley & Sons, Inc., Chichester (1990)
2. Binder, R.V.: Testing object-oriented systems: models, patterns, and tools. Addison-Wesley Longman Publishing Co., Inc., Amsterdam (1999)
3. Bourhfir, C., Dssouli, R., Aboulhamid, E., Rico, N.: Automatic executable test case generation for extended finite state machine protocols. In: IWTCS 1997, pp. 75–90 (1997)
4. Cheng, K.T., Krishnakumar, A.S.: Automatic functional test generation using the extended finite state machine model. In: DAC 1993, pp. 86–91. ACM Press, New York (1993)
5. Dai, Z.R., Deussen, P.H., Busch, M., Lacmene, L.P., Ngwangwen, T., Herrmann, J., Schmidt, M.: Automatic Test Data Generation for TTCN-3 using CTE. In: ICSSEA (2005)
6. Object Management Group. Object Constraint Language (OCL), version 2.0 (2005)
7. Object Management Group. Unified Modeling Language (UML), version 2.1 (2007)
8. Hamie, A., Civello, F., Howse, J., Kent, S.J.H., Mitchell, R.: Reflections on the object constraint language. In: Bézivin, J., Muller, P.-A. (eds.) UML 1998. LNCS, vol. 1618, pp. 162–172. Springer, Heidelberg (1999)
9. Hierons, R., Harman, M., Fox, C., Ouarbya, L., Daoudi, M.: Conditioned slicing supports partition testing. In: Software Testing, Verification and Reliability (2002)
10. Reactive Systems Inc. Reactis, http://www.reactive-systems.com
11. Kansomkeat, S., Rivepiboon, W.: Automated-generating test case using UML statechart diagrams. In: SAICSIT 2003, pp. 296–300 (2003)
12. Kosmatov, N., Legeard, B., Peureux, F., Utting, M.: Boundary coverage criteria for test generation from formal models. In: ISSRE 2004, pp. 139–150. IEEE, Los Alamitos (2004)
13. Legeard, B., Peureux, F., Utting, M.: Automated Boundary Testing from Z and B. In: Eriksson, L.-H., Lindsay, P.A. (eds.) FME 2002. LNCS, vol. 2391, pp. 21–40. Springer, Heidelberg (2002)
14. Leirios: LTG/UML, http://www.leirios.com
15. Liskov, B.: Keynote address - data abstraction and hierarchy. In: SIGPLAN, pp. 17–34 (1988)
16. Offutt, J., Abdurazik, A.: Generating tests from UML specifications. In: France, R.B., Rumpe, B. (eds.) UML 1999. LNCS, vol. 1723, pp. 416–429. Springer, Heidelberg (1999)
17. Richters, M., Gogolla, M.: On formalizing the UML object constraint language OCL. In: Ling, T.-W., Ram, S., Li Lee, M. (eds.) ER 1998. LNCS, vol. 1507, pp. 449–464. Springer, Heidelberg (1998)
18. Weißleder, S.: ParTeG (Partition Test Generator), http://parteg.sourceforge.net
19. Samuel, P., Mall, R.: Boundary Value Testing based on UML Models. In: ATS 2005, pp. 94–99. IEEE Computer Society, Los Alamitos (2005)

20. Sokenou, D.: Generating Test Sequences from UML Sequence Diagrams and State Diagrams. In: INFORMATIK 2006, pp. 236–240 (2006)
21. Telcordia Technologies. AETG, http://aetgweb.argreenhouse.com
22. Telelogic. Rhapsody Automated Test Generation, http://www.telelogic.com
23. Le Traon, Y.: Design by contract to improve software vigilance. IEEE Trans. Softw. Eng. 32(8), 571–586 (2006)
24. Utting, M., Legeard, B.: Practical Model-Based Testing: A Tools Approach. Morgan Kaufmann Publishers Inc., San Francisco (2006)
25. VerifySoft Technology. Conformiq Test Generator, http://www.verifysoft.com/
26. Ziemann, P., Gogolla, M.: Validating OCL specifications with the USE tool — an example based on the BART case study. In: FMICS 2003 (2003)

Putting Performance Engineering into Model-Driven Engineering: Model-Driven Performance Engineering

Mathias Fritzsche[1] and Jendrik Johannes[2]

[1] SAP Research CEC Belfast, BT370QB Belfast, United Kingdom
mathias.fritzsche@sap.com
[2] Technische Universität Dresden, D-01062, Dresden, Germany
jendrik.johannes@tu-dresden.de

Abstract. Late identification of performance problems can lead to significant additional development costs. Hence, it is necessary to address performance in several development phases by performing a performance engineering process. We show that Model-Driven Engineering (MDE) specifics can be utilised for performance engineering. Therefore, we propose a process combining MDE and performance engineering called Model-Driven Performance Engineering (MDPE).

Additionally we present our first experiences in application of MDPE concepts.

1 Introduction

Usability of software applications is highly dependent on how the resulting software system performs and if the resulting software fulfils performance related requirements. A software's performance, which is defined as "the degree to which an application or component meets its objectives for timelines" [1], is however seldom analysed before the actual system is implemented and performance of the running system can be measured.

Examples like the development of the Information System for the German Police called "Inpol-Neu" [2], which was published in the mass-media, show that addressing performance in a late phase of software development can lead to significant additional development effort. "Inpol-Neu" was planned to go productive in spring 2001. End of 2001, performance tests for the integrated system indicated that the system was not able to fulfil performance-related requirements. A reduced version of "Inpol-Neu" went live at 18th August 2003. The example of "Inpol-Neu" indicates the importance of addressing the performance of an integrated application throughout the whole development lifecycle.

Earlier performance analysis can be done through *performance engineering*, which is not well integrated into most software development processes. This paper investigates how to improve the integration of performance engineering into the development process of complex software applications. It argues that by moving from *Code-Centric Development* (CCD) to *Model-Driven Engineering*

H. Giese (Ed.): MoDELS 2007 Workshops, LNCS 5002, pp. 164–175, 2008.

(MDE) many of the causes for poor integration of performance engineering can be prevented. Based on this observation, it proposes an extension of MDE that we call *Model-Driven Performance Engineering* (MDPE).

The paper is structured as follows: Section 2 reviews performance engineering techniques for CCD and delineates extended possibilities of performance engineering by utilisation of MDE. Following these observations, we propose a *Model-Driven Performance Engineering* (MDPE) process in Section 3. Section 4 summarises first experiences of applying MDPE and introduces a tool architecture for future implementations. Section 5 compares our approach with related concepts and highlights its unique properties.

2   Background

This section provides a comparison of extending both *Code-Centric Development* (CCD) and *Model-Driven Engineering* (MDE) with performance engineering.

2.1   Extending Code-Centric Development with Performance Engineering

Different established performance analysis techniques like Queuing Networks [3], Layered Queuing Networks [4], Queuing Petri Nets [5], and FMC-QE [6] use formal performance models for performance predictions. Other approaches for evaluation are simulation-based [7], where models of a system are executed in a simulation.

It is evident that performance prediction at design time requires analysis models defining the structure and behaviour of the analysed system, resource requirements, branch probabilities, and details about *factors due to contention of resources*. Semi-formal models are commonly used in CCD, but mainly to support human understanding, communication, and documentation of a system. Therefore CCD requires models only to be sufficient to support human interpretation. They are not used as development artefacts for forward engineering from models to executable code.

In more detail, a semi-formal specification of models makes tool support in terms of transformations, consistency checks, and repository functionality difficult. Therefore, models in CCD are not kept in sync after the code is implemented or the system is refined and are thrown away. Analysis models for performance, design models, and code have to be developed separately using specific knowledge about performance modelling concepts like the Queuing Theory. Therefore these approaches are rarely used in industrial projects.

In terms of performance, a "fix it later approach" is commonly used for CCD as described in [1] and [8]. This can lead to significant correction costs as seen on the example of "Inpol-Neu". This is supported by our experience with SAP's development lifecycle called *Product Innovation Lifecycle* (PIL) [9]. SAP's PIL mainly addresses performance in early phases of requirement specification and after integration of already implemented components. Performance predictions in intermediate stages of the development process are not performed.

We claim that this is because performance engineering solutions for CCD are not minimally intrusive in terms of missing automation and of missing formalisation: it is necessary to explicitly define models for performance engineering. This requires additional investment and performance engineering expertise that industry is not willing to provide. The next section argues that the same problems can be avoided by utilisation of MDE.

2.2 Extending Model-Driven Engineering with Performance Engineering

In MDE, a formalisation of modelling enables the usage of models as development artefacts in forward engineering from models to executable code. Modelling languages for *development models*[1] are formally defined with the help of meta modelling languages such as MOF [10]. This makes models machine-readable, which enables broad tool support as provided by the Eclipse Modelling Framework (EMF) [11] or SAP's Modelling Infrastructure MOIN [12].

Such tools offer automated transformation between models of different abstractions, between models specifying different view points, or from highly detailed models to platform specific code. Through this, different development artefacts can be kept in sync, saving effort and shifting effort from coding to modelling. By using transformations, performance models based on development models of different stages of refinement can be generated and performance engineering for each of these refinement stages becomes possible without much additional effort. This effort does not focus on modelling itself, but on annotating of separately defined performance information—like specification of resource requirements on already existing structural and behavioural models.

Based on these observations, the following section proposes an extended MDE process: *Model-Driven Performance Engineering* (MDPE).

3   Model-Driven Performance Engineering (MDPE)

The requirement of a short time to market in combination with an increasing complexity of software systems calls for a reasonable performance engineering process that utilise features of MDE as argued in Sect. 2. A solution that provides a high degree of automation is required to handle big and complex models of enterprise software. The flexibility in MDE wrt. different levels of abstraction and models of different domains, calls for a similar flexible solution for performance engineering. Earlier initial performance feedback with minimal effort should be supported as well as maximal performance feedback with extended (but still cost-efficient) effort. Such stepwise feedback should be given at any stage over the whole development lifecycle. To meet these requirements we propose a solution which is based on the *Software Performance Engineering* (SPE) [1] approach and utilises MDE specifics.

---

[1] We use the term *development model* in this paper to distinguish between models as development artefacts and formal *performance models*.

SPE integrates different steps of performance engineering repeatedly at different stages of the development process. The idea is to generate early performance feedback; starting at the stage of requirement analysis. SPE is a stepwise process that distinguishes two kinds of performance models, a Software Execution model and a System Execution model.

The first one is represented in an execution graph [1]. This graph is a flow graph extended with resource demands and branching probabilities. It enables analysis in the absence of delays because of factors due to contention for resources like multiple users. Results of the analysis are the mean, best-case, and worst-case response time. The System Execution model is based on the Software Execution model extended with details about contention for resources (like deployment information and multi-user scenarios). The model can be represented as a Queuing Network [1]. The output of the analysis of this more complex performance model is the prediction of the utilisation of resources and detailed a performance prediction such as identification of bottle necks. Additionally, SPE includes the specification of patterns and anti-patterns for software architectures to minimise poor architectural decisions from a performance perspective [1,13].

Fig. 1 delineates our idea of MDPE which is based on SPE but utilises specifics of MDE. The proposed process is an extension of MDE which enables SPE-like performance engineering by utilisation of MDE concepts as described in Sect. 2. In comparison to related approaches utilising model driven techniques [14,15,16,17], our approach enables stepwise performance feedback which can be repeated at different stages of refinement in a MDE process.

In MDPE, performance analysis is performed at each refinement step of the MDE process. Each time, performance feedback can be produced stepwise. Thus, we take two orthogonal dimensions of refinement in MDPE into account: One dimension to refine the performance models, and another dimension to refine the development models in a traditional MDE process.

Initial automated performance feedback is based on structural information from development models only (cf. *Static Model Analysis* in Fig. 1). This feedback will include the identification of performance anti-patterns and identification of model-based performance metrics to enable comparability of models from

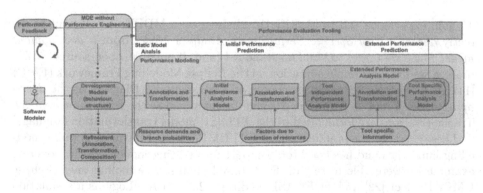

Fig. 1. MDPE concept as Block Diagram [18]

the performance perspective. An example of a simple model-based performance metric is the number of actions in a UML activity diagram.

The next analysis steps are based on performance analysis models. These can be derived from development models by enriching them with additional performance related information which requires involvement of the user. Following the concept of SPE, we distinguish between two kinds of performance models:

The *Initial Performance Analysis Model* is derived from development models enriched with the resource demands of actions and probabilities of branches in behavioural models. The computation of this model is simple. Only resource demands under consideration of branch probabilities have to be added. This simple analysis enables *Initial Performance Prediction* which includes declaration of the mean, best-case, and worst-case response time. Initial Performance Analysis Models are conceptually the same as Software Execution Models in SPE.

The *Extended Performance Analysis Model* is comparable to a System Execution Model in SPE. It is a further enriched Initial Performance Analysis Model, annotated with information about contention for resources. The *Extended Performance Prediction* based on this model enables more precise results. Additionally, resource utilisation can be prognosticated. The price for these more detailed results is a more complex analysis.

Dependent on the size, characteristics and domains of the modelled system, different simulative or analytical evaluation techniques will be necessary to take factors due to contention of resources into account and to minimise possible failures in performance prediction. Therefore it is planned to evaluate performance based on Extended Performance Analysis Models by using different concepts and tools. For the implementation of this approach we require the definition of a *Tool-Independent Performance Analysis Model* like KLAPER [19]. This model will be the basis for several *Tool-Specific Performance Analysis Models* taking tool-specific information into account.

The next section describes our first experiences with using MDPE concepts to identify requirements for an implementation of the proposed process.

4   Initial Experiences and Future Work

To gain experience and to identify the challenges in MDPE, we attempt to directly derive a *Tool Specific Performance Analysis Model* from a *development model*. Since we target to build on standard (and, if possible, open-source) MDE tooling, we base our implementation on the Eclipse Modelling Framework (EMF) [11]. As a concrete Scenario, we choose an UML Activity Diagram as the *development model* and an AnyLogic [20] simulation model as the *performance model*. Transformations are formulated in the ATL [21] model transformation language.

These choices have practical reasons: 1) UML is one of the most popular modelling languages and has good tool support for creating models. In the concrete example we were able to rely on EMF-based open-source tooling only (Eclipse UML2 Project [22] and TOPCASED editors [23]). 2) AnyLogic is a simulation tool which supports the creation of graphical representations of simulations and do on-the-fly analysis by simulation. This is suitable for first experimentations. 3) ATL was chosen, because it is the standard transformation language for EMF models.

First, we required means to enrich the UML diagram with performance information. To this end, we decided to use the UML profile for schedulability, performance, and time specification (SPT) [24]. In this profile, the stereotype PStep with a set of tagged values is defined. It can be annotated to a variety of UML elements. In our experimentation we only used the tagged values HostExecutionDemand, Repetition, and Probability.

Figure 2 displays an UML activity diagram where all actions have been annotated with a HostExecutionDemand—indicating their mean duration. The initial node was annotated with a Repetition value for the arrival rate. Each of the control flows from the decision node are annotated with a Probability value.

Second, we determined that the simplest analysis we could do is "running" the activity diagram in a simulation. In AnyLogic, we modelled a library of elements that correspond to activity diagram elements: We defined their semantics with respect to the simulation and gave graphical representations to make it easy for the developer to relate the simulation to the original diagram.

The AnyLogic library elements representing actions, decision, initial, and final nodes can be seen in Figure 3. The bar in front of an action represents the queue of unprocessed signals at the current simulation timestamp. A bar at a final node indicates the amount of arrived signals at the current simulation timestamp. An action that is currently active is filled.

Third, as the most challenging step, a transformation was written in ATL. It was expected that the transformation is straightforward, since we have made

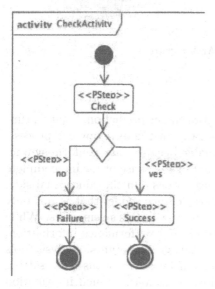

Fig. 2. An UML activity diagram

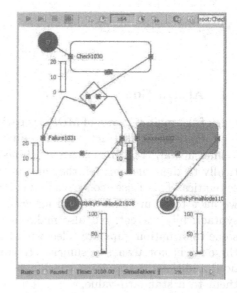

Fig. 3. A derived AnyLogic transformation

the required types of UML model elements available in AnyLogic through the provided library. However, it proved to be non-trivial to provide a complete transformation. The resulting transformation consists of 750 lines of ATL code, which are all hand-written. The implementation, together with example models and a detailed description of the example was released on the ATL Use Cases web page[2].

The simulation model from Figure 3 was created by the transformation without additional efforts. The figure shows the simulation running at a concrete timestamp (3108 time units have passed). A possible bottleneck of the system can be observed by monitoring the simulation: the queue in front of the Success action is growing but never shrinking.

In the following we discuss observations we made by creating this first implementation and their consequences for an MDPE tool architecture. This architecture is sketched in Fig. 4 and will be explained in the next sections.

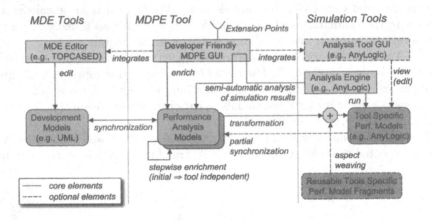

Fig. 4. MDPE Tool Architecture

4.1   Abstraction

One of the main benefits of MDPE is early performance prediction. That is, running analysis on abstract system definitions early in the development process. While such abstract models are machine-readable because they conform syntactically to their metamodel, they are not formal in the sense of having complete semantics. This raises conceptual and technical issues: On the conceptual side, we have to assure that we end up with a performance model that is not only syntactically correct, but also makes sense wrt. the analysis semantics. While some information gaps are filled with the additional performance information, these might not always be sufficient to run an analysis. Sometimes, analysis tools need additional parameters which can be derived by other means (e.g., setting them to a standard value, when it is considered harmless). Such information

---

[2] http://www.eclipse.org/m2m/atl/usecases

often cross-cuts the whole performance model. Practically, this is often the case in the transformation to AnyLogic. As a consequence, static information had to be repeatedly inserted at different points in the transformation. It would be desirable to separate this information into model fragments formulated in the analysis formalism and then weave them into the transformation result using Aspect-Oriented Modelling techniques (cf. lower right corner of Fig. 4).

4.2   Location and Definition of Performance Information

In the example we applied a profile to add performance information to the UML model directly. While that is a valid approach when UML is used to do performance modelling[3], the UML models handled are development models of our systems. Thus adding the performance information there pollutes the model with additional information that is of little value for the ongoing MDE design process.

Thus, this information should be added to the Initial and Extended Performance Analysis Models only (cf. Fig. 1). For these models we plan to develop a metamodel—not from scratch, but based on an existing work. Parts from UML together with the SPT profile [24] are a promising candidate to build on.

Since one of our aims is to let the software modeller do analysis without consulting performance engineering experts, the provision of performance information should be tool-supported and automated as much as possible. Consequently, we do not plan to provide a graphical editor for our performance models. They should rather be produced from development models and automatically acquired or user defined performance data. For the last case we anticipate providing tool-guidance for developers by providing wizards or similar means (cf. upper middle of Fig. 4). This user interface should offer extension points to integrate with performance data sources (e.g., collected performance data from experiences in a company). In some cases, it might be useful to integrate with MDE and analysis GUIs if possible, since it is an easy way to give better feedback to the user (cf. upper part of Fig. 4). For instance, observing an actual running simulation in AnyLogic and getting a visualisation of relations to the development model can leverage understanding of analysis results for non-performance experts.

4.3   Structural Discrepancies

In the example, the analysis formalism was easily aligned with activity diagrams (by providing an AnyLogic library). Such correspondences between development and performance model elements might not always exist. It is not clear if this is a problem. Missing correspondences might also indicate that useful analysis can not be done in this combination. Nevertheless, we have to keep this in mind when designing a tool-independent performance metamodel, because it aims at combining arbitrary MDE formalisms with arbitrary performance engineering formalisms. It is clear that not all MDE models are useful for MDPE (e.g., static UML class diagrams without attached behaviour). But there is a subset of MDE formalisms which should be supported.

---

[3] UML can be used for performance modelling by applying one of the standardised profiles SPT [24] or MARTE [25].

4.4 Transformation and Synchronisation

Our experience with providing a single ATL transformation has shown that the definition of the relationships between formalisms is not a trivial task and that it is difficult to ensure stable and complete transformations using this "single transformation" approach. Additionally, it is often required to not only transform, but update already transformed models, which is very important when refining models based on analysis results. Thus, a synchronisation mechanism is needed. In particular between development and performance analysis models, since structural changes, caused by analysis results, should reflect automatically on the design (cf. lower left corner of Fig. 4). Synchronisation between the tool-independent and tool-dependant performance models is also useful when the model structure can be changed directly in the analysis tool, which can be done, for instance, in AnyLogic (cf. lower right corner of Fig. 4). However, the analysis engines can also be hidden. The results they deliver have to be analysed, for instance by anti-pattern matching, to propose structural changes to the modeller (cf. upper middle of Fig. 4). Another related issue is versioning of models. It is required to run subsequent analysis on altered models, compare them, and choose the best design.

Some issues could be addressed by using additional features of ATL like several input and output models and high-level transformations. The ATL based tool Atlas Model Weaver (AMW) [26] could help with the synchronisation issue, since it allows the definition of relationships between models and the automatic generation of ATL transformation for both directions. Application of the Epsilon Platform [27] that supports several model-managing tasks is also considered. Another promising approach is Triple Graph Grammars [28] which offers solutions to incremental model synchronisation. We are in contact with researchers and developers of all the mentioned approaches. Some of us are involved in the development of the Reuseware Composition Framework [29,30] which is momentarily extended for aspect-oriented modelling and could also be applied for tasks in MDPE. It has yet to be decided which transformation and synchronisation technologies should be used. MDPE is definitely a good application and use-case for several of these technologies. Thus, our work will also contribute to this area.

5 Related Work

Current ideas in combining MDE and performance engineering are addressing different aspects. Various authors, e.g. [14,15] propose use of transformations for generating performance models from annotated UML models in an automatic way. For instance [17], depicts how to map definitions of composite processes specified in Business Process Execution Language (BPEL) [31].

In [19] a language, called KLAPER, for performance models is proposed which is independent of the performance analysis technique like Queuing Petri Nets or Layered Queuing Models. Such a language simplifies performance evaluation of the same development models with the help of different performance analysis techniques.

In [16] a process that combines Model-Driven techniques and performance engineering is introduced which is called Software Performance Model-Driven Architecture (SPMDA). The SPMDA approach enables two kinds of performance models which are transformed from two fixed refinement steps into a Model-Driven Process. According to this, SPMDA does not enable stepwise performance engineering in terms of providing stepwise performance feedback for each refinement step in the development process.

To enable a minimally intrusive solution, it is not only necessary to automate generation of performance models, it is also important that a modeller can decide how much effort he invests in performance engineering. Therefore, we require stepwise performance feedback for each refinement step in a development process which includes earlier initial (maximal) performance feedback with minimal (extended) effort as shown for the Code Centric performance engineering approach.

The MDPE approach is based on SPE concepts. As in SPE the approach is stepwise by combining identification of anti-patterns for performance and different kinds of performance models. The approach is also usable for different stages in a development process to provide performance feedback throughout the whole development lifecycle. In comparison to SPE a high degree of automation can be reached because MDPE is based on formal development models with extensive tool support. This allows, for instance, automated generation of different *Tool Specific Performance Analysis Models* to minimise failures in performance prediction.

6   Conclusion

In this paper we proposed to extend Mode-Driven Engineering to Model-Driven Performance Engineering. This approach utilises Mode-Driven techniques to enable stepwise performance feedback. This includes earlier initial (maximal) performance feedback with minimal (extended) effort. The approach is repeatable at different stages of refinement in a Mode-Driven Engineering process. MDPE is applicable if behaviour models of the system are available on abstraction levels where performance data can be defined based on experiences or measurements on existing systems. As a consequence, the possibility of performing early analysis could increase the acceptance of behavioural modelling in a MDE process.

We clarified that putting this process into industrial practices requires tools with high automation. Our first experiments identified requirements for such a tool architecture which we will continue to evolve and improve. For instance, a synchronisation mechanism between different development and analysis models is required to adequately integrate analysis results into the development process. To define transformations to analysis models, the semantics of the development models have to be clearer than they often are in traditional MDE processes.

Acknowledgement

This research has been co-funded by the European Commission within the 6th Framework Programme project MODELPLEX contract number 034081 (cf. http://www.modelplex.org).

References

1. Smith, C.U.: Performance Solutions: A Practical Guide To Creating Responsive, Scalable Software. Addison-Wesley, Reading (2002)
2. Jakob Vo, J.R., Tretkowski, I.: Das polizeiliche Informationssystem INPOL (2002)
3. Bolch, G., Greiner, S., de Meer, H., Trivedi, K.: Queuing Networks and Markov Chains: Modeling and Performance Evaluation with Computer Science Applications. John Wiley & Sons Inc., New York, USA (1998)
4. Woodside, C.M., Neilson, J.E., Petriu, D.C., Majumdar, S.: The stochastic rendezvous network model for performance of synchronous client-server-like distributed software. IEEE Transactions on Computers 44(1), 20–34 (1995)
5. Bause, F.: "QN + PN = QPN" - combining queueing networks and petri nets, Technical Report no. 461, Dept. of CS, University of Dortmund, Germany (1993)
6. Zorn, W.: Fmc-qe: A new approach in quantitative modeling. In: Proc. of MSV 2007 (June 2007)
7. Robinson, S.: Simulation: The Practice of Model Development and Use. John Wiley & Sons Inc., New York (March 2004)
8. Dugan, R.F.: Performance lies my professor told me: the case for teaching software performance engineering to undergraduates. SIGSOFT Softw. Eng. Notes 29(1), 37–48 (2004)
9. SAP, A.G.: Product innovation lifecycle from Ideas to Customer Value, Whitepaper Version 1.1, EXTERNAL VERSION, p. 34 (July 2004)
10. OMG: MetaObject Facility (MOF) specification version 2.0 (January 2006), http://www.omg.org/cgi-bin/doc?formal/2006-01-01
11. Budinsky, F., Brodsky, S.A., Merks, E.: Eclipse Modeling Framework. Pearson Education (2003)
12. Michael Altenhofen, T.H., Kusterer, S.: Ocl support in an industrial environment (2006)
13. Smith, C.U., Williams, L.G.: New software performance antipatterns: More ways to shoot yourself in the foot. In: Int. CMG Conference, Computer Measurement Group, pp. 667–674 (2002)
14. D'Ambrogio, A.: A model transformation framework for the automated building of performance models from uml models. In: WOSP 2005: Proceedings of the 5th international workshop on Software and performance, pp. 75–86. ACM Press, New York (2005)
15. Gu, G.P., Petriu, D.C.: Xslt transformation from uml models to lqn performance models. In: WOSP 2002: Proceedings of the 3rd international workshop on Software and performance, pp. 227–234. ACM Press, New York (2002)
16. Cortellessa, V., Marco, A.D., Inverardi, P.: Software performance model-driven architecture. In: SAC 2006: Proceedings of the 2006 ACM symposium on Applied computing, pp. 1218–1223. ACM Press, New York (2006)
17. D'Ambrogio, A., Bocciarelli, P.: A model-driven approach to describe and predict the performance of composite services. In: WOSP 2007: Proceedings of the 6th international workshop on Software and performance, pp. 78–89. ACM Press, New York (2007)
18. Knopfel, A., Grone, B., Tabeling, P.: Fundamental Modeling Concepts: Effective Communication of IT Systems. John Wiley & Sons, Chichester (2006)
19. Grassi, V., Mirandola, R., Sabetta, A.: From design to analysis models: a kernel language for performance and reliability analysis of component-based systems. In: WOSP 2005: Proceedings of the 5th international workshop on Software and performance, pp. 25–36. ACM Press, New York (2005)

20. XJ Technologies: AnyLogic — multi-paradigm simulation software (June 2007), http://www.xjtek.com/anylogic/
21. ATLAS Group: ATLAS transformation language (June 2007), http://www.eclipse.org/m2m/atl/
22. The Eclipse Foundation: Eclipse UML2 (June 2007), http://www.eclipse.org/uml2/
23. The Topcased Project Team: TOPCASED (June 2007), http://www.topcased.org
24. OMG: UML profile for schedulability, performance, and time specification (January 2005), http://www.omg.org/docs/formal/03-09-01.pdf
25. OMG: UML profile for modeling and analysis of real-time and embedded systems (2007)
26. The AMW Project Team: Atlas Model Weaver (June 2007), http://eclipse.org/gmt/amw/
27. The Epsilon Project Team: Epsilon Platform (June 2007), http://eclipse.org/gmt/epsilon/
28. Schürr, A.: Specification of graph translators with triple graph grammars. In: Mayr, E.W., Schmidt, G., Tinhofer, G. (eds.) WG 1994. LNCS, vol. 903, pp. 151–163. Springer, Heidelberg (1995)
29. Software Technology Group, Technische Universität Dresden: Reuseware Composition Framework (June 2007), http://www.reuseware.org
30. Henriksson, J., Johannes, J., Zschaler, S., Aßmann, U.: Reuseware – adding modularity to your language of choice. In: TOOLS EUROPE 2007, pp. 127–146 (October 2007): Special Issue of the Journal of Object Technology 6(9)
31. Alves, A., Arkin, A., Askary, S., Bloch, B., Curbera, F., Goland, Y., Kartha, N., Sterling, Knig, D., Mehta, V., Thatte, S., van der Rijn, D., Yendluri, P., Yiu, A.: Web services business process execution language version 2.0. OASIS Committee Draft (May 2006)

7th International Workshop on Ocl4All: Modelling Systems with OCL

David Akehurst[1], Martin Gogolla[2], and Steffen Zschaler[3]

[1] Thales Scotland
dave@akehurst.net
[2] Technische Universität Bremen
gogolla@informatik.uni-bremen.de
[3] Technische Universität Dresden
szschaler@acm.org

Abstract. This year's OCL workshop at the MODELS conference looked out to usages of OCL outside the direct context of UML or beyond the capabilities of standard OCL. It was a very interesting and successful workshop, which apart from the presentation of 10 papers a lively discussion on various topics surround current usage of OCL was held. Six main topics recurred throughout the discussions: (1) Means and uses of transformation to other languages, (2) Support for side-effects and executability, (3) Continuing need for OCL, (4) Providing extensions to the standard, (5) Platform independence of the language, (6) Formality of the language. This summary report presents the results of the workshop and the discussions.

1 Introduction

Ocl4All (2007) is the seventh UML/MODELS workshop on the Object Constraint Language (OCL). As with its previous editions, this year's OCL workshop has been held under a specific theme: Using OCL in an extended system-modelling context. Since the inception of OCL, the world of modelling has changed. While the Unified Modelling Language (UML) is still of great importance, many software-development projects use other, often so-called domain-specific languages for their models. In this situation, OCL must go beyond its tight connection to UML or it must eventually fail. And, indeed, we see a strong movement for extensions of OCL that bring it beyond its original concepts both in its relation to UML and in the basic principles underlying the language. At the same time, the current OCL 2.0 standard already spans some 230 pages making it quite hard to ensure consistency both in the standard and in its implementations. Therefore, the OCL community needs to start looking for ways of systematically modularising and extending the language. The 2007 issue of the OCL workshop aimed to discuss cases of using OCL outside of UML, problems encountered and solutions proposed. The workshop was very lively, in a mixture of presentations and discussions. Out of a submitted 14 papers, 10 were

H. Giese (Ed.): MoDELS 2007 Workshops, LNCS 5002, pp. 176–181, 2008.

accepted. The accepted papers have been published in a special edition of Electronic Communications of the EASST, an on-line journal [1]. In this workshop summary, we first present a short overview of the papers and then go on to the main points of discussion and the conclusions reached at the workshop.

2   Workshop Papers

Here, we give a short overview for each paper taken from the abstracts provided by the authors.

2.1   William Robinson: Extended OCL for Goal Monitoring [2]

Monitoring human-computer interaction aids the analysis for understanding how well software meets its purpose. In particular, monitoring human-computer interactions with respect to a users goal model helps to determine user satisfaction. By formalizing a goal model, runtime monitors can be automatically derived. The REQMON system monitors the satisfaction of goal models. Recently, an OCL compiler was developed for REQMON. The OCL was extended slightly to address temporal and real-time constraints. Now, goal models can be represented in the extended OCL, from which runtime monitors can be compiled. The resulting REQMON system appears to be easier to use.

2.2   Pierre Kelsen et al.: Specifying Executable Platform-Independent Models Using OCL [3]

Model-driven architecture aims at describing a system using a platform-independent model in sufficient detail so that the full implementation of the system can be generated from this model and a platform model. This implies that the platform-independent model must describe the static structure as well as the dynamic behavior of the system. We propose a declarative language for describing the behavior of platform-independent models based on a hybrid notation that uses graphical elements as well as textual elements in the form of OCL code snippets. Compared to existing approaches based on action languages it is situated at a higher level of abstraction and, through a clean separation of modifier operations and query operations, simplifies the comprehension of the behavioral aspects of the platform-independent system.

2.3   Ke Jiang et al.: Using OCL in Executable UML [4]

Executable UML allows precisely describing the software system at a higher level of abstraction. The executable models can be translated to a less abstract programming language completely or executed directly. Object Constraint Language (OCL), as a formal specification language, is a standard published along with UML. It is primitively used to describe constraints for UML models. In this paper, we explore some general features of executable UML and propose using OCL in executable UML. We extend OCL to support actions with side-effect in order to precisely model behavior. We also discuss some open issues.

2.4   David Akehurst et al.: OCL: Modularising the Language [5]

The Object Constraint Language (OCL) was originally designed as an 'add-on' to the Unified Modelling Language (UML) in order to facilitate writing textual constraints complementing the graphical specifications. Since its original standardisation many extensions have been added to the language and many more have been proposed. The original structure of the OCL definition has not been formed, however, with a view of extensibility. Still, OCL can be redesigned in such a manner that it becomes easy to extend the language. In this paper we present a modular redefinition of OCL and illustrate how it supports extension. This new approach to the design of OCL enables you to consistently extend or customise OCL to your own needs.

2.5   Mirco Kuhlmann et al.: Analyzing Semantic Properties of OCL Operations by Uncovering Interoperational Relationships [6]

The OCL (Object Constraint Language) as part of the UML (Unified Modeling Language) is a rich language with different collection kinds (sets, multi-sets, sequences) and a large variety of operations defined thereon. Without negating the strong correlation between both fields we can say that these operations have their origin partly in logic (like the operations forAll and exists) and partly in computer science, in particular database systems (like the operation select). Some of these operations may be expressed in terms of other operations. This paper presents a systematic study of relationships which hold between OCL features like the mentioned operations. Apart from presenting the relationships between operations in a conceptual way, the relationships are described by a formal metamodel allowing systematic and computer supported access to the operation relationships by querying an underlying formal description.

2.6   David Akehurst et al.: C# 3.0 Makes OCL Redundant! [7]

Other than its 'platform independence' the major advantages of OCL over traditional Object Oriented programming languages has been the declarative nature of the language, its powerful navigation facility via the iteration operations, and the availability of tuples as a first class concept. The recent offering from Microsoft of the "Orcas" version of Visual Studio with C# 3.0 and the Linq library provides functionality almost identical to that of OCL. This paper examines and evaluates the controversial thesis that, as a result of C# 3.0, OCL is essentially redundant, having been superseded by the incorporation of its advantageous features into a mainstream programming language.

2.7   Milan Milanović et al.: Sharing OCL Constraints by Using Web Rules [8]

This paper presents an MDE-based approach to interchanging rules between the Object Constraint Language (OCL) and REWERSE I1 Rule Markup Language

(R2ML). The R2ML tends to be a standard rule markup language by following up the W3C initiative for Rule Interchange Format (RIF). The main benefit of this approach is that the transformations between languages are completely based on the languages' abstract syntax (i.e., metamodels) and in this way we keep the focus on the language concepts rather than on technical issues caused by different concrete syntax. In the current implementation, we have supported translation of the OCL invariants into the R2ML integrity rules. While most of the OCL expression could be represented in the R2ML and other rule languages, we have also identified that collection operators could only be partially supported in other rule languages (e.g., SWRL).

2.8   Florian Heidenreich et al.: A Framework for Generating Query Language Code from OCL Invariants [9]

The semantical integrity of business data is of great importance for the implementation of business applications. Model-Driven Software Development (MDSD) allows for specifying the relevant domain concepts, their interrelations and their concise semantics using a plethora of modelling languages. Since model transformations enable an automatic mapping of platform independent models (PIMs) to platform specific models (PSMs) and code, it is reasonable to utilise them to derive data schemas and integrity rules for business applications. Most current approaches only focus on transforming structural descriptions of software systems while semantical specifications are neglected. However, to preserve also the semantical integrity rules we propose a Query Code Generation Framework that enables Model-Driven Integrity Engineering. This framework allows for mapping UML models to arbitrary data schemas and for mapping OCL invariants to sentences in corresponding declarative query languages, enforcing semantical data integrity on implementation level. This supersedes the manual translation of integrity constraints and, thus, decreases development costs while increasing software quality.

2.9   Matthias Bräurer et al.: Model-Level Integration of the OCL Standard Library Using a Pivot Model with Generics Support [10]

OCL 2.0 specifies a standard library of predefined types and associated operations. A model-level representation of the library is required to reference its elements within the abstract syntax model created by an OCL parser. Existing OCL engines build this model in the implementation code which severely limits reusability, flexibility and maintainability. To address these problems, we show how a common pivot model with explicit support for template types can help to externalize the definition of the standard library and integrate it with instances of arbitrary domain-specific modeling languages. We exemplify the feasibility of our approach with a prototypical implementation for the Dresden OCL2 Toolkit and present a tailored EMF editor for modeling the OCL types and operations. We limit our discussion to the model level, i.e., we do not consider an implementation of the standard library for an execution engine.

2.10   Emine Aydal: Evaluation of OCL for Large-Scale Modelling: A Different View of the Mondex Smart Card Application [11]

OCL is used to add rigour to UML/MOF models, and in particular can be used to express behavioural details (e.g., operation pre- and postconditions, class invariants) of such models. The applicability and utility of OCL can be assessed by applying it to realistic applications and by investigating its capabilities both in terms of language characteristics and tool support. With this in mind, in this paper we model functional requirements for the Mondex Smart Card Application using UML Diagrams, demonstrate how system invariants as well as operation pre- and post-conditions are specified in OCL, and explore the degree to which OCL tool support can be used to create and validate these models. Moreover, we discuss how these pre- and post-conditions can be validated, in part by discussing how test cases can be selected from the OCL specifications created.

3   Workshop Discussions

There were a number of recurring topics that occurred throughout the presentations and discussion of the workshop: (1) Transformation to other languages, (2) Support for side-effects and executability, (3) Is OCL redundant, (4) Providing extensions to the standard, (5) Platform independence, (6) Is it a formal language?

The transformation of OCL to other languages was directly raised in two papers [8,9] regarding the conversion to web rule languages and to SQL. Open world vs closed world assumptions was a distinguishing point between these two papers. The SQL paper stayed in a semantics with closed world assumption whilst the web rule paper switched to open world. OCL uses a closed world assumption therefore translating to an open world language causes problems in particular with negations.

There was extensive discussion on whether OCL should support side-effects. This related to other discussions on making OCL more easily extensible so that side-effect concepts (amongst others) can be added if required. There was clear agreement that OCL is currently intended to be side-effect free. The discussion took two directions, one regarding whether or not it would be useful and the other on potential problems it would cause. There was no agreement on whether it would be useful; the main argument for side-effect was the goal of full code generation, however the counter argument revolved around OCL being declarative and not focusing on implementation. Potential problems were discussed in the areas of object identity, query operations and local let expressions.

Triggered by paper [7], discussion occurred on the potential redundancy of OCL in the context of other programming languages such as C# and Ruby, which support some of the same features. The main two arguments in favour of OCL were the potential for verification and validation support and the small size of OCL.

Many papers discussed extensions to OCL [2,3,4] and there was common agreement that a standard mechanism for enabling these extensions to be clearly and easily defined was required. This is related to other discussions and papers on redefining the OCL standard in a more modular fashion. There were two papers that discussed the requirements for the OCL standard library to be replaceable [5,10].

The question of whether OCL is platform independent was discussed. This related to discussion on translating OCL to other languages and issues about the standard library. No definitive conclusion was reached.

Finally a long discussion was held on whether OCL is a formal language. The discussion mainly revolved around the provision of a formal semantics for OCL. Past work has provided a formal semantics for parts of and different versions of OCL. The current standard certainly does not provide a full formal semantics. Thus we agreed that OCL is a semi-formal language as it is currently defined.

References

1. Akehurst, D.H., Gogolla, M., Zschaler, S. (eds.): Ocl4All: Modelling Systems with OCL. Electronic Communications of the EASST, vol. 9 (2008),
   http://eceasst.cs.tu-berlin.de/index.php/eceasst/issue/view/16
2. Robinson, W.: Extended OCL for goal monitoring. [1],
   http://eceasst.cs.tu-berlin.de/index.php/eceasst/issue/view/16
3. Kelsen, P., Pulvermueller, E., Glodt, C.: Specifying executable platform-independent models using OCL. [1],
   http://eceasst.cs.tu-berlin.de/index.php/eceasst/issue/view/16
4. Jiang, K., Zhang, L., Miyake, S.: Using OCL in executable UML. [1],
   http://eceasst.cs.tu-berlin.de/index.php/eceasst/issue/view/16
5. Akehurst, D.H., Zschaler, S., Howells, G.: OCL: Modularising the language. [1],
   http://eceasst.cs.tu-berlin.de/index.php/eceasst/issue/view/16
6. Kuhlmann, M., Gogolla, M.: Analyzing semantic properties of OCL operations by uncovering interoperational relationships. [1],
   http://eceasst.cs.tu-berlin.de/index.php/eceasst/issue/view/16
7. Akehurst, D.H., Howells, G., Scheidgen, M., McDonald-Maier, K.: C# 3.0 makes OCL redundant! [1],
   http://eceasst.cs.tu-berlin.de/index.php/eceasst/issue/view/16
8. Milanović, M., Gašević, D., Giurca, A., Wagner, G., Devedžić, V.: Sharing OCL constraints by using web rules. [1],
   http://eceasst.cs.tu-berlin.de/index.php/eceasst/issue/view/16
9. Heidenreich, F., Wende, C., Demuth, B.: A framework for generating query language code from OCL invariants. [1],
   http://eceasst.cs.tu-berlin.de/index.php/eceasst/issue/view/16
10. Bräuer, M., Demuth, B.: Model-level integration of the OCL standard library using a pivot model with generics support. [1],
    http://eceasst.cs.tu-berlin.de/index.php/eceasst/issue/view/16
11. Aydal, E.G., Paige, R.F., Woodcock, J.: Evaluation of OCL for large-scale modelling: A different view of the Mondex purse. [1],
    http://eceasst.cs.tu-berlin.de/index.php/eceasst/issue/view/16

Model-Level Integration of the OCL Standard Library Using a Pivot Model with Generics Support

Matthias Bräuer and Birgit Demuth

Dresden University of Technology
Software Technology Group
01062 Dresden, Germany
{matthias.braeuer,birgit.demuth}@inf.tu-dresden.de

Abstract. OCL 2.0 specifies a standard library of predefined types and associated operations. A model-level representation of the library is required to reference its elements within the abstract syntax model created by an OCL parser. Existing OCL engines build this model in the implementation code which severely limits reusability, flexibility and maintainability. To address these problems, we show how a common pivot model with explicit support for template types can help to externalize the definition of the standard library and integrate it with instances of arbitrary domain-specific modeling languages. We exemplify the feasibility of our approach with a prototypical implementation for the Dresden OCL2 Toolkit and present a tailored EMF editor for modeling the OCL types and operations. We limit our discussion to the model level, i.e., we do not consider an implementation of the standard library for an execution engine.

1   Introduction

The Object Constraint Language (OCL) [1] specifies a standard library of types and associated operations. This includes primitive types such as **Integer** or **String**, collection types like **Set** or **Bag** as well as a number of special types which are important for the OCL type system (**OclAny**, **OclVoid**, and **OclType**). Among the predefined operations on these types are arithmetic, boolean and set-theoretic operations. All types in the standard library are instances of abstract syntax classes. These are located one level above the type definitions in the four-layered meta hierarchy of the OMG MOF architecture [2]. Since OCL allows querying of both metamodels and models, the standard types exist either on the M2 or the M1 layer.

Now, when building the abstract syntax model from a textual OCL expression, an OCL parser needs to have access to the elements of the standard library. This is necessary, for instance, to properly locate operations defined for the implicit supertype **OclAny** or to create user-defined collection and tuple types. Existing OCL engines, such as the current release of the Dresden OCL2 Toolkit [3] or the

H. Giese (Ed.): MoDELS 2007 Workshops, LNCS 5002, pp. 182–193, 2008.
© Springer-Verlag Berlin Heidelberg 2008

Kent OCL Library [4], usually build an internal representation of the standard library programmatically, e.g, using the API of a model repository.

Hiding the structure of the standard library inside the implementation code of the engine triggers a number of problems. First, the *reusability* of the library definition is severely impaired, because it is tied to a particular implementation language and platform. Porting the OCL engine to another programming language thus requires an entire rewrite of the code that creates the library. Second, the *flexibility* of the "in-code" approach is relatively low, because the model of the standard library cannot conveniently be validated, altered, extended, or modularized. This is disadvantageous if the underlying execution platform (i.e., an interpreter or code generator) does not support some of the standard library types and operations. In this case, adapting the library definition on the model level by removing the corresponding elements would be helpful. Finally, the implementation of the OCL engine tends to become fairly complex leading to decreased *maintainability*. For instance, the Dresden OCL2 Toolkit in its current release contains a helper class with more than 400 lines of code alone to manage the model of the standard library.

As an answer to these problems, we propose the novel approach of creating the OCL standard library as an instance of a so-called *pivot model*, which can be viewed as a "universal language covering a certain domain" [5]. In this paper, we define a pivot model as an intermediate metamodel used for aligning the metamodels of arbitrary domain-specific modeling languages (DSL) with that of OCL. By directly supporting *generics* in this metamodel, modeling all of the template types and operations in the OCL standard library becomes possible. We have implemented this approach using the Eclipse Modeling Framework (EMF) [6], which allowed us to build a highly functional editor for the pivot model and employ EMF's default XMI serialization capabilities. Providing the predefined OCL types within an OCL engine therefore reduces to a simple model file import. Concrete collection types can be created from the corresponding templates by binding their type parameters with the required element type.

The remainder of this paper is structured as follows: In Sect. 2, we briefly review the challenges for a model-level integration of the OCL standard library in the light of two existing OCL engines. We continue by describing the design of a suitable pivotal metamodel addressing these issues in Sect. 3. In Sect. 4, we present a practical evaluation of our approach. We highlight the visual editor used for modeling the standard library and describe an illustrative example. A brief account of related work is provided in Sect. 5. Finally, Sect. 6 concludes on our work and shows up further research.

2   Background

Based on observations from two well-known implementations of the OCL standard, namely the Dresden OCL2 Toolkit and the Kent OCL Library, we can identify two major challenges for a model-level integration of the standard library in an OCL engine. In brief, these are:

1. Operations and parameters in the standard library instantiate the corresponding metaclasses from the UML metamodel [7]. When OCL is integrated with domain-specific modeling languages developed within so-called language workbenches [8] or via UML profiles, we cannot rely on a common format for the library any more.
2. The standard library contains template types and operations that are parameterized with a type parameter. Most modeling languages do not support a declarative definition of these generic elements.

In the following, we will discuss these two issues in greater detail.

2.1   OCL for Domain-Specific Modeling Languages

In recent years, the importance of domain-specific languages (DSLs) for describing systems has increased and a convergence with model-driven approaches such as the OMG MDA initiative [9] can be witnessed [10]. As a result, the original scope of OCL being an add-on to UML [11] has widened to support constraints and queries over object-based modeling languages in general [12].

An obvious solution to these new challenges is the introduction of a pivotal metamodel that abstracts over the metamodels of arbitrary domain-specific languages and provides exactly those features required for an integration with OCL. Both of our reference OCL engines work this way. The Dresden OCL2 Toolkit in its current version employs a so-called *Common Model* [13] to adapt the metamodels of UML 1.5 as well as MOF 1.4, while the Kent OCL Library supports UML 1.4, Ecore (the metamodel used by EMF), and Java via a central *Bridge* model [14].

Unfortunately, both solutions fail to decouple the model of the OCL standard library from the adapted metamodel. In the Dresden OCL2 Toolkit, the predefined library operations and their parameters are instances of the corresponding UML or MOF metaclasses, while in the Kent OCL Library they instantiate metamodel-specific adapter classes. Both approaches demand a programmatic creation of the standard library types and operations. Consequently, to model the standard library externally, we need to find a way to instantiate these elements independently from any adapted metamodel.

2.2   Generics in the OCL Standard Library

The predefined collection types in the standard library are actually *template types* with the type parameter T [1, p. 144]. As an example, consider the sum operation of the OCL Collection type whose return parameter is typed with the element type of the collection. We say that a concrete type Collection(Integer) is created from the template Collection(T) by substituting, or *binding*, T with the type Integer. Since element types may be nested, there is an infinite number of collection types which have to be dynamically created when parsing a particular OCL expression.

However, not only types can have type parameters. Consider the product operation of `Collection(T)` which returns the cartesian product of two collections: `product(c2:Collection(T2)):Set(Tuple(first:T,second:T2))`. Note that the concrete signature of this operation (in particular, its return type) not only depends on the binding of the type parameter T, but also on the type of the argument c2. This is an example of a so-called *generic operation* [15]. Further note that the return type of the product operation is itself a template type, namely `Set(T)`, whose type parameter T is bound with the generic type `Tuple(first:F, second:S)`. The actual type of the type parameters F and S is determined at runtime, based on the binding for T and T2, respectively. In this case, we call T and T2 *type arguments* for the generic tuple type.

Finally, some of the predefined operations in the library have return types that depend on the object they are invoked on. Examples are `OclAny::asSet` (returning a singleton set containing the object) and `OclAny::allInstances` (returning the set of all instances of a type). Both operations have `Set(T)` as their return type, but the concrete binding for T cannot be determined until the source type of the operation call is known.

To remove the definition of the standard library from the implementation code and specify it declaratively, a mechanism to model generic types and operations is required. Moreover, the engine needs to support the binding of generic elements at runtime to dynamically create concrete types while parsing an OCL expression.

3   The Design of a Pivot Model with Generics Support

We are currently reengineering the Dresden OCL2 Toolkit to increase its reusability and flexibility and to provide the foundations for future research into the integration of OCL with arbitrary domain-specific languages. To this end, we have redesigned and reimplemented large parts of the toolkit's infrastructure [16]. The new architecture features a more flexible model repository adaptation mechanism. It is based on a pivot model that results from a careful analysis of previous approaches (cf. Sect. 2.1) and the `Core::Basic` package of UML 2.0. So far, we have integrated both EMF and the Netbeans Metadata Repository [17] and implemented bindings for Ecore, MOF and UML. The main elements of the new pivot model are shown in Fig. 1.

A comprehensive discussion of the new architecture is outside the scope of this paper. However, for a better understanding of the following paragraphs we would like to draw attention to one noteworthy feature that sets it apart from existing OCL implementations: A layered architecture now eliminates any dependencies from the pivot model to the OCL metamodel. Thus, the support for model-level generics, which we will describe below, is only an enabling technology for modeling the template types in the OCL standard library. All necessary functionality is already contained in the implementation of the pivot model metaclasses and can easily be leveraged for alternative model querying languages.

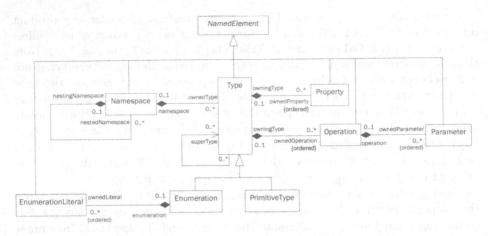

Fig. 1. The main elements of the pivot model

Figure 2 summarizes how the pivot model introduces template types and operations as first-class model entities. The design is loosely based on the generics support in EMF 2.3 [18] which closely mirrors the generic capabilities of Java 5 [15]. The key idea is to introduce a new abstraction called **GenericElement** which classifies elements that may contain one or several **TypeParameter**s.

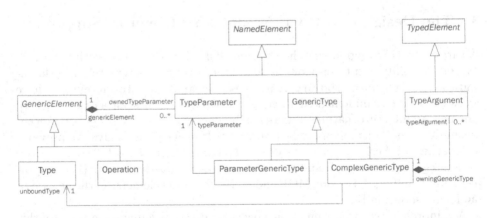

Fig. 2. Generics in the pivot model

The type parameters of a generic element may be *bound* with a concrete type, which means that all occurrences of the parameter in the definition of the generic element are replaced with this type (Fig. 3). In the case of a **Type** instance, this will affect all properties and operations (including their parameters) declared for this type.

In line with other metamodels, the pivot model generalizes properties, operations and parameters with an abstract metaclass **TypedElement** that declares

Fig. 3. Binding the type parameters of generic elements

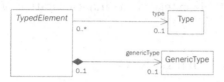

Fig. 4. Typed elements and generic types

a reference to a type. Now, as illustrated in Fig. 4, we allow typed elements to alternatively reference a `GenericType`. Generic types exist in two flavours (cf. Fig. 2). A `ParameterGenericType` simply references a `TypeParameter`, as in the case of the return parameter of the sum operation mentioned in Sect. 2.2. A `ComplexGenericType`, by contrast, references another Type with unbound type parameters as well as a number of `TypeArguments` that will replace the type parameters during binding. In the example of the `product` operation, the return parameter contains a complex generic type referencing the unbound type `Tuple(first:F,second:S)` and defining two type arguments T and T2. This example shows nicely that type arguments, being typed elements themselves, can have a generic type as well. Through this design, an unlimited nesting of generic types becomes possible.

It turns out that supporting generic types for typed elements does not suffice yet. Consider the OCL collection type `Sequence(T)`. This template type extends `Collection(T)`. Intuitively, binding type parameter T of `Sequence(T)` with a concrete type, say `String`, should result in `Sequence(String)` extending `Collection(String)`. Yet, the design developed so far does not cover this special case. The key observation here is that the two type parameters T are not the same. In fact, it is perfectly legal to label the type parameter of the sequence type with S instead of T. Correctly binding both subtype `Sequence(S)` and supertype `Collection(T)` requires S to be a `TypeArgument` of `Collection(T)`. This intuition leads to the introduction of a new association between `Type` and `GenericType` denoting the generic supertypes of a type (Fig. 5). Then, binding a type will cause all generic supertypes to be bound as well. If all type parameters of a generic super type are bound (i.e., it is not generic any more), it can be safely added to the regular `superType` reference list (cf. Fig. 1).

Fig. 5. Generic supertype

On a side note, it is worth highlighting that in contrast to EMF, our pivot model does not know the notion of a *raw type*, i.e., a "fallback" type that is assumed to exist for any type parameter in an unbound generic type. This is a direct consequence of our aim to avoid any dependencies from the pivot model to the OCL metamodel. Otherwise, OclAny as the root of the OCL type system would have been a logical choice. To guarantee proper type conformance checking, we have suitably extended the implementation of the OCL collection metaclasses instead.

4   Practical Evaluation

The previous section presented the design of a pivot model with explicit support for generics. Now, we can proceed with showing its application. We have realized the new infrastructure of the Dresden OCL2 Toolkit as a set of Eclipse plug-ins. To create implementation classes for the pivot model elements, we employed the metamodeling and code generation facilities of the Eclipse Modeling Framework. This yielded the following advantages:

1. Except for some behavioral features that have to be implemented manually, the pivot model implementation generated by EMF is already fully functional and can be instantiated. Contrary to previous approaches, we do not depend on an integration with a particular DSL to create an instance of the OCL standard library. By realizing the same interfaces, our standard library model is compatible with any metamodel binding that is created for the pivot model.
2. The XMI serialization capabilities of EMF enable us to effectively save and load the standard library which improves reusability.
3. EMF can generate a highly customizable tree editor for a metamodel. In the next section, we show how a heavily adapted version of the default pivot model editor allows the user to conveniently view, edit and alter the model of the standard library.

4.1   Visually Modeling the OCL Standard Library

Figure 6 partly shows the model of the standard library in the adapted pivot model editor. This model, which contains all types and operations defined in the OCL 2.0 specification, is part of the new toolkit infrastructure. Users may, however, replace the default library with a modified version when integrating a new domain-specific language with the engine. For instance, if a DSL does not know the concept of an ordered set, the OrderedSet type can be safely removed from the library model. This ensures that all valid abstract syntax models created by a parser will indeed execute on the domain-specific target platform.

The look and feel of the pivot model editor resembles that of the EMF Ecore editor. However, we have simplified the modeling of generics to hide complexity from the user. When creating typed elements (properties, operations, and parameters), declared type parameters of the containing generic element show

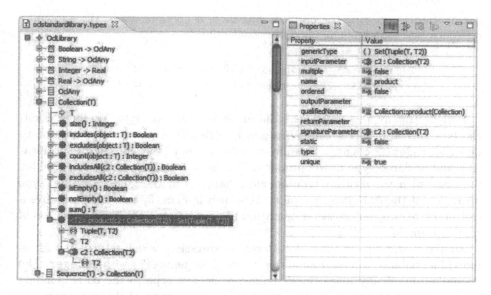

Fig. 6. The model of the OCL standard library

up in the list of possible types. The editor automatically creates the necessary **ParameterGenericType** instance in this case. If a template type is selected (e.g., for the **c2** parameter of the **product** operation), a complex generic type and corresponding type arguments are added. Similarly, the editor allows to specify the type arguments when extending generic supertypes.

The root of the model is an instance of a special facade interface called **OclLibrary**, which provides the necessary means for an OCL parser to retrieve the predefined standard library types when building the abstract syntax model from an OCL expression.

4.2 Binding Template Types during OCL Parsing

In the following, we demonstrate the feasibility of our approach with a simple example that involves the binding of generic OCL collection types while parsing an OCL expression. Figure 7 depicts the model we will base the example scenario on.

Now, consider the following OCL expression which specifies the derived attribute **totalBalance** in class **Person**. Note that the second invocation of the

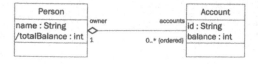

Fig. 7. The example model

dot operator (accessing the property **balance** of all elements in the **accounts** reference list) represents an implicit *collect* iterator.

```
context Person::totalBalance : int
derive: self.accounts.balance->sum()
```

Parsing this expression triggers the following template type bindings: First, the type of the property call expression referring to **accounts** is evaluated to be **OrderedSet(Account)**. This directly stems from the multiplicity specification and declared type of the property. The actual binding of the **OrderedSet** template with the element type **Account** happens in the **getOrderedSetType** operation of the **OclLibrary** facade. As shown in Sect. 3, this solely requires a call to the **bindTypeParameter** operation implemented in the **Type** metaclass of the pivot model.

Similarly, the type of the *collect* iterator expression, which returns the list of individual balance values, results from binding **Sequence(T)** with **Integer**. The engine automatically maps the domain-specific **int** type to the corresponding OCL standard library type. As a result, the return type of the **sum** operation becomes **Integer**. To conclude this discussion, Fig. 8 shows the abstract syntax model of the example expression as it is visualized in the DSL-agnostic model browser that is part of the new toolkit infrastructure. Notice that not only the **Sequence** template has been bound, but also its generic supertype **Collection(T)**.

It is worth highlighting here that the method presented in this paper solely addresses the static structure of the OCL standard library. To realize the dynamic semantics and actually execute the expression in Fig. 8, we still rely on an *instance-level* (M0) implementation of the predefined types and operations. To this end, we have redesigned the existing Java library of the Dresden OCL2 Toolkit to support a flexible integration of arbitrary DSLs via a set of factory interfaces. In addition, an OCL interpreter based on the new infrastructure has been developed to complement the components on the model level.

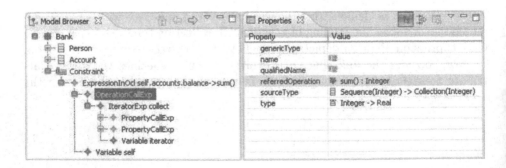

Fig. 8. The abstract syntax model of the example expression

5   Related Work

To the best of our knowledge, there is no published work that deals with the model-level integration of the OCL standard library as described in this paper. Akehurst et al. [12] hint at this possibility, but simply suggest to import a UML package containing the standard library types. Therefore, they do not address the problems outlined in Sect. 2. However, they propose a mechanism to detach the implementation of the standard library types and operations on the *instance level*. The ideas from this work may complement our approach and further simplify the integration of different domain-specific languages.

Another technique that aims at aligning OCL with custom domain-specific languages on the instance level has been presented in [19]. Unfortunately, the authors employ a custom expression language that is akin but not equal to OCL. Furthermore, they build on top of a model management framework and execution engine which does not support a model-level integration of the standard library.

Lastly, the latest release of the Eclipse MDT OCL project [20] features a highly innovative way of integrating OCL with different modeling languages. Instead of a pivot model, a generic environment interface defines type parameters for all metamodeling concepts required by OCL. Unfortunately, this otherwise elegant approach necessitates a concrete specialization of the entire OCL metamodel as well as the OCL standard library for each custom DSL binding. The predefined operations of the standard types have to be created within the implementation code yielding the disadvantages highlighted in Sect. 1.

6   Conclusions and Future Work

In this paper, we have presented a novel technique for integrating the OCL standard library on the model level. Contrary to previous approaches, we support a declarative rather than a programmatic definition of the predefined types and operations thereby improving reusability, flexibility, and maintainability. In addition, our method eases the integration of different domain-specific languages with OCL, because the pivot model provides an intermediate abstraction layer for a variety of metamodels. Therefore, instantiating elements of the library model is independent of a particular DSL binding and solely requires a suitable implementation of the pivot model interfaces. We have demonstrated the feasibility and usefulness of our approach through an example that was realized using newly developed components of the Dresden OCL2 Toolkit.

We are currently working on porting the tools of the Dresden OCL2 Toolkit to the new infrastructure. Our aim is to leverage the increased flexibility provided by our approach for other OCL-based languages defined by the OMG. Examples are the *Query/View/Transformation* (QVT) [21] language and the upcoming *Production Rule Representation* (PRR) [22] standard. This may open up interesting perspectives for areas as diverse as model transformation and business rule execution.

Finally, our solution still faces some limitations that are worthwhile to address. For instance, our pivot model currently lacks the expressive power to model the iterator expressions for the OCL collection types. In fact, detaching the definition of iterators requires a different approach altogether since the corresponding well-formedness rules for the abstract syntax are currently heavily intertwined with the concrete syntax. Similarly, we have not yet found a satisfying answer to the problem of binding generic operations whose return type depends on contextual information (e.g., `allInstances` and `asSet` in `OclAny` or `flatten` in the collection types). Even though we are able to model the signature of these operations, we still have to check for them explicitly in the code. Thus, the implementation of the OCL abstract syntax elements (M2) still contains a few details of the standard library structure (M1).

Acknowledgment. The authors would like to thank Florian Heidenreich, Christian Wende and Steffen Zschaler for their fruitful discussions and contributions to the Dresden OCL2 Toolkit.

References

1. Object Management Group (OMG): Object Constraint Language, Version 2.0 (2006)
2. Object Management Group (OMG): Meta Object Facility (MOF) Core Specification, Version 2.0 (2006)
3. Technische Universität Dresden, Department of Computer Science: (Dresden OCL Toolkit), http://dresden-ocl.sourceforge.net
4. University of Kent at Canterbury, Department of Computing: (Kent Object Constraint Language Library), http://www.cs.kent.ac.uk/projects/ocl
5. Kappel, G., Kapsammer, E., Kargl, H., Kramler, G., Reiter, T., Retschitzegger, W., Schwinger, W., Wimmer, M.: On Models and Ontologies - A Layered Approach for Model-based Tool Integration. In: Mayr, H.C., Breu, R. (eds.) Proceedings of Modellierung 2006, GI-Edition, Innsbruck, Austria, March 22-24, 2006. Lecture Notes in Informatics (2006)
6. Budinsky, F., Steinberg, D., Merks, E., Ellersick, R., Grose, T.J.: Eclipse Modeling Framework, 1st edn. Eclipse Series. Addison Wesley Longman, Amsterdam (2003)
7. Object Management Group (OMG): Unified Modeling Language: Superstructure Specification, Version 2.0 (2005)
8. Fowler, M.: Language Workbenches: The Killer-App for Domain Specific Languages? White Paper (2005),
   http://www.martinfowler.com/articles/languageWorkbench.html
9. Object Management Group (OMG): MDA Guide Version 1.0.1 (2003),
   http://www.omg.org/docs/omg/03-06-01.pdf
10. Bézivin, J., Jouault, F., Kurtev, I., Valduriez, P.: Model-Based DSL Frameworks. In: Companion to the 21st Annual ACM SIGPLAN Conference on Object-Oriented Programming, Systems, Languages, and Applications, OOPSLA 2006, Portland, Oregon, USA, pp. 602–616. ACM Press, New York (2006)
11. Warmer, J., Kleppe, A.: The Object Constraint Language, Getting Your Models Ready for MDA, 2nd edn. Object Technology Series. Addison-Wesley Longman, Amsterdam (2003)
12. Akehurst, D., Howells, W., McDonald-Maier, K.: UML/OCL – Detaching the Standard Library. In: Proceedings OCLApps 2006: OCL for (Meta-) Models in Multiple Application Domains, MoDELS/UML 2006, Genova, Italy, pp. 205–212 (2006)

13. Loecher, S., Ocke, S.: A Metamodel-Based OCL-Compiler for UML and MOF. Electronic Notes in Theoretical Computer Science, 43–61 (2004)
14. Akehurst, D., Patrascoiu, O.: OCL 2.0 – Implementing the Standard for Multiple Metamodels. Electronic Notes in Theoretical Computer Science, 21–41 (2004)
15. Bracha, G.: Generics in the Java Programming Language. Technical report, Sun Microsystems (2004),
    http://java.sun.com/j2se/1.5/pdf/generics-tutorial.pdf
16. Bräuer, M.: Design and Prototypical Implementation of a Pivot Model as Exchange Format for Models and Metamodels in a QVT/OCL Development Environment. Technical report, Technische Universität Dresden (2007)
17. Netbeans.org: Metadata Repository (MDR) (2003)
18. Merks, E., Paternostro, M.: Modeling Generics With Ecore. In: EclipseCon 2007, Santa Clara, California, USA, IBM Corp. (2007) (Tutorial Slides),
    http://www.eclipsecon.org/2007/index.php?page=sub/&id=3845
19. Kolovos, D.S., Paige, R.F., Polack, F.A.: Towards Using OCL for Instance-Level Queries in Domain Specific Languages. In: Proceedings OCLApps 2006: OCL for (Meta-) Models in Multiple Application Domains, MoDELS/UML 2006, Genova, Italy, pp. 26–37 (2006)
20. Eclipse.org: (Model Development Tools (MDT) OCL component),
    http://www.eclipse.org/modeling/mdt/?project=ocl
21. Object Management Group (OMG): Meta Object Facility (MOF) 2.0 Query/View/Transformation (QVT) Specification (2005)
22. Object Management Group (OMG): Production Rule Representation Request For Proposal Draft 1.0 (2003)

Evaluation of OCL for Large-Scale Modelling: A Different View of the Mondex Purse

Emine G. Aydal, Richard F. Paige, and Jim Woodcock

University of York, UK
{aydal,paige,jim}@cs.york.ac.uk

Abstract. OCL is used to add rigour to UML/MOF models, and in particular can be used to express behavioural details (e.g., operation pre- and postconditions, class invariants) of such models. The applicability and utility of OCL can be assessed by applying it to realistic applications and by investigating its capabilities both in terms of language characteristics and tool support. With this in mind, in this paper we model functional requirements for the Mondex Smart Card Application using UML Diagrams, demonstrate how system invariants as well as operation pre- and post-conditions are specified in OCL, and explore the degree to which OCL tool support can be used to create and validate these models. Moreover, we discuss how these pre- and post-conditions can be validated, in part by discussing how test cases can be selected from the OCL specifications created.

1 Introduction

The Unified Modeling Language (UML) is accepted as a de facto standard for software and system modelling. It offers a rich set of notations for modeling both the static and dynamic aspects of an object-oriented system [5]. The Object Constraint Language (OCL), developed by Warmer as a business modeling language within IBM [10], is a declarative language that can be used to describe model behaviour, as well as metamodel constraints.

In this paper we present an exemplar of system modelling, using OCL together with UML. This is carried out for the purposes of evaluating the utility of OCL for realistic systems modelling. The evaluation is in terms of both the language and its existing tool support. Moreover, we also consider how the constraints, pre- and postconditions specified in OCL can be validated, via an overview of strategies for selecting test cases from models.

The system we model using UML and OCL is the Mondex Smart Card Application. We thus commence with an overview of the system under investigation.

1.1 Mondex Smart Card Application

The Mondex Smart Card Application, also known as Mondex Purse, is a global electronic payment scheme providing digital form of cash and coins. It offers

H. Giese (Ed.): MoDELS 2007 Workshops, LNCS 5002, pp. 194–205, 2008.

immediate transfer of value without signature, PIN or transaction authorization between card holders in currencies allowed [2].

Mondex is an important step also in the implementation of the Grand Challenge Programme, i.e., a multi-national, long-term, research programme that aims to create a substantial and useful body of code that has been verified to the highest standards [3]. One of the main objectives of this programme is to populate a repository of formally specified and verified codes that are useful in practice and serve as examples for the future applications. The first case study proposed to be included in this repository is the Mechanical Verification of Mondex. Different groups are involved in Mondex Challenge globally and produced distinct versions of the software by using different modeling/specification languages. A group at the Massachusetts Institute of Technology used Alloy; the University of Southampton applied Event-B; a group at the University of Bremen used OCL; Escher Technologies chose Perfect Developer; RAISE is used at the University of the United Nations Macao and the Technical University of Denmark; and finally Z is used by a group at the University of York [3]. The work from all these groups was based on the monograph that outlined the specifications, refinement and proof details of Mondex in Z [4]. It is important to note that this monograph focused on a subset of the actual requirements, so as to concentrate on security/mission-critical requirements.

In this study, we have followed a different path than the studies mentioned above and started by creating the model of the system from informal requirements detailed in [2]. By doing so, we covered some of the functional requirements that were omitted in [4] as well as all the other studies based on this monograph.

The main goal of our study is to test some of the formally verified versions of Mondex by using model-based testing techniques and tools. Formal verification brings a significant amount of trust to the produced code, but it is a very long and rigorous process. Significant amount of time is spent in writing the formal specifications and verifying the systems correct, therefore it would be beneficial if the testing time can be reduced by generating effective test cases by using the models created early in the process. Successful implementation of this study would also demonstrate the invaluable contribution of model-based testing in a more formal context.

1.2   Contribution

The main contribution of the paper lies within the complicated details of the modelling and the validation stage of a real life software application, Mondex Smart Card Application. We present the difficulties encountered whilst specifying the model behaviour with OCL by using the USE tool. Frame variables, messaging between objects, derived attributes, constants are some of the concepts we discuss in detail. We also explain how the system invariants and pre-/post-conditions of operations are handled, and how the system is validated by using the scenario-based technique. This technique is based on automatic snapshots technique introduced by Gogolla et al in [7] and [8]. Automatic snapshots technique has only been applied to invariants so far.

In this paper, we also explore the relationship between testing and the use of OCL, and explain our plans in extending the technique mentioned above to cover pre-/post-conditions with the aim of test data selection. When achieved, this new approach may allow testers to carry out the test data selection process during modelling instead of implementation stage, thus reduce the time for testing and provide a language-independent form for test cases.Whilst explicating these, we demonstrate how the tool chosen for this study is used and what sort of improvements are required to make the process more efficient.

In the rest of this report, the modelling stage of the experiment is explained in Section 2. Section 3 focuses on how scenario-based validation of the model is carried out in this study and how techniques used in validation can be applied to test data selection. Finally, Section 4 outlines the lessons learned and provide concrete suggestions to the issues mentioned throughout the paper.

2   Modelling Mondex Smart Card Application

In this experiment, we have modeled the system by making use of UML diagrams. We have created use case diagrams, use case scenarios, class and state diagrams of the system. To strengthen the meaning of our diagrams and to specify the system constraints as well as pre/postconditions of operations, we used OCL expressions. Our current system consists of 8 classes, 31 operations, 30 invariants and 197 pre/postconditions. This number excludes utility classes such as *Date* and their associated operations.

In the first phase of modelling, we separated the system into broadly defined modules that address different functions of the system. Brief descriptions of these modules are given below.

Payment deals with the functional requirements related to money transfers.
Logging   records the transactions and the errors.
Recovery   handles the exceptions in case of a failure during a payment.
Currency Management   deals with the currency-related features.
Operational Control   manages the authentication-related issues.
Data Display and Customisation   lets the user to view and customise certain data held by the Purse.

We then created use case diagrams and complemented each diagram with well-defined scenarios. Each scenario is also linked to relevant modules and requirements. Before creating further UML Diagrams, we searched for modeling tools that allowed defining the invariants and pre-/post-conditions in OCL. We considered *OCL Compiler by University of Dresden (OCLCUD)* which is a tool that can be used independently as the OCL compiler or as part of the free UML modeling tool Argo/UML, *UML Specification Environment (USE)*, which is a tool implemented by Mark Richters in University of Bremen, where the models, invariants, pre-/post-conditions can be specified textually, and *OCL Compiler*, produced by Cybernetic Intelligence GMBH, that analyses OCL expressions which appear in the UML model. There are other OCL-compatible tools such as *Octopus* by Klasse Objecten; *KeY* by University of Karlsruhe, Chalmers University of Technology, Gothenburg, and the University of Koblenz; *OCLE* by Babes Bolyai University; *ModelRun* by BoldSoft(Borland).

Most of the tools listed are capable of syntactic checking of OCL Expressions and verification of Invariants for a given instance of the model. In addition to these, they all have additional features addressing different needs such as generation of Java code from OCL expressions, providing compliancy with MOF, etc. After careful consideration, we decided to use the tool *USE* especially due to its capabilities in generating automatic snapshots of the system and in validating pre-/post-condition through scenarios. It also allows the creation of re-usable artifacts through series of commands saved in files.

After having selected the tool, we have defined the class diagram and focused on the invariants of the system. Table 1 lists some of the invariants and respective OCL expressions considered during this stage.

Table 1. Examples to Invariants

Inv. Name	Invariant Desc.
iCurrList	The currency assigned to a pocket must be included in the currency list of the purse. inv iCurrList: avCurrencies->includesAll(pockets.currency)
iTransferLimit	The transfer limit cannot exceed the transfer limit ceiling value. inv iTransferLimit: self.TransferLimit <= self.TransferLimitCeiling
iNoException	Number of exceptions logs is fixed. inv iNoException: exceptionlogs->size() <= cNoException
iDefPocket	At a given time, number of the default pockets is at most one. inv iDefPocket: pockets->select(Default=true)->size() = 1
iNoPocket	Each purse can hold several currencies. Each currency is held in a different pocket and the number of pockets is fixed for a given purse. inv iNoPocket: pockets->size() <= cNoPocket

Invariants

The USE tool does not provide a consistency check for the invariants, i.e., there is no way of verifying whether there are conflicting and inconsistent invariants. However, one of the features the tool provides is that it can check whether all the invariants hold for an instance of the model. In addition,the USE tool does not allow the user to create incorrect bindings between objects. For instance, if the user attempts to create a link between two objects where no association is defined or if the link being created conflicts with the multiplicity rules, then the tool gives immediate warning. The invariant check list is also updated after each action, and therefore the user gets immediate feedback from the tool about the current status of the system.

In this study, we created instances of our model where all the invariants are satisfied. This gave us the confidence that there are no conflicting invariants. However, we are aware that there may still be *restricting* invariants, i.e., the effect of some invariants may be stronger than others in which case further refinement may be required. For example, if invariant x states that $a > 0 \wedge a < b$ and a second invariant reads $a < c$ where $c < b$, then clearly second invariant actually restricts the borders defined by the first invariant and the variable a can only be in the range $[0,c]$ when these two invariants are combined. One may think that as long as the invariants are satisfied, the *restricting* invariants would not cause a problem. However, one of our plans in testing our model is to use the invariants as our test data selection criterion and clearly the range of variables is of crucial value in such a process.

After having created the invariants, we have formed a traceability matrix in order to trace the relation between requirements, modules, use cases, constants and invariants. The traceability matrix has revealed the requirements that have been missed out or those that need to be addressed in a later stage.

Pre-/Post-conditions

In the next stage of system modelling, we focused on pre- and post-conditions of the operations. The states of the system are also taken into account since not all the operations are allowed in different states of the system. One down side of the tool used is that it is not possible to use state-related functions such as the one shown in Version1 below, therefore, in order to introduce the states of the system to our model, we created a *state* variable to our main class and checked the value of this variable each time we needed to check the state of the system, as shown below.

pre Version1: self.oclInState(Unlocked)
pre Version2: self.LockingState = 'Unlocked'

Another issue encountered at this stage is the distinct set of variables used in the definition of the pre- and post-conditions, because each operation requires or restricts the modification of different variables. These variables are also called the *frame variables* [5]. Post-conditions must not only describe all the changes to frame variables, but also make sure that frame variables that do not change are mentioned as unchanged. This second factor revealed some of the missing post-conditions. For instance, the fourth and the fifth post-conditions written for the operation *EraseExceptionLog*, listed in Table 2, are found as the result of this consideration.

One of the assumptions taken at this point is that all the variables except frame variables stayed unchanged during the course of the operation. For the example given in Table-2, we only mentioned the frame variables in the post-conditions and did not create post-conditions in the form of $a = a@pre$ for the rest of the variables. We believe the recognition of this concept in OCL (and UML) tools would help to prevent the post-condition-related errors caused by this assumption.

Another point of concern addressed during the determination of post-conditions has been the *messaging* issue. OCL provides *HasSent* (' ˆ ') operator to allow communication between operations [6]. This operator is used

Table 2. Operation : EraseExceptionLog()

context MondexPurse:: EraseExceptionLog(p_SequenceNumber : Real) : Boolean

pre EraseExceptionLogPre1:
     self. PurseProviderFlag = true
 pre EraseExceptionLogPre2:
     self.LockingState = 'Unlocked' or self.LockingState = 'Locked'
 pre EraseExceptionLogPre3:
     exceptionlogs->select(SequenceNumber = p_SequenceNumber)->size()= 1

post EraseExceptionLogPost1:
     exceptionlogs->size() = exceptionlogs@pre->size() - 1
 post EraseExceptionLogPost2:
     exceptionlogs->select(SequenceNumber = p_SequenceNumber)->size()= 0
 post EraseExceptionLogPost3:
     self._NumberOfUnusedExceptions = self._NumberOfUnusedExceptions@pre + 1
 post EraseExceptionLogPost4:
     self.LockingState = self.LockingState@pre
 post EraseExceptionLogPost5:
     self.PurseProviderFlag = self.PurseProviderFlag@pre

when an operation x is called during the execution of another operation y and postcondition of y returns true only if the operation x returns true. The USE tool does not recognise the *HasSent* operator, therefore, we extend the frame of the callee operation by adding the frame of the called operation. Table 3 presents an example to how *HasSent* operator is used in our case study.

In this example, the operation *ChangePersonalCode* returns true if the personal code is changed and required actions are carried out. However, if at the end of the operation, the personal code does not seem to have changed,i.e., the purse user has entered the code incorrectly more than the times allowed, then the purse is expected to lock itself out by calling *ChangeTheStateToLockedOut* and as a result, *ChangePersonalCode* returns false. In our model, we reflected

Table 3. An example of how *HasSent* operator is handled

context MondexPurse::ChangePersonalCode() : Boolean

post ChangePersonalCodePost1:
     % Personal Code changes, desired affects are applied and operation returns true.
     or
     (PersonalCode = PersonalCode@pre and
        self ^ ChangeTheStateToLockedOut() and
        result = false)

...or
     (PersonalCode = PersonalCode@pre and
        self._ NumberOfIncorrectEntries = self.PersonalCodeAttempts and
        self.LockingState = 'LockedOut' and
        result = false)

this by inserting the post-conditions of *ChangeTheStateToLockedOut* operation into the post-conditions of *ChangePersonalCode* operation. This technique, as mentioned above, enlarges the frame variables set of *ChangePersonalCode* by adding the variables *_NumberOfIncorrectEntries* and *PersonalCodeAttempts*. In addition to this, to support the workaround further, in the scenarios written for the validation of pre-/post-conditions of operations, we created nested calls to operations, therefore when a new operation is called from within an operation, the preconditions of called operation are checked automatically.

3   The Validation and Test Data Selection

Pre- and post-conditions determine the accessibility and validity rules for a given operation. Their contribution to a software development process is invaluable not only in modeling and implementation phases, but also in testing.

In [9], Korel et al introduced a test data generation technique where the test case specification is defined in terms of *assertion violation*. According to [9], finding an assertion violation may reveal a fault in the program, a faulty pre-condition or an erroneous assertion. They tackle the problem of finding program input on which an assertion is violated by reducing it to finding program input on which a selected statements is executed. In this study, one of our aims is to use pre- and post-conditions as test data selection criterion early in modelling phase instead of waiting for the code to be produced in implementation phase. With this idea in mind, the following section presents how the validation of pre- and post-conditions is being done in our experiment. We then discuss our plans in extending these validation activities to test data selection.

Scenario-based Validation of Pre/Post-conditions

The objective of this process is to present that given the right inputs, the system can enter and exit operations successfully. In other words, the strength of the pre- and post-conditions are well balanced, so that the access to/exit from operations are not prevented by too strong pre-/post-conditions. To address this issue, we make use of the operation execution capability of USE tool. The tool allows the user to check pre-/post-conditions by calling an operation on an instance of the model. The pre-conditions are checked when the *openter* command is executed. If the pre-conditions are satisfied, the operation is put into call stack. After the execution of the statements between enter and exit points, the tool checks the post-conditions and the return value when the *opexit* command is run. Further details about these operations are given in [1].

During this experiment, we first formed a base object model of the system that satisfies all the invariants to ensure that the scenarios are built on top of a valid state of the system. We then examined the type of commands required in a scenario and found the following categories:

- Setting/Creation of frame variables/objects/operation parameters
- Access to the operation with the correct list of parameters on a given object

– Modification/Deletion of frame variables/objects
– Exit the operation with return value

Note that the term *scenario* is used instead of a *snapshot* in this study. We use the term snapshot for a randomly created object model of the system where as the scenarios are defined in such a way that they serve a purpose. The scenarios can also be seen as tuned versions of snapshots that satisfy a property. Table 4 gives the scenario created to satisfy the pre- and post-conditions of the *EraseExceptionLog()* function given in Table 2. As shown in Table 4, we first created a new exception log record and linked it to Purse1. Other variables related to state and user of the purse are also set according to the preconditions of the operation. After entering the operation, the log is erased and the number of unused exceptions is incremented by one.

Table 4. Scenario for the validation of EraseExceptionLog()

Operation	<EraseExceptionLog.cmd>
Setting The Frame Variables	! create exLog1 : ExceptionLog ! set exLog1.SequenceNumber :− 100 ... ! insert(Purse1,exLog1) into Exception ! set Purse1.PurseProviderFlag := true ! set Purse1.LockingState := 'Unlocked' ! set Purse1.. NumberOfUnusedExceptions := 6
Enter the operation	! openter Purse1 EraseExceptionLog(100)
Modification of Frame Variables	! destroy Purse1.exceptionlogs->select(SequenceNumber=100) ! set Purse1.. NumberOfUnusedExceptions := 7
Exit the operation	! opexit true

The commands in Table 4 are collected in EraseExceptionLog.cmd file. Analogous to this operation, the scenarios for the rest of the operations are also created as .cmd files and are executed in USE command line. After each execution, the invariants of the system are also checked in order to avoid any plausible conflict.

The drawback of this process was that we had to find the frame variables set as well as the right values for these variables to satisfy the targeted assertions. The next section explains our plans in making this process more automatic by using the pre/post-conditions as a way of selecting test data for the system.

Test Data Selection

The main purpose of writing pre-/post-conditions is to ensure the correct functioning of the system by checking the status of the system on the entry and exit point of the operations. Within this context, in this section, we explain our plans using pre-/post-conditions in the selection of test data with the aim of exercising the system in crucial points to find faulty situations.

In [7] and [8], Gogolla et al present how to integrate ASSL (*A Snapshot and Sequence Language*) elements to generate scenarios. They also generate test cases that exercise certain invariants and *validation* cases that proves that no scenario can be found that satisfies the negated version of an invariant.

We plan to apply this technique to the pre-/post-conditions of our system. One big advantage is that there will be scenarios that satisfy a negated version of a pre-/post-condition and these scenarios will still be valid for the system. For instance, the user may attempt to run an operation that can not be run in the current state of the system. In such a case, the pre-condition of the operation must fail and the system must inform the user of the situation. This is a perfectly valid scenario that can be generated by negating a pre-condition and introducing it as a property to be satisfied.

One main difference of our plan in applying the technique outlined in [7] seems to appear in mapping pre-/post-conditions to the scenarios. Table 5 shows an example to this mapping in the case of *EraseExceptionLog* operation.

Table 5. Mapping between Scenario View and Operation View

SCENARIO VIEW	OPERATION VIEW
! insert(Purse1,exLog1) into Exception	pre: exceptionlogs-> select(SequenceNumber = p_SequenceNumber)->size()= 1
! set Purse1.PurseProviderFlag := true	pre : self.PurseProviderFlag = true
! set Purse1.LockingState := 'Unlocked'	pre : self.LockingState = 'Unlocked'
! destroy Purse1.exceptionlogs-> select(SequenceNumber = 100)	post : exceptionlogs->size() = exceptionlogs@pre->size() - 1 post : exceptionlogs->select (SequenceNumber = p_SequenceNumber) ->size()= 0
! set Purse1._NumberOfUnusedExceptions := 7	post : self._NumberOfUnusedExceptions = self._NumberOfUnusedExceptions@pre+1

The second column presents the *Operation View* where the pre-/post-conditions of the operation are defined where as the first column, *Scenario View*, gives the statements that match the respective pre-/post-conditions in a scenario. As shown in Table 5, the mappings concerning value check, such as the ones in the second and third row, are straightforward. On the other hand, the ones that involve addition or deletion of an association or an object require more thorough understanding of the semantics which makes the mapping rather complicated. This issue is further discussed in Section 4.

The following section summarises the lessons learned so far and outlines the suggestions addressing the improvements of OCL tools, particularly USE tool, to cater for the requirements mentioned in this paper.

4   Conclusion

In this paper, we have presented our experience with the USE tool in modeling and validating Mondex Purse by using UML diagrams and OCL expressions. We believe that OCL is indispensable for use with UML in describing model behaviour and finding evidence for model validation. Especially after having monitored the scenario-execution capabilities for pre-/post-conditions provided by USE, based on OCL, we see great potential for OCL to be also used in test data selection context.

Other OCL- and tool-related observations made during this study are listed below under various subtitles.

Invariants. The invariants are well integrated into the model structure in USE tool. We believe the existence of a *invariant consistency check* component in OCL tools will greatly improve the process of validation by removing the necessity to create the instances of a model and shorten the process of re-checks when invariants are modified.

Constants. The constants for a system may be fixed in a later stage of the development or even during application loading. It would be helpful to be able to differentiate constants from variables in the modeling stage and to have a user interface similar to the invariants screen, where system constants are listed.

Derived Attributes. OCL supports the definition of derived attributes, but this concept is hardly integrated into the tools. To overcome this problem, we created invariants ensuring the right values of derived attributes. However, to remove the task of creating extra, invariant-like structures, the tools must handle the automatic setting/modification of derived attributes.

Frame Variables. We believe that the integration of the concept of frame variables into OCL tools would enhance the process of pre-/post-condition determination. This is also supported by Kassios on his recent work that focuses on dynamic frames and dependencies [12]. Implementation and integration of dynamic frames to current OCL tools may introduce a new era for pre-/post-condition handling. The idea of including all the variables involved in an operation also supports the idea of completeness of the pre/post-conditions for an operation. Once this new scheme is introduced, OCL tools must also guarantee that variables except the frame variables do not change during the course of an operation by checking the pre and post states of the objects without the user intervention.

HasSent (^)Operator. As mentioned in Section 2, *HasSent* operator is used when an operation x is called during the execution of another operation y and postcondition of y returns true only if the operation x returns true. This operator is beneficial for both keeping track of function flow and for checking the pre-/post-condition consistency between two operations. Especially to reveal the infeasible/unreachable functions, the addition of this feature to OCL tools has utmost importance. We believe the tool developers can make use of the *Inline function* concept in implementing this operator in OCL tools.

Pre-/Post-conditions and Scenarios. It is our belief that the technique introduced for finding scenarios for invariants in [7] and [8] has great potential for adjustment to pre-/post-conditions in the context of test data selection. However, there are several issues that needs careful consideration.

As observed in Table 5, mapping from Operation View to Scenario View is not a trivial task in many cases. In fact, there is a third layer where Pascal-like ASSL procedures are used in generating several objects, links by using loops, and a fourth layer where these procedures, invariants and scenarios are actually executed. Figure 1 is a simplified version of a deployment diagram given in [7].

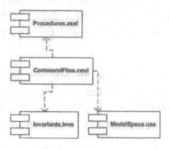

Fig. 1. Deployment Diagram for USE

In the components given in Figure 1, we can observe three syntactically different languages. The *.use* file contains the definition of classes, associations, invariants, pre-/post-conditions. The definition of classes and associations are specific to USE tool, but the definition of invariants and pre-/post-conditions are written in OCL. The *.invs* file also contains invariants written in OCL. These invariants do not hold for all the states of the system, but are necessary in generating scenarios with specific properties. The *.assl* files provide the procedure definitions used in generating n number of objects that may be linked to other objects. Finally, the *.cmd* file provides the means of communicating with the tool by loading/reading other files and is specific to USE.

Although these components seem to target different objectives, their functionalities overlap. For instance, in ASSL, if an instance of the association *paymentlogs* will be created between the objects MondexPurse1 and PaymentLog1, the syntax reads *Insert(paymentlogs,[MondexPurse1],[PaymentLog1]*, where as the same effect would be produced if the following command is run in USE Command line: *!insert(MondexPurse1,PaymentLog1) into paymentlogs*. We believe that it is crucial to minimise such syntactical differences between semantically-similar languages especially if they are used in collaboration with each other. The alternative and the ideal solution would be to create a uniform integrated language that is compliant with UML, OCL and other related OMG standards.

In addition, assertion-accepting programming languages such as Spec# and JML toolset can also be taken into account in formalising the *scenario description language*. These languages are used in implementation level, but it would definitely be beneficial for model-based software development and testing if this level of compliancy and compatibility between the scenario description language (ASSL and USE commands in our case), constraint language (OCL) and modeling language (UML) can be achieved in the modeling stage.

Last words. As mentioned in [11], besides improved tool support and a clear and concise language description, OCL would benefit from more convincing examples and application scenarios. We believe our experience and findings will help to shed light to future users of UML and OCL, as well as tool developers, and we will continue to report further observations on the matter.

References

1. Gogolla, M., Richters, M.: Using the UML Specification Environment(USE) (2002), http://citeseer.ist/psu.edu/531031.html
2. Introduction to Mondex Purse Operation, Tech. report., Mondex International Limited (1999), https://mol.mastercard.net/mol/molbe/public/login/ebusiness/smart_cards/mondex/
3. Woodcock, J., Banach, R.: The Verification Grand Challenge, Computer Society of India Communications (2007)
4. Stepney, S., Cooper, D., Woodcock, J.: An Electronic Purse: Specification, Refinement and Proof. Oxford University Computing Laboratory, Tech Report (2000)
5. Sendall, S., Strohmeier, A.: Specifying System Behaviour in UML, Technical Report DI/00/343, EPFL (2000)
6. Warmer, J., Kleppe, A.: The Object Constraint Language, Getting Your Models Ready for MDA, Wesley (2003)
7. Gogolla, M., Bohling, J., Richters, M.: Validation of UML and OCL Models by Automatic Snapshot Generation. In: Stevens, P., Whittle, J., Booch, G. (eds.) UML 2003. LNCS, vol. 2863, Springer, Heidelberg (2003)
8. Gogolla, M., Buettner, M., Richters, M.: USE:UML Specification Environment for Validating UML and OCL, Science of Computer Programming (2006)
9. Korel, B., Al-Yami, A.M.: Assertion-oriented automated test data generation. In: Proceedings of the 18th International Conference on Software Engineering (ICSE), pp. 71–80. IEEE, Los Alamitos (1996)
10. The Object Constraint Language (viewed 06/2007), http://www.um.es/giisw/ocltools/ocl.htm
11. Baar, T., Chiorean, D., Correa, A., Gogolla, M., Hussmann, H., Patrascoiu, O., Schmitt, P.H., Warmer, J.: Tool Support for OCL and Related Formalism - Needs and Trends, Technical Report, MODELS 2005 (2005), http://www.db.informatik.uni-bremen.de/publications/Baar_2005_OCLWS.ps
12. Kassios, I.T.: Dynamic Frames: Support for Framing, Dependencies and Sharing without Restrictions, In: FM 2006, pp. 208-283 (2006)

Second International Workshop on Models@run.time

Nelly Bencomo[1], Robert France[2], and Gordon Blair[1]

[1] Computing Department, Lancaster University., InfoLab21,
Lancaster, UK, LA1 4WA
[2] Computer Science Department, Colorado State University
Fort Collins, CO, USA, 80523-1873
{nelly,gordon}comp.lancs.ac.uk, france@cs.colostate.edu

Abstract. The second edition of the workshop Models@run.time was co-located with the ACM/IEEE 10th International Conference on Model Driven Engineering Languages and Systems. The workshop took place in the lively city of Nashville, USA, on the 2nd of October, 2007. The workshop was organised by Nelly Bencomo, Robert France, and Gordon Blair and was attended by at least 25 people from 7 countries. This summary gives an overview of the presentations and lively discussions that took place during the workshop.

Keywords: model-driven engineering, reflection, run-time systems.

1 Introduction

Research on model-driven software development has mainly focused on the use of models at design, implementation, and deployment stages of development. This work has produced relatively mature techniques and tools that are currently being used in academia and industry. However, the use of model-driven approaches for validating and monitoring run-time behaviour can also produce significant benefits. A key benefit is that models can be used to provide a richer semantic base for runtime decision-making related to system adaptation and other runtime concerns. For example, models can be used to help determine when a system should move from a consistent architecture to another consistent architecture. Model-based monitoring and management of executing systems can also play a significant role as we move towards implementing the key self-* properties associated with autonomic computing (i.e. self-management, self-optimization, self-healing, and self-protection)[3].

Goal

The goal of this workshop was to understand the relationship between models produced during development and models used to support and enable run-time monitoring and adaptation of software. Key research topics of the workshop were (1) to study how models produced during development can be effectively leveraged during run-time, (2) how model-driven approaches can be applied to managing and monitoring the execution and operation of systems, (3) to what extent can model-driven engineering be used to tame the complexity of developing and managing

H. Giese (Ed.): MoDELS 2007 Workshops, LNCS 5002, pp. 206–211, 2008.
© Springer-Verlag Berlin Heidelberg 2008

adaptive software. This is the second in a series of MODELS workshops on this topic. The workshop successfully brought together researchers from different communities including researchers working on model-driven software engineering, software architectures, computational reflection, adaptive systems, autonomic and self-healing systems, and requirements engineering. At least twenty-five people attended from France, Germany, Norway, South Korea, The Nertherlands, UK and the US.

The call for papers invited submissions on a number of focus topics including: relevance and suitability of different model-driven approaches to monitoring and managing systems during run-time, compatibility (or tension) between different model-driven approaches, the role of reflection in maintaining the causal connection between models and run-time systems, experience related to the use of run-time models to adapt software systems, and the management and modelling of runtime variability using models.

In response to the call for papers, nine (9) papers were submitted, of which (6) papers were accepted. Each submitted paper was reviewed by at least 3 program committee members. After discussions two papers were selected as the best papers. The decision took into account the relevance of the papers to the goals of the workshop, the impact on the discussion and results, and the quality of the papers and presentations. These two papers were extended and improved taking into account the discussions and conclusions of the workshop and are published in this proceeding.

2 Workshop Format

The workshop was designed to facilitate focused discussion on the use of models during run time. It was structured into presentation and work (discussion) sessions. The opening presentation was given by Nelly Bencomo and Robert France. Nelly set the context of the workshop describing the general goal and presented the results of the 1st edition of the workshop in MODELS'06 [2] and the related workshop M-ADAPT (Model-driven Software Adaptation) at ECOOP'07 [1]. Robert continued by describing the specific goals of the second edition of the workshop and stating key questions to kick off the discussion and call for the inspiration and motivation needed during the rest of the day. After the opening presentation, the paper sessions followed. There were 6 papers divided in 3 sessions.

The workshop was structured into presentations during the morning and discussion sessions in the afternoon. During the presentation session, papers were presented by two speakers, the first speaker was an author of the paper and the second speaker (reader) was an independent reader. Second readers provided another view on the contents of the paper, placing it in relation to the workshop topics and research questions.

To ensure effectiveness of the format of the workshop, presentations were limited to 25 minutes, 15 minutes presentation by the first speaker, 5 minutes by the second reader and 5 minutes for questions. Presentation sessions were cochaired by Oystein Haugen and Arnor Solberg. After the presentations, specific research interests and questions were discussed. The partial results of this discussion were used to split the participants into two groups to allow focused debate and dialogue during the afternoon. The workshop was closed by a final discussion, including an evaluation of the workshop itself made by the attendees. Details of the sessions are provided in Sections 3 and 4 below. The workshop proceeded smoothly, with all attendees keenly contributing through constructive and friendly debate. Attendees enjoy and praised the idea of the second readers.

3   Session Summaries

The 6 papers were divided into the following three categories according to their topics and contributions:

Error detection and Self Healing
- "*A Modeling Framework for Self-Healing Software Systems*", by Michael Jiang, Jing Zhang, David Raymer, and John Strassner, second reader: Jules White
- "*Model-Based Run-Time Error Detection*", by Jozef Hooman, and Teun Hendriks, second reader: James Hill

Monitoring and Verification
- "*System Monitoring using Constraint Checking as part of Model Based System Management*", by Christian Hein, Tom Ritter, and Michael Wagner, second reader: Matthias Gutheil
- "*AMOEBA-RT: Run-Time Verification of Adaptive Software*", by Ji Zhang, Betty Cheng, and Heather Goldsby, second reader: Jozef Hooman

Techniques and Approaches
- "*Coherent Support for Models at Run-Time through Orthogonal Classification*", by Atkinson Colin and Matthias Gutheil, second reader: Olivier Barais
- "*Control-theory and models at runtime*", by Pierre-Alain Muller and Olivier Barais, second reader: Aniruddha Gokhale

Robert and Nelly took notes of specific questions and topics raised during the presentations. After the presentations, individual questions made by the participants were gathered. Following the questions stated by the attendees and the notes taken by Robert and Nelly, discussions groups were established. Attendees left the room to start the exchange of ideas over meals.

4   Discussions

After lunch each group came into the room and shared ninety minutes of lively discussions. Both groups addressed different topics. The first group discussed the *infrastructure* needed to support *the use of models during runtime*. The second group focused on *theoretical concepts and languages needed to define and work with models during runtime*. Slides summarizing the reports were produced by the leader discussant of each breakout session (Oystein Haugen and Jules White respectively). As the two breakout groups reassembled to summarize their work it is worthy of note that the ideas of the paper "Control theory and models at runtime" by Muller and Barais had influence on both discussion groups.

Summary of discussion in the "Infrastructure Group"

The discussions in this group focused on what support is needed to effectively support the use of models during runtime. As a first step, the ways in which models were used in the papers presented at the workshop were discussed. The papers presented at the workshop mainly focused on *verification* (Zhang et al., Hein et al.), *error detection and correction* (Hooman et al.), and *self-healing* (Jiang et al.). In this context, runtime models specify the expected behaviours of the running application. These techniques use a "supervisor component" which observes the system in order to detect any deviation from its expected behaviour. Any deviation reveals a failure in the running application. If the objective is verification or error detection, the failure is reported to the user. In the case of self-healing, the supervisor automatically adapts the running application.

Philippe Lahire, one of the participants, suggested that a model@runtime is a model that is coupled with a controller that uses information from a running system to perform some control on the running system. The controller can be viewed as a separate model or can be considered to be part of the runtime model. The functionality provided by a controller is linked to the type of information captured in the runtime model, which, in turn, is tied to the type of adaptation supported by the model. He suggested that it would be useful to classify the properties that a runtime model must have to support particular types of adaptations (e.g., self-healing, self-protection) in the context of particular types of systems (e.g., information, embedded, distributed systems).

The discussions also led to the identification of other uses of runtime models. For example, runtime models can be used to support adaptation to environment changes, runtime updating of system components, or the graceful degradation of some functionalities. For each kind of adaptation, specific runtime models have to be defined. For example, in the case of adaptation to a changing environment, the models have to capture the variation points of the application and define rules to choose the appropriate variants according to the information coming from the environment. In the case of runtime updates of components, the model could capture the dependencies between running components and rules to safely upgrade them.

Given that there are various purposes for models at runtime (and corresponding types of models), the discussions then focused on identifying a common infrastructure to support the use of runtime models. The papers presented at the workshop (and the examples that came up in the discussions) all included a "supervisor component" around the runtime model. This component is called "runtime awareness" in the work of Hooman et al. and identified as the Observer/Controller pair in the control theory analogy proposed by Muller et al.. The supervisor component monitors data coming from the running application, makes decisions based on the observations and performs required adaptations on the running application. The supervisor thus consists of three activities: *Observe*, *Decide*, and *Adapt*.

For observation, the supervisor needs access to data coming from the running system. These data can be the inputs and outputs of the system but access to system internal data or environment information might also be required. For decision-making, the supervisor processes the information collected by observation using a decision model. This model defines appropriate responses for specific behaviours of the system. If needed, the decision can either lead to a user notification or trigger an adaptation of the running application.

Adaptation in this context, consists of changing the running system at runtime. It is not required for all systems and it cannot always be automated. In some cases, for example, error detection, debugging and verification, the user is notified and is responsible for modifying the system.

Summary of discussion in the "Concepts and Languages Group"

To start their discussions, this group considered it was pertinent to define what a model at runtime means. The group came up with the following definition: *"an abstraction at a higher level of representation than code that is used to derive adaptation through monitoring and feedback mechanisms."*

Using this concept, several use cases for models were identified.

- Model-based recovery
- System management
- Models for feedback
- Models for manipulating variability
- Determining what instrumentation to generate
- Models as an interface to a system rather than code manipulation

The group also concluded that current technologies like interceptors, AOP, constraint logic programming, control theory, and model checking techniques are useful to support the use of runtime models. This means that there is no need to come with new technologies in a short term.

Reflection was, as in the first edition of this workshop, stated as a capability needed when dealing with models to monitor and drive the execution of systems. In this sense, runtime models would be used to manipulate the system itself using introspective and intercession capabilities. It was discussed that the concept of meta-level would perhaps be interpreted in a different way in the context of models at runtime. Until now, meta-programming and reflection have been studied mainly at the coding level. At this point an open research question arised: what would be the parallel at the modelling level? The comparison would seem to be allowing the meta-model to change at runtime in order to adapt to new requirements or quality of service specifications. The above would require the meta-model to be continuously evaluated and understood during execution. This was contrasted with the current approach where a meta-model is interpreted somehow statically with no updates once the system starts. It was also pointed out that performance is an issue to take into account when using reflection. The ideas expressed by Pierre-Alain and Olivier paper about control theory seems to fit nicely with what was discussed.

As the two breakout groups reassembled to summarize their work and exchange reached conclusions, it was interesting to see how both groups identified dynamic software adaptation as a significant research area where the use of models at runtime can be useful. In this context, models can be used to (i) manipulate the system itself, e.g., adding a component to the model has the effect of changing the underlying code; and (ii) verify the behaviour of the system during execution (using for example reflection).

Final Remarks

A general wrap-up discussion was held at the end of the workshop. The organizers asked for feedback on the workshop and a number of useful ideas were suggested. Attendees confirmed that they were very pleased with the papers, presentations and discussions carried out during the workshop. The inclusion of second readers was considered successful and useful. It was concluded that the research community should be encouraged to continue the study the issues related to models at runtime and its relevance for the development of seld-adaptive systems. It was suggested that the organizers should consider the presentation of small demos that show the use of models at runtime in a possible next edition of this workshop. The workshop was closed with a warm "thank you" from the organizers to all participants for a successful workshop. After the workshop finished many of the attendees went for a well deserve dinner to continue talking.

Acknowledgments. We would also like to thank the members of the program committee who acted as anonymous reviewers and provided valuable feedback to the authors: Betty Cheng, Fabio M. Costa, Federal University of Goias, Brazil, Van Den Berg Aswin, John C. Georgas, Gang Huang, P.F.Linington, Andrey Nechypurenko, Eugenio Scalise, Rui Silva Moreira, Arnor Solberg, Marten van Sinderen, Thaís Vasconcelos Batista, Jules White. We also would like to thank Aniruddha Gokhale, Oystein.Haugen, Jim Hill. We specially thank to Philippe Lahire, Jeff Gray, Franck Fleurey, and Heather Goldsby for the feedback and ideas provided for this summary. Last but not least, the authors of all submitted papers are thanked for helping us making this workshop possible.

References

1. Blair, G., Bencomo, N., France, R., Cebulla, M.: Proceedings of the First Workshop on Model-driven Adaptation (M-ADAPT 2007) at ECOOP 2007, Bericht Nr. 2007 - 10 (2007)
2. Blair, G., Bencomo, N., France, R.: Summary of the Workshop Models@run.time at MoDELS 2006. In: Nierstrasz, O., Whittle, J., Harel, D., Reggio, G. (eds.) MoDELS 2006. LNCS, vol. 4199, Springer, Heidelberg (2006)
3. Kephart Jeffrey, O., Chess David, M.: The Vision of Autonomic Computing. In: IEEE Computer, pp. 41–50. IEEE Computer Society Press, Los Alamitos (2003)

AMOEBA-RT: Run-Time Verification of Adaptive Software *

Heather J. Goldsby, Betty H.C. Cheng**, and Ji Zhang

Department of Computer Science and Engineering
Michigan State University, 3115 Engineering Building
East Lansing, Michigan 48824 USA
{hjg,chengb,zhangji9}@cse.msu.edu

Abstract. Increasingly, software must dynamically adapt its behavior in response to changes in the supporting computing, communication infrastructure, and in the surrounding physical environment. Assurance that the adaptive software correctly satisfies its requirements is crucial if the software is to be used in high assurance systems, such as command and control or critical infrastructure protection systems. Adaptive software development for these systems must be grounded upon formalism and rigorous software engineering methodology to gain assurance. In this paper, we briefly describe AMOEBA-RT, a run-time monitoring and verification technique that provides assurance that dynamically adaptive software satisfies its requirements.

1 Introduction

Increasingly, software must adapt its behavior in response to changes in the supporting computing, communication infrastructure, and in the surrounding physical environment [1]. As such, extensive work has been done to develop adaptation mechanisms and infrastructure to enable dynamic adaptation at run time [1]. In addition, a number of research projects have been investigating software engineering techniques to support dynamic adaptation [2,3,4,5,6,7]. Assurance that the adaptive software correctly satisfies its requirements is crucial if the software is to be used in high assurance systems, such as command and control or critical infrastructure protection systems. We previously introduced the Adapt-operator extended Linear Temporal Logic (A-LTL) [8] to formally specify adaptation properties for adaptive software. We consider adaptive software to be a system comprising a number of steady-state programs and adaptations among these steady-state programs. Specifically, a *steady-state program* is a non-adaptive program suited for a specific set of environmental conditions, and an *adaptation* is a transition from one steady-state program (the *source program*) to another

* This work has been supported in part by NSF grants EIA-0000433, CNS-0551622, CCF-0541131, IIP-0700329, CCF-0750787, Department of the Navy, Office of Naval Research under Grant No. N00014-01-1-0744, Siemens Corporate Research, and a Quality Fund Program grant from Michigan State University.
** Corresponding author.

H. Giese (Ed.): MoDELS 2007 Workshops, LNCS 5002, pp. 212–224, 2008.
© Springer-Verlag Berlin Heidelberg 2008

steady-state program (the *target program*). [1] For our approach, the developer specifies the adaptation properties, designs the steady-state programs and the adaptations among these steady-state programs, and then executes the adaptive system. In this paper, we describe AMOEBA-RT a run-time monitoring and verification technique to verify that dynamically adaptive software adheres to A-LTL and LTL properties.

Our objective is to provide assurance that an adaptive system adheres to its critical *adaptation properties* that can be expressed in A-LTL and LTL. Model checking is an attractive means to verify that every possible path through a system adheres to functional properties. Recent research efforts have demonstrated the use of static *model checking* to verify critical properties in adaptive software [7, 9]. We previously developed the AMOEBA model checker [10] that modularly verifies A-LTL and LTL adaptation properties in adaptive software, thereby, significantly reducing the complexity of model checking of adaptive software. However, as the scale and thus complexity of adaptive programs increase, model checking techniques encounter the *state explosion problem*, where the size of the program's state space is far greater than that which can be effectively analyzed. Thus, even modular static model checking techniques are insufficient to provide assurance that a complex adaptive program adheres to its adaptation properties. Run-time verification [11, 12, 13, 14] is an attractive complement to static verification. Run-time verification monitors executions of a software system and uses a model checker to verify that the behavior of a software system adheres to a set of formal specifications, including temporal logic properties. Since only one execution path is examined at a time, assurance is provided and yet the state explosion problem is effectively avoided. Currently, to the best of our knowledge, there does not exist a run-time model checker that verifies adaptation properties specified in A-LTL and LTL.

In this paper, we introduce AMOEBA-RT, an A-LTL and LTL run-time model checker for adaptive software. In AMOEBA-RT, the run-time state information of an adaptive program is collected and analyzed at run time for adherence to the formal specifications. To that end, the adaptive software program is instrumented using an aspect-oriented approach [15] to collect run-time state information. As such, the aspect-oriented approach is non-invasive, meaning that the source code for the adaptive software is not directly altered. At run-time, the instrumented code sends the collected state information to a run-time model checking server that runs as a separate process in parallel. The run-time model checking server uses an automaton-based approach to determine whether the state information received from the adaptive program satisfies the adaptation properties specified in A-LTL and LTL.

AMOEBA-RT has been used to verify and detect execution errors in a number of adaptive components in wireless communication and distributed data processing applications, including an adaptive Java pipeline program [10]. The remainder of the paper is organized as follows. In Section 2 we provide background information on the adapt-operator extended LTL, three commonly-used adaptation semantics, and the analysis of adaptation properties. In Section 3, we briefly introduce the AMOEBA-RT architecture.

---

[1] These definitions provide an abstract specification of adaptive system behavior. The adaptive system may be realized through a variety of adaptation mechanisms, such as those mentioned in [1]. Additionally, control theory may be used to implement the adaptive system provided that all of the adaptations and steady-state programs have been identified prior to deployment.

In Section 4, we illustrate the run-time verification using the adaptive Java pipeline example. Lastly, Section 5 summarizes the paper and discusses future work.

2 Specifying Adaptation Properties

This section describes the formal specification language used to specify adaptation properties, A-LTL, and illustrates how A-LTL can be used to specify commonly occurring adaptation semantics. AMOEBA-RT can then check for adherence to these adaptation properties at run-time.

To specify adaptation requirements, we previously proposed A-LTL (Adapt operator-extended LTL) [8], an extension to LTL with the adapt operator ($\xrightarrow{\Omega}$). Informally, a software program satisfying "$\phi \xrightarrow{\Omega} \psi$" (read as ϕ adapts to ψ with adaptation constraint Ω) means that the program initially satisfies ϕ, and at a certain state A, it fulfills all the obligations demanded by ϕ and stops being constrained by ϕ, and in the next state B, starts to satisfy ψ, where ϕ and ψ are two temporal logic formulae. The state sequence (A, B) satisfies Ω, where Ω is an LTL formula evaluated on a sequence of two states. Formal details of A-LTL may be found elsewhere [8].

Based on results presented in the literature [16, 17, 18] and our own experience [19], we summarize three commonly-used semantics for adaptation. We assume that the local properties of the source program and the target program have both been specified in LTL. We specify the adaptation from the source program to the target program with A-LTL. For some adaptations, the source/target program behavior may need to be constrained during the adaptation process. For example, a source program may need to stop receiving incoming packets in order to clear the data buffer.

We assume the adaptive system has moderate *computational reflection* capability [20], i.e., it is aware of its adaptation and the currently running steady-state program. This capability can be achieved by simply introducing *flag propositions* in the program to identify its current steady-state program or adaptation status. We assume that a decision maker system component is available to translate environment changes into specific adaptation requests. Our specification technique describes the expected program behavior in response to these requests. We use an atomic proposition A_{REQ} to represent the receipt of an adaptation request from the decision maker.

In the following, we summarize three commonly occurring basic adaptation semantic interpretations from the literature [16, 17, 18, 19] specified in terms of A-LTL. There are potentially many other adaptation semantics. In all three adaptation semantics, we denote the source and the target programs local properties as S_{SPEC} and T_{SPEC}, respectively. If applicable, the restriction condition during adaptation is R_{COND}. We assume that the flag propositions are included in the program specifications. We use the term *fulfillment states* to refer to the states where all the obligations of the source program are fulfilled (i.e., S_{SPEC} is satisfied), thus making it safe to terminate the source behavior and ensuring that the system does not become inconsistent. We illustrate these semantics using a GSM-oriented audio streaming encoding and decoding protocol, which is a signal processing-based forward error correction protocol. There are two participants in this protocol, the sender and the receiver. Each participant has two encoding/decoding programs: GSM(1,2), which should be used when loss rate is low, and GSM(1,3), which should be used when loss rate becomes high. The global invariant is that all packets should be encoded using GSM. An extended version of this example is presented in [9].

One-Point Adaptation. Under one-point adaptation semantics, after receiving an adaptation request A_{REQ}, the program adapts to the target program T_{SPEC} at a certain point during its execution. The prerequisite for one-point adaptation is that the source program S_{SPEC} should always eventually reach a fulfillment state during its execution.

$$(S_{SPEC} \wedge \Diamond A_{REQ}) \xrightarrow{\Omega} T_{SPEC}. \tag{1}$$

Formula 1 states that the program initially satisfies S_{SPEC}. After receiving an adaptation request, A_{REQ}, it waits until the program reaches a fulfillment state, i.e., all obligations generated by S_{SPEC} are satisfied. Then the program stops being obligated to satisfy S_{SPEC} and starts to satisfy T_{SPEC}. This adaptation semantics is explicitly or implicitly applied by most approaches (e.g., [16, 17, 19]) to deal with simple cases that do not require constraining the source behavior or overlapping the source and target behavior. For example, once the loss rate becomes high, the sender and receiver immediately adapt from GSM(1,2) to GSM(1,3).

Guided Adaptation. Under guided adaptation semantics, after receiving an adaptation request, the program first constrains its source program behavior by a restriction condition, R_{COND}, and then adapts to the target program when it reaches a fulfillment state. This semantics is suitable for adaptations whose source programs do not guarantee reaching a fulfillment state within a given amount of time. The restriction condition should ensure that the source program will finally reach a fulfillment state.

$$(S_{SPEC} \wedge (\Diamond A_{REQ} \xrightarrow{\Omega_1} R_{COND})) \xrightarrow{\Omega_2} T_{SPEC}. \tag{2}$$

Formula 2 states that initially S_{SPEC} is satisfied. After an adaptation request, A_{REQ}, is received, the program should satisfy a restriction condition R_{COND} (marked with $\xrightarrow{\Omega_1}$). When the program reaches a fulfillment state of the source, the program stops being constrained by S_{SPEC}, and starts to satisfy T_{SPEC} (marked with $\xrightarrow{\Omega_2}$). The *hot-swapping* technique introduced by Appavoo *et al* [16] and the safe adaptation protocol [19] use the guided adaptation semantics. For example, once the loss rate becomes high, the sender waits until its buffer is empty (the restriction condition) and then transfers from GSM(1,2) to GSM(1,3). The receiver transfers from GSM(1,2) to GSM(1,3) when it receives the first packet encrypted using GSM(1,3).

Overlap Adaptation. Under overlap adaptation semantics, the target program behavior starts before the source program behavior stops. During the overlap of the source and the target behavior, a restriction condition is applied to safeguard the correct behavior of the source and target programs. This adaptation semantics is appropriate for the case when continuous service from the adaptive system is required. The restriction condition should ensure that the source program reaches a fulfillment state.

$$\begin{aligned}&\left((S_{SPEC} \wedge (\Diamond A_{REQ} \xrightarrow{\Omega_1} R_{COND})) \xrightarrow{\Omega_2} true\right) \\ &\wedge \left(\Diamond A_{REQ} \xrightarrow{\Omega_1} (T_{SPEC} \wedge (R_{COND} \xrightarrow{\Omega_2} true))\right). \end{aligned} \tag{3}$$

Formula 3 states that initially S_{SPEC} is satisfied. After an adaptation request, A_{REQ}, is received, the program should start to satisfy T_{SPEC} and also satisfy a restriction condition, R_{COND} (marked with $\overset{\Omega_1}{\longrightarrow}$). When the program reaches a fulfillment state of the source program, the program stops being obliged by S_{SPEC} and R_{COND} (marked with $\overset{\Omega_2}{\longrightarrow}$). The *graceful adaptation protocol* introduced by Chen *et al* [17] and the *distributed reset protocol* introduced by Kulkarni *et al* [18] use the overlap adaptation semantics. For example, once the loss rate becomes high, the sender immediately transfers from GSM(1,2) to GSM(1,3). However, the receiver executes both GSM(1,2) to GSM(1,3) in parallel until all of the packets encoded using GSM(1,2) have been processed.

3 Run-Time Model Checking

Run-time model checking has been proposed as a means to gain the verification benefit of model checking while avoiding the state explosion problem. In general, run-time verification monitors the run-time behavior of a software system and checks its conformance to a requirements specification defined as a temporal logic property [21]. During the execution of the software, an execution trace is generated and analyzed by a model checker to verify its conformance to the formal specification. A common implementation of run-time model checkers [11, 12, 13, 21, 14] is to use a property automaton running in parallel with the adaptive software. Given a formal specification, the *property automaton* is constructed in such a way that it accepts exactly the set of executions that satisfy the specification.

In this paper, we propose AMOEBA-RT, which extends the AMOEBA model checker [10] with support for run-time verification of adaptation properties A-LTL and LTL. AMOEBA-RT is designed to gain the verification benefit of model checking for complex adaptive systems, while avoiding the state explosion problem. Specifically, AMOEBA-RT provides a means to continuously monitor and verify the behavior of a software system either during development or after the system has been deployed. When an error is detected, the software may either file an error report, or attempt to repair the error automatically. AMOEBA-RT has two primary capabilities: First AMOEBA-RT uses an aspect-oriented technique to produce execution traces by instrumenting and monitoring the executing adaptive software. Second, AMOEBA-RT uses a run-time model checker to verify that the adaptive software adheres to its adaptive properties. In the following, we provide additional details about each capability.

3.1 Run-Time Monitoring

AMOEBA-RT instruments the adaptive system to achieve run-time monitoring. Figure 1 depicts the overall architecture of AMOEBA-RT. The instrumented code collects information about the run-time state of the adaptive software and transmits the information to the run-time model checking server. The instrumentation is achieved using *AspectJ* [15], an aspect-oriented extension to the Java programming language. In AspectJ, each crosscutting concern is defined in an *aspect* comprising *pointcuts* and *advice*. A *pointcut* identifies a set of points (named *join points*) in a program, such as invocations of a certain function, assignments to a certain variable, etc. An *advice* comprises the type of the advice (*before*, *after*, or *around*), a set of pointcuts, and a code segment. A before/after advice causes the AspectJ compiler to insert the code segment before/after every join point in the program matched by the pointcuts. An around advice causes the AspectJ compiler to replace the join points matched by the pointcuts with the code segment. Our AMOEBA-RT instrumentation defines pointcuts around method calls that indicate a change in run-time state and uses advice to collect the state information and transmits it to the run-time model checking server. Currently, the developer must identify the relevant method calls and define pointcuts and advice for each adaptation.

Our approach is non-invasive in that the AspectJ compiler compiles the Java source files and an aspect file specifying the instrumentation, and then generates instrumented Java bytecode files. The Java bytecode files are then executed on a general JVM. During run-time, the instrumentation code collects run-time state information and sends the information to the run-time model checking server in sequence. When the adaptive program terminates, an end of execution message ('EOE') is attached to the end of the sequence and sent to the run-time model checking server.

3.2 Run-Time Analysis

As depicted in Figure 1, the AMOEBA-RT run-time model checking server checks the conformance of the sequence of state information received from the instrumented code with the adaptation requirements specified in A-LTL/LTL. Specifically, the model checker uses a property automaton running in parallel with the adaptive software. Given an A-LTL/LTL specification, the A-LTL interpreter generates a *property automaton*, which is an automaton that accepts exactly the set of executions that satisfy the A-LTL/LTL specification. Therefore, the model checker accepts the execution trace generated by the executing adaptive software if and only if the trace satisfies the specification.

AMOEBA-RT constructs a property automaton for the property being verified by extending the logic rewrite rules introduced by Bowman and Thompson [22]. In the property automaton, each node comprises two fields, 'p' and 'q,s' where p is a propositional logic formula indicating the condition satisfied by the node itself, and q is an A-LTL formula indicating the property that must be satisfied by its next states. The next

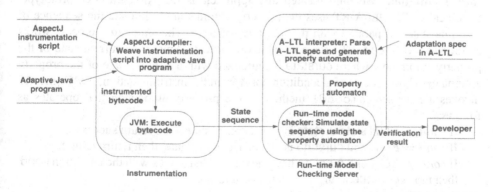

Fig. 1. The dataflow diagram for AMOEBA-RT verification

nodes $t_1, t_2, \cdots, t_k$ of a node s are non-overlapping, i.e., the p values of these nodes are logically disjoint. Therefore, the property automata constructed are deterministic, i.e., we can always choose the appropriate next node based on the conditions in the current state. If a run-time execution path is accepted by the property automaton, then it satisfies the specification. In this way, the property automaton serves to verify a given execution sequence at run-time.

Formally, a *property automaton* is a tuple (S, S_0, T, P, N), where: S is a set of states. S_0 is a set of initial states where $S_0 \subseteq S$. $T : S \rightarrow 2^S$ maps each state to a set of next states. $P : S \rightarrow proposition$ represents the propositional conditions that must be satisfied by each state. $N : S \rightarrow formula$ represents the conditions that must be satisfied by all the next states of a given state.

Given a set of A-LTL/LTL formula Φ, we generate a property automaton $PROP(\Phi)$ with the following features: For each member $\phi \in \Phi$, create an initial state $s \in S_0$ such that $P(s) = true$, $N(s) = \phi$. Let pe, p_i, and q_i be propositional formulae. For each state $s \in S$, let the partitioned normal form [22] of $N(s)$ be $(pe \wedge empty) \vee \bigvee_i (p_i \wedge \bigcirc q_i)$, then it has a successor $s'_i \in S$ for each p_i field with $P(s'_i) = p_i$ and $N(s'_i) = q_i$. The $(pe \wedge empty)$ part of the partitioned normal form depicts the condition when a sequence is *empty*, where $empty \equiv \neg \bigcirc true$ [22], and pe is a proposition that must be true when the state is the last state. In the $\bigvee_i (p_i \wedge \bigcirc q_i)$ part of the formula, the propositions p_i partitions $true$ (i.e., the propositions p_i are mutually exclusive), and q_i is the corresponding condition that must hold when p_i holds in the current state.

A path of a property automaton is an infinite sequence of states $s_0, s_1, \cdots$ such that $s_0 \in S_0$, $s_n \in S$, and $s_i, s_{i+1} \in T$, for all i ($0 \leq i < n$). We say a path of a property automaton $s_0, s_1, \cdots$, *simulates* an execution path of a program $s'_1, s'_2, \cdots$, if $P(s_i)$ *agrees with* s'_i for all i ($0 < i$). We say a property automaton *accepts* an execution path from initial state $s \in S_0$, if there is a path in the property automaton starting from s that simulates the execution path. It can be proved [10] that the property automaton constructed above, from initial state $s \in S_0$, accepts exactly the set of executions that satisfy $N(s)$.[2] Thus, we are able to use the property automaton to verify that an execution path satisfies Φ.

Implementation. We implemented this approach as the AMOEBA-RT prototype. Specifically, AMOEBA-RT uses the property automaton to simulate the sequence of run-time states in parallel with the adaptive software. The simulation process works as follows: AMOEBA-RT uses a variable curstate to denote the current state of the property automaton, where curstate is initialized with the initial state of the property automaton. Upon receipt of a condition cond from the instrumentation, AMOEBA-RT invokes a moveNext(cond) method of the property automaton that operates as follows:

- If $cond = EOE$ and curstate is an accepting state, then return success.
- If $cond = EOE$ and curstate is not an accepting state, then return failure.
- If $cond \neq EOE$ and curstate has a next state that agrees with the condition cond, then move curstate to the next state and return success.

---

[2] We ignore the eventuality constraint [23] (a.k.a self-fulfillment [24]) at this point. However, later steps will ensure eventuality to hold in our approach.

– If $cond \neq EOE$ and curstate does not have a next state that agrees with the condition cond, then return failure.

If the property automaton returns *success* at the end of an execution trace, then the execution trace adhered to the A-LTL property. Otherwise, if a violation of the property automaton is encountered, the run-time model checking server returns *failure*, and the state sequence (i.e., a counter-example) is recorded in a bug report. The bug report may first be used to alert a human operator that the system requires immediate attention [12]. Second, the bug report is analyzed by the developers. If the bug report describes valid behavior, then the property must be corrected. If the bug report describes incorrect system behavior, such as an invalid adaptation, then the developer must modify the system itself, e.g., by disallowing the invalid adaptation.

Run-time verification occurs at run time. The overhead incurred by the instrumentation code includes the evaluation of monitored state conditions and the transmission of these conditions to the run-time model checking server. Its effect on the performance of the run-time adaptive system depends on the density of the instrumentation points, the number of conditions to be monitored at each point, and the encoding of the conditions to be transmitted. In our experiments, the performance overhead incurred by run-time verification is largely imperceptible ($< 1\%$).

4   An Illustrative Example

In some multi-threaded Java programs, such as proxy servers, data are processed and transmitted from one thread to another in a pipelined fashion. The Java pipeline is implemented using a pair of piped I/O classes, which can be **synchronous** (i.e., the pipeline waits for a response) or **asynchronous** (i.e., the pipeline continues to receive data) functions. Previously [25] we have studied optimization techniques and proposed an asynchronous Java pipeline design to be run on a multi-processor machine. By eliminating synchronization overhead, the asynchronous version gains a speed up rate of 4.83 over the synchronous implementation when the CPU load is low [25]. However, when the CPU load is high, the synchronous implementation performs better. The data transmission is achieved by accessing shared buffers. A sync buffer and an async buffer are used for the synchronous and asynchronous pipeline components, respectively. Previously, we have constructed an adaptive version of the Java pipeline classes where the system can monitor CPU workload and use an adaptation decision maker to select the optimal implementation for specific run-time conditions.

We specify the adaptation requirements for the adaptive Java pipeline program in A-LTL as follows. Before adaptation, the system (i.e., the source program) is required to input data from the synchronized pipeline in response to the outputs. That is, for each output data x in the synchronous mode, the system must eventually input data x. In LTL:

$$\Box(SyncOutput(x) \rightarrow \Diamond SyncInput(x)). \tag{4}$$

The program behavior after adaptation can be specified in a similar manner. The system (i.e., the target program) is required to input data from the asynchronous pipeline in response to the outputs. In LTL:

$$\square(AsyncOutput(x) \rightarrow \lozenge AsyncInput(x)). \tag{5}$$

For both the synchronous and asynchronous pipelines, when an output event occurs, an input obligation is generated. In other words, if the output is generated, then there should be a subsequent input event to read the generated output, thus discharging the input obligation. Formulae (4) and (5) state that an execution must fulfill all input obligations before it terminates.

In the adaptation from the source program to the target program, we allow the write operation of the asynchronous pipeline to overlap with the read operation of the synchronous pipeline. Therefore, we apply the overlap adaptation semantics introduced in Section 2 to the specification of the adaptation. During the overlapped period, the restriction condition is that the synchronous pipeline should not output data, and the asynchronous pipeline should not input data. The requirement for the adaptation from the source to the target can be specified using the overlap adaptation semantics as follows:

$$(((\square(SyncOutput \rightarrow \lozenge SyncInput) \wedge (\lozenge A_{REQ}$$
$$\overset{\Omega}{\longrightarrow} \square \neg SyncOutput))$$
$$\overset{\Omega}{\longrightarrow} true)$$
$$\wedge (\lozenge A_{REQ}$$
$$\overset{\Omega}{\longrightarrow} (\square(AsyncOutput \rightarrow \lozenge AsyncInputs) \wedge (\square \neg AsyncInput$$
$$\overset{\Omega}{\longrightarrow} true)))). \tag{6}$$

This formula states that the system should adapt from the source program (in the synchronous mode) to the target program (in the asynchronous mode) in response to the adaptation request A_{REQ}. The source and target programs overlap. During the overlapped period, the source must not output data, and the target must not input data. The output obligation generated in the synchronous mode must be fulfilled before the adaptation completes.

4.1 Instrumentation and Model Checking

To monitor the run-time execution conditions of the adaptive Java pipeline program, we use aspect-oriented programming to insert instrumentation code into the adaptive system. Currently, the AspectJ script for instrumentation is generated manually; future work will explore automated support.

In this example, the "instrumentation concern" is encapsulated in an `Instrumentation` aspect, saved in a file named `Instrumentation.aj`. Specifically, we define a pointcut `Main` to identify the `main()` method of the adaptive Java pipeline program. Figure 2 (a) depicts the *before advice* we defined for the `Main` pointcut. Specifically, at the very beginning of the entire program, we insert code to initialize the property automaton in the run-time model checking server by sending an A-LTL formula to the server. The `AmoebaChecker` class implements a stub that is responsible for the communication with the model checking server. Its constructor

```
1  before() :Main() {
2    AmoebaChecker.checker = new AmoebaChecker ("192.168.1.101", 2211,
3    "(((([](SyncOutput-><>SyncInput) /\\ (<>AREQ _>[] !SyncOutput)) _>true)
4      /\\ (<>AREQ _> ([] (AsyncOutput-> <> AsyncInput) /\\
5      ([]!AsyncInput _> true ))))" ); }
                                      (a)
1  after() :Main { AmoebaChecker.checker.terminate(); }
                                      (b)
1  public pointcut sync_output() : withincode (*sync.PipedInputStream.receive(..))
2  && get (byte[] buffer );
                                      (c)
1  before() : sync_output() { checker.nextState ("SyncOutput"); };
                                      (d)
```

Fig. 2. Instrumentation Code

method takes three parameters: The first two parameters specify the IP address and the port number for the model checking server, respectively. The third parameter specifies the A-LTL property to be verified. Figure 2(b) depicts the after advice we defined for the Main pointcut. Specifically, at the very end of each execution, we insert code to send an ''EOE'' message to the run-time model checking server to terminate the model checking.

Second, we use pointcuts to identify the locations of the adaptive Java pipeline program at which the sync shared buffer and the async shared buffer are accessed and therefore should be instrumented. Figure 2 (c) illustrates the pointcut definition for the SyncOutput message. Line 1 defines that the pointcut is within the receive() method of the async piped input and sync piped input classes. Line 2 defines that the pointcut is at the location where the buffer is accessed. When the buffers are accessed for read/write, an input/output message will be generated and sent to the run-time model checking server through network communication. Figure 2(d) shows the advice definition for SyncOutput. This code defines that it is a *before advice* for the sync_output pointcut. Before each access to the sync buffer, the advice inserts instrumentation code that invokes the nextState() method of the checker, which sends the SyncOutput message to the run-time model checking server.

We executed the instrumented adaptive Java program and verified the program against the overlap adaptation requirement in Formula (6) using AMOEBA-RT. To demonstrate that the model checker is actually effective in detecting errors, in a second experiment, we deliberately introduced some errors in the adaptive system. Specifically, we observed the obligation fulfillment is ensured by the buffer empty check in the sync piped input component, which is manifested as "if" statements at a number of locations in the code. We removed one of these "if" statements from the sync piped input component. This time, AMOEBA-RT detected violations of the property in Formula (6) in some of the random executions. As a response to the violations, AMOEBA-RT recorded the execution paths in a bug report that is currently processed offline. The bug reports documents counter-examples, that is, the paths of execution that lead to a property violation. The bug report in the above experiment showed that during those execution paths, the property was indeed violated.

5   Conclusions

In this paper, we introduced AMOEBA-RT, a run-time verification approach for adaptive software. AMOEBA-RT provides a means to continuously monitor and verify the post-release behavior of a software system. When an error is detected, the software may either file an error report, or attempt to repair the error automatically.

There are numerous possible directions for future work. First, we are investigating the use of counter-examples generated by AMOEBA-RT as input to the decision-making process for adaptation. Ideally, the adaptive system would be able to detect property violations and then adapt to repair itself. Second, currently our restriction conditions are safety conditions. We are considering additional types of restriction conditions, such as non-functional requirements. Additionally, we are interested in enabling a developer to visualize the run-time execution path of the adaptive system on the design models [26]. We envision that this capability could be used to better understand the relationship between environmental conditions and adaptation, as well as the need for additional steady-state systems. Finally, we are exploring how AMOEBA and AMOEBA-RT can be used to guide the automatic generation of steady-state programs using digital evolution [27].

References

1. McKinley, P.K., Sadjadi, S.M., Kasten, E.P., Cheng, B.H.C.: Composing adaptive software. IEEE Computer 37(7), 56–64 (2004)
2. Métayer, D.L.: Software architecture styles as graph grammars. In: Proceedings of the 4th ACM SIGSOFT symposium on Foundations of software engineering, pp. 15–23. ACM Press, New York (1996)
3. Taentzer, G., Goedicke, M., Meyer, T.: Dynamic change management by distributed graph transformation: Towards configurable distributed systems. In: Selected papers from the 6th International Workshop on Theory and Application of Graph Transformations, pp. 179–193. Springer, Heidelberg (2000)
4. Hirsch, D., Inverardi, P., Montanari, U.: Graph grammars and constraint solving for software architecture styles. In: Proceedings of the third international workshop on Software architecture, pp. 69–72. ACM Press, New York (1998)
5. Oreizy, P., Medvidovic, N., Taylor, R.N.: Architecture-based runtime software evolution. In: Proceedings of the 20th International Conference on Software Engineering, pp. 177–186. IEEE Computer Society, Los Alamitos (1998)
6. Taylor, R.N., Medvidovic, N., Anderson, K.M., Whitehead Jr., E.J., Robbins, J.E.: A component- and message-based architectural style for GUI software. In: Proceedings of the 17th International Conference on Software Engineering, pp. 295–304. ACM Press, New York (1995)
7. Kramer, J., Magee, J.: Analysing dynamic change in software architectures: a case study. In: Proc. of 4th IEEE International Conference on Configurable Distributed Systems, Annapolis (1998)
8. Zhang, J., Cheng, B.H.C.: Using temporal logic to specify adaptive program semantics. Journal of Systems and Software (JSS), Architecting Dependable Systems 79(10), 1361–1369 (2006)

9. Zhang, J., Cheng, B.H.C.: Model-based development of dynamically adaptive software. In: Proceedings of IEEE International Conference on Software Engineering (ICSE 2006), Shanghai,China (2006)
10. Zhang, J., Cheng, B.H.C.: Modular model checking of dynamically adaptive programs. Technical Report MSU-CSE-06-18, Computer Science and Engineering, Michigan State University, East Lansing, Michigan (2006), http://www.cse.msu.edu/~zhangji9/Zhang06Modular.pdf
11. Havelund, K., Rosu, G.: Monitoring Java programs with Java PathExplorer. In: Proceedings of the 1st Workshop on Runtime Verification, Paris, France (2001)
12. Lee, I., Kannan, S., Kim, M., Sokolsky, O., Viswanathan, M.: Runtime assurance based on formal specifications. In: Proc. Parallel and Distributed Processing Techniques and Applications, pp. 279–287 (1999)
13. Drusinsky, D.: The temporal rover and the atg rover. In: Proceedings of the 7th International SPIN Workshop on SPIN Model Checking and Software Verification, London, UK, pp. 323–330. Springer, Heidelberg (2000)
14. Feather, M.S., Fickas, S., Van Lamsweerde, A., Ponsard, C.: Reconciling system requirements and runtime behavior. In: Proceedings of the 9th International Workshop on Software Specification and Design, p. 50. IEEE Computer Society, Los Alamitos (1998)
15. The AspectJ Team: The AspectJ(TM) programming guide (2007), http://eclipse.org/aspectj
16. Appavoo, J., Hui, K., Soules, C.A.N., et al.: Enabling autonomic behavior in systems software with hot swapping. IBM Systems Journal 42(1), 60 (2003)
17. Chen, W.K., Hiltunen, M.A., Schlichting, R.D.: Constructing adaptive software in distributed systems. In: Proc. of the 21st International Conference on Distributed Computing Systems, Mesa, AZ (2001)
18. Kulkarni, S.S., Biyani, K.N., Arumugam, U.: Composing distributed fault-tolerance components. In: Proceedings of the International Conference on Dependable Systems and Networks (DSN), Supplemental Volume, Workshop on Principles of Dependable Systems, pp. W127–W136 (2003)
19. Zhang, J., Yang, Z., Cheng, B.H.C., McKinley, P.K.: Adding safeness to dynamic adaptation techniques. In: Proceedings of IEEE ICSE 2004 Workshop on Architecting Dependable Systems, Edinburgh, Scotland, UK (2004)
20. Maes, P.: Concepts and experiments in computational reflection. In: Conference proceedings on Object-oriented programming systems, languages and applications, pp. 147–155. ACM Press, New York (1987)
21. Barringer, H., Goldberg, A., Havelund, K., Sen, K.: Program monitoring with ltl in eagle. In: 18th International Parallel and Distributed Processing Symposium, Parallel and Distributed Systems: Testing and Debugging - PADTAD 2004, IEEE Computer Society Press, Los Alamitos (2004)
22. Bowman, H., Thompson, S.J.: A tableaux method for Interval Temporal Logic with projection. In: de Swart, H. (ed.) TABLEAUX 1998. LNCS (LNAI), vol. 1397, pp. 108–123. Springer, Heidelberg (1998)
23. Vardi, M., Wolper, P.: An automata-theoretic approach to automatic program verification. In: Proceedings of the 1st Symposium on Logic in Computer Science, Cambridge, England, pp. 322–331 (1986)
24. Lichtenstein, O., Pnueli, A.: Checking that finite state concurrent programs satisfy their linear specification. In: Proceedings of the 12th ACM SIGACT-SIGPLAN symposium on Principles of programming languages, pp. 97–107. ACM Press, New York (1985)

25. Zhang, J., Lee, J., McKinley, P.K.: Optimizing the Java pipe I/O stream library for performance. In: Pugh, B., Tseng, C.-W. (eds.) LCPC 2002. LNCS, vol. 2481, Springer, Heidelberg (2005)
26. Goldsby, H., Cheng, B.H.C., Konrad, S., Kamdoum, S.: A visualization framework for the modeling and formal analysis of high assurance systems. In: Proceedings of the ACM/IEEE 8th International Conference on Model Driven Engineering Languages and Systems, Genova, Italy (2006)
27. Goldsby, H.J., Knoester, D.B., Cheng, B.H.C., McKinley, P.K., Ofria, C.A.: Digitally evolving models for dynamically adaptive systems. In: Proceedings of the IEEE ICSE Workshop on Software Engineering for Adaptive and Self-Managing Systems (SEAMS), Minneapolis, Minnesota (2007)

Model-Based Run-Time Error Detection*

Jozef Hooman[1,2] and Teun Hendriks[1]

[1] Embedded Systems Institute, Eindhoven, The Netherlands
jozef.hooman@esi.nl, teun.hendriks@esi.nl
[2] Radboud University Nijmegen, The Netherlands

Abstract. The reliability of high-volume products, such as consumer electronic devices, is threatened by the combination of increasing complexity, decreasing time-to-market, and strong cost constraints. As an approach to maintain a high level of reliability and to avoid customer complaints, we present a run-time awareness concept. Part of this concept is the use of models for run-time error detection. We have implemented a general awareness framework in which an application and a model of its desired behaviour can be inserted. It allows both time-based and event-based error detection at run time. This method, coupled to local recovery techniques, aims to minimize any user exposure to product-internal technical errors, thereby improving user-perceived reliability.

Keywords: reliability, error detection, embedded systems, models, run-time verification.

1   Introduction

Modern consumer electronics devices, such as TVs or smart phones, contain vast amounts of intelligence encoded in either software or dedicated hardware. Hundreds of engineers develop and improve these "computers in disguise" for global markets but facing plenty of local variations. Complexity and open connectivity make it exceedingly difficult to guarantee total product correctness under all operating conditions. The final aim of our work is to improve user-perceived reliability of these devices by run-time awareness, i.e., allow a device to correct at run time important, user-noticeable, failure modes. This paper presents an approach to provide run-time error detection as a first step towards awareness.

The work described here is part of the Trader project in which academic and industrial partners collaborate to optimize the reliability of high-volume products, such as consumer electronic devices. The main industrial partner of this project is NXP Semiconductors (formerly Philips Semiconductors), with a focus on audio/video equipment (e.g., TVs and DVD players). NXP provides the problem statement and relevant case studies which are taken from the TV domain. A current high-end TV is a very complex device which can receive analog

---

* This work has been carried out as part of the Trader project under the responsibility of the Embedded Systems Institute. This project is partially supported by the Dutch Ministry of Economic Affairs under the Bsik program.

H. Giese (Ed.): MoDELS 2007 Workshops, LNCS 5002, pp. 225–236, 2008.

and digital input from many possible sources and using many different coding standards. It can be connected to various types of recording devices and includes many features such a picture-in-picture, teletext, sleep timer, child lock, TV ratings, emergency alerts, TV guide, and advanced image processing. Similar to other domains, we see a convergence to additional features such as photo browsing, MP3 playing, USB, games, databases, and networking. Correspondingly, the amount of software in TVs has seen an exponential increase from 1 KB in 1980 to 24 MB in current high-end TVs. Also the hardware complexity is increasing rapidly to support, for instance, real-time decoding and processing of high-definition (HD) images for large screens, large data streams, and multiple tuners. Correspondingly, a TV is designed as a system-on-chip with multiple processors and dedicated hardware accelerators, to meet stringent real-time requirements of, for instance, HDTV-quality input at rates up to 120 Hz.

In addition, there is a strong pressure to decrease time-to-market, i.e., the increasing complexity of products has to be addressed in shorter innovation cycles. To realize many new features quickly, components developed by others have to be incorporated. This includes so-called third-party components, typically realizing audio and video standards, but also in-house developed components supplied by other business units. Moreover, there is a clear trend towards the use of downloadable components, to increase product flexibility and to allow new business opportunities (selling new features, games, etc.).

Given these trends, the complexity of hardware and software, and the large number of possible user settings and types of input, exhaustive testing is impossible. Moreover, the product has to tolerate certain faults in the input (e.g., deviations from coding standards or bad image quality). Hence, it is extremely difficult to continue producing products at the same reliability level. The cost of non-quality, however, is high, because it leads to many returned products, it damages brand image, and reduces market share.

The main goal of the Trader project is to prevent faults in high-volume products from causing customer complaints. Hence, the focus is on run-time error detection and correction, minimizing any disturbance of the user experience of the product. The main challenge is to realize this without increasing development time and, given the domain of high-volume products, with minimal additional hardware costs and without degrading performance.

This paper is structured as follows. In Sect. 2 the main approach is described. We list the main research questions in Sect. 3. Section 4 contains current results. In Sect. 5 we discuss related work. Concluding remarks can be found in Sect. 6.

2   Approach

In observing failures of current products, it is often the case that a user can immediately observe that something is wrong, whereas the system itself is completely unaware of the problem. Inspired by other application domains, such as the success of helicopter health and usage monitoring [1], the main approach in Trader is to give the system a notion of run-time awareness that its customer-perceived behavior is (or is likely to become) erroneous. In addition, the aim is to provide the system with a strategy to correct itself in line with customer expectations. The concept of run-time awareness and correction as pursued by the Trader project is depicted in Fig. 1.

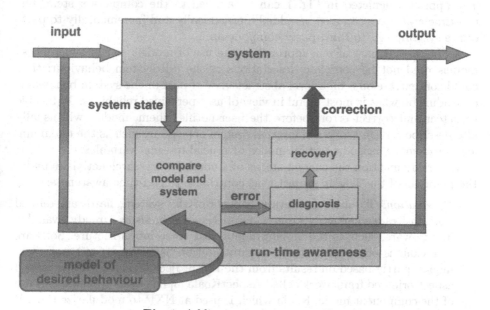

Fig. 1. Adding awareness at run time

We list the main ingredients of our run-time awareness approach, giving examples from the TV-domain:

- *Observation*: observe relevant inputs, outputs and internal system states. For instance, for a TV we may want to observe keys presses from the remote control, internal modes of components (dual/single screen, menu, mute/unmute, etc), load of processors and busses, buffers, function calls to audio/video output, sound level, etc.
- *Error detection*: detect errors, based on observations of the system and a model of the desired system behaviour. For a TV, this could be done using a state machine which describes mode changes in response to remote control commands. An alternative is to use a model of expected load and memory usage and compare this with the actual system behaviour.
- *Diagnosis*: in case of an error, find the most likely cause of the error, e.g. using architectural models of the system. Examples are diagnosis techniques that record data about executed parts of the system and the (non)occurrence of errors or techniques that use architectural models that include faulty behaviour. These techniques can be applied at various levels of granularity, from fine-grained fault-localization in blocks of C-code to course-grained diagnoses of large components.

– *Recovery*: correct erroneous behaviour, based on the diagnosis results and information about the expected impact on the user. Possible corrections include restarting particular components, resetting internal modes/variables, rescheduling software components, etc.

The approach depicted in Fig. 1 can be applied to the complete system, but run-time awareness can also be added hierarchically and incrementally to parts of the system, e.g., to third-party components.

An important part of our approach is the use of models at run time. These models need not be complete descriptions of the full system behaviour; they could concentrate on a high-level abstract view of part of the system behaviour, depending on what is most useful in view of user-perceived reliability. To be able to detect and correct errors before the user notifies them, models will usually also describe certain aspects of internal system behaviour, such as the maximum load or memory usage in certain modes or crucial internal variables.

We briefly mention the current status of a number of research activities under the umbrella of the Trader project that contribute to run-time awareness:

– *Observation*: To observe relevant aspects of the system, hardware-related work in Trader currently aims at exploiting mechanisms already available in hardware, such as the on-chip debug and trace infrastructure. Software behaviour is observed by code instrumentation using aspect-oriented techniques, partly based on results from the ESI-project Ideals [2]. A specialized aspect-oriented framework called AspectKoala [3] has been developed on top of the component model Koala which is used at NXP to modularize the TV software.
– *Error detection*: Various techniques for error detection are investigated such as hardware-based deadlock detection and range checking. An approach which checks the consistency of internal modes of components turned out to be successful to detect teletext problems due to a loss of synchronization between components [4].
– *Diagnosis*: The diagnoses techniques developed within Trader are based on so-called program spectra [5]. The first applications in the TV domain are encouraging and the technique is currently refined by using it for debugging.
– *Recovery*: To allow independent recovery of parts of the system, a framework for local recovery has been developed [6]. A few first experiments in the multimedia domain show that, after some refactoring of the system, independent recovery of parts of the system is possible without large overhead. Another part of the recovery research concentrates on task migration. This includes, for instance, the migration of tasks from one processor to another to improve image quality in case of overload situations (e.g., due to intensive error correction on a bad input signal).

In addition, there are controlled experiments with TV users to capture user-perceived failure severity, that is, to get an indication of the level of user-irritation caused by a product failure. In the remainder of this paper we focus on model-based error detection, and refer to [7] for more information on other research within Trader.

3   Research Questions

We list a number of research questions concerning the embedding of error detection in concrete industrial products. In Sect. 3.1 we address the problem of getting suitable models. Section 3.2 discusses the use of these models for run-time error detection.

3.1   Modeling

There are several questions related to the models to be used at run time:

- Which part of the system has to be modeled? For a complex price-sensitive device such as a TV, it is cost-inhibitive to check the complete system behaviour at run time. Hence, a choice has to be made based on the likelihood of errors and the impact on the user. Moreover, it is relevant to take into account which errors can be treated by the diagnosis and the recovery parts of the awareness framework.
- Which models are most suitable for run-time error detection? For instance, which type of models is convenient and what is the right level of abstraction? Although we focus on user-perceived behaviour, some architectural modeling will be relevant to enable early detection of errors, i.e., before a user observes a failure.
- How to obtain suitable models? Typically, in the area of embedded systems, the number of models available in industry is limited. The required overall system behaviour is usually not modeled and models have to be reconstructed using a lot of implicit domain knowledge (comparable to the experiences described Sect. 4 of [8]).
- How to increase the confidence in the model; how to evaluate model quality and fidelity?

3.2   Using Models at Run Time

The use of models at run time for error detection raises a number of questions:

- How to obtain the relevant observations from the system? Note that this involves both hardware and software parts of the system. Typically, there are several processors and state information is often distributed. Hence, a question is how to get a consistent snapshot of the global state of the system.
- How to avoid detecting non-existing errors? The concept is to compare system observations (e.g., output, states, load) with the values specified in the model of desired system behaviour, henceforth also called the specification model. False errors might occur due to a number of reasons such as i) the use of an incorrect model, ii) an incorrect implementation of the model, iii) a comparison at a wrong moment in time when the system is not stable. This leads to the questions mentioned in the following points.
- How to preserve model semantics in the implementation at run time?

- When to compare system observations with the model? When the system is unstable, e.g., it is performing an action which takes some time, comparison may lead to wrong results. How to decide when the system is in a stable state? Is it possible to get notifications from the system or should stability be deduced indirectly, e.g., by observing return values or changing data structures? Should comparison be done time-driven, event-driven, or by a combination?
- When to report an error exactly? Should system and specification match exactly, or is a certain tolerance allowed? How much difference is allowed? Should a single deviation lead to an error or are a few consecutive deviations needed before an error is generated?

Observe that many of these questions are related. For instance, the decision what to model depends on the type of errors one wants to detect, which errors are recoverable, and what can be observed about the system in an effective way (without too much costs or performance loss). In our context, an important factor is also the user perception of which failures are irritating and which type of recovery is acceptable for users.

4   Results on Model-Based Error Detection

We present the current results of the Trader project on model-based error detection. First, in Sect. 4.1, we discuss work on obtaining a model of desired system behaviour, related to the questions in Sect. 3.1. Next, in Sect. 4.2, we present a framework for run-time model-based error detection to obtain more insight in the issues mentioned in Sect. 3.2.

4.1   Experiences with Modeling Desired System Behaviour

Since the TV domain is our source of inspiration and the focus is on user-perceived reliability, the first aim was to make a model that captures the user view of a particular type of TV in development. The model should capture the relation between user input, via the remote control, and output, via images on the screen and sound. Such a model did not exist. Neither could it be derived easily from the TV requirements, which, in common industrial practice, were distributed over many documents and databases.

Concerning the control behaviour of the TV, a few first experiments indicated that the use of state machines leads to suitable models. But it also revealed that it was very easy to make modeling errors. Constructing a correct model was more difficult than expected. Getting all the information was not easy, and many interactions were possible between features. Examples are relations between dual screen, teletext and various types of on-screen displays that remove or suppress each other. Hence, we aim at executable models to allow quick feedback on the user-perceived behaviour and to increase the confidence in the fidelity of the model. In addition, we exploit the possibilities of formal model-checking and test scripts to improve model quality.

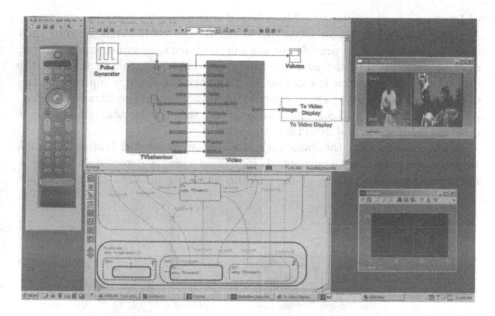

Fig. 2. Simulation of model of TV behaviour

Besides the control behaviour, a TV also has a complex streaming part with a lot of audio and video processing. Typically, this gets most attention in the requirements documentation. We would like to model this on a more abstract level, with emphasis on the relation with the control part.

These considerations led to the use of Matlab/Simulink [9]. The Stateflow toolbox of Simulink is used for the control part and the Image and Video Processing toolbox for the streaming part. A snapshot of a simulation is depicted in Fig. 2. The Simulink model is shown in the middle, at the top, with on the left a (blue) Stateflow block called "TVbehaviour" and on the right, an image processing block called "Video". The Stateflow block is a hierarchical and parallel state diagram. It is partly shown on the bottom, where the active states are dark (blue). External events are obtained by clicking on a picture of a remote control, shown on the left. Output is visualized by means of Matlab's video player and a scope for the volume level, shown on the bottom right side in Fig. 2.

The visualization of the user view on input and output of the model turned out to be very useful to detect modeling errors and undesired feature interactions. Since the model was changed frequently, we experimented with the tool Reactis [10] to generate test scripts to check conformance after model changes. This tool can also be used to validate model properties. Related functionality is provided by the Simulink Design Verifier.

4.2   A Framework for Run-Time Model-Based Error Detection

To foster quick experimentation with the use of models at run time inside real industrial products, e.g. a TV where the control software is implemented on top of Linux, we have developed a Linux-based framework for run-time awareness. A particular System Under Observation (SUO) can be inserted, needing only minimal adaptations to provide certain observations concerning input, output, and internal states to the awareness monitor. The specification model of the desired system behaviour is included by using the code generation possibilities of Stateflow. Hence, it is easy to experiment with different specification models. The awareness part also contains a comparator that can be adapted to include different comparison and detection strategies.

Before implementing the framework, it has been modeled in Matlab/Simulink to investigate the main concepts. A high-level view is depicted in Figure 3, illustrating the comparison of the volume level. To simulate the comparison

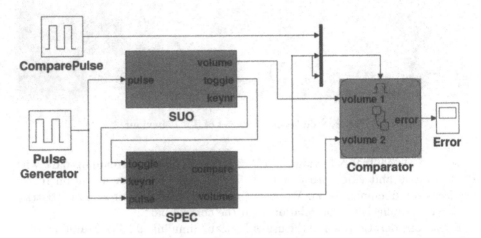

Fig. 3. Model of model-based error detection

strategy, we also made a second model for the SUO, this time a more detailed architectural model which also includes timing delays to simulate the execution time of internal actions. A few observations based on simulations are listed below:

– Our initial specification models had to be adapted to include best-case and worst-case execution times. To capture uncertainties in the system behaviour, we added intermediate states to represent that the system might be in transition from one mode to another.
– Part of the comparison strategy is included in the specification model, to be able to use domain knowledge about processing delays and intermediate states. To this end, the specification generates events to start and to stop the comparison (modeled by the "compare" signal in Fig. 3).
– The comparator should not be too eager to report errors; small delays in system-internal communication might easily lead to differences during a short amount of time. Hence, current comparators only report an error if differences persist during a certain amount of time or occur a consecutive number of times. A trade-off has to be made between taking more time to

avoid false errors and reporting errors fast to allow quick repair. This also influences the frequency with which comparisons take place (modeled by the "ComparePulse" in Fig. 3).

The design of the awareness framework is shown in Fig. 4. The SUO and the awareness monitor are separate processes communicating via Unix domain sockets. The SUO has to be adapted slightly, to send messages with relevant input and output (which may also include internal states) to Input and Output Observers. The Stateflow Coder of Simulink is used to generate C-code from a Stateflow model of the desired behaviour. This code is included in the Stateflow Model Implementation component and executed by the Model Executor. Based on event notifications from the Input Observer, the Model Executor provides input to the code of the model. It also receives output from the model. Information about relevant input and output is stored in the Configuration component.

The Comparator compares model output with system output which is obtained from the Output Observer. For each observable value, the user of the framework can specify (1) a threshold for the allowed maximal deviation between specification model and system, and (2) a limit for the number of consecutive deviations that are allowed before an error will be reported. Another

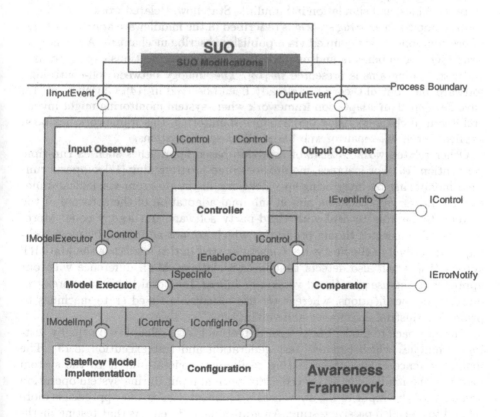

Fig. 4. Design of awareness framework in Linux

parameter is the frequency with which time-based comparison takes place. This can be combined with event-based comparison by specifying in the specification model when comparison should take place and when not (e.g., when the system is in an unstable state between certain modes). The Model Executor obtains this information from executing the implementation of the model and uses it to start and stop the Comparator. The Controller initiates and controls all components, except for the Configuration component which is controlled by the Model Executor.

5   Related Work

Traditional fault-tolerance techniques such as Triple Modular Redundancy and N-version programming are not applicable in our application domain of high-volume products, because of the cost of the required redundancy. Related work that also takes cost limitations into account can be found in the research on fault-tolerance of large-scale embedded systems [11]. They apply the autonomic computing paradigm to systems with many processors to obtain a healing network. Similar to our approach is the use of a kind of controller-plant feedback loop, state machines, and simulation in Simulink/Stateflow. Related work on adding a control loop to an existing system is described in the middleware approach of [12] where components are coupled via a publish-subscribe mechanism. A method to wrap COTS components and monitor them using specifications expressed as a UML state diagrams is presented in [13]. The analogy between self-controlling software and control theory has already been observed in [14]. Garlan et al [15] have developed an adaptation framework where system monitoring might invoke architectural changes. Using performance monitoring, this framework has been applied to the self-repair of web-based client-server systems.

Other related work consists of assertion-based approaches such as run-time verification [16]. For instance, monitor-oriented programming [17] supports run-time monitoring by integrating specifications in the program via logical annotations. In our approach, we aim at minimal adaptation of the software of the system, to be able to deal with third-party software and legacy code. Moreover, we also monitor timing properties which are not addressed by most techniques described in the literature. Closely related in this respect is the MaC-RT system [18] which also detects timeliness violations. Main difference with our approach is the use of a timed version of Linear Temporal Logic to express requirements specifications, whereas we use executable timed state machines to promote industrial acceptance and validation.

Our approach to model-based error detection is also related to on-the-fly testing techniques which combine test generation and test execution [8,19]. The main difference is that these testing techniques generate input to the system based on the model, whereas we consider normal input during system operation and forward this input to the awareness component. Hence, our approach is more related to so-called passive testing. An additional difference is that testing methods concentrate on testing the input/output interface, whereas our focus is on fast error detection (preferably before output failures occur) which often leads to the monitoring of internal implementation details such as internal variables or load.

6 Concluding Remarks

Clearly, we have not yet answered all research questions mentioned in Sect. 3. Concerning the modeling questions of Sect. 3.1 we have mainly followed the well-known state machine approach to model the control behaviour of embedded systems. To increase both the industrial acceptance and the confidence in the correctness of the models, model execution and an intuitive visualization of input/output behaviour turned out to be essential. Convenient tool support has been obtained by using Matlab/Simulink/Stateflow which allows efficient code generation from models.

To investigate the questions in Sect. 3.2 about the use of models at run time, we developed a framework which allows quick experiments with run-time awareness. Currently, the framework is used for awareness experiments with the open source media player MPlayer [20]. It was easy to insert both the MPlayer and an abstract high-level Stateflow model of its desired behaviour in the framework, without degrading the performance of the MPlayer. Although some injected errors could be detected, more work is needed to investigate which types of errors can be detected, how false errors can be avoided, and how the approach scales to larger models. Moreover, we also intend to investigate the use of more architectural information in the model to detect errors earlier, before they affect the user-perceived behaviour.

Current work also includes connections with diagnosis and recovery techniques. The first results indicate that more research is needed to clarify the relation between the types of errors that can be detected and those that can be corrected by the local recovery techniques developed within Trader. Moreover, future work will address issues concerning the synchronization between the techniques, e.g., to avoid error detection during recovery and to ensure a re-synchronization between system and model after recovery.

Acknowledgments. Many thanks goes to Chetan Nair for his work on the implementation of the awareness framework in Linux. The members of the Trader project are gratefully acknowledged for many fruitful discussions on reliability and the awareness concept. We thank the anonymous reviewers for many useful comments and suggestions for improvement.

References

1. Cronkhite, J.D.: Practical application of health and usage monitoring (HUMS) to helicopter rotor, engine, and drive systems. In: AHS, Proc. 49th Annual Forum, vol. 2, pp. 1445–1455 (1993)
2. Embedded Systems Institute: Ideals project (2007), http://www.esi.nl/ideals/

3. van de Laar, P., Golsteijn, R.: User-controlled reflection on join points. Journal of Software 2(3), 1–8 (2007)
4. Sözer, H., Hofmann, C., Tekinerdogan, B., Aksit, M.: Detecting mode inconsistencies in component-based embedded software. In: DSN Workshop on Architecting Dependable Systems (2007)
5. Zoeteweij, P., Abreu, R., Golsteijn, R., van Gemund, A.: Diagnosis of embedded software using program spectra. In: Proc. 14th Conference and Workshop on the Engineering of Computer Based Systems (ECBS 2007), pp. 213–220 (2007)
6. Sözer, H., Tekinerdogan, B.: Introducing recovery style for modeling and analyzing system recovery. In: Proc. Working IEEE/IFIP Conference on Software Architecture (WICSA) (2008)
7. Embedded Systems Institute: Trader project (2007), http://www.esi.nl/trader/
8. Larsen, K., Mikucionis, M., Nielsen, B., Skou, A.: Testing real-time embedded software using UPPAAL-TRON: an industrial case study. In: 5th ACM Int. Conf. on Embedded Software (EMSOFT 2005), pp. 299–306. ACM Press, New York (2005)
9. The Mathworks: Matlab/Simulink, (2007), http://www.mathworks.com/
10. Reactive Systems: Model-Based Testing and Validation with Reactis (2007), http://www.reactive-systems.com/
11. Neema, S., Bapty, T., Shetty, S., Nordstrom, S.: Autonomic fault mitigation in embedded systems. Engineering Applications of Artificial Intelligence 17, 711–725 (2004)
12. Parekh, J., Kaiser, G., Gross, P., Valetto, G.: Retrofitting autonomic capabilities onto legacy systems. Cluster Computing 9(2), 141–159 (2006)
13. Shin, M.E., Paniagua, F.: Self-management of COTS component-based systems using wrappers. In: Computer Software and Applications Conference (COMPSAC 2006), pp. 33–36. IEEE Computer Society, Los Alamitos (2006)
14. Kokar, M.M., Baclawski, K., Eracar, Y.A.: Control theory-based foundations of self-controlling software. IEEE Intelligent Software, 37–45 (1999)
15. Garlan, D., Cheng, S., Schmerl, B.: Increasing System Dependability through Architecture-based Selfrepair. In: Architecting Dependable Systems, Springer, Heidelberg (2003)
16. Colin, S., Mariani, L.: Run-time verification. In: Broy, M., Jonsson, B., Katoen, J.-P., Leucker, M., Pretschner, A. (eds.) Model-Based Testing of Reactive Systems. LNCS, vol. 3472, pp. 525–555. Springer, Heidelberg (2005)
17. Chen, F., D'Amorim, M., Rosu, G.: A formal monitoring-based framework for software development and analysis. In: Davies, J., Schulte, W., Barnett, M. (eds.) ICFEM 2004. LNCS, vol. 3308, pp. 357–372. Springer, Heidelberg (2004)
18. Sammapun, U., Lee, I., Sokolsky, O.: Checking correctness at runtime using real-time Java. In: Proc. 3rd Workshop on Java Technologies for Real-time and Embedded Systems (JTRES 2005) (2005)
19. van Weelden, A., Oostdijk, M., Frantzen, L., Koopman, P., Tretmans, J.: On-the-fly formal testing of a smart card applet. In: Int. Conf. on Information Security (SEC 2005), pp. 565–576 (2005)
20. MPlayer: Open source media player (2007), http://www.mplayerhq.hu/

Second International Workshop on Multi-Paradigm Modeling: Concepts and Tools

Juan de Lara[1], Tihamér Levendovszky[2], Pieter J. Mosterman[3], and Hans Vangheluwe[4]

[1] Universidad Autónoma de Madrid, Spain
jdelara@uam.es
[2] Budapest Univ. of Technology and Economics, Hungary
tihamer@aut.bme.hu
[3] The MathWorks, Inc.
Pieter.Mosterman@mathworks.com
[4] McGill University (Montréal), Canada
hv@cs.mcgill.ca

Abstract. The comprehensive use of models in design has created a set of challenges beyond that of supporting one isolated design task. In particular, the need to combine, couple, and integrate models at different levels of abstraction and in different formalisms is posing a set of specific problems that the field of Computer Automated Multi-Paradigm Modeling (CAMPaM) is aiming to address. This paper summarizes the results of the 2nd Workshop on Multi-Paradigm Modeling: Concepts and Tools.

1 Introduction

Computational modeling has become the norm in industry to remain competitive and be successful [23]. As such, Model-Based Design of, for example, embedded software has enterprise-wise implications and modeling is not limited to isolated uses by a single engineer or team. Instead, it has reached a proliferation much akin to large software design, with requirements for infrastructure support such as version control, configuration management, automated processing, etc.

The comprehensive use of models in design has created a set of challenges beyond that of supporting one isolated design task. In particular, the need to combine, couple, and integrate models at different levels of abstraction and in different formalisms is posing a set of specific problems that the field of Computer Automated Multi-paradigm Modeling (CAMPaM) is aiming to address [16,22].

The essential element of multi-paradigm modeling is the use of explicit models throughout. This leads to a framework with models to represent the syntax of formalisms used for modeling, models of the transformations that represent the operational semantics, as well as model-to-model transformations for inter-formalism transformation [12]. These models are then used to facilitate generative tasks in a language engineering, such as evolving a domain-specific modeling formalism as its requirements change, but also in a tool engineering space, such as automatic generation of integrated development environments. Moreover, an

H. Giese (Ed.): MoDELS 2007 Workshops, LNCS 5002, pp. 237–246, 2008.

explicit model of a model transformation allows analyses such as termination characteristics, consistency, and determinism [4].

Thus, CAMPaM addresses two orthogonal problem directions:

1. *Multi-Formalism Modeling* [21], concerned with the coupling of, and transformation between, models described in different formalisms. In Figure 1, a part of the "formalism space" is depicted in the form of a formalism transformation graph (FTG). The different formalisms are shown as nodes in the graph. The arrows denote a homomorphic relationship "can be mapped onto". The mapping consists of transforming a model in the source formalism into one in the target formalism preserving certain pertinent properties.

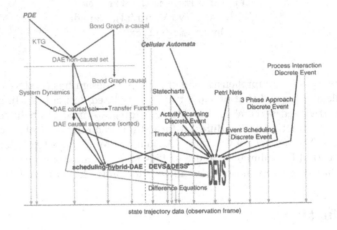

Fig. 1. The Formalism Transformation Graph (FTG)

The specification of a composite system may include the coupling of heterogeneous components expressed in different formalisms. For the analysis of its properties the composite system must be assessed by looking at the *whole* multi-formalism system. Components may have to be transformed to a common formalism, which can be found in the FTG [21]. Formalisms can be meta-modelled and the transformations denoted by the arrows of the FTG can be modelled as model transformations.

In contrast, in the *co-simulation* approach [6], each component is simulated with a formalism-specific simulator. Interaction because of component coupling is resolved at the trajectory (simulation data) level. Questions about the overall system can only be answered at the level of input/output (state trajectory). It is no longer possible to answer symbolic, higher-level questions which could be answered within the formalisms of the individual components.

2. *Model Abstraction*, concerned with the relationship between models at different levels of abstraction. Models described in either the same or in different formalisms can be related through the abstraction relationship, and its dual,

refinement. A foundation for the notion of abstraction, is the *information contained* in a model M, defined as the different questions (properties) $P = I(M)$ that can be asked concerning the model ($|P|$ and $p, p' \in P : p \neq p'$). These questions either result in true or false ($M \models p$ or $M \not\models p$).

A relation between two models M_1 and M_2 can have the character of an *abstraction*, *refinement*, or *equivalence* relative to a non-empty set of questions (properties) P.

- In case of an *equivalence*, it is required that for all $p \in P$ holds: $M_1 \models p \iff M_2 \models p$. This is written $M_1 =_P M_2$.
- If M_1 is an *abstraction* of M_2 with respect to P it holds for all $p \in P$: $M_1 \models p \Rightarrow M_2 \models p$. This is written $M_1 \sqsupseteq_P M_2$.
- Furthermore, M_1 is said to be a *refinement* of M_2 iff M_1 is an *abstraction* of M_2. This is written $M_1 \sqsubseteq_P M_2$.

Further discussion of this is included in the summary of the 1st Workshop on Multi-Paradigm Modeling: Concepts and Tools in 2006 [7].

To address the problems from the use of multiple formalisms and multiple levels of abstraction, meta-modeling and model transformation are used. *Meta-Modeling* [23] is based on the explicit modeling of modeling formalisms. Formalisms are described as models using meta-formalisms that are expressive enough to describe other formalisms' syntax and semantics. Examples are the Entity Relationship formalism and UML class diagrams. Model transformation is based on the explicit modeling of model transformations.

2 The Workshop

The objective of the workshop was to provide a forum to discuss the concepts as well as the tool building aspects required for multi-paradigm modeling. It was oriented to researchers and practitioners working in the modeling, simulation and analysis of complex systems, dealing with multiple paradigms in a model-driven manner. This includes tool vendors, academic researchers which address tool building as well as users of these tools.

This year workshop included five research paper presentations and one invited talk by Gabor Karsai (ISIS/Vanderbilt University) entitled "Multi-paradigm Modeling: Some past projects, lessons learned, and research challenges". The presentation addressed how the model-based engineering of large-scale embedded information systems often necessitates the use of different, heterogeneous modeling paradigms. Multiple-aspect, multi-paradigm, domain-specific models capture not only the physical and functional views of the hardware and the software architecture, but they should also represent interactions among different physical domains, as well as non-functional aspects such as faults and their effects, safety properties, and many others. The presentation highlighted the experience from four different projects in the past fifteen years, where multi-paradigm modeling had to be used to solve complex design and operational problems. Various examples were given for the modeling paradigms used in specific engineering systems. The research issues discussed included the problems of interacting engineering domains, the integration of models and their modeling languages, and the semantics of modeling paradigms and their precise specification.

The papers were presented in two sessions, both chaired by Pieter Mosterman. The first session was entitled MPM Concepts and Applications and included three papers:

- "ModHel'X: A Component-Oriented Approach to Multi-Formalism Modeling", by C. Hardebolle and F. Boulange [9]. In this paper, the authors address two important issues: to provide support for the specification of the semantics of a modeling formalism, and to allow the specification of the interactions between parts of a model described using different modeling formalisms. For this purpose, they present the ModHel'X system, which focuses on model execution, including simulation, code generation and real-time execution.
- "From UML State Charts to DEVS State Machines using XML", by J.L. Risco-Martín, S. Mittal, B. Zeigler and J.M. de la Cruz [18]. In this contribution, the authors present an integrated approach towards using UML state machines transformed as DEVS [24] models. The transformation mechanism is available as an upcoming standard, State Chart XML (SCXML) that provides a generic execution environment based on CCXML and Harel State tables. The transformation is ilustrated by taking a UML state machine and augmenting it with information during the process using SCXML to make it DEVS capable. The obtained DEVS models are indeed Finite Deterministic DEVS, able to be encoded as a W3C XML schema.
- "Applying Multi-Paradigm Modeling to Multi-Platform Mobile Development", by L. Lengyel, T. Levendovszky and C. Hassan [14]. In this work, the authors introduce some CAMPaM ideas in their meta-modeling and model transformation framework, the Visual Modeling and Transformation System (VMTS). The concepts are illustrated with an example in model-based development for mobile platforms.

The second session was entitled MPM Tools, and included two papers:

- "Towards Parallel Model Transformations", by G. Mezei, H. Charaf, T. Levendovszky [15]. In this contribution, the authors tackle the problem of efficiency of graph transformation by proposing the execution of model transformations in parallel. The paper presents algorithms to find and apply steps of the transformations in parallel, and an implementation is given the Visual Modeling and Transformation System (VMTS).
- "Domain-specific Model Editors with Model Completion", by S. Sen, B. Baudry and H. Vangheluwe [20]. In this paper, the authors propose an integrated software system capable of generating recommendations for model completion of partial models built in arbitrary domain-specific model editors. The automatic completion is powered by a Prolog engine whose input is a constraint logic program derived from the specification (meta-model with constraints) of the modeling language to which the partial models belong.

3   Working Group Results

The workshop included two working group discussion sessions.

3.1   Consistency

This working group consisted of K. Cerans, B. Latronico, D. Matheson, E. Syriani, and H. Vangheluwe. The discussion focused on *model consistency*.

In the development of complex systems, *multiple views* on the system-to-be-built are often used. These views typically consist of models in *different formalisms*. Different views usually pertain to various *partial aspects* of the overall system. In a multi-view approach, individual views are (mostly) less complex than a single model describing all aspects of the system. As such, multi-view modeling, like modular, hierarchical modeling, simplifies model development. Most importantly, it becomes possible for individual experts on different aspects of a design to work in isolation on individual, possibly domain-specific views without being encumbered with other aspects. These individual experts can work mostly independently, thereby considerably speeding up the development process. This approach does however have a *cost* associated with it. As individual view models evolve, inconsistencies between different views are often introduced and those need to be corrected.

Ensuring consistency between different views requires periodic concerted efforts from the model designers involved. In general, the *detection* of inconsistencies and *recovering* from them is a tedious, error-prone and manual process. Automated techniques can alleviate the problem and this has been investigated in the Concurrent Engineering community over the last two decades [2]. These solutions were often based on some form of constraint propagation between the different views. Al-Anzi and Spooner [1] give a classification of inconsistencies that may occur in the context of Concurrent Engineering. Easterbrook *et. al* [3] introduce the notion of ViewPoints and describe how consistency between them can be checked. In the Software Engineering community, the consistency between different views of a design has also been studied extensively [5,8].

For the sake of the discussions, a working definition of consistency was proposed: A set of models M is consistent with respect to a set of consistency constraints C over M if all constraints in C are satisfied. M is inconsistent when at least one of the constraints in C is not satisfied. Consistency constraints may pertain to *syntax* as well as to *semantics* of models. In the former case, the constraints may pertain to the *structure* of models or to *values* of model attributes. In the case of semantics, the consistency constraints are defined over the *semantic domain*. This implies that models may have to be simulated to check consistency.

Whereas checking consistency constraints over a set of models can be done in isolation, often one starts from a consistent set of models and then *incrementally* makes changes to some of the models (usually one at a time). In this case, inconsistencies should be detected and where possible, modifications to (other) models in M must be made to maintain consistency. As such, changes in one model are *propagated* to other models. Which changes need to be made is determined by the consistency constraints. It is noted that a consistency check of a set of models in isolation can sometimes be performed by incrementally constructing the set from an empty set, keeping consistency at each intermediate step.

Triple Graph Grammars (TGGs) [19] were proposed as a reasonable starting point for automating consistency checking and enforcement, at least at a structural level (and initially, only for two models). In TGGs, two meta-model graphs are connected via a correspondence graph. This declarative model allows for checking consistency of the models, both with the meta-models and with each other. Furthermore, a collection of unidirectional change propagation rules can be inferred from the TGG model [10]. Related work has demonstrated this and has shown how conflict situations can be detected [11]. Furthermore, potential rules to resolve a conflict can be presented to the user for manual intervention. At the level of attribute relationships, a declarative specification would be desirable and Modelica (www.modelica.org) was suggested as a starting point.

3.2 Simulation

This working group consisted of C. Hardebolle, T. Levendovszky, P.J. Mosterman, and J.L. Risco-Martín.

The discussion focused on models of time for the execution of models that are designed using different formalisms. A concrete application example is formed by the networked power window control system that is sketched in Fig. 2. In the example a bus, depicted by a double straight line at the bottom, connects three controllers; a window controller, a lights controller, and a mirror controller. These three controllers may be implemented by different microcontrollers. To connect the controllers to the physical part of the system, actuators and sensors are employed. This is illustrated for the power window system where the controller actuates the window by a dc motor and obtains feedback measurements from a current sensor [17].

In the design of such a networked embedded system, a number of different formalisms are routinely employed. For example, the physics of the window movement includes the dynamics because of the window mass, the lift mechanism, and friction coefficients, and may be best modeled using differential equations, either as a system of ordinary differential equations (ODE) or as a system of

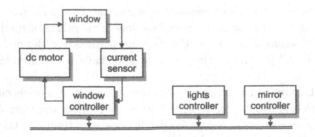

Fig. 2. A networked power window control system

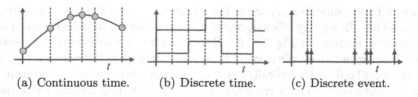

(a) Continuous time.   (b) Discrete time.   (c) Discrete event.

Fig. 3. State trajectories

differential and algebraic equations (DAE). This is schematically presented in Fig. 3(a), which shows a behavior that varies continuously with respect to time.

The behavior of the controller, on the other hand, often is implemented as periodic using a given sample time to determine the period. The controller may implement a number of tasks that may execute with different periods. This is illustrated in Fig. 3(b), where the sample time is represented by the distance in time between the dashed lines. Two tasks are shown, one at the bottom with a period of two and one at the top with a period of three.

The window controller may obtain its setpoint commands (i.e., whether to move the window up, down, or not at all) from a user operated switch that is located elsewhere in the vehicle. The commands are then communicated over a network that is also utilized by other control systems. To study the effects of the network and to determine the quality of service, the events at which data is transferred across the network are modeled. This is depicted in Fig. 3(c) by events that occur at points in time that may be arbitrarily spaced. This illustrates how over certain intervals of time, the event density may be high, whereas at other times the event density may be low.

The discussion centered around three different types of temporal semantics of models

- continuous-time, $\dot{x}(t) = f(x(t), u(t), t(t))$
- discrete-time, $x(t_k + h) = f(x(t_k), u(t_k), t_k)$
- discrete-event, $x(t_k + h_k) = f(x(t_k), u(t_k), t_k)$

This classification has been discussed in detail by Zeigler, Kim, and Praehofer [24] The working group concentrated specifically on the efficient generation of behaviors of the separate computational systems in isolation and in combination.

Continuous-time systems are typically executed by discretizing the continuous trajectory by using a numerical integration routine, embodied by a *solver*. The discretized points in time are indicated in Fig. 3(a) by the circles along the continuous trace. To efficiently execute an ODE, a specific solver has to be selected based on the characteristics of the behavior that the ODE embodies.

Discrete-time systems that represent embedded control can often be executed based on a static schedule, for example derived to be rate-monotonic. This results in little overhead in determining when a period starts (e.g., by doing an integer comparison) but the sample time that is employed may result in scheduled points in time at which no changes in the system occur. This is illustrated in Fig. 3(b) by the first sample hit where no change in either of the two tasks occurs.

To avoid such superfluous sample time hits, an event calendar can be implemented which allows very efficient handling of variable event densities such as in discrete-event systems. In Fig. 3(c) it is illustrated how for a discrete-event system values in between two events may be considered irrelevant. This in contrast with the zero-order hold that is typically applied in discrete-time systems. The event calendar to handle such variable event density consists of a data structure that has to very efficiently order new events based on their future time of occurrence. Similarly, scheduled events that are retracted have to be found with low time complexity.

This leads to three different types of execution engines, each with their respective benefits and drawbacks. Where a continuous-time execution engine can efficiently determine the step size based on differential equations, the integration mechanism is overly complex for determining the sample time hits in a discrete time system. A static schedule is more efficient, even in the face of superfluous sample time hits. However, in case of discrete-event systems, the sample time would have to be chosen arbitrarily small, which would result in excessive superfluous events whilst still resulting in error in the exact event time. While for discrete-event systems an event calendar is more efficient, such a heavy-weight data structure is excessively complex for executing a discrete-time system. Likewise, the static scheduling as implemented for discrete-time systems is often not applicable for continuous-time simulation as it would result in a fixed time-step of the numerical integration. A notable exception is real-time simulation where such a fixed time-step is a necessity.

The discussion then was directed towards potential solutions to obtain the best of each of the separate execution technologies without arriving at a conclusive assessment of the best approach.

4 Workshop Participants

Tihamér Levendovszky. BUDAPEST UNIVERSITY OF TECHNOLOGY AND ECONOMICS, HUNGARY
Eugene Syriani. MCGILL UNIVERSITY, CANADA
Hans Vangheluwe. MCGILL UNIVERSITY, CANADA
Janis Barzdins. UNIVERSITY OF LATVIA, LATVIA
Ryan Thibodeaux. VANDERBILT UNIVERSITY, USA
Dan Matheson. INTEGWARE, USA
José Luis Risco Martín. UNIVERSIDAD COMPLUTENSE DE MADRID, SPAIN
Pieter van Gorp. ANTWERP UNIVERSITY, BELGIUM
Cécile Hardebolle. ÉCOLE SUPÉRIEURE D'ÉLECTRICITÉ, FRANCE
Sumant Tambe. VANDERBILT UNIVERSITY, USA
Akshay Dabholkar. VANDERBILT UNIVERSITY, USA
Jon Oldevik. SINTEF, NORWAY
Karlis Cerans. UNIVERSITY OF LATVIA, LATVIA
Pieter J. Mosterman. THE MATHWORKS, INC., USA
Thomas Kühne. VICTORIA UNIVERSITY OF WELLINGTON, NEW ZEALAND
Joanna Chimiak-Opoka. UNIVERSITY OF INNSBRUCK, AUSTRIA
Elizabeth Latronico. BOSCH, USA

5   Program Committee

Peter Bunus. LINKÖPING UNIVERSITY
Michel Chaudron. EINDHOVEN UNIVERSITY OF TECHNOLOGY
Jean-Marie Favre. UNIVERSITY OF GRENOBLE
Holger Giese. UNIVERSITÄT PADERBORN
Mirko Conrad. THE MATHWORKS, INC.
David Hill. BLAISE PASCAL UNIVERSITY
Jozef Hooman. EMBEDDED SYSTEMS INSTITUTE
Gabor Karsai. VANDERBILT UNIVERSITY
Thomas Kühne. VICTORIA UNIVERSITY OF WELLINGTON
Klaus Müller-Glaser. UNIVERSITY OF KARLSRUHE
Hessam S. Sarjoughian. ARIZONA STATE UNIVERSITY
Mamadou K. Traoré. BLAISE PASCAL UNIVERSITY
Jeroen Voeten. EINDHOVEN UNIVERSITY OF TECHNOLOGY
Hans Vangheluwe. MCGILL UNIVERSITY

5.1   External Reviewers

Ernesto Posse. MCGILL UNIVERSITY
Philipp Graff. UNIVERSITY OF KARLSRUHE

Acknowledgements

The activities described in this paper supported, in part, by the Information Technology Innovation and Knowledge Centre. This paper was supported by the János Bolyai Research Scholarship of the Hungarian Academy of Sciences, and the Spanish Ministry of Science and Education, project MOSAIC (TSI2005-08225-C07-06). The Canadian National Sciences and Engineering Research Council (NSERC) and the Canadian research network MITACS are gratefully acknowledged for their support.

References

1. Al-Anzi, F.S., Spooner, D.L.: Classification and consistency of behavior in complex object design views for concurrent engineering. In: Proc. Int. Conf. on Data and Knowledge Systems for Manufacturing and Engineering, IEEE Comp. Soc. Press, Los Alamitos (1996)
2. Dewan, P., Riedl, J.: Toward computer-supported concurrent software engineering. IEEE Computer 26, 17–27 (1993)
3. Easterbrook, S., Finkelstein, A., Kramer, J., Nuseibeh, B.: Coordinating distributed viewpoints: The anatomy of a consistency check. Int. Journal on Concurrent Engineering: Research & Applications 2, 209–222 (1994)
4. Ehrig, H., Ehrig, K., Prange, U., Taentzer, G.: Fundamentals of Algebraic Graph Transformation. Springer, Heidelberg (2006)

5. Finkelstein, A., Gabbay, D., Hunter, A., Kramer, J., Nuseibeh, B.: Inconsistency handling in multiperspective specifications. IEEE Transactions on Software Engineering 20, 569–578 (1994)
6. Fishwick, P., Zeigler, B.P.: A Multimodel Methodology for Qualitative Model Engineering. ACM Transactions on Modelling and Computer Simulation 1(2), 52–81 (1992)
7. Giese, H., Levendovszky, T., Vangheluwe, H.: Summary of the Workshop on Multi-Paradigm Modeling: Concepts and Tools. Models in Software Engineering, 252–262 (2007)
8. Grundy, J., Hosking, J., Mugridge, W.B.: Inconsistency management for multiple-view software development environments. IEEE Transactions on Software Engineering 24, 960–981 (1998)
9. Hardebolle, C., Boulanger, F.: ModHel'X: A Component-Oriented Approach to Multi-Formalism Modeling. In: [13], pp. 49–60 (2007)
10. Königs, A.: Model Transformation with Triple Graph Grammars. In: Model Transformations in Practice Satellite Workshop of MODELS 2005, Montego Bay, Jamaica (2005)
11. Königs, A., Schürr, A.: Tool Integration with Triple Graph Grammars - A Survey. Elec. Notes in Theo. Comp. Science, vol. 148, pp. 113–150. Elsevier, Amsterdam (2006)
12. de Lara, J., Vangheluwe, H.: Defining visual notations and their manipulation through meta-modelling and graph transformation. J. Vis. Lang. Comput. 15(3-4), 309–330 (2004)
13. de Lara, J., Levendovszky, T., Mosterman, P.J.: Proc. of the Workshop on Multi-Paradigm Modeling: Concepts and Tools. BME-DAAI Tech. Rep. Series Vol. 1. Budapest Univ. of Tech. and Economics Dep. Automation and Applied Informatics (2007)
14. Lengyel, L., Levendovszky, T., Hassan, C.: Applying Multi-Paradigm Modeling to Multi-Platform Mobile Development. In: [13], pp. 9–22 (2007)
15. Mezei, G., Charaf, H., Levendovszky, T.: Towards Parallel Model Transformations. In: [13], pp. 23–34 (2007)
16. Mosterman, P.J., Vangheluwe, H.: Guest Editorial: Special issue on computer automated multi-paradigm modeling. ACM TOMACS 12(4), 249–255 (2002)
17. Mosterman, P.J., Sztipanovits, J., Engell, S.: Computer Automated Multi-Paradigm Modeling in Control Systems Technology. IEEE Transactions on Control System Technology 12(2), 223–234 (2004)
18. Risco-Martín, J.L., Mittal, S., Zeigler, B., de la Cruz, J.M.: From UML State Charts to DEVS State Machines using XML. In: [13], pp. 35–48 (2007)
19. Schürr, A.: Specification of Graph Translators with Triple Graph Grammars. In: Mayr, E.W., Schmidt, G., Tinhofer, G. (eds.) WG 1994. LNCS, vol. 903, pp. 151–163. Springer, Heidelberg (1995)
20. Sen, S., Baudry, B., Vangheluwe, H.: Domain-specific Model Editors with Model Completion. In: [13], pp. 61–74 (2007)
21. Vangheluwe, H.: DEVS as a common denominator for multi-formalism hybrid systems modelling. In: IEEE Int. Symposium on Computer-Aided Control System Design, Anchorage, Alaska, pp. 129–134. IEEE Computer Society Press, Los Alamitos (2000)
22. Vangheluwe, H., de Lara, J., Mosterman, P.J.: An Introduction to Multi-Paradigm Modelling and Simulation. In: Proc. AI Simulation&Planning, pp. 9–20 (2002)
23. Völter, M., Stahl, T.: Model-Driven Software Development. Willey (2006)
24. Zeigler, B., Kim, T., Praehofer, H.: Theory of Modeling and Simulation: Integrating Discrete Event and Continuous Complex Dynamic Systems. Academic Press, London (2000)

ModHel'X: A Component-Oriented Approach to Multi-Formalism Modeling*

Cécile Hardebolle and Frédéric Boulanger

SUPELEC – Computer Science Department,
3 rue Joliot-Curie, Gif-Sur-Yvette Cedex, France
{cecile.hardebolle,frederic.boulanger}@supelec.fr

Abstract. We present ModHel'X, an approach to multi-formalism modeling which addresses two important issues in this field: (a) providing support for the specification of the semantics of a modeling formalism, and (b) allowing the specification of the interactions between parts of a model described using different modeling formalisms. ModHel'X is based on the concept of Model of Computation and focuses on the execution of models, considered as the computation of one possible behavior of the model. The structural elements of a modeling language are described by specializing the meta-model of ModHel'X whereas its semantics, i.e. the corresponding model of computation, is described by specializing the predefined stages of a generic execution model. Using the same mechanisms, designers can specify the semantic adaptation that is suitable at each interface between heterogeneous parts of their model. Finally, ModHel'X comes with an execution engine which is able to interpret heterogeneous models for simulation.

1 Introduction

Complex systems are inherently heterogeneous because of the diverse nature of their numerous parts: hardware, software, digital, analog, reused or specifically designed IPs (Intellectual Properties), etc. Modeling such systems requires multiple modeling formalisms, adapted to the nature of each part of the system, the aspect on which the model focuses (functionality, time, power consumption...) and to the level of abstraction at which the system, or one of its parts, is studied. As emphasized by [1], having a global model of such a system all along the design process is necessary in order to answer questions about properties of the whole system, and in particular about its behavior. Such a model is said to be *multi-formalism* [2].

Different aspects of multi-formalism modeling (or heterogeneous modeling) have been studied: mathematical foundations [3], tools for validation [4] or simulation [5]. A central problem is to establish the meaning of the composition of heterogeneous parts of a model and to ensure their correct inter-operation when using the model to answer questions about the designed system [6].

---

* This work has been performed in the context of the Usine Logicielle project of the System@tic Paris Région Cluster (www.usine-logicielle.org)

H. Giese (Ed.): MoDELS 2007 Workshops, LNCS 5002, pp. 247–258, 2008.

We believe that the first step to be taken for solving this problem is to provide means for the precise specification of the semantics of the modeling formalisms that we want to use. Indeed, except for a few mathematically founded languages, the semantics of a modeling language is often described using natural language, what may lead to ambiguities and to diverse interpretations by different tools along the design chain. When combining different modeling languages in a model, ambiguities in the semantics of one of them make it impossible to define the overall semantics of the model. In this context, semantic variations as found in UML are acceptable only if the variation used is explicitly stated. In ModHel'X, we propose a set of tools for allowing the executable specification of the semantics of a modeling formalism without referring to any model instance (i.e. at the meta-modeling level [2]). In order to facilitate the combination of multiple modeling languages in models, our approach relies on component-oriented and hierarchical modeling [7]. The encapsulation principle is a major advantage for heterogeneous modeling since its purpose is to hide the internal mechanisms of the components. In this context, hierarchy is a structural way of combining the heterogeneous parts of a model, as well as a simple abstraction mechanism.

The second step to obtain a meaningful multi-formalism model of a system is to provide support for the specification of the semantic adaptation between model parts that use different modeling formalisms. An important constraint is that no model part should be modified to become compatible with the other parts of the multi-formalism model. This is particularly important when the model parts are provided by different technical teams or by suppliers for instance. In ModHel'X, the adaptation mechanism is decoupled from the model parts which are being integrated. A second issue is that the semantic adjustment between heterogeneous parts of a model depends not only on the formalisms at stake but also on the system which is modeled. Usual adaptation patterns between modeling formalisms often exist, but they are not unique and may need parameter adjustments since they represent default adaptations which do not necessarily fit directly a particular context. For example, integrating a model part which focuses on the notion of time with another which does not, may imply to customize the adaptation which is realized on the notion of time so that it is coherent with the expected behavior of the system. ModHel'X permits the description of adaptation patterns and allows the designer to choose the most suitable one in a given model. These descriptions may be reused in different contexts, and parameters allow their adaptation to specific applications.

The remainder of the paper is organized as follows. In Section 2 we review some of the related work and motivate our approach. Section 3 details and illustrates the main principles of ModHel'X. We discuss some specific aspects of our approach in Section 4, before concluding.

2   Existing Multi-Formalism Approaches and Motivations

In meta-modeling approaches such as Kermeta [8], the abstract syntax of a modeling language is described as a meta-model. The elements of this meta-model have methods whose semantics is defined in an imperative language. Each modeling language has a different meta-model in Kermeta. In the context of heterogeneous modeling, the definition of the combination of several modeling languages using such approaches implies either the definition of a meta-model which is the union of all the meta-models of the involved languages, or the definition of transformations from each meta-model to a meta-model chosen among them. Defining a union meta-model seems neither reasonable nor scalable since it implies the modification of the meta-model and of the associated model transformations each time an additional modeling language is taken into consideration. The second method is much more interesting since it is more flexible: the target meta-model can be chosen according to the question that must be answered about the system. Such an approach is implemented in the $ATOM^3$ tool [9]. However, the way the different heterogeneous parts of the model are "glued" together does not seem to be addressed by this approach, nor by other approaches based on model transformation [10,11] which have other advantages otherwise. In particular, in [11], it is stated that it is possible to formally define the semantics of a modeling language by defining a mapping to an already formally defined modeling language.

Another approach for defining the semantics of a modeling language, is to define the constructs of the language in a fixed abstract syntax – or meta-model – which is component oriented (as in [7]) and to consider that the semantics of the language is given by its "Model of Computation" (MoC). Such an approach is implemented in Ptolemy [1]. A model of computation (called "domain" in Ptolemy) is a set of rules for interpreting the relations between the components of a model. In this approach, the meta-model is the same for each language and what defines the semantics of the language is the way the elements of this meta-model are interpreted by the corresponding MoC. Heterogeneous models are organized into hierarchical layers, each one involving only one MoC. Thanks to this architecture, MoCs (i.e. modeling languages) are combined in pairs at the boundary between two hierarchical levels. The main drawback of the Ptolemy approach is that the way MoCs are combined at a boundary between two hierarchical levels is fixed and coded into the Ptolemy kernel. This implies that a modeler has either to rely on the default adaptation performed by the tool, or to modify the design of parts of its model (by adding adaptation components) in order to obtain the behavior he expects.

The approach we propose is based on the concept of *model of computation (MoC)* as defined in [1]. Our MOF meta-model, which is inspired by the abstract syntax of Ptolemy, contains special constructs for making the interactions between heterogeneous MoCs explicit and easy to define. In order to interpret a model in ModHel'X, it is necessary to describe its structure using our meta-model. Then, we define an interpretation of the elements of our meta-model which matches the semantics of the original language. Such an interpretation is what we call a Model of Computation. The interpretation of a model according to a MoC gives the same behavior as the interpretation of the original model according to the semantics of its modeling language. The same concepts used to define MoCs are used to define how different MoCs are "glued" together in heterogeneous models, at the boundary between two hierarchical layers. The execution engine of ModHel'X relies on the precise specification of the models of computation and of their interactions to determine without ambiguity the behavior of multi-formalism models.

Like Ptolemy, BIP (Behavior, Interaction, Priority) [4] also takes advantage of a hierarchical and component-oriented abstract syntax. It provides formally defined mechanisms for describing combinations of components in a model using heterogeneous interactions. BIP does not consider components as black boxes and has access to the description of their behavior. This allows the formal verification of properties on the model. It is important to note that, in BIP, the description of the interactions between components is made at the M1 level.

The "42" approach [12] seems closer to ours. Based on the synchronous paradigm, 42 generates the code of the MoCs (called "controllers") from the contracts of the components (described using automata), the relations between their ports and additional information related to activation scheduling. The strength of this approach lies in the description of the behavioral contract of components. However, such a description may not be available (in the case of an external IP for instance) or may not be easy to establish, in the case of continuous time behaviors for example.

Metropolis [13] also relies on the concept of model of computation, but it focuses on MoCs related to process networks. It originates from trace algebras [14] and is closely related to the tag semantics approaches [3,15]. In Metropolis, the modeling of the function is separated from the modeling of the architecture. A mapping mechanism is provided to produce platform specific models. Metropolis includes tools for verification, simulation and synthesis.

3   Modeling Heterogeneous Systems with ModHel'X

3.1   Black Boxes and Snapshots

In ModHel'X, we adopt a component-oriented approach in which we consider components as black boxes, called *blocks*, in order to decouple the internal model of a component from the model of the system in which it is used. Therefore, the behavior of a block is observable only at its interface: nothing is known about what is happening inside the block, and in particular whether the block is even computing something at a given moment.

In addition, instead of "triggering" the behavior of a block, we only *observe* its interface. When we need to observe a block, we ask it to provide us with a coherent view of its interface at this moment. A block can therefore be active even when we do not observe it. This is a key point in our approach because it allows us to embed asynchronous processes in a model without synchronizing them: we simply observe them at instants suitable for the embedding model. The behavior of a block or a model is therefore a sequence of observations. An observation of a model is defined as the combination of the observations of its blocks according to a MoC. This definition holds at all the levels of a hierarchical model. The observation of the top-level model, i.e. the model of the overall system, is a *snapshot* [16] which defines the exact state of the interface of each block at a given instant. We detail the way a snapshot is obtained using the rules expressed by a MoC in Section 3.4.

3.2   Time

The notions of time used in different models of computation are varied (real time, logical clocks, partial order on signal samples, etc.), and ModHel'X must support all of them. Moreover, in an heterogeneous model, different notions of time are combined and each part of the model may have its own time stamp in a given snapshot. Therefore, the succession of snapshots is the only notion of time which is shared by all MoCs and which is predefined in ModHel'X. On this sequence of instants, each MoC can define its own notion of time.

A snapshot of a model is made whenever its environment (i.e. the input data) changes, but also as soon as any block at any level of the hierarchy needs to be observed, for instance because its state has changed. To this end, each component of an heterogeneous model can give constraints on its own time stamp at the next snapshot. For instance, in a timed automaton, a time out transition leaving the current state must be fired even if no input is available. This can be achieved by requiring, when entering this state, that the next snapshot occurs before the timeout expires. This feature is a major departure from the Ptolemy approach, where the root model drives the execution of the other layers of the hierarchy.

Times in two MoCs may be synchronized by the interaction pattern at the boundary of two hierarchical levels. Thus, time constraints can propagate through the hierarchy up to the top level model.

3.3   A Generic Meta-model for Representing the Structure of Models

The generic meta-model that we propose, shown on Figure 1, defines abstract concepts for representing the structural elements of models. Since our goal is to support the widest possible range of modeling languages, the concepts that we define can seem very similar to concepts found in other modeling approaches, in particular component-oriented ones. Each of the concepts of our meta-model can be specialized in order to represent notions that are specific to a given modeling language, but their semantics is given by the MoCs which interprets them.

In the *structure* of a *model*, *blocks* are the basic units of behavior. *Pins* define the interface of models and blocks. The interactions between blocks are represented by *relations* between their pins. Relations are unidirectional and do not have any behavior: they are interpreted according to the MoC in order to determine how to combine the behaviors of the blocks they connect. For instance, a relation can represent a causal order between two blocks as well as a communication channel.

In Modhel'X, data is represented by *tokens*. The concept of token can be specialized for each model of computation. For instance, in a discrete event

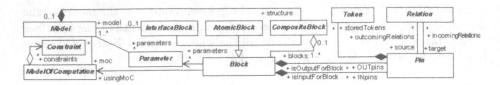

Fig. 1. Generic meta-model for representing the structure of models

model, tokens may have a value and a time-stamp, while in a data-flow model, they carry a value only. The type of the value which is carried by a token is not taken into account by the MoC, which is only in charge of delivering the tokens by interpreting the relations between the blocks.

The behavior of a block can be described either using a formalism which is external to our framework (e.g. in C or Java), yielding an *atomic block*, or by a ModHel'X model. To handle the latter case, we have introduced a special type of block called an *interface block*, which implements hierarchical heterogeneity: the internal model of an interface block may obey a MoC which is different from the MoC of the model in which the block is used. Interface blocks are a key notion in our framework since they are in charge of adapting the semantics of their inner and outer models of computation. They allow the explicit specification of the interactions between different MoCs.

3.4   An Imperative Semantics for MoCs and Their Interactions

Computing a snapshot of an heterogeneous model requires to compute the observation of all its parts, which may use different MoCs i.e. different notions of time, control or data. The issue of the consistency of such an observation is similar to the definition of the state of a distributed system [16]. In ModHel'X, we have chosen to define a model of computation as an algorithm for computing observations of the model to which it is associated. For each observation, the algorithm asks the blocks of the model to *update* the state of their interface. The results of the update (output data) are propagated to other blocks by *propagation* operations. We want our execution engine to be deterministic, therefore we observe the blocks sequentially. To ensure the consistency of the computed behavior with the control and concurrency notions of the original model, the MoC must include *scheduling* operations which determine the order in which to update the blocks.

Figure 2 represents the generic structure of our algorithm. This structure is a fixed frame which "standardizes" the way MoCs can be expressed in ModHel'X, but the contents of its elements is left free. Therefore, for each MoC, the semantics of the operations of this algorithm has to be described, using an imperative syntax, in order to define the scheduling and propagation "policies" specific to the MoC (non necessary operations can be left empty). The left part of the figure shows the loop which computes the succession of snapshots in the execution of the model. In the computation of a snapshot, the computation of an observation of one block brings into play the scheduling and propagation operations

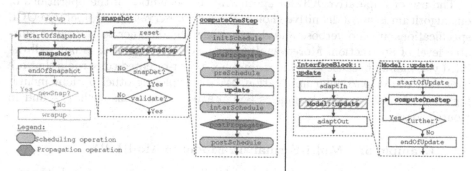

Fig. 2. Generic execution algorithm

Fig. 3. Update on an interface block and its internal model

mentioned above and is called a *step* (represented on the right part of Figure 2 under the name `computeOneStep`). The algorithm loops on successive steps until the snapshot is entirely determined (i.e., for most MoCs, when the state of all the outputs of the executed model is known). A given block may be updated several times in this loop, what allows the use of non-strict [17] blocks for the computation of fixed point behaviors. Therefore, ModHel'X supports MoCs in which cyclic dependencies are allowed.

The execution of a model traverses the hierarchy thanks to the delegation of the operations of interface blocks to their internal model. Snapshots are realized only at the top level, which represents the whole system. An internal model is only asked to provide a coherent view of its behavior when its interface block is updated. The update operations of interface blocks and models are shown on Figure 3. The `adaptIn` and `adaptOut` operations of an interface block allow the modeler to specify explicitly how the semantics of the internal and the external MoCs are adapted before and after the update of its internal model. This may include the adaptation of data, time or control. The `startOfUpdate` and `endOfUpdate` operations in the update of a model are used respectively to take new inputs from the interface block into account, and to provide it with newly determined outputs. The observation of a model may be partial (if it models a non-strict component). The loop which computes the observation must stop when the `further` operation indicates that no more outputs can be determined.

3.5 Implementation and Validation

We have experimented our approach in a prototype based on the Eclipse EMF framework [18]. We use the ImperativeOCL [19] language, an imperative extension of OCL, for describing the semantics of the operations of our algorithm. No interpreter being available for the moment, we translate it into Java. We have successfully implemented several MoCs, such as Finite State Machines (FSM), Discrete Events (DE) and *charts [20]. We are developing a library of MoCs in order to further the validation of our approach. We are currently working on the UML Statecharts and the Synchronous Dataflow (SDF) MoCs.

The use of ImperativeOCL for specifying the semantics of the operations of our algorithm is not a definitive choice. We have observed that ImperativeOCL specifications are too verbose and do not allow the designer to work at a suitable level of abstraction. Moreover, ImperativeOCL's semantics is not well defined yet, mainly because it includes complex object-oriented constructs that are irrelevant to our particular application. We are exploring other options including model transformation languages and pre/post conditions such as found in Hoare's logic.

3.6   Example of a Multi-Formalism Model in ModHel'X

To illustrate our approach, and in particular the semantic adaptation between a timed and an untimed MoC, we consider a simple hierarchical and heterogeneous model of a coffee machine which works as follows: first the user inserts a coin, then he presses the "coffee" button to get his coffee after some preparation time.

In this model, we take into account the date of the interactions between the user and the machine: insert a coin, push a button, deliver the coffee. Therefore, we use the Discrete Events (DE) MoC, which is implemented, for instance, by SimEvents (The MathWorks) or VHDL. We represent our user by an atomic block, whose behavior is written in Java. We model the coffee machine as an automaton (with UML Statecharts for instance), because at this stage of the design process, we focus on the logic of its behavior. We consider here a simple version of this MoC called FSM (Finite State Machines), which is similar to the one presented in [8]. Figure 4 shows the global model resulting from the combination of the DE and FSM models. Such a combination is a classical example, which is well addressed by tools like Ptolemy. However, we will see that it is possible to handle the interactions between DE and FSM differently with ModHel'X.

The representation of the structure of the DE model in ModHel'X is straightforward. The representation of the FSM model is more involved because a transition may have two associated behaviors: the evaluation of its guard and its action. Since blocks are the basic units of behavior in ModHel'X, a transition is represented using a block for its guard linked to a block for its action. Relations between guards represent the states.

In DE, when a snapshot is taken, the current time is determined according to the time stamps of the input events and on the time constraints produced by the blocks. At each computation step, we consider the blocks which have posted

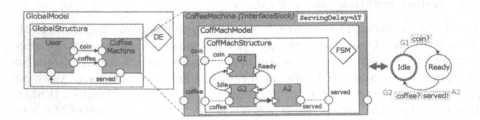

Fig. 4. Global model of the coffee machine and coffee machine automaton

a time constraint for the current time and the blocks which are the target of events. We update a minimal element of these blocks according to a topological sort in order to respect causal dependencies. Listing 1.1 shows the code of the **initSchedule** operation for the DE MoC. This is the only scheduling operation for this MoC, the others (**pre**, **inter** and **postSchedule**) being left empty.

DE and FSM share the notion of event. However, FSM has no notion of time attached to events. So, when a DE event enters FSM, the interface block has to remove its time stamp to make it look like an FSM event. When an FSM event enters DE, the interface block has to give it the "right" time stamp. An acceptable way to proceed is to give it the same time stamp as the most recent incoming event (in particular, this is what is done by Ptolemy). We provide an interaction pattern which realizes this adaptation. However, for our coffee machine, this behavior does not model the serving delay, which is an important characteristic of the model. Therefore, we add a **ServingDelay** parameter to the coffee machine and we modify the pattern so that the time stamp of the **served** event is the sum of the time stamp of the **coffee** event and the **ServingDelay** (see the **adaptOut** operation on Listing 1.2.

Listing 1.1. DEMoC::initSchedule(m:Model)

```
// Search for blocks having produced a constraint at the current time
OrderedSet(Block) blocklist := self . constraints
    →select(c: Constraint | c. constraintTime=self. currentTime)→collect(c: Constraint | c. author);
if ( blocklist →notEmpty()){ // If blocks have produced constraints at the current time...
        self . topologicalSort ( blocklist , m.structure); // Topological sort on these blocks
        self . currentBlock := blocklist →first(); // Choose the first one to update
        // Then remove the corresponding constraint
        self . constraints := self . constraints →reject(b:Block|b=self. currentBlock);
}else{ // ... else, search for blocks that have to receive events
        blocklist := self . activeEventList →collect(e:Event|e. destinationPin . isInputForBlock)
        if ( blocklist →notEmpty()){ // If there are blocks to update
            self . topologicalSort ( blocklist , m.structure); // Topological sort on these blocks
            self . currentBlock := blocklist →first(); // And choose the first one to update
        }
}
```

Listing 1.2. CoffeeMachine::adaptOut()

```
self . model. structure . pinsOut→select(pInt:Pin | pInt . storedTokens→notEmpty())
    →forEach(pInt:Pin){ // Check all the output pins of the internal model
        self . pinsOut→forEach(pExt:Pin){ // If FSM events have been produced by the internal model...
            pExt.storedTokens→append( // ... they become DE events on the outputs of the block
                new DEEvent( // ... with time stamps = last stored time stamp + serving delay
                    self .tLastDEevt + self . parameters→select(name="servingDelay")));
        }
        pInt .storedTokens→clear(); // FSM events are cleared
}
```

4 Discussion

4.1 Intended Workflow and Required Effort for Using ModHel'X

There are two prerequisites to the use of the ModHel'X framework. First, an expert of a modeling language has to describe the structural and semantic elements of this language using our meta-model and our imperative syntax. Since our goal is not to replace existing modeling tools, this expert also defines transformations from the original meta-model of the language to our generic meta-model. This is the difficult part of the work because the semantics of modeling tools is often known intuitively, through the experience we have of the tools. Second, for each pair of MoCs that may interact in heterogeneous models, experts should define interaction patterns, which model standard ways of combining models that obey these MoCs. The interaction policy actually used in a particular model will be a specialization of one of these patterns, tuned using parameters.

These steps represent the main effort needed to benefit from the ModHel'X approach. The first step is done once and for all for each modeling language. It is necessary to define at least one semantic adaptation policy for each pair of MoCs that one intends to use together. However, there is no need to define such a policy for any pair of MoCs, first because there may be no sense in making some MoCs interact, second because even when they are used together in a model of a system, some models of computation never interact directly. The number of useful combinations of MoCs is therefore much lower than the number of combinations that are theoretically possible for N MoCs.

4.2 Supported Models of Computation

Considering that a given structure of model can be interpreted as an automaton or as a discrete event model depending on the MoC which is associated to it can seem somewhat extreme. However, this choice has proven to be powerful since a tool like Ptolemy supports, on this basis, paradigms as different as finite state machines, ordinary differential equations or process networks.

In the same way, ModHel'X can support a large range of models of computation. This includes MoCs for continuous behaviors, which are approximated by the computation of a series of discrete observations. ModHel'X also supports models of computation that allow cyclic dependencies in models. Such dependencies are solved by iterating toward a fixed point, as in the Synchronous Reactive domain of Ptolemy. The fixed point is reached only if all blocks are monotonous according to a partial order defined by the model of computation. Last, even if the execution engine of ModHel'X is deterministic (it is designed to compute one of the possible behaviors of a model), non deterministic MoCs are supported but require the use of pseudo-random functions in their specification.

4.3 Comparison between ModHel'X and Ptolemy

Ptolemy was our main source of inspiration, but we have extended it on several aspects. One of our main contributions is the explicit specification of the interactions between MoCs (see Section 3.4). Moreover, our approach is based on the observation of blocks and not on the triggering of actors. Thanks to this change of paradigm and to the introduction of time constraints, the execution of a ModHel'X model is not necessarily driven by its root level. Indeed, a block at any level of the hierarchy of the model can produce a constraint on the time stamp of its next observation, what will force the execution machine to compute a snapshot at this time, even if no new input is available for the model. Finally, the definition of our abstract syntax as a MOF meta-model allows us to rely on model transformation tools from the MDE community to exchange models with other tools in the design chain.

5   Conclusion

We have presented an approach to multi-formalism modeling that (a) provides support for the specification of the semantics of a modeling formalism through the concept of model of computation, and (b) allows the definition of the interactions between heterogeneous parts of a model through a special modeling construct and using an imperative syntax. This approach relies on the black-box and the snapshot paradigms to compute the observable behavior of a model by combining the behaviors observed at the interface of its components. A generic meta-model for representing the structure of hierarchical heterogeneous models has been proposed. On this basis, models of computation are described by giving a specific semantics to the operations of a generic algorithm which computes series of snapshots of models which conform to the proposed meta-model.

We are currently developing the MoC library of our prototype in order to further the validation of our approach. The rigid structure of the execution algorithm of ModHel'X is a first step toward the definition of MoCs in a fixed frame with formal semantics. However, for the moment, our imperative syntax is still too close to Java to have a formal semantics. Therefore, ModHel'X cannot be used for model-checking or demonstrating properties. We are currently studying several possibilities for replacing ImperativeOCL with a more concise and formal language. Moreover, we are considering the use of a formal framework for founding the semantics of our execution algorithm.

References

1. Eker, J., Janneck, J.W., Lee, E.A., Liu, J., Liu, X., Ludvig, J., Neuendorffer, S., Sachs, S., Xiong, Y.: Taming heterogeneity – the Ptolemy approach. Proceedings of the IEEE, Special Issue on Modeling and Design of Embedded Software 91(1), 127–144 (2003)
2. Mosterman, P.J., Vangheluwe, H.: Computer automated multi-paradigm modeling: An introduction. Simulation: Transactions of the Society for Modeling and Simulation International 80(9), 433–450 (2004), Special Issue: Grand Challenges for Modeling and Simulation
3. Lee, E.A., Sangiovanni-Vincentelli, A.L.: A framework for comparing models of computation. IEEE Trans. on CAD of Integrated Circuits and Systems 17(12), 1217–1229 (1998)

4. Basu, A., Bozga, M., Sifakis, J.: Modeling heterogeneous real-time systems in BIP. In: 4th IEEE International Conference on Software Engineering and Formal Methods (SEFM 2006), pp. 3–12 (2006)
5. Fritzson, P., Engelson, V.: Modelica — A unified object-oriented language for system modeling and simulation. In: Jul, E. (ed.) ECOOP 1998. LNCS, vol. 1445, pp. 67–90. Springer, Heidelberg (1998)
6. Henzinger, T.A., Sifakis, J.: The embedded systems design challenge. In: Misra, J., Nipkow, T., Sekerinski, E. (eds.) FM 2006. LNCS, vol. 4085, pp. 1–15. Springer, Heidelberg (2006)
7. Bruneton, E., Coupaye, T., Stefani, J.: The fractal component model specification (2004)
8. Muller, P.A., Fleurey, F., Jézéquel, J.M.: Weaving executability into object-oriented meta-languages. In: Proceedings of the 8th ACM/IEEE International Conference on Model Driven Engineering Languages and Systems (MODELS/UML 2005), pp. 264–278 (2005)
9. de Lara, J., Vangheluwe, H.: $ATOM^3$: A tool for multi-formalism modelling and meta-modelling. In: Kutsche, R.-D., Weber, H. (eds.) ETAPS 2002 and FASE 2002. LNCS, vol. 2306, pp. 595–603. Springer, Heidelberg (2002)
10. Levendovszky, T., Lengyel, L., Charaf, H.: Software Composition with a Multi-purpose Modeling and Model Transformation Framework. In: IASTED on SE, Innsbruck, Austria, pp. 590–594 (2004)
11. Karsai, G., Agrawal, A., Shi, F., Sprinkle, J.: On the use of graph transformations for the formal specification of model interpreters. Journal of Universal Computer Science, Special issue on Formal Specification of CBS 9(11), 1296–1321 (2003)
12. Maraninchi, F., Bouhadiba, T.: 42: Programmable models of computation for a component-based approach to heterogeneous embedded systems. In: 6th ACM International Conference on Generative Programming and Component Engineering (GPCE 2007), pp. 53–62 (2007)
13. Balarin, F., Lavagno, L., Passerone, C., Vincentelli, A.L.S., Sgroi, M., Watanabe, Y.: Modeling and designing heterogeneous systems. Advances in Concurrency and System Design (2002)
14. Burch, J.R., Passerone, R., Sangiovanni-Vincentelli, A.L.: Overcoming heterophobia: Modeling concurrency in heterogeneous systems. In: Proceedings of the second International Conference on Application of Concurrency to System Design, p. 13 (2001)
15. Benveniste, A., Caillaud, B., Carloni, L.P., Sangiovanni-Vincentelli, A.L.: Tag machines. In: Proceedings of the 5th ACM International Conference On Embedded Software (EMSOFT 2005), pp. 255–263. ACM, New York (2005)
16. Chandy, K.M., Lamport, L.: Distributed snapshots: Determining global states of distributed systems. ACM Transactions on Computer Systems 3(1), 63–75 (1985)
17. Meyer, B.: Introduction to the Theory of Programming Languages. Prentice Hall, Hemel Hempstead (U.K.) (1990)
18. Eclipse Foundation: (Eclipse Modeling Framework (EMF))
19. OMG: Meta Object Facility (MOF) 2.0 Query/View/ Transformation specification (2005)
20. Hardebolle, C., Boulanger, F., Marcadet, D., Vidal-Naquet, G.: A generic execution framework for models of computation. In: Proceedings of the 4th International Workshop on Model-based Methodologies for Pervasive and Embedded Software (MOMPES 2007), at the European Joint Conferences on Theory and Practice of Software (ETAPS 2007), pp. 45–54. IEEE Computer Society, Los Alamitos (2007)

Domain-Specific Model Editors with Model Completion

Sagar Sen[1,2], Benoit Baudry[1], and Hans Vangheluwe[2]

[1] IRISA/INRIA,
Campus universitaire de Beaulieu
Rennes, France
{ssen,bbaudry}@irisa.fr
[2] School of Computer Science,
McGill University
Montreal, Quebec, Canada
hv@cs.mcgill.ca

Abstract. Today, integrated development environments such as Eclipse allow users to write programs quickly by presenting a set of recommendations for code completion. Similarly, word processing tools such as Microsoft Word present corrections for grammatical errors in sentences. Both of these existing systems use a set of constraints expressed in the form of a grammar to restrict/correct the user. Taking this idea further, in this paper we present an integrated software system capable of generating recommendations for model completion of partial models built in arbitrary domain specific model editors. We synthesize the model editor equipped with automatic completion from a modelling language's declarative specification consisting of a meta-model and constraints on it along with a visual syntax. The automatic completion feature is powered by a Prolog engine whose input is a constraint logic program derived from some models. The input logic program is obtained by a model transformation from models in multiple languages: the meta-model (as a class diagram), constraints on it (as constraint logic clauses), and a partial model (in the domain specific language). The Prolog engine solves the generated logic program and the solution(if there is one) is returned to the model editor as a set of recommendations for properties of the partial model. We incorporate automatic completion in the generative tool AToM[3] and use SWI-Prolog for constraint representation and satisfaction. We present examples using an illustrative visual language of Finite State Machines.

1 Introduction

Generative modelling tools such as AToM[3] (A Tool for Multiformalism Metamodelling) [3],GME(Generic Modelling Environment)[5], GMF (Eclipse Graphical Modelling Framework)[4] can synthesize a domain specific visual model editor from a declarative specification of a domain specific modelling language. A declarative specification consists of a meta-model, a set of constraints on all possible instances (or models) of the meta-model, and a visual syntax that describes

H. Giese (Ed.): MoDELS 2007 Workshops, LNCS 5002, pp. 259–270, 2008.
© Springer-Verlag Berlin Heidelberg 2008

how language elements(objects and relationships) manifest in the model editor. The designer of a model uses this model editor to construct a model on a canvas. This is analogous to a using an integrated development environment(IDE) to enter a program or a word processor to enter sentences. However, IDEs such as Eclipse present recommendations for completing a program statement when possible based on its grammar and existing libraries [2]. Similarly, Microsoft Word presents grammatical correction recommendations if a sentence does not conform to natural language grammar. Can we extrapolate similar technology for partial models constructed in a model editor for a domain specific modelling language(DSML)?

The major difficulty for providing completion capabilities in model editors is to integrate heterogeneous sources of knowledge in the computation of the possible solutions for completion. The completion algorithm must take into account the concepts defined in the meta-model for the DSML, the constraints expressed on this meta-model and the partial model built by a domain expert. The difficulty is that these three sources of knowledge are obviously related(they refer to the same concepts) but are expressed in different languages, sometimes in different files, and in most cases by different people and at different moments in the development cycle as they are separable concerns.

In this paper, we propose an automatic transformation from all these sources of knowledge to a *constraint logic program* (CLP).The generated program can then be fed in a Prolog engine that provides the possible solutions for completing the model. Our transformation is integrated in the software tool AToM³. The meta-model for a DSML is built directly in AToM³'s model editor using its class diagram formalism. The constraints on this meta-model are defined with Prolog in a separate file. Using this information and a description of the concrete visual syntax(specified in an icon editor) for a modelling language, AToM³ synthesizes a visual model editor for the DSML. The partial model can be built and edited in the generated model editor and the designer can ask for recommendations for possible completions.

An overview of our methodology is presented in Section 2. In Section 3 we present how domain specific modelling languages are specified and model editors for them are synthesized in MDE using meta-models, constraints and visual syntax. We also present in Section 3 an example of a partial model and a complete model in our chosen domain. Using the meta-model,constraints, and partial model we present the transformation to a constraint logic program in Section 4. We present examples of model completion recommendations generated for partial models in Section 5. We conclude in Section 6 with limitations of our work and we layout future directions.

2   Methodology Overview

Synthesis of model editors elicit the involvement of several different experts and users. We identify the involvement of language designers, domain experts or users of a DSML, visual syntax designers for automatic synthesis of model editors.

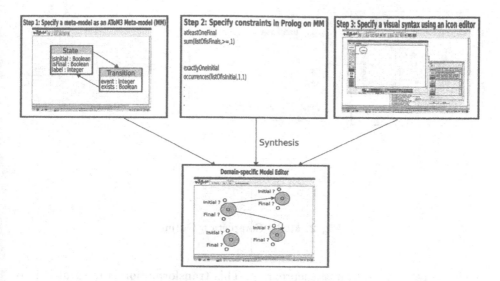

Fig. 1. Steps Taken by a DSML Designer to Synthesize a Model Editor in AToM[3]

- *Language Designers* interact with the domain experts to specify the concepts in a DSML in the form of a meta-model which is an AToM[3] class diagram [1] (meta-model from now on). Next, the designer specifies a set of Prolog clauses on the properties defined in the meta-model. We use SWI-Prolog for constraint representation.
- *Visual Syntax Designers* construct annotated icons that represent the different concepts in the meta-model. The icon for a class may be annotated with its property values. In Figure 1 we summarize how the meta-model, constraints,and visual syntax is used to synthesize a model editor for a DSML.
- *Domain Experts and Users* build models in the model editor that is synthesized from the meta-model, constraints, and visual syntax specifications. They also help the language designer define the concepts in the meta-model.

A domain expert uses the synthesized model editor to build models. He creates a model by inserting objects and building relationships between objects. He/she also sets values for properties. The model is simply a graph or a partial model until it conforms to its modelling language by satisfying all the constraints imposed on the modelling language. Manually performing such a task can be extremely tedious and sometimes impossible due to the size of the domains of model properties and complexity of constraints.

To automate the completion of a partial model we introduce a model transformation to construct a generative algorithm from the knowledge provided in the meta-model and constraints. The algorithm takes apartial model asinput

---

[1] AToM[3] class diagram is a subset of UML class diagram for meta-modelling and has sufficient expressiveness for *bootstrapping*.

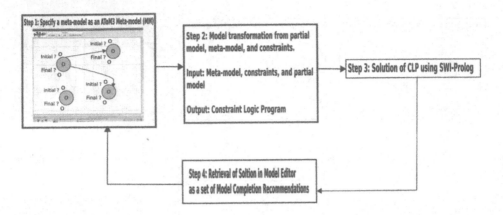

Fig. 2. Model Completion Outline

andgene rates a constraintlogicprogram. This transformation is integrated into AToM^3 so that it can be used for completion of models in any domain specific language.

Logic programming tool developers have built **Prolog** compilers [6] that can perform computer algebra and constraint satisfaction on an input constraint logic program. Such a **Prolog** compiler is invoked by AToM^3 and the synthesized CLP is solved and the results (if they exist) are returned to the model editor as recommendations. We use **SWI-Prolog** [6] for compiling the constraint logic program. In Figure 2 we outline how we complete partial models in AToM^3.

Now that we have outlined our overall methodology we go ahead and study each aspect of the methodology in detail leading to examples that illustrate the working of the idea. We illustrate our methodology using the guiding example of a **Finite State Machine (FSM)** modelling language.

3   Specifying a Domain Specific Modelling Language

In this section we explain the steps taken to declaratively specifying a domain specific modelling language. We use **Finite State Machines (FSM)** as a running example for a modelling language. A FSM modelling language is a visual language with circles representing states and directed arrows representing transitions between states. To define a modelling language and to generate visual model editor from it requires three inputs:

1. A Meta-model as an AToM^3 class diagram
2. A Set of **Prolog** Constraints on the meta-model
3. A Visual Syntax

We briefly describe these in the following sub-sections.

3.1 Meta-model

A model consists of objects and relationships between them. The meta-model of the modelling language specifiesthetypes of all the objects and theirpossibleinter relationships. The type of an object is referred to as a class. The meta-model for the FSM modelling language is presented in Figure 3. The classes in the meta-model are **State** and **Transition**.

In this paper we use the class diagram formalism in AToM^3 for specifying a meta-model. The class diagram formalism can specify itself and hence exhibits the property of *bootstrapping*. We use the visual language notation of class diagrams to specify the meta-model for the FSM modelling language in Figure 3.

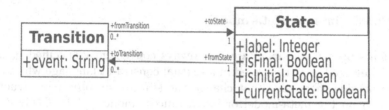

Fig. 3. The Finite State Machine Meta-model

Each class in the meta-model has *properties*. A property is either an *attribute* or a *reference*. An attribute is of primitive type which is either Integer, String, or Boolean. For instance, the attributes of the class **State** are isInitial and isFinal both of which are of primitive type Boolean. An example domain of values for the primitive attributes is given in Table 1. The String variable can be a finite set consisting of a null string, and finite length strings that specify a set of strings. In this paper, we consider a finite domain for each attribute. The domain is specified in the meta-model and all the models that are instances of the meta-model know of the domain for each attribute.

Describing the state of a class of objects with only primitive attributes is not sufficient in many cases. Modelling many real-world systems elicits the need to model complex relationships such as modelling that an object contains another set of objects or an object is related to another finite set of objects. This set

Table 1. Domains for Primitive Datatypes

Type	Domain
Boolean	$\{0, 1\}$
Integer	$\{MinInt, .., MaxInt\}$
String	$\{"a", "b", "c", "event1", ..\}$

of related objects is constrained by a *cardinality*. When a class is related to
another class, the related classes refer to each other via *references*. For instance,
in Figure 3 the classes **State** and **Transition** refer to each other via references
annotated with uni-directional relationships. The cardinality constraints are also
annotated with the relationship.

Apart from attributes and references, objects can inherit properties from other
classes. The attributes and references of a class called a super class are inherited
by derived classes. Similarly a derived class inherits the references in the super
class. There is no inheritance in our FSM meta-model, nevertheless we consider
transformation of inheritance relationships in the transformation presented in
Section 4.

3.2   Constraints on Meta-model

Constraints on a meta-model are not always conveniently specified using diagrams. They are better expressed in a textual constraint language who's semantics has no side-effect (does not change the state of an object or structure of
the model) on the meta-model or its instances (models). The OMG standard
for constraint specification is Object Constraint Language (OCL) however in our
current work we use constraint logic programming clauses in the form of Prolog
statements. These constraints are initially specified on meta-model properties.
The transformation generates a set of constraints on a lists of properties (those
influencing the constraint) in the partial model.

We use the CLP bounds library to specify constraints on properties with finite
domain. There are several predicates in the standard Prolog library. For instance,
one of the constraints for the FSM modelling language is:

– **atLeastOneFinalState** Variables: listOfisFinal is the list of all isFinal attributes
  for all states in the model. **Prolog** Constraint: sum(listOfisFinal,¿=,1) Explanation: The attribute isFinal is a boolean and the list of isFinals contains the
  values of all attributes in the partial model. The constraint ensures that the
  sum of the isFinals is greater than or equal to 1. This enforces the constraint
  that there is at least one Final state.

Other constraints include exactly one initial state, and a unique label for a
state object. To define constraints for arbitrary DSMLs we point the reader
to the SWI-Prolog referencemanual [6]. The language and the libraries have
been developed for two decades and we have a large repository of constraints
to work with including facility to use a foreign language to define an arbitrary
boolean function. Prolog has powerful mechanisms such as *domain reduction*. For
instance, constraint alldifferent(listOfVariables) ensures the automatic reduction
in the domain of variables in listOfVariables such that the each variable in the list
has a domain with values notinthedomain of the others. Thetextual specification
of constraints is typically specified in an different file from the class diagram
meta-model itself.

3.3   Visual Syntax

The final step(in specifying a DSML for synthesizing a model editor) we take is to specify the concrete visual syntax of the class of objects in the meta-model. The visual syntax specifies what an object looks like on a 2D canvas. An icon editor in AToM³ is used to specify the visual syntax of the classes in the meta-model.

An icon editor is used to specify the visual syntax of meta-model concepts such as classes and relationships. The icon for **State** is a circle annotated with three of its attributes(isFinal, isInitial, and label). The connectors in the diagram are points of connection between **State** objects and **Transition** objects.

The visual syntax can also by dynamically changed based on the properties of the model for example. In an iconic visual modelling language such FSM the first step taken in specifying a visual syntax is drawing an icon that represents a class of objects. If needed it is annotated with text and its properties. Connectors are added to the visual object so that it can be connected to other objects if they are related.

4   Transformation from Declarative Specification and a Partial Model to **CLP**

We present the transformation of the different parts of a partial model to a CLP using the meta-model and constraints asinput. The essential idea to generate CLPs constitutes the following steps:

1. Create variables to represent properties of a partial model
2. Define a domain on these variables.
3. Define constraints on these variables.
4. Finally, insert the label(SetOfVariables) clause toperformback-tracking search.

We associate a *finite domain* for each variable in the constraint logic program (CLP) hence, making it a *constraint logic program in finite domain* (CLP(FD)).We use the clp_bounds library in SWI-Prolog to express domains and constraints in CLP(FD). We generate a conjunction of constraints in Prolog. The conjunction is given by a "," operator. Finally, we insert the label predicate at the end of the program to perform back-tracking to find the value assignment/labeling of variables so as to generate completions for the partial model.

4.1   Transforming an Object

We now discuss how objects in a partial model are transformed to CLP. We illustrate this with a concrete example to enhance the reader's understanding. Consider the object shown in Figure 4. It is a **State** object. The attributes of a **State** object are isFinal, isInitial, currentState, and label. Each attribute also has a domain. The attributes isFinal, isInitial and currentState in the **State** object has a boolean domain of $[0, 1]$. The label attribute has an integer domain of $[0, 1, 2, .., MaxNumberOfStates]$.

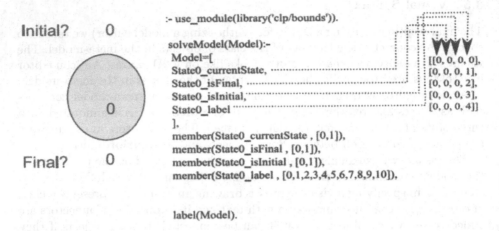

Fig. 4. (a) Object (example of a **State** object (b) Generated CLP code (c) Five **Prolog** solutions for each variable

In the transformation first each attribute has a unique identity which is given by OwningObjectName_attributeName. This unique ID is used to create a variable and is added to a list of variables in the CLP. If Model is the set of variables in the partial model. Then the variable State0_isFinal is included in this list:

$$Model=[..., State0\_isFinal,...],$$

Next, we associate a domain with a variable already included in the list of model variables. This is done using the member Prolog predicate. For instance, the domain for the variable State0_isFinal is manifested in Prolog as follows:

$$member(State0\ isFinal,[0,1])$$

We obtain the domain information for an attribute from the meta-model of the modelling language.

The CLP code generated for a **State** object is shown in Figure 4 (b). Solving the Prolog program gives a set of arrays with the result for the value assignment of each variable. This is shown in Figure 4 (c).

4.2   Transforming an Association

Next, we consider the transformation of an association in partial model to Prolog clauses. Consider the associations in Figure 5 (a). Two **State** objects are connected by two **Transition** objects. The existence of these relationships is determined by boolean *existence variables* such as Transition0_exists and Transition1_exists. In general, these variables are synthesized for all association in the partial model. We obtain the cardinality constraint for each association from the meta-model. In the partial model we look for all associations with the same

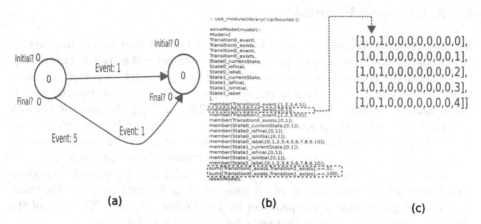

Fig. 5. (a) Association between **State** objects and a **Transition** (b) Generated CLP code (c) Cardinality constraint determines the value of an existence variable

source and destination object. We impose a cardinality constraint on all associations with the same source and destination. We synthesize two **Prolog** clauses to impose the cardinality constraint on a list of existence variables for the associations with the same source and destination. The example in Figure 5 (a) has its code generated in Figure 4 (b).

The cardinality constraints are imposed as sum of existence variables as follows:

$$\text{sum}([\text{Transition0 exists}, \text{Transition1 exists}], >=, 0),$$
$$\text{sum}([\text{Transition0 exists}, \text{Transition1 exists}], =<, 100),$$

The solution obtained for completing the partial model is shown in Figure 5 (c).

4.3 Generating Constraints

Finally, we insert constraints defined on the meta-model. A constraint C is expressed on properties p1,p2,...pN of a meta-model MM. In a partial model we identify all properties that are constrained by C and generate a list of variables (those already generated as described in Sections 4.1 and 4.2).

For instance, to ensure that every **State** object in the partial model has a unique label we generate the following constraint which is added as a conjunction to the constraints already generated:

$$\text{all different}([\text{State0\_label}, \text{State1\_label}, ..])$$

The all_different clause ensures that he value of each element in the list it receives as input is unique.

5   A Running Example

In this section, we present an example of a partial model that we use to generate model completion recommendations. In Figure 6 we present a partial model with two generated recommendations. For the same partial model we performed more tests. We generate 5 model completion recommendations. We randomly shuffle the domain constraints in the generated CLP. The shuffling changes the priority order in which values for properties are chosen by Prolog and has an effect on the result of model completion. We do not study this variability in detail. However, we present the time taken for generating 5 recommendations in Table 2.

For our example the time taken to generate a solution for the model is reasonably acceptable with an average of 2.5 seconds. A large portion of the time taken involves pre-processing of the problem by the Prolog compiler. The rest of the time is taken to find value assignments for constraint satisfaction.

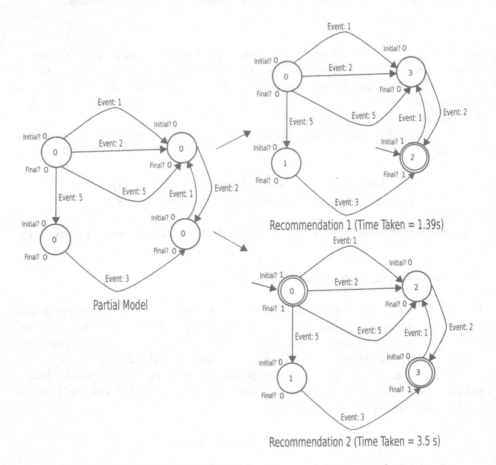

Fig. 6. A Partial Model and Two Proposed Recommendations

Table 2. Generated Recommendations

Recommendation	CPU Time
1	1.3
2	0.55
3	3.34
4	3.50
5	3.72

6   Conclusion

In this paper we present a framework for generating model completion recommendations in model editors. We illustrate our approach with the simple example of the FSM modelling language. At present we specify the meta-model as an AToM^3 class diagram (which is subset of UML class diagrams with sufficient facility for *bootstrapping*). Constraints on the meta-model are directly specified in Prolog. We also demonstrate, using a reasonably complex example, the working of our approach. However, there is room for several improvements.

Currently we only support constraint satisfaction of constraints from the metamodel and constraints of the modelling language. We wish to extend this by introducing *user-specific objective functions* and other constraints such as model transformation pre-conditions. This could lead to synthesis of interesting models for tasks such as model transformation testing and design space exploration. It would also be interesting to see how constraints from multiple paradigms can co-exist in the same environment and how they can be solved to get meaningful results.

Also, we start from a partial model with a fixed number of objects. In other words the *dimensionality* given by the object space is fixed. We plan to separate the notion of object space and property space to allow the synthesis of objects that add to a partial model before we go ahead and find values for proper ties as explained in this article.

Finally, we plan to use high-level constraints to formally communicate knowledge between modelling domains(multi-paradigm modelling) or scientific knowledge in general.

References

1. Apt, K.R., Wallace, M.G.: Constraint Logic Programming with ECLiPSe. Cambridge University Press, Cambridge (2007)
2. Ko, A.J., Aung, H.H., Myers, B.A.: Design requirements for more flexible structured editors from a study of programmers' text editing, CHI 2005 (2005),
http://portal.acm.org/citation.cfm?id=1056808.1056965

3. Vangheluwe, H., de Lara, J.: Domain-Specific Modelling with $AToM^3$. In: Tolvanen, J.-P., Sprinkle, J., Rossi, M. (eds.) The 4th OOPSLA Workshop on Domain-Specific Modeling, Vancouver, Canada, October 2004, p. 8 (2004)
4. Ehrig, K., Ermel, C., Hansgen, S.: Generation of visual editors as eclipse plug-ins. In: Proceedings of the 20th IEEE/ACM international Conference on Automated software engineering, pp. 134–143 (2005)
5. Ledeczi, A.R., Bakay, A., Maroti, M., Volgyesi, P., Nordstrom, G., Sprinkle, J., Karsai, G.: Composing Domain-Specific Design Environments in Computer, pp. 44–51 (2001)
6. Wielemaker, J.: SWI-Prolog 5.6.35 Reference Manual (2007), http://gollem.science.uva.nl/SWI-Prolog/Manual/

Third Intenational Workshop on Quality in Modeling

Ludwik Kuzniarz[1], Lars Pareto[2], Jean Louis Sourrouille[3], and Miroslaw Staron[2]

[1] Blekinge Institute of Technology
Ronneby, Sweden
[2] IT University of Göteborg
Göteborg, Sweden
[3] INSA Lyon, LIESP,
F-69621, France

Abstract. Introduction of Model Driven Development (MDD) raises new challenges in software quality management related to shifting the focus to models from text documents and code. The goal of this workshop was to gather researchers and practitioners interested in the emerging issues of quality in the context of MDD and to provide a forum for discussions of emerging issues related to software quality in MDD. An intended outcome of the workshop was an initial elaboration of a unified quality model for models. The paper reports activities performed in the workshop and the main results achieved throughout the workshop as well as during the follow-up activities. The workshop was divided into two parts: presentation part, where paper contributions were presented and discussed, and working part, where a guided discussion was conducted aimed at elaboration of a common quality model. The working part was preceded by an introductory presentation setting up a frame for the discussion, followed by concise position statements of the participants, and discussion towards formulation of a common quality model. As a follow-up activity, the contributions from the working part were combined into a common quality model published as a technical research report and highlighted in the paper. Future research directions and planned activities are also outlined.

1 Introduction

Model Driven Development (MDD) introduces changes to the known and accepted perception of software quality. In short, software quality is often defined as the degree to which the software conforms to stakeholder needs, product requirements, and product-component (internal) requirements. This notion of quality is valid in modeling too, but as models are used in more contexts than code (e.g., for domain analysis, architectural work, design documentation) quality concepts need to be extended to accommodate also for these uses. That models are graphical, and sometimes purposefully incomplete or semantic-free, also bring out quality aspects not present in the context of software development rooted in a view on software as code.

The goal of this workshop is to gather practitioners and researchers working in the area of modeling to discuss issues of quality in modeling. Several presentations

H. Giese (Ed.): MoDELS 2007 Workshops, LNCS 5002, pp. 271–274, 2008.

during the workshop show that this is an important topic and that a significant effort needs to be put before arriving at a mature quality framework/model for quality in modeling.

2 Presentations

The first half of the workshop contained presentations of position papers. The topics of the presentations included such aspects as:

- quality assessment of models used at several companies,
- an overview of available quality frameworks which can be applied for models,
- a critical appraisal of design patterns in UML models,
- implementing a family of model consistency checkers, and
- alternative models for the design review activity.

The discussions around these papers reflected the topics of the workshop – how to define the common quality model for models and modeling.

3 Working Session on Quality Model

In the same spirit as the presentations, the second part of the workshop contained a working session with the purpose of establishing a common quality model. The existing work of Pareto and Boquist [1] was the starting point for the discussions and the origin of the idea.

The session was prepared in advanced: the participants were asked to answer a set of questions and present their views during the workshop. The questions were:

- **Q1** What qualities of models and modelling matter?
- **Q2** How do they relate?
- **Q3** How can they be measured?

Each question was accompanied with instructions that detailed the intention with the question and provided formats for answering the question. In the instructions for Q1, participants were asked to produce a list of quality attributes and to classify these as belonging to either of the following general areas of quality (based on the quality framework of ISO9126[1]):

- *Project quality* relating to how well an organization executes the software process that involves modelling.
- *Process quality* relating to how well the software development process supports modelling (i.e. how well does the process state who should use which models when for what)?

---

[1] For historical reasons, the framework deviates slightly from ISO9126 in that it distinguishes process from project qualities. We do not regard this as significantly affecting the outcome .

- *Product quality* relating to "technical" properties of the model itself; these may be "white box" properties or "black box" properties.
- *Quality in use* relating to how well users of models can achieve their goals in some particular contexts of use.

Contributions varied in nature. Some were rearrangements of past research results within the bounds of the given framework, other brought poorly understood quality areas much in need for research, e.g., the need for abstraction metrics, and the need for a notion of unified modelling elements.

4 The Common Model

The post workshop activities (refer to Pareto [2] for details), resulted in the set of quality attributes shown in Figure 1.

As this outcome of the working session shows, there are almost 50 distinguishable qualities that researchers in model quality are concerned with.

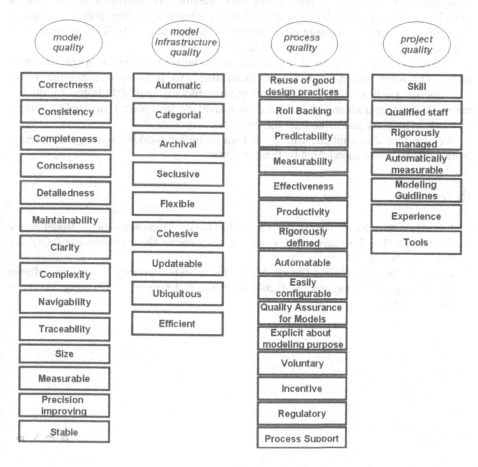

Fig. 1. Modeling Related Quality Attributes

The discussions during the working session provided the initial quality model, and also outlined several new research directions. The initial model, however, seems to reflect general trends in software engineering, for example raising the issue how to "measure" the level of abstraction of a model or how to provide units for normalization (similar to the notion of Line of Code) of models.

5 Research Directions

The development of a common quality model for MDD requires further empirical studies and theoretical work. From the discussions around the quality model one could notice that there are still "white spots" in this field. One of these is the notion of a size of the model – how to measure it and how to reason about it. Another is the issue of the complexity and consistency of models.

An important research direction is the evaluation and definition of quality characteristics in the context of MDD. The sample of respondents in the workshop represents only a subset of researchers and practitioners interested in the area of modeling. Although this is the correct (and necessary) starting point, it requires extending the sample to capture other aspects of perceived quality. This, nevertheless, once again calls for empirical studies in the area.

It seems that the next natural step for the workshop is to focus on operationalizing quality characteristics in order to make them usable for industry with minimal effort (i.e. not demanding customizations of quality models and definitions of quality metrics). This operationalization could improve the acceptance of quality related methods in industry and make their use more wide-spread.

We also intend to continue with the set-up including working sessions in the next workshops as it was appreciated by the participants.

References

1. Pareto, L., Boquist, U.: A Quality Model for Design Documentation in Model-centric Projects. In: The 3rd International Workshop on Software Quality Assurance (SOQUA), Portland, USA (2006)
2. Pareto, L. (ed.): A Unified Quality Model for Models. Research Reports in Software Engineering and Management, Vol. 2008:01. 2008, IT University of Göteborg: Göteborg, Sweden (2008)

Developing a Quality Framework for Model-Driven Engineering

Parastoo Mohagheghi and Vegard Dehlen

SINTEF, P.O. Box 124 Blindern,
N-0314 Oslo, Norway
{parastoo.mohagheghi,vegard.dehlen}@sintef.no

Abstract. This paper presents some related work on quality frameworks and requirements for evaluating them. It also discusses characteristics of model-driven engineering that are important when building a quality framework, such as its use of models in several stages of development and maintenance, generation of other artifacts from models and its multi-abstraction level approach that requires consistency and traceability. We present a 7-step process on how to define a quality framework that is adapted to model-driven engineering, and which integrates quality engineering with quality evaluation. As an example, the framework is applied on transformation quality. We maintain that the transformation process and transformation mapping should be discussed separately, as they require different approaches, and suggest quality goals, quality-carrying properties to achieve the quality goals and methods for evaluating these properties.

Keywords: Model-driven engineering, quality, transformation, metrics.

1 Introduction

More attention is paid to the quality aspects in Model-Driven Engineering (MDE) along with the growing importance of modeling in software development. Some challenging issues (especially for complex or large systems and special domains) are the increasing complexity that we need to understand and handle, the need for reliable systems and approaches that can verify and preserve quality requirements, as well as the dynamic adaptation and management of systems using transformations at runtime. Our research on the "Quality in MDE" project in SINTEF (http://quality-mde.org/) focuses on developing a quality framework applicable for MDE that includes quality goals, means or quality-carrying properties to achieve them, and evaluation methods. The research questions include:

1. *What quality aspects are important in MDE? Are there any differences in quality goals and activities when using MDE compared to other approaches?*
2. *How can quality goals be achieved and evaluated?*
3. *How can MDE improve the quality of developed software?*

H. Giese (Ed.): MoDELS 2007 Workshops, LNCS 5002, pp. 275–286, 2008.
© Springer-Verlag Berlin Heidelberg 2008

This paper gives some answers to the above questions and defines an initial framework for defining and evaluating quality in MDE. It further discusses the quality of transformations as an example of applying the framework. This paper is a revised and shortened version of a paper presented at the 2nd workshop on Quality in Modeling co-located with MODELS 2007 and we refer to the workshop version for more discussions on the requirements of quality frameworks.

The paper is organized as follows. Section 2 presents some definitions of software quality, the different purposes of modeling, work on quality frameworks and characteristics of MDE that are important when defining a quality framework. Section 3 presents our quality framework and Section 4 applies it on the transformation quality. The paper is concluded in Section 5.

2 Background

2.1 Definitions of Quality and Relation to Modeling Purposes

According to IEEE, software quality as an attribute is (1) the degree to which a system, component, or process meets specified requirements, and (2) the degree to which a system, component, or process meets customer or user needs or expectations [10]. ISO 9126-1 defines quality as a set of features and characteristics of a product or service that bear on its ability to satisfy stated or implied needs [11]. Evaluating quality based on the goals or needs is also emphasized by Claxton and McDougal who write that assessing the quality of anything – models included – has two parts. One comes from measuring the right things, in the right way, with the right yardsticks. But the heart of quality comes from the second aspect; judging something based on its intended function and purpose [2]. So the search for quality (in modeling) starts by asking, "What's the purpose of a model?" as models are in fact developed for various purposes.

Kühne classifies models as being either *descriptive* (capture some knowledge; e.g. requirements or domain analysis) or *prescriptive* (aka specification models; used as blueprints of a possible or imaginary system) [13]. In other words, a model can exist later or earlier than its original. Hesse thinks that in the software engineering field, a model often plays a double role: describing a part of an application domain and prescribing a piece of software for that domain [8]. Daniels defines three kinds of models based on their purposes [4]:

- *Conceptual models* describe a situation of interest in the world, such as a business operation or factory process.
- *Specification models* define what a software system must do, the information it must hold, and the behavior it must exhibit. They assume an ideal computing platform.
- *Implementation models* describe how the software is implemented, considering all the computing environment's constraints and limitations.

Different types of models have of course different quality goals, where a "quality goal" is defined as a clear definition of what quality means to a stakeholder and that can be measured in a meaningful way. For example, conceptual models should be understandable for external stakeholders but not necessarily detailed. However, it is not often straightforward to define quality goals for each purpose of modeling or aspect, because:

- Some quality goals are in conflict with one another. For example using the same modeling language for different models reduces the need for learning new languages. On the other hand, we want to use different modeling features in each model (for example, the implementation model has to take the programming environment into account [4]) and using the same modeling language might therefore not be appropriate. Paige et al. believe that users may profit from using different languages for different purposes and combining them [21].
- Some quality goals crosscut models or activities. For example, if our conceptual model contains the concept of *customer*, our software will contain direct representations of customers, and our software customers will have similar attributes to their real-world counterparts. We want this correspondence because it improves traceability between requirements and code, and because it makes the software easier to understand [4].

Thus any research on quality in MDE should take into account the various modeling purposes, relations of purposes to quality goals and the dependencies or conflicts between them. In MDE, models are refined progressively and transformed to new models or code. In [19], we discussed that the quality of models depends on the quality of modeling language(s) used, the quality of tools used for modeling, the knowledge of developers of the problem in hand and their experience of modeling languages and tools, the quality of the modeling processes and the quality assurance techniques applied to discover faults or weaknesses. We also add the quality of activities performed on the models such as transformations to the above list, and discuss it in more details throughout this paper.

2.2 What Characterizes Model-Driven Engineering?

The characteristics of MDE that are important when defining a quality framework are:

- *Use of models in several stages of software development*: Models are used from early development phases to testing, simulation and code generation. Models are often incomplete, imprecise and inconsistent early in the software development life-cycle and get gradually more precise and complete. Models can be non-executable or executable (even early analysis models can be executable).
- *Models on different levels of abstraction and from different viewpoints*: An example is the OMG MDA's viewpoints of Computational Independent Models (CIM), versus Platform Independent Models (PIM) and Platform Specific Models (PSM) [20]. Relations between these models are important when evaluating them for some quality characteristics. For example, refined models have additional classes and methods that can increase complexity metrics. Another example is structural models vs. behavioral models. This is a characteristic of e.g. UML and not necessarily all modeling languages. The multi-view and multi-abstraction level development approach means that each of the diagrams and abstraction levels might require specific quality goals and metrics. Lange describes this for the model

size metrics that varies on various diagrams and abstraction levels [15]. Mellor and Balcer refer to several challenging issues that inevitably arise from the multi-view and multi-notational approach of UML in MDE [18]:

o *Consistency*: The models of various views need to be syntactically and semantically compatible with each other (i.e., horizontal consistency).

o *Transformation and evolution*: a model must be semantically consistent with its refinements (i.e., vertical consistency).

o *Traceability*: A change in the model of a particular view should lead to corresponding consistent changes in the models of other views.

o *Integration*: Models of different views may need to be seamlessly integrated before software production.

• *Activities are performed on models by tools*: Models undergo transformations and refinements. Many activities have models as input, output, or both. The quality of such activities can preserve, improve or reduce the quality of models. Model transformation is applied by tools, and during a transformation output models are supplied with information not present in the input model. Examples are domain-specific information or the platform concept during the PIM to PSM transformation. Models should therefore be complete and precise but not include unnecessary or redundant information [23].

• *Generation of code and other artifacts from models*: This means that evaluating the quality of models is more important in MDE than in traditional software development, where the code is mostly evaluated for quality.

• *Developing Domain Specific Languages (DSLs) and models*: DSLs have existed for a while and Domain Specific Modeling Languages are also getting more popular as a means to increase productivity and tailor the development environment to a domain. Selecting any approach for developing a DSL such as defining a metamodel or a UML profile needs knowledge of language and tool design and appropriate quality guidelines.

Thus a quality framework in MDE should take into account the role of models, languages, tools, transformations and their appropriateness for the domain and modeling purposes. *Model-driven Quality Assurance (MDQA)* is often defined as the automatic quality assurance that is based on models such as using system models for testing and verification (see e.g., http://www.mdqa.org/). In this paper, we suggest the notion of *Model-Driven Quality Engineering (MDQE)* meaning taking advantage of MDE to prevent and discover quality defects as early as possible in the software development lifecycle. MDE lends itself to quality engineering because of two reasons. First, models are primary software artifacts in MDE and several other artifacts are generated from models. Thus developing high quality models improves the quality of e.g., test cases and code that may be fully or partly generated from models. Second, quality engineering is enhanced by the extensive use of tools in transforming models to other models or code. Tools can analyze and monitor models for various characteristics. An example is discussed by Haesen and Snoeck in relation with consistency checking which can be done *by analysis* (an algorithm detects inconsistencies between deliverables), *by monitoring* (meaning that a tool has a monitoring facility that checks every new specification), and *by construction or by generation* (meaning that a tool generates one deliverable from another and guarantees semantic consistency) [7]. Another example is using tools for checking rules or constraints during modeling or transformations as proposed in [1]. Rules and constraints can also be defined on metamodels.

2.3 Related Work on Quality Frameworks

In this section, we present some work on quality frameworks that either address the quality of models or quality in MDE, or may be used in building such a framework for MDE.

ISO/IEC 14598 International Standard (Standard for Information technology - Software product evaluation - Part 1: General overview) defines the term *quality model* as "the set of characteristics and relationships between them, which provides the basis for specifying quality requirements and evaluating quality". ISO 9126 is an example of a widely used software quality model [11]. We use the term *quality framework* in our work to avoid any confusion between quality model and model quality.

Dromey proposes a five step approach in constructing a quality model [5]:

1. Identify a set of high-level quality attributes for the product like reliability or maintainability.
2. Identify the product components. Examples are modules, requirements or relations.
3. Identify and classify the most significant, tangible, quality-carrying properties for each component. These are properties that result in manifestation of the high-level quality attributes.
4. Propose a set of axioms for linking product properties to quality attributes. This is not an easy task and the links cannot always be empirically verified.
5. Evaluate the model, identify its weaknesses and refine it.

To identify high-level quality attributes, one may ask:

- What are the most important usages of this product?
- What kind of defects we want to avoid for these usages?

Trendowicz and Punter discuss quality models for software product lines [25]. The activities during development of a quality model or framework are shown in Figure 1. The definition of goals, characteristics and sub-characteristics should be done iteratively and involve the stakeholders. This procedure goes on for as long as there is a set of measurable sub-characteristics defined. A sub-characteristic is measurable when it is possible to attach it to a particular component of a product line and define one or more corresponding metrics (which can be quantitative, qualitative evaluation or a combination of both); thus similar to the tangible quality-carrying properties in the Dromey's process. Reviewing should guarantee that the quality model is feasible and not too complex. The final step is actually execution. They further write that quality models should be *flexible* (to be tailored to a specific organization and project), *reusable* and *transparent* (clear insight into their rationale as well as the meaning of the characteristics and relations among them).

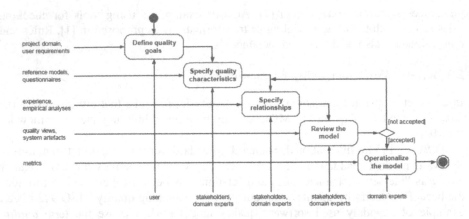

Fig. 1. Activities during development of quality models as defined in [25]

A framework that is applied on conceptual models is first presented by Lindland et al. [16] and later extended by Krogstie et al. and applied for evaluating the quality of modeling languages (see for example [12]). Lindland et al. divided quality goals into *syntactic* (adherence to the language rules or syntax), *semantic* (relevance to the problem domain and containing statements that are correct and relevant) and *pragmatic* (understandability of a model by stakeholders).The framework separates quality goals from means to achieve them. For example having formal syntax in a language is a means to achieve syntactic quality. Means are similar to quality-carrying properties in the Dromey's process. Solheim and Neple have simplified and adapted this framework to MDE [23]. They further identify *transformability* and *maintainability* as two quality goals that are important in MDE, which are in turn decomposed into several characteristics.

Lange and Chaudron identify two primary use of models; either development or maintenance [14]. They further define some purposes of modeling for each phase (e.g., analysis and prediction are done in the development phase) and relate some quality characteristics to each purpose. These characteristics are further related to metrics that are mainly on the detailed design level. Of other work on the quality of models we can mention [2] on the quality of data models (a data model is a model describing parts of business) and [26] on the quality of UML 2.0 models.

In addition to models, modeling languages has been subject of research, as in [6, 12 and 21]. The three works have some language quality requirements in common such as having minimal set of concepts that are precisely defined, uniqueness of concepts and understandability, while they complement each other in other aspects. Another difference is when they are applied. Paige et al. [21] recommend their principles for designing modeling languages, while Krogstie et al. [12] and Grossman [6] have defined criteria for evaluating modeling languages.

Putting all the related work together provides requirements for quality frameworks and a list of quality goals for some aspects such as models and languages, while other aspects such as processes, activities and tools are less studied. There is also a need for more empirical studies and evaluation of the frameworks.

3 Defining a Quality Framework for MDE

In the previous section we presented some work on quality frameworks, MDE characteristics, and on the quality of models and modeling languages. In this section, we present a process for defining a quality framework in MDE which is illustrated in Figure 2.

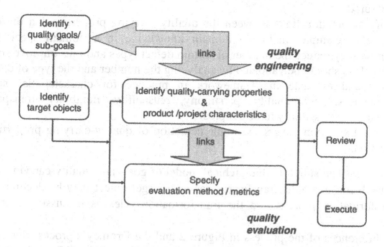

Fig. 2. Steps in developing a quality framework for MDE; specifying both quality engineering and quality evaluation

We define the steps as:

1. Identify *quality goals*. Examples of quality goals are maintainability, reuse or increased productivity. Identifying quality goals should involve all stakeholders and reflect the purposes of modeling and the priorities of the project.
2. Identify *target objects* that can impact the quality goals. Proper target objects can be the software development approach or process, models, metamodels, languages, tools, transformations or the quality assurance techniques.
3. Identify the *quality-carrying properties* of the target objects and the *product or project characteristics* that they help to achieve. For example the possibility to generate code from models is a quality-carrying property of the modeling tool that reduces the amount of manual coding and provides more consistent code. Identifying the quality-carrying properties is based on several aspects such as:
   o Purpose of the target object.
   o Lifecycle phase (stages of development, maintenance or run-time).
   o Isolated or in relation with other objects: it may be a need to integrate models / languages/ tools/ activities with other models / languages/ tools / activities, or they may need to exchange data. Integration may require consistency, portability, traceability, compatibility etc.
   o Scale of the project.

o Domain-specific or general.

o Lifetime (long-living or not): lifetime has impact on the need for training, documentation, or maintainability.

As discussed by Trendowicz and Punter [25], relations should also be identified.

4. Specify how to evaluate the quality-carrying properties and characteristics; e.g., measuring quantitatively by metrics or subjective evaluation, inspections using checklists or interviewing the users. Specify links that validates that the right thing is measured.

5. Specify association links between the quality-carrying properties and the quality goals. For example, including domain knowledge in a domain specific code generator may reduce the number of certain defect types and thus improve software quality. This should be validated by analyzing the number and the type of defects.

6. Review and evaluate the framework in practice for characteristics such as completeness, orthogonality, parsimony, reusability, flexibility, transparency, relevance and possibility to be adopted.

7. Execute: Execution covers the implementation of quality-carrying properties and evaluation.

The process can support a hierarchical model of goals and quality-carrying properties as well. For example, transformations as a target object may be decomposed to the transformation process and the transformation rules as discussed in the next section.

The differences of the process in Figure 2 and the Dromey's process described in Section 2.3 are introducing target objects in the MDE context, adding the evaluation step and the requirements for evaluating the quality framework. We also work on identifying the quality-carrying properties and the product / project characteristics that MDE can support; i.e., MDQE.

4 Quality of Transformations

4.1 Motivation

A key point in MDE is the transformation of models. This approach has been proven useful both during the development and the maintenance of software systems, allowing refinements, new views or system code to be generated from models. Transformations automate tasks that are either too tedious or complex for most developers to consistently and reliably implement [9]. One can – and should – therefore engineer and evaluate the quality of the transformation itself. For instance, it is important that the output model maintains the properties of the input model, e.g. the transformation produces consistent models [17 and 24].

Other reasons for considering the quality of transformations are due to reuse and runtime concerns. Just like software components and services should be reused when building new systems, so should transformations be reused when developing new transformations. A relevant example of a transformation repository is the ATL Transformation zoo, which is a part of the Eclipse project[1]. Having access to quality

---

[1] http://www.eclipse.org/m2m/atl/atlTransformations/

criteria for transformations would allow meaningful comparison of transformation quality according to a set of chosen quality metrics. When using transformation at runtime, additional quality attributes come into play. In some systems, e.g. safety-critical ones, response times are usually important and, thus, the transformations have to adhere to constraints on timeliness. Also, during runtime adaptation it is even more important that the transformations maintain consistency and reliability among system configurations.

4.2 Applying the Quality Framework

The quality framework for MDE presented in Figure 2 suggests starting with identifying quality goals and target objects. Improving software quality and increase-ing the productivity of software developers are the high-level quality goals which may be achieved by the transformation activity in MDE as the high-level target object. Further, one may discuss the quality of transformations itself. This section suggests target objects for transformation quality.

Kühne writes that a transformation is information on a mapping from one model to another, created by a transformation engineer, for the transformation engine, in order to automate a transformation process [13]. So a transformation can be regarded as a model that describes a transformation function. Hesse, on the other hand, writes that although a transformation can be modeled if one wants to do so, the static model of a transformation should not be confused with its dynamic original [8]. In his view, transformations are processes and not models. These views show how transformations

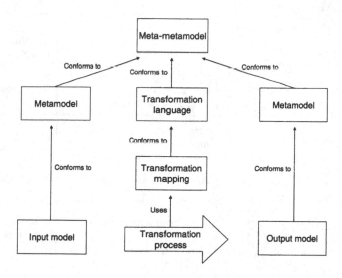

Fig. 3. A transformation is described by its transformation mapping. It takes a model as input and produces a different model as output (we can also view code as a model). Each model – the transformation mapping included – conforms to a metamodel.

have both a dynamic and a static part. To us, a *transformation* denotes the process, while a *transformation specification, model* or *mapping* refers to the description of this process. In our opinion, these parts are equally relevant when considering quality, and they require different approaches.

Figure 3 depicts the transformation process which can be regarded as an operator; i.e., output model=Trans(input model), with numerous properties. As can be seen, there are also additional elements involved in a transformation, which are all candidates for target objects. Our main focus, however, is on the transformation process and mapping. In Table 1 we view these two dimensions of a transformation as the target objects and suggest lower level quality goals with quality-carrying properties and evaluation techniques. These suggestions are not considered as exhaustive.

Table 1. Applying the quality framework on the quality of transformations

Target Object	Quality Goal	Quality-carrying Property	Evaluation
Transformation process	*High performance*	Effective transformation engine [3]	Measure performance
		Select appropriate transformation approach [3]	Measure performance
Transformation model / rules	*Preservation of consistency*	Enforce consistency by tools [7]	Consistency analysis tool, measuring consistency before and after transformation
	Reusability	Modularization, i.e. specialize and chain transformations, and rule inheritance	Inspection
	Simplicity	Few number of rules, i.e. modularization	Measure complexity in the number or size of rules
		Appropriate algorithm	Measure the complexity of algorithms
		Simple output models	Measure complexity and size of the output model [22]
	Compactness	Generic transformations [27]. They contain rules where types of some object types are variables, allowing a single generic rule to handle several situations.	Inspection

5 Conclusion and Future Work

The MDE approach allows us to automate many activities in software development. Since models in MDE are expected to get progressively more complete, precise and executable during development, they can be used to evaluate and verify the quality of design, fix errors and eliminate unwanted complexity, preferably at the early stages of software development. We defined a process for defining a quality framework and based on existing literature, we provided some initial observations on transformation quality related to MDQE.

However, much work is still needed in all the stages defined in Figure 2. We will build further on the quality framework presented here to identify quality goals, quality-carrying properties and evaluation methods for aspects that affect the quality of models and are relevant for our partners in the MODELPLEX project (www.modelplex.org). One of such aspects is identifying quality criteria for Domain-Specific Languages (DSLs) appropriate for modeling large and complex systems. Suggestions for future work on transformations are further analysis of what affects the quality of transformations and to gather empirical evidence on associations between the proposed quality-carrying properties and the quality of generated software. Especially important is the development of tool support for quality engineering, as tools are such an important part of MDE. This would support the execution part of the MDE quality framework.

References

1. Berenbach, B.: Evaluation of Large, Complex UML Analysis and Design Models. In: 26th Int'l Conference on Software Engineering (ICSE 2004), pp. 232–241 (2004)
2. Claxton, J.C., McDougall, P.A.: Measuring the Quality of Models. In: The Data Administration Newsletter (TDAN.com) (visited on June 22 2007), http://www.tdan.com/i014ht03.htm
3. Cuadrado, J.S., Molina, J.G.: Building Domain-Specific Languages for Model-Driven Development. IEEE Softw. 24(5), 48–55 (2007)
4. Daniels, J.: Modeling with a Sense of Purpose. IEEE Softw. 19(1), 8–10 (2002)
5. Dromey, R.G.: Concerning the Chimera. IEEE Software 13(1), 33–43 (1996)
6. Grossman, M., Aronson, J.E., McCarthy, R.V.: Does UML Make the Grade? Insights from the Software Development Community. Info and Softw Tech. 47, 383–397 (2005)
7. Haesen, R., Snoeck, M.: Implementing Consistency Management Techniques for Conceptual Modeling. In: Third International Workshop, Consistency Problems in UML-based Software Development III – Understanding and Usage of Dependency Relationships, pp. 99–113 (2004)
8. Hesse, W.: More Matters on (Meta-) Modeling: Remarks on Thomas Kühne's "Matters". J. Softw Syst Model 5, 387–394 (2006)
9. IBM, http://www.ibm.com/developerworks/rational/library/apr05/brown/index.html
10. IEEE 610.12 IEEE Standard Glossary of Software Engineering Terminology
11. ISO- International Organization for Standardization, ISO/IEC 9126-1, http://www.iso.org/iso/iso_catalogue/catalogue_tc/catalogue_detail.htm?csnumber=2274
12. Krogstie, J.: Evaluating UML Using a Generic Quality Framework. In: UML and the Unified Process, pp. 1–22. Idea Group Publishing (2003)

13. Kühne, T.: Matters of (Meta-) Modeling. J. Softw. Syst. Model 5, 369–385 (2006)
14. Lange, C.F.J., Chaudron, M.R.V.: Managing Model Quality in UML-based Software Development. In: 13th Int'l Workshop on Software Technology and Engineering Practice (STEP 2005), pp. 7–16 (2005)
15. Lange, C.F.J.: Model Size Matters. In: Kühne, T. (ed.) MoDELS 2006. LNCS, vol. 4364, p. 5. Springer, Heidelberg (2007)
16. Lindland, O.I., Sindre, G., Sølvberg, A.: Understanding Quality in Conceptual Modeling. IEEE Software 11(2), 42–49 (1994)
17. Liu, Z., Jifeng, H., Li, X., Chen, Y.: Consistency and Refinement of UML Models. In: Third International Workshop, Consistency Problems in UML-based Software Development III – Understanding and Usage of Dependency Relationships, pp. 23–40 (2004)
18. Mellor, S.J., Balcer, M.J.: Executable UML: a Foundation for Model-Driven Architecture. Addison-Wesley, Reading (2002)
19. Mohagheghi, P., Aagedal, J.Ø.: Evaluating Quality in Model-Driven Engineering. In: Workshop on Modeling in Software Engineering (MISE 2007), In: Proc. of ICSE 2007, p. 6 (2007)
20. Object Management Group's Model Driven Architecture, http://www.omg.org/mda/
21. Paige, R.F., Ostroff, J.S., Brooke, P.J.: Principles for Modeling Language Design. Info. and Softw. Tech. 42, 665–675 (2000)
22. Saeki, M., Kaiya, H.: Model Metrics and Metrics of Model Transformations. In: The First Workshop on Quality in Modeling, pp. 31–45 (2006)
23. Solheim, I., Neple, T.: Model Quality in the Context of Model-Driven Development. In: 2nd International Workshop on Model-Driven Enterprise Information Systems (MDEIS 2006), pp. 27–35 (2006)
24. Straeten, R.: Formalizing Behaviour Preserving Dependencies in UML. In: Third International Workshop, Consistency Problems in UML-based Software Development III – Understanding and Usage of Dependency Relationships, pp. 71–82 (2004)
25. Trendowicz, A., Punter, T.: Quality Modeling for Software Product Lines. In: 7th ECOOP Workshop on Quantitative Approaches in Object-Oriented Software Engineering (QAOOSE 2003), p. 7 (2003)
26. Unhelkar, B.: Verification and Validation for Quality of UML 2.0 Models. Wiley, Chichester (2005)
27. Verró, D., Pataricza, A.: Generic and Meta-Transformations for Model Transformation Engineering. In: Baar, T., Strohmeier, A., Moreira, A., Mellor, S.J. (eds.) UML 2004. LNCS, vol. 3273, pp. 290–304. Springer, Heidelberg (2004)

Doctoral Symposium

Claudia Pons

LIFIA, CONICET, University of La Plata
Buenos Aires, Argentina
cpons@info.unlp.edu.ar

Abstract. The MoDELS 2007 Doctoral Symposium provided a forum for Ph.D. students, conducting research in model-driven software engineering, to discuss their goals, methodology and results at an early stage in their research, in a critical but supportive and constructive environment. The symposium offered an opportunity for the eight student participants to interact with other students at a similar stage in their careers and with the mentoring board composed of five experts in the software modeling field. The students received practical guidance for the completion of the dissertation research and motivation for a research career. This summary offers an overview of the activities that occurred at the Symposium.

1 Introduction

Model-driven software engineering (MDE) is a dynamic new field of research, creating a paradigm shift in the way software applications are designed and maintained. This paradigm proposes the use of models as the basic building blocks, which are used to design and build software. This process is achieved by successively applying model transformations until the executable code is obtained. MDE builds on ideas and experiences from many different fields to produce the novel research needed to drive this paradigm shift.

The MoDELS 2007 Doctoral Symposium provided a forum for PhD. students, conducting research in MDE, to discuss their goals, methodology and results at an early stage in their research, in a critical but supportive and constructive environment. The symposium offered an opportunity for student participants to interact with other students at a similar stage in their careers and with established researchers in the software modeling community. The closed character of this symposium (participation on invitation only) was a premise for deep and constructive discussions.

Each presentation was organized as a mock thesis-defense, with a committee of 5 mentors providing extensive feedback and advice for completing a successful PhD thesis. The research topics presented by student during the symposium covered hot topics in the MDE field such as version control for models, modeling language semantics, methodologies for developing model transformations, model composition, aspects in models, etc.

This year we received 12 submissions from 6 countries. Submissions were judged on originality, overall contribution, technical merit, presentation quality and relevance

H. Giese (Ed.): MoDELS 2007 Workshops, LNCS 5002, pp. 287–292, 2008.
© Springer-Verlag Berlin Heidelberg 2008

to the conference topics. The symposium was intended for students who had already settled on a specific research topic (closely related to model-driven engineering) and had obtained initial results, but still had enough time remaining before their final defence so that they might benefit from the symposium experience. Each submission was reviewed by two mentors from the Selection Committee. The committee finally selected 9 proposals (although one of the students was unable to attend the symposium).

The closing session of the symposium was a panel discussion that was organized in conjunction with the Educator's Symposium. The main topic of the panel was what to teach (and learn) in modeling in order to feel the needs for a research career in industry and/or academia.

2 Organization and Committees

The Symposium was held in conjunction with the ACM/IEEE 10th International Conference on Model Driven Engineering Languages and Systems. It was organized as a whole- day event on October 1st, 2007 in Nashville (TN), USA. The home page of the symposium is at:
    http://sol.info.unlp.edu.ar/models2007ds/

Mentoring Committee

   Jordi Cabot (Universitat Oberta de Catalunya, Spain)
   Alexandre Correa (Universidade Federal do Rio de Janeiro, Brazil)
   Ileana Ober (Université Paul Sabatier, Toulouse, France)
   (chair) Claudia Pons (Universidad Nacional de La Plata, Argentina)
   Dániel Varró (Budapest University of Technology and Economics, Hungary)

Selection Committee

   David Akehurst (University of Kent at Canterbury, UK)
   Thomas Baar (Ecole Polytechnique Fédéral de Lausanne, Switzerland)
   Jean-Michel Bruel (Université de Pau, France)
   Maja D'Hondt (Université des Sciences et Technologies de Lille, France)
   Tom Mens (University of Mons-Hainaut, Belgium)
   Ana Moreira (Universidad Nova de Lisboa, Portugal)
   Ivan Porres (Åbo Akademi University, Findland)

We would like to thank everyone who contributed to the success of the Symposium, specially the experts comprising the committees who supported the review process and the mentoring activities.

3 Summary of Student Presentations

Each student prepared a short paper that was published in the Symposium Proceedings, online at http://CEUR-WS.org/Vol-262. The participating students, along with the titles of their presentations and their affiliation, are (in alphabetical order):

- **Kerstin Altmanninger.** Johannes Kepler University, Linz, Austria.
  Models in Conflict – Towards a Semantically Enhanced Version
  Control System for Models.
- **Michelle Crane.** Queen's University, Kingston, Ontario, Canada.
  Slicing the Three-layer Architecture: A Semantic Foundation
  for Behavioural Specification.
- **Gunter Mussbacher.** University of Ottawa, Canada.
  Aspect oriented User Requirements Notation
- **Hongzhi Liang.** School of Computing, Queen's University, Canada.
  Scenario integration via the transformation and manipulation
  of higher-order graphs.
- **Torbjörn Lundkvist.** Åbo Akademi University, Finland.
  Definition of Visual Language Editors Using Declarative Languages.
- **Jon Oldevik.** University of Oslo, Norway.
  Semantics Preserving Model Composition.
- **Rick Salay.** University of Toronto, Canada.
  Towards a Formal Framework for Multimodeling in Software Engineering.
- **Andres Vignaga.** Universidad de Chile, Chile.
  Methodological Approach to Developing Model Transformations.

This section offers a brief summary of the student presentations. Further information can be found in [1].

First presentation: Michelle Crane presented a research proposal whose overall goal is to contribute to the definition of a formal semantics for UML, and indeed visual behavioral modeling languages in general. Specifically, Michelle's work aims to validate the three-layer semantic architecture, used as a way of explaining the behavioral semantics of UML. The validation includes a definition of the semantics of UML actions and activities, as well as a prototype interpreter.

Second presentation: The doctoral work of Kerstin Altmanninger was focused on "Version Control Systems" (VCS). She explained that for a widespread success of the model-driven paradigm, appropriate tools such as "Version Control Systems" (VCS) are required to adequately support a model-based development process. First attempts to model-based versioning, however, perform conflict detection mainly on basis of a syntactic representation of models without exploiting their semantics. Consequently, Kerstin's proposal consists in defining an approach towards a semantically enhanced VCS, which enables for semantic conflict detection allowing not only a more precise conflict detection but also the determination of a conflict's reason, which can simplify the merge process. This is achieved by introducing the concept of semantic views which explicate a certain aspect of a modeling language's semantics relevant for conflict detection.

Third presentation: Rick Salay's doctoral research is motivated by the fact that the relations between models are seldom just generic "mappings" but instead usually realize an incremental modeling step of some kind. Thus, we have steps like translations, projections, refactorings, refinements, decompositions, merges, the taking of sub-models or aspects, etc. In each case, the relation contains the details of how the elements of the component models in the step are related. These details constitute the syntactic and semantic aspects of a relation while the modeling step enacted by it is its "pragmatic" aspect. In order to provide tool support for modeling with many models, a formalism is required that treats model relations and sets of interrelated models, including their pragmatic aspects, as first class entities that can be typed, characterized using metamodels, reasoned about and manipulated using operators. To achieve this Rick proposes an approach with two key facets. Firstly, a set of interrelated models can be viewed as a kind of hierarchical model – a multimodel. Secondly, relations types can be classified using meta-types corresponding to the typical modeling steps that arise in software engineering. Together, these provide a unified framework in which to express modeling scenarios within software engineering.

Fourth presentation: Torbjörn Lundkvist discussed his work on how to reduce the effort of designing visual interactive editors that can be customized for several domain-specific visual languages. In the context of this research work, a high level of reuse of configurable general editor components is considered to reduce the effort of designing editors for domain specific environments. This research work aims to show that this can be achieved by defining a general language independent editor architecture that is configured to a specific language notation by the use of declarative languages. A declarative language can be used to describe what a system should be like, not how to implement it. He believes this brings many benefits, as the information expressed in a declarative language can be reused by many different components in a tool. The focus of this research work is finding methods that allow the definition of a visual language editor based on declarative languages. This problem can be decomposed into several related areas, including the definition of languages and visual notations, how to edit and manipulate structures expressed in these languages, and the definition of query and model transformation languages.

Fifth presentation: Hongzhi Liang spoke at the Symposium about the integration of different models, such as scenarios. He remarked that this integration is an important component of the requirements engineer's work. If manually performed, the integration operation is error-prone and time consuming. Thus, an integrated computer-aided environment would be desirable. In his work he proposes a framework based on mathematical category theory machinery of algebraic operations with higher-order graphs that provides formalization and a generic pattern for scenario integration. In order to evaluate the proposed framework, Hongzhi has instantiated the framework and is currently developing an experimental tool.

Sixth presentation: The presentation by Andres Vignaga introduced his work on the definition of a methodology specifically aimed at developing and evolving model transformations. The focus will be set on design and implementation activities; however the scope shall include the entire life-cycle. A development process is built on best practices collected throughout the experience of the community. For model transformations, a collection of best practices is still to be completed. To that end, general Software Engineering best practices may serve, at least, as an inspiration. This claim demonstrated to be particularly valid, for example, in model transformation testing. However, adapting existing application development methodologies to the model transformation domain would result unnecessary restrictive. Andres considers more appropriate to come up with a solution that freely combines established knowledge of traditional development with research in the model transformation area, from an MDE-minded point of view. The solution will be a full-edged process expressed as a SPEM model. He proposes a lifecycle based on an iterative and incremental model, and structured in phases; at least one for construction and one for evolution. The scope of the proposed activities includes requirements, analysis, design, implementation, testing and management. Activities will be associated to process roles and input and output work products, organized into disciplines, and refined into steps. Whenever possible, the proposal shall also provide guidance on process elements, especially for activities, steps and work products. Activities and steps will be described in detail, and the procedure for generating output work products from input work products will be made explicit. Work products, in turn, will be precisely described, enabling automatic work product manipulation.

Seventh presentation: Jon Oldevik discussed his work on Semantics Preserving Model Composition. He remarked that separation of concerns (SoC) and modularization are well established strategies for managing complex specifications. However, although software is designed with SoC in mind, the language mechanisms at hand often lead to tangling and scattering of concerns. This has motivated a range of language extensions to support concern specification, such as aspects and subjects in programming and modeling. The current trend is modularization of cross-cutting concerns into units, e.g. aspects that can later be composed by some transformation process (composition/merging/weaving). An important issue in this process is how the semantics of the models/programs is preserved. The focus of Jon's work is on composition and configuration of software specifications from a modeling perspective. Standard mechanisms in modeling (e.g. in UML) provide composition and configuration with well understood characteristics. Examples from UML are class redefinitions, composite structures, composite states, structured activities, interaction decomposition, and package merge. This work goes beyond those by exploring modeling and composition of concerns at a collaboration level, focusing on their architecture and interaction dimensions. The semantics governing such compositions and their results is of particular interest in this regard. Jon proposes to address how generative techniques can be used for implementing the compositions and guide semantics preservation, and also address what semantics preservation means in different modeling and composition contexts.

Eighth presentation: Gunter Mussbacher introduced a proposal on aspect oriented user requirements notation (AoURN). This notation extends the user requirements notation (URN) with aspects and thus unifies goal-oriented, scenario based, and aspect-oriented concepts in one framework. Minimal changes to URN ensure that requirements engineers can continue working with goal and scenario models expressed in a familiar notation. At the same time, concerns in goal and scenario models, regardless of whether these concerns crosscut or not, can be managed across model types. Typical concerns in URN are non-functional requirements (NFRs), use cases and stakeholder goals. As AoURN expresses concern composition rules with

URN itself, it is possible to describe rules in a highly flexible way that prove the modularity, reusability, scalability, and maintainability of URN models. Considering the strong overlap between NFRs and crosscutting concerns, aspects can help bridge the gap between goals and scenarios.

4 Conclusion

The fruitful exchange among mentors and students at the Symposium provided mutual benefit toward addressing promising research ideas for future exploration. After each student presentation, mentors offered words of general advice and suggestions regarding all facets of research. Mentors challenged the student to think about potential weaknesses in his/her thesis. Apart from the technical advices, the following topics were mentioned in the selection reviews and during the symposium,

- *The importance of a literature search.* A characteristic of a good literature search is that it does more than simply enumerate references; a good literature search provides a comparative description that offers a discussion of the advantages and disadvantages of the related work.
- *The importance of setting the focus of the thesis.* It was suggested to the students that they always be able to define their research problem concisely, as well as the associated questions on why the problem is important. The key challenges of the problem need to be understood and explained well to others.
- *The importance of the validation of the results.* The validation of the results of the research is a critical part of evaluating the impact of the contribution and proving the merit of the approach to others.
- *The importance of publishing the results.* Publishing provides feedback from research peers that may be useful to influencing the direction of the dissertation. Also, writing throughout the PhD process eases the trouble of having to write a large dissertation at the end. Writing helps to provide structure to incubating ideas and also offers a historical account of the decisions and rationalizations made along the way.

Additional information can be found in the home page of the symposium, at:
http://sol.info.unlp.edu.ar/models2007ds/

Reference

1. Pons, C. (ed.): Doctoral Symposium at MoDELS 2007 Proceedings. CEUR Workshop Proceedings, vol. 262 (2007), http://CEUR-WS.org/Vol-262, ISSN 1613-0073

Models in Conflict – Towards a Semantically Enhanced Version Control System for Models

Kerstin Altmanninger

Department of Telecooperation, Johannes Kepler University Linz, Austria
kerstin.altmanninger@jku.at

Abstract. For a widespread success of the model-driven paradigm, appropriate tools such as "Version Control Systems" (VCS) allowing for consistency maintenance between concurrently edited model versions are required to adequately support a model-based development process. Initial attempts for graph-based versioning of model artifacts are either tightly coupled to the modeling environment, not flexible with respect to the used modeling language or cannot interpret the model's semantics. On basis of those characteristics, the goal of the outlined thesis presented in this paper is to provide mechanisms to detect conflicting modifications between parallel edited model versions more accurately. By reducing falsely indicated conflicts and by finding additional semantic conflicts, the resolution process can be simplified by means of appropriate techniques for comparison, conflict detection, conflict resolution and merge.

1 Introduction

The shift from code-centric to model-centric software development places models as first class entities in "Model-driven Software Development" (MDSD) processes. A major prerequisite for the wide acceptance of MDSD are proper methods and tools which are available for traditional software development, such as build tools, test frameworks or "Version Control Systems" (VCS). Considering the latter, *optimistic* VCS which do not rely on pessimistic methods (such as locking) are particularly essential when the development process proceeds in parallel such that different developers concurrently modify a model, which may result in concurrent, potentially conflicting modifications. Hence, such conflicting modifications need to be resolved in terms of a model check-in process of the VCS by appropriate techniques for model *comparison, conflict detection, conflict resolution* and *merging*.

In case model developers use different modeling environments to edit their model artifacts and hence the employed modeling tools are not tightly coupled to the VCS, certain approaches that rely on tracking model modifications (e.g., operation-based mechanisms) are not applicable. Instead, a *loosely-coupled* VCS for model artifacts has to be provided which operates in a state-based manner. However, in the light of a growing number of "Domain Specific Languages"

H. Giese (Ed.): MoDELS 2007 Workshops, LNCS 5002, pp. 293–304, 2008.

(DSLs), a *flexible* approach, which can be adapted to the used modeling language, is desirable since most of the VCS for models (e.g., like the commercial tool IBM Rational Software Architect[1] and Odyssey-VCS [1]) solely concentrate on versioning UML models.

For dealing with concurrent modifications on models and specifically for the identification of conflicts, it is necessary not only to consider the logical structure of models in terms of a graph-based representation but also to "understand" the *model's semantics*. For example, concurrent modifications on a model may not result in an obvious conflict when syntactically different parts of the model (e.g., different model elements) were edited. Nevertheless, they may interfere with each other due to side effects [2], thus yielding an actual conflict, which, without considering the model's semantics, would remain hidden. Furthermore, certain conflicts which would be detected by a structural difference computation are not necessarily conflicts because in modeling languages often more than one possibility exists to model a specific case. E.g., in UML activity diagrams, decision nodes as well as conditional nodes are two equivalent ways to express alternative branches in a process, which could in fact result in a conflict if two developers edit a model concurrently by using such different but semantically equivalent modeling concepts. Valuable conflict reports, however, are essential for model developers in order to ensure the correctness of the merged version and consequently to avoid finally merged model artifacts which are not in the model developers intent. Therefore, in this paper, an optimistic, loosely coupled and flexible "Semantically enhanced **Mo**del **Ver**sion Control System" (SMoVer)[2] is laid out which is able to provide some "understanding" of the model's semantics in order to achieve accurate conflict reports by reducing falsely indicated conflicts and by finding additional semantic conflicts.

The remainder of this paper is structured as follows: Section 2 identifies the problems encountered by existing approaches. In Section 3, the research hypotheses are given and the goal of the thesis, presented in this paper, is laid out. In Section 4, the conceptional design of SMoVer is explained. The actual realization status of SMoVer is presented in Section 5 and a comparison to existing VCS is given in Section 6. Finally, Section 7 discusses further prospects beyond the scope of the outlined thesis and Section 8 gives a conclusion.

2   Problem Identification

The challenges emerging when realizing an optimistic, loosely coupled and flexible semantically enhanced VCS for model artifacts, for which an accurate conflict detection process has to be employed, span over the following issues.

Firstly, a check-in process which allows to detect and resolve conflicting modifications between parallel developed model versions [3,4] has to be provided. Secondly, to realize a loosely coupled VCS, the exchange of model artifacts between the VCS and the used modeling environments by model developers has to be

---

[1] http://www-306.ibm.com/software/awdtools/architect/swarchitect/
[2] http://smover.tk.uni-linz.ac.at/

enabled. Thirdly, techniques for a language independent and therefore flexible VCS and finally semantic enrichment techniques and strategies for the VCS's check-in process, for a more precise determination and resolution of conflicts, are needed.

Considering the check-in process in more detail, the succeeding challenges arise. Starting with the first phase of the check-in process, *model comparison* should not rely on text- or tree based approaches (like e.g., CVS[3], Subversion[4] and CoEd [5]) since they do not take the logical structure of models into account which is required for effective model comparison. Hence, existing graph-based approaches have to be employed. Furthermore, for the model comparison process techniques like the use of identifiers (IDs) for model elements or heuristics need to be considered in order to identify created, deleted and updated elements between model versions. In the *conflict detection* phase conflicts should not solely be identified due to the syntactical structure of models but additionally some "understanding" about the artifacts to be versioned should be provided to properly identify conflicts. This is already done by approaches [2,4] in the area of programming languages. They are, however, typically restricted to specific programming languages and therefore cannot immediately be reused in the realm of models. In addition, these approaches rely on formal semantics whereas existing modeling languages, such as UML, commonly do not exhibit a formal description of their semantics not least since being hard and costly to define [6]. Therefore, the *conflict detection* phase requires a more specific approach where semantics can be defined particularly for the purpose of detecting conflicts more precisely. *Conflict resolution*, however, commands for an appropriate identification of the reasons of conflicts, especially when going beyond just supporting syntactical conflict detection. Hence, conflicts need to be visualized and reported adequately to model developers. Model *merging*, finally, must produce a consistent new model which is based on the results of the previous phases and which can be facilitated by model transformations.

3   Research Hypotheses and Goal of the Approach

To tackle the identified challenges in order to achieve a merged model versions with the greatest possibility to be in all developers intents, the following hypotheses have been defined:

- *Model comparison* can be successfully achieved by applying existing graph-based comparison techniques and has to rely on 3-way comparison approaches comprising the concurrently edited model versions and their common ancestor. Therefore, comparison techniques must not solely rely on either using identifiers or heuristics and need to consider any possible change which can be undergone by a model element.
- *Conflict detection* can be conducted on top of the before calculated difference sets and can not rely on full formal specifications of the semantics underlying

---

[3] http://www.nongnu.org/cvs/
[4] http://subversion.tigris.org/

a model since only certain aspects are relevant. Therefore, conflict detection can benefit from the definition of semantics allowing to find conflicts more precisely i.e., by avoiding falsely indicated syntactic conflicts, by finding previously undiscovered semantic conflicts and by finding more precisely defined conflicts.

– *Conflict resolution* can be empowered by reasoning on the semantics of the conflicts detected. Furthermore, adequate visualization techniques have to be provided for model developers.

Hence, the goal of the thesis can be reflected in three areas:

– *Development* of *concepts and techniques* for establishing an optimistic, loosely coupled and flexible semantically enhanced VCS which enables finding and resolving conflicts between model versions more accurate by reducing falsely indicated conflicts and by detecting additional semantic conflicts.
– *Implementation* of *SMoVer* which incorporates the concepts and techniques established by using state of the art technologies and standards (cf. Subsection 5.2).
– *Evaluation* of the quality of the conflict detection and resolution process of SMoVer. Firstly, on basis of a comparison of the loosely coupled approach to other loosely coupled and tightly coupled VCSs for models and secondly, of the power of expressiveness of the technique for semantic enrichment introduced by this approach for different modeling languages.

4 SMoVer - Conceptual Design

In the light of the previously mentioned goals of the approach, SMoVer is proposed. In the following, the conceptual design of the system is explained.

Fig. 1 visualizes a common scenario in a VCS, where two model developers Sally & Harry create personal working copies of a model (V) out of the repository ❶. After they modified their personal working copies with their preferred modeling environment, both want to check-in their version later on to the repository. However, if Sally commits her changed model (V') to the repository first,

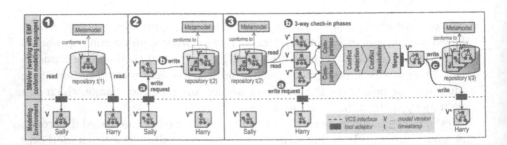

Fig. 1. Workflow in a loosely coupled and flexible VCS

the check-in process can proceed since the current revision in the repository is the direct ancestor of the incoming working copy (Fig. 1, ❷). Harry attempts to commit his changed model (V") later whereas he has to apply a 3-way check-in process because the last revision in the repository is not the one he has checked-out previously (Fig. 1, ❸). This means, the two model versions of Sally and Harry have to be compared with respect to their common ancestor version in the repository, in order to ensure consistency between the parallel edited model versions. This comparison process, however, is based on a graph-based *structural difference* computation between the model versions. The actual comparison of model elements is based on an ID designated in the metamodel. Conflicts, however, may origin due to *creation*, *deletion* or *update* of model elements. By inspecting the structural features, namely the *attributes* and *references* of a model element, one can determine whether the model element as a whole has been updated. In particular four different *update strategies* to detect structural changes in a graph that are of interest for conflict detection are considered:

- **Attribute update (ATT):** The value of an attribute has been changed.
- **Reference update (REFS):** The set of referenced model elements has been changed. For example, new model elements have been created or deleted. Therefore the following possible combinations can be identified: Create-Create (CC), Create-Delete (CD), Delete-Create (DC), Delete-Delete (DD).
- **Role update (ROL):** A model element is referenced or de-referenced by another model element. Again, the four possible combinations of create and delete can be enumerated (CC, CD, DC, DD).
- **Referenced element update (REF):** A referenced model element has undergone an update (e.g., an attribute, reference or role update).

To make this process of detecting conflicts explicit, the following OCL expressions define the derivation of the corresponding conflict sets. In more detail, the conflict set (Con) contains all conflicting model elements and is a union of three further sets that represent update-update (UpdCon), create-create (CrCon) and update-delete (DelCon) conflicts accordingly. The *isUpdated* function determines updated model elements and the function *areNotEqual* checks for the equality (as opposed to the identity) of two model elements.

To represent the model's semantics, so-called *semantic view definitions* are introduced in order to make certain semantic aspects explicit. To start with, the

```
Creates '=(V'-V)
Creates "=(V"-V)
Updates '=V->select (e | e . isUpdated (V,V')
Updates "=V->select (e | e . isUpdated (V,V")
Deletes '=(V-V')
Deletes "=(V-V")

CrCon  =Creates '->intersection (Creates ")->select (e | e . areNotEqual (V',V"))
UpdCon=Updates '->intersection (Updates ")->select (e | e . areNotEqual (V',V"))
DelCon=(Updates '->intersection (Deletes "))->union (Updates "->intersection (Deletes '))

Con=UpdCon->union (CrCon->union (DelCon))
```

Listing 1.1. OCL constraints for the determination of conflict sets

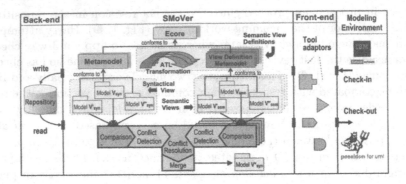

Fig. 2. Conceptual design of SMoVer

basis of the approach is the metamodel which describes the syntax of the models to be versioned. Additionally, to be able to provide semantic conflict detection, a *metamodel representing a certain view* of interest has to be defined. On basis of those metamodels, a *transformation* can be specified such that rules of a model transformation relate the elements of the metamodel (abstract syntax) to which the original model conforms to and the elements of the metamodel representing the definition of the view of interest , the so-called *semantic view*. As a consequence of the transformation realizing a semantic mapping, conflict detection can be carried out on both, model and semantic view (cf. Fig. 2). Conflicts that are determined purely upon the comparison of model versions are *syntactic conflicts* whereas a *semantic conflict* is detected between the representations of the model versions in a semantic view. The actual detection of conflicts in both the original model and the view works analogous to the graph-based detection of structural conflicts.

Compared to the definitions of semantics for programming languages [7] the translational approach, by means of semantic view definitions, is similar to a *translational semantics* specifications. In a translational approach, which can be considered as a special case of denotational semantics, constructs of one language map onto constructs of another, usually simpler language such as machine instructions. Similarly, in SMoVer, a translation into a semantic view that defines a certain facet of interest is proposed for the purpose of conflict detection.

In the following example (cf. Fig. 3) Sally & Harry are working concurrently on a WSBPEL [8] model. Therefore, a language developer previously defined the metamodel and the according IDs and update strategies in SMoVer. Additionally (s)he also set up a semantic view definition which purpose is to detect static semantic conflicts due to addition of "Activities" in a "Sequence" on the same position whereby the model versions cannot be merged because it is not clear which "Activity" comes first. This conflict could also be detected in the syntax if the update strategy REFS:C is considered but then all concurrent insert operations of "Activities" in a "Sequence" would be reported as a conflict whereas probably most of them are no actual conflicts. Therefore the language developer created a view of interest for this circumstance which allows to find the actual

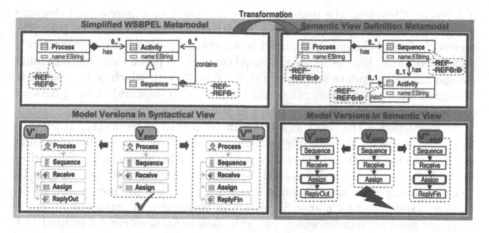

Fig. 3. Conflict detection example

conflicts more accurately than in the syntax. Hence, as shown in Fig. 3, Sally & Harry both insert an "Activity" on the end of the "Sequence" whereas a static semantic conflict arises (Con={Assign(REFS:CC)}) in the semantic view by applying the before mentioned conflict detection algorithm.

However, various view definition possibilities exist for which a categorization is proposed according to three semantic aspects important for versioning, namely: *Equivalent concepts, static semantics* and *behavioral semantics.* Through the definition of "equivalent concepts", which allow the expression of identical meaning in different ways to achieve convenient modeling and readability, falsely indicated conflicts can be avoided. Through the definition of static semantics, which describe static characteristics of a model (like inheritance, constraints [9], or relationships), additional "static semantic conflicts" can be detected. In contrast, through the definition of behavioral semantics, with which the ability arises to detect concurrent changes of the behavior of a model artifact (e.g., by using dependency graphs [2,4,10] or by transforming the model in a different modeling language [11]), additional "behavioral semantic conflicts" emerge.

5   SMoVer - Realization Status

In the following subsections, the realization status of the aforementioned goals are laid out to evince the stated hypotheses.

5.1   Concepts and Techniques

Considering the main purpose of SMoVer in providing accurate conflict reports and the previously defined characteristics of the system, the following concepts and techniques for the check-in phases can be identified.

In a loosely coupled context, the implementation of the algorithm for the *comparison phase* should be a metamodel independent approach to derive model differences. Therefore, the decision has been made to compare model elements using IDs for each element in order to detect model modifications [12]. The representation of changes is grouped in creation, deletion, and changes like in related work [13]. Moreover, the proposed comparison phase considers a detailed categorization of update strategies (cf. Section 4) with which it is possible to fine-grain the kind of modification and therefore also to provide a more detailed conflict report in the succeeding phase of the check-in process.

As mentioned in the previous section and in preceding works [12,14] the *conflict detection phase* is realized by a determination of conflict sets between three versions of a model artifact. Therefore the first work in this context [12] describes the techniques and strategies needed for conflict detection. The second one [14] gives an overview on how to define and work with multiple semantic view definitions exemplified by a specific modeling language and categorizes them in three semantic aspects for which semantic view definitions can be utilized. Additionally it is demonstrated that the proposed conflict detection process allows fine-tuning of the conflicts reported and an increase in effectiveness by reducing falsely indicated syntactic conflicts, by detecting undiscovered semantic conflicts and by more precisely defined semantic conflicts than reported in the syntax. Therefore, from a purely conceptual point of view, the activities needed to be covered by this phase are completed.

For the *conflict resolution phase*, two main conceptual decisions have to be made about the following two challenges. Firstly, how the semantic conflicts can be efficiently traced back from the semantic view and being reported in the syntactical representation and secondly, how the conflicts can be visualized in the VCS to fully support the model developer during the resolution process. Regarding the second activity "visualization", it has to be investigated if the VCS can make use of the concrete syntax of models during this phase and how this concrete syntax can be preserved in the system for specific modeling environments.

5.2 Implementation

In order to define the abstract syntax of a modeling language and a desired semantic view definition, a metamodeling architecture is needed. The "Eclipse Modeling Framework" (EMF)[5] provides Ecore, which is a simplified version of the OMG's metamodeling standard "Meta Object Facility" (MOF) that constitutes the M3 layer, has been chosen. EMF covers persistence support with an XMI serialization mechanism and a reflective API for manipulating EMF models. The creation of a semantic view from a model artifact is realized through the "Atlas Transformation Language" (ATL) [15], which is a QVT-like model-to-model transformation language. Accordingly, the top of Fig. 2 shows the usage of this metamodeling stack in the context of the implementation architecture.

The comparison of the concurrently edited model versions with their common ancestor version is carried out on a generic graph representation of the respective models and views. For this purpose, the EMF reference implementation of

---

[5] http://www.eclipse.org/modeling/emf/

"Service Data Objects" (SDO)[6] is used. SDO is a general framework to realize standardized access to potentially heterogeneous data sources such as databases, XML files or models serialized in XMI. SDO allows to create "datagraphs" from EMF models, which are convenient for comparison purposes as SDO's mechanism to establish the difference between two graphs. These so called "change summaries" are used in SMoVer to store modifications between versions, which are then used by the actual conflict detection mechanism. Hence, the underlying algorithm implements the comparison strategies mentioned in Section 4 and establishes the relevant sets of conflicting elements. Both, the comparison and merge component of the implementation are therefore carried out with Java on top of SDO, EMF and ATL for model transformations in the semantic view(s) and to produce a consistent merged model version.

Summing up, currently not implemented because no concepts and techniques have been defined yet are the tracing back of the computed semantic conflicts in the syntax and visualization techniques which will be focused on in the future.

5.3 Evaluation

For evaluating the feasibility of the approach it is planned to apply a series of case studies firstly, on the *effectiveness of the loosely coupled semantically enhanced check-in phases* applicable on various modeling languages and secondly, on the *power of expressiveness of semantic view definitions* in order to be able to identify semantic conflicts.

To start with, for the loosely coupled check-in phases it will be investigated how effective they are compared to other loosely coupled and tightly coupled VCS for models (cf. Section 6). In a first step, the evaluation is conducted on basis of a syntactic comparison and conflict detection techniques and in a second step with the help of semantic view definitions in order to derive semantic conflicts for exploring the approache's limitations utilized on a specific modeling language. On basis of this comparison between SMoVer and other loosely and tightly coupled VCS, a comprehensive statement about the effectiveness of the approach for a specific modeling language can be made. Nevertheless, an evaluation conducted on one specific modeling language is not sufficient. Because different modeling languages have different power of expressiveness, several modeling languages have to be analyzed for view definition possibilities. The knowledge derived from this evaluation is an overview for which modeling languages this semantically enhanced approach is more (eventually UML) or less (e.g., some DSLs) valuable.

6   Related Work

The most closely related graph-based approach considering model versioning which works in a state-based manner and provides semantic awareness during the conflict detection process is laid out by *Cicchetti et al.* [16]. They propose

---

[6] http://www.eclipse.org/modeling/emf/?project=sdo

to leverage conflict detection and resolution by adopting design-oriented descriptions endowed with custom conflict specifications. Hence, several conflicting situations, which can not be captured by a priori structural conflict detection mechanism can be specified that they refer to as "domain specific conflicts". The developers, however, are forced to enumerate all wrong cases in form of weaving models, which negatively affects the usability and scalability of the approach. Therefore, in the work of *Cicchetti et al.*, each modification, which is not allowed to preserve a design pattern and the design pattern itself have to be specified in a weaving pattern (as they exemplified for the singleton design pattern). Anyway, the approach of *Cicchetti et al.* focuses on the detection of previously undiscovered conflicts in terms of domain specific conflicts only, whereas behavioral semantic conflicts and the detection of previously falsely indicated conflicts as provided by SMoVer are not considered. In addition, so far, the work of *Cicchetti et al.* is solely applicable on UML models as opposed to SMoVer which is flexible by being able to deal with all kind of Ecore-based modeling languages.

Another loosely coupled, semantically enhanced approach called *SemVersion* is presented by *Völkel* [17], which is based on RDF, proposing the separation of language specific features (e.g., semantic difference) from general features (e.g., structural difference or branch and merge). To perform the semantic difference, the semantics of the used ontology language are taken into account. Therefore, assuming using an RDF Schema as the ontology language and two versions (A and B) of an RDFS ontology, *SemVersion* uses RDF Schema entailment on model A and B and infers all possible triples. Now, a structural difference on A and B can be calculated in order to obtain the semantic difference. The approach of *Völkel*, however, does not consider behavioral semantic conflicts and is not flexible to operate on any modeling language.

VCSs which detect conflicts solely due to structural comparison of concurrent edited model versions without incorporating semantics are numerous [18,1,19]. To start with, *Alanen & Porres* [18] provide state-based difference calculation and merging algorithms with which the functionality of a VCS for MOF-based models can be realized. This approach is therefore not tightly coupled to a specific modeling environment and enables developers the parallel editing of model artifacts with their preferred tooling. *Oliveira et al.* [1] presents a graph-based VCS for versioning UML models called *Odyssey-CVS*, aiming to support different UML-based CASE tools in evolving their artifacts. However, *Oliveira et al.* is not flexible in the used modeling language because it can only be applied to UML models. Similarly the tightly coupled approach of *Oda & Saeki* [19] and the commercial tool *IBM Rational Software Architect* are also limited to UML models by the *IBM Rational Software Architect* and additionally ER models by *Oda & Saeki*.

7   Future Challenges

Future challenges are numerous but since current researches in this area are still in the beginning not encountered in context of the outlined thesis presented in this paper. Firstly, as the proposed VCS is loosely coupled to the modeling environment XMI is used to exchange models. Because of the fact that different modeling environments export different XMI representations, so-called tool adaptors for a common XMI representation are essential. Secondly, in a longer prospect, a fully functional semantically enhanced VCS also needs to support versioning capabilities for huge model artifacts which have associations to other models in the same context. Therefore functionalities have to be provided to support versioning beyond one artifact. Thirdly, as metamodels evolve over time, for industrial settings the defined metamodels in the VCS also need to be defined as being able to be versioned. Hence, a smoothly technique has to be invented with which this can be realized considering that all models and according transformations have to be adapted to the new metamodel version as well. The migration of instances is in fact a well known problem from the area of schema evolution [20] e.g., in the field of database systems. Fourthly, an important prerequisite of a VCS for models are visualization techniques needed for the conflict resolution process in order to provide the developer with an adequate overview on the model elements. The challenges which has to be dealt with is how to work with the concrete syntaxes of the different model environments and how those data can be versioned in order to satisfy the the demands of developers.

8   Conclusion

In this paper an optimistic, loosely coupled and flexible VCS called SMoVer, which is extensible to incorporate the semantics needed for the conflict detection process between model versions, is presented. By means of transforming a model into a semantic view, conflicts due to equivalent concepts can be eliminated and hidden static and behavioral semantic aspects can be explicated. Therefore, various semantic view definitions can be established, consequently all of them covering a different semantic aspect. The conflict detection algorithm is applicable on the syntax and all semantic views in the same way. Hence, the joint use of semantic view definitions expressing certain semantic aspects of a modeling language and the employment of graph-based comparison techniques on models and views allows for an accurate conflict detection between versions of model artifacts. This is archived by reducing falsely indicated conflicts and by finding additional semantic conflicts.

References

1. Oliveira, H., Murta, L., Werner, C.: Odyssey-VCS: a flexible version control system for UML model elements. In: Proc. of the 12th Int. Workshop on Software Configuration Management (SCM), ACM Press, New York (2005)
2. Thione, G.L., Perry, D.E.: Parallel changes: Detecting semantic interferences. In: Proc. of the 29th Annual Int. Computer Software and Applications Conf (COMPSAC), vol. 1, pp. 47–56. IEEE Computer Society, Los Alamitos (2005)
3. Westfechtel, B.: Structure-oriented merging of revisions of software. In: SCM, pp. 68–79 (1991)

4. Mens, T.: A state-of-the-art survey on software merging. IEEE Trans. Software Eng. 28(5), 449–462 (2002)
5. Bendix, L., Larsen, P.N., Nielsen, A.I., Petersen, J.L.S.: CoEd – a tool for versioning of hierarchical documents. In: Magnusson, B. (ed.) ECOOP 1998 and SCM 1998. LNCS, vol. 1439, Springer, Heidelberg (1998)
6. Harel, D., Rumpe, B.: Meaningful modeling: What's the semantics of "semantics"? Computer 37(10), 64–72 (2004)
7. Slonneger, K., Kurtz, B.: Formal Syntax and Semantics of Programming Languages: A Laboratory Based Approach. Addison-Wesley Longman Publishing Co., Inc., Boston (1995)
8. OASIS: Web services business process execution language (WSBPEL) standard version 2.0 (April 2007),
   http://docs.oasis-open.org/wsbpel/2.0/wsbpel-v2.0.pdf
9. Object Management Group (OMG): OCL 2.0 specification (June 2005)
10. Shao, D., Khurshid, S., Perry, D.E.: Evaluation of semantic interference detection in parallel changes: an exploratory experiment. In: Proc. of the 23rd IEEE Int. Conf. on Software Maintenance, Paris, France (2007)
11. Ryndina, K., Küster, J.M., Gall, H.: Consistency of business process models and object life cycles. In: Proc. of the 1st Workshop on Quality in Modeling (2006)
12. Altmanninger, K., Bergmayr, A., Kotsis, G., Reiter, T., Schwinger, W.: Models in conflict – detection of semantic conflicts in model-based development. In: Proc. of the 3rd Int. Workshop on Model-Driven Enterprise Information Systems (MDEIS), pp. 29–40. INSTICC Press (2007)
13. Toulmé, A.: Presentation of EMF compare utility. In: Eclipse Modeling Symposium (2006)
14. Altmanninger, K., Bergmayr, A., Kotsis, G., Schwinger, W.: Semantically enhanced conflict detection between model versions in SMoVer by example. In: Int. Workshop on Semantic-Based Software Development in conjunction with the Int. Conf. on Object-Oriented Programming, Systems, Languages, and Applications (OOPSLA) (2007)
15. Allilaire, F., Bézivin, J., Jouault, F., Kurtev, I.: ATL – eclipse support for model transformation. In: Proc. of the Eclipse Technology eXchange Workshop (eTX) of the European Conf. on Object-Oriented Programming (ECOOP) (2006)
16. Cicchetti, A., Rossini, A.: Weaving models in conflict detection specifications. In: Proc. of the 2007 ACM Symposium on Applied Computing (SAC), Seoul, Korea, pp. 1035–1036. ACM Press, New York (2007)
17. Völkel, M.: D2.3.3.v2 SemVersion – versioning RDF and ontologies (2006), http://www.aifb.uni-karlsruhe.de/Publikationen/showPublikation?publ_id=1163
18. Alanen, M., Porres, I.: Version control of software models. In: Yang, H. (ed.) Advances in UML and XML-Based Software Evolution, Idea Group Publishing (2005)
19. Oda, T., Saeki, M.: Generative technique of version control systems for software diagrams. In: Proc. of the 21st IEEE Int. Conf. on Software Maintenance (2005)
20. Roddick, J.F., de Vries, D.: Reduce, reuse, recycle: Practical approaches to schema integration, evolution and versioning. In: Roddick, J.F., Benjamins, V.R., Si-said Cherfi, S., Chiang, R., Claramunt, C., Elmasri, R.A., Grandi, F., Han, H., Hepp, M., Lytras, M., Mišić, V.B., Poels, G., Song, I.-Y., Trujillo, J., Vangenot, C. (eds.) ER Workshops 2006. LNCS, vol. 4231, pp. 209–216. Springer, Heidelberg (2006)

Aspect-Oriented User Requirements Notation: Aspects in Goal and Scenario Models

Gunter Mussbacher

SITE, University of Ottawa, 800 King Edward, Ottawa, ON, K1N 6N5, Canada
gunterm@site.uottawa.ca

Abstract. Technologies based on aspects and applied at the early stages of software development allow requirements engineers to better encapsulate crosscutting concerns in requirements models. The Aspect-oriented User Requirements Notation (AoURN) extends the User Requirements Notation (URN) with aspects and thus unifies goal-oriented, scenario-based, and aspect-oriented concepts in one framework. Minimal changes to URN ensure that requirements engineers can continue working with goal and scenario models expressed in a familiar notation. At the same time, concerns in goal and scenario models, regardless of whether these concerns crosscut or not, can be managed across model types. Typical concerns in URN are non-functional requirements (NFRs), use cases, and stakeholder goals. As AoURN expresses concern composition rules with URN itself, it is possible to describe rules in a highly flexible way that is not restricted by any specific composition language. Aspects can improve the modularity, reusability, scalability, and maintainability of URN models. Considering the strong overlap between NFRs and crosscutting concerns, aspects can help bridge the gap between goals and scenarios. On the other hand, Early Aspects (EA) research can benefit from a standardized way of modeling concerns with AoURN.

Keywords: Aspect-oriented Requirements Engineering, Aspects, Use Case Maps, Goal-oriented Requirement Language, User Requirements Notation.

1 Introduction

By the end of the 1990s, Aspect-Oriented Programming (AOP) [10] allowed software engineers to better encapsulate, at the implementation level, crosscutting concerns (i.e. aspects) which are notoriously difficult to modularize with a single dominant modularization technique alone (e.g. with object-oriented concepts). During the last decade, the research community has shifted its emphasis more to Early Aspects (EA) [8] by investigating ways of addressing crosscutting concerns in requirements and design models. Two of the most common requirements engineering models are goal-oriented and scenario-based models. The User Requirements Notation (URN) [2, 16, 17] is the first and currently only standardization effort that combines goal and scenario models in one language. The Aspect-oriented URN (AoURN) [11, 12, 13, 14] aims to extend URN

H. Giese (Ed.): MoDELS 2007 Workshops, LNCS 5002, pp. 305–316, 2008.
© Springer-Verlag Berlin Heidelberg 2008

with aspect concepts to better manage crosscutting concerns in goal and scenario models. AoURN unifies goal-oriented, scenario-based, and aspect-oriented concepts in one framework.

AoURN consists of Aspect-oriented Use Case Maps (AoUCM), first introduced in [11], and the Aspect-oriented and Goal-oriented Requirement Language (AoGRL), first introduced in [13]. A detailed description of AoUCM and its matching and composition algorithms is available in [12], while AoURN's flexible and exhaustive composition rules based on URN itself are discussed in [13,14]. Qualitative and quantitative assessments of the modularity, reusability, scalability, and maintainability of AoURN are available in [12,14] and [13], respectively. This paper presents AoURN as a whole for the first time, further aligning AoUCM and AoGRL with each other, and discusses the relationship of aspects in goal and scenario models.

In the remainder of this paper, Sect. 2 gives an overview of URN and related work on EA. Section 3 describes AoURN, while Sect. 4 discusses the relationship of aspects in goal and scenario models as illustrated by a sample AoURN model. Section 5 concludes the paper and identifies future work.

2   Background

2.1   User Requirements Notation

The User Requirements Notation (URN) [2,16,17], a standardization effort of the International Telecommunication Union (ITU-T Z.150 Series), contains two complementary modeling languages for goals and scenarios. The Goal-oriented Requirement Language (GRL) is a visual modeling notation for business goals and non-functional requirements (NFRs) of many stakeholders, for alternatives to be considered, for decisions that were made, and for rationales that helped make these decisions. GRL supports reasoning about goals and NFRs with the help of GRL *strategies*. A strategy describes a particular configuration of alternatives in the GRL model. An *evaluation mechanism* propagates these low-level decisions regarding alternatives to satisfaction ratings of high-level stakeholder goals and NFRs. A reusable goal model is called a *GRL catalogue*.

Use Case Maps (UCMs) are a visual scenario notation that focuses on the causal flow of behavior optionally superimposed on a structure of components. UCMs depict the interaction of architectural entities while abstracting from message and data details. UCMs support the definition of *scenarios* including pre- and post-conditions. A scenario describes a specific path through the UCM model where only one alternative at any choice point is taken. Given a scenario definition, a *traversal mechanism* can highlight the scenario path or transform the scenario into a message sequence chart (MSC). Essentially, the traversal mechanism turns the scenario definitions into a test suite for the UCM model.

URN links indicated by small triangles can link any two URN model elements. In particular, links from GRL models to UCM models establish traceability between goal and scenario models in URN. URN is the first and currently only standardization effort to address explicitly, in a graphical way, and in one language goals and scenarios, and the links between them. Current tool support for URN is available with the Eclipse-based jUCMNav tool [15]. Over the last decade, GRL and UCMs have successfully been used for service-oriented, concurrent, distributed, and reactive systems such as telecommunications systems, agent systems, e-commerce systems, operating systems, health information systems, and business process modeling [16].

2.2 Goal-Oriented Requirement Language

The *Goal-oriented Requirement Language* (GRL) [2, 15, 16] combines the Non-Functional Requirements (NFR) framework [6] and i* framework [19] to support reasoning about goal models. The syntax of GRL (Fig. 1) is based on the syntax of the i* framework. A GRL goal graph is an AND/OR graph of *intentional elements* that optionally reside within an *actor boundary*. An *actor* represents a stakeholder of the system. A goal graph shows the high-level business goals and non-functional requirements of interest to a stakeholder and the alternatives for achieving these high-level elements. A goal graph also documents rationales (*beliefs*) important to the stakeholder.

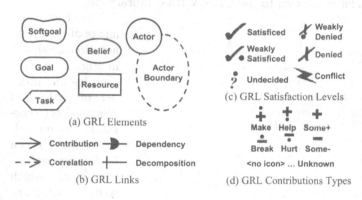

(a) GRL Elements

(b) GRL Links

(c) GRL Satisfaction Levels

(d) GRL Contributions Types

Fig. 1. Basic Elements of GRL Notation

Various kinds of *links* connect the elements in a goal graph, allowing an element to be decomposed into sub-elements, indicating desired impacts and side effects of one element on another element, and modeling relationships between actors (one actor depending on another actor for something). A more complete coverage of the notation elements is available in [2, 15].

From the NFR framework, GRL borrows the notion of an evaluation mechanism that supports reasoning about the goal graph. The decisions of stakeholders are typically documented in the goal graph by the assignment of satisfaction levels (Fig. 1.c) to alternatives (e.g. the chosen alternative is set to Satisficed whereas all other alternatives are set to Denied). Based on these initial settings and the various links with various contribution types (Fig. 1.d), the satisfaction ratings are propagated to higher-level goals and non-functional requirements of stakeholders. jUCMNav keeps track of these initial settings separate from goal graphs in *strategies*. Several strategies can be defined for a goal model, allowing trade-off analyses to be performed by exploring and comparing various

configurations of alternatives. GRL also takes into account that not all high-level
goals and non-functional requirements are equally important to the stakeholder.
Therefore, jUCMNav supports the definition of *evaluation attributes* for intentional elements such as *priority* (high, medium, low, none), which are also taken
into account when evaluating strategies for the goal model [15].

2.3   Use Case Maps

Use Case Maps (UCMs) [2, 4, 16] are ideally suited for the description of functional requirements and, if desired, high-level design. Paths describe the causal
flow of behavior of a system (e.g. one or many use cases). By superimposing paths
over components, the architectural structure of a system can be modeled. In general, components describe any kind of structural entity at any abstraction level
(e.g. classes or packages but also systems, actors, sub-systems, objects, aspects,
hardware). As many scenarios and use cases are integrated into one combined
UCM model of a system, it is possible to use UCM specifications as a base for
further analysis. Undesired interactions between scenarios can be detected, performance implications can be analyzed, testing efforts can be driven based on the
UCM model, and various architectural alternatives can be analyzed. For further
information, the reader is referred to the URN Virtual Library [16].

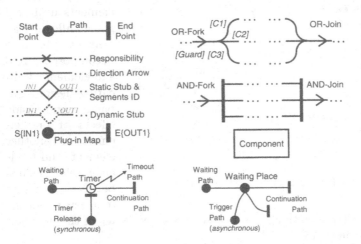

Fig. 2. Basic Elements of UCM Notation

The basic ele-
ments of the UCM
notation are shown
in Fig. 2. A *map*
contains any num-
ber of *paths* and
components (struc-
tural   elements).
UCM models can
be decomposed us-
ing *stubs* which
contain sub-maps
called   *plug-ins.*
Plug-in maps are
reusable units of
behavior and struc-
ture. *Plug-in bind-
ings* define the con-
tinuation of a path
on a plug-in by connecting in-paths and out-paths of a stub with start and end
points of its plug-ins, respectively. A stub may be *static* which means that it
can have at most one plug-in, whereas a *dynamic* stub may have many plug-ins
which may be selected at runtime. A *selection policy* decides which plug-ins of a
dynamic stub to choose at runtime. A more complete coverage of the notation
elements is available in [2, 4].

2.4   Overview of Related Work on Early Aspects

As the Aspect-oriented User Requirements Notation (AoURN) [11, 12, 13, 14] makes use of goal and scenario models, we will briefly review aspect-oriented approaches to requirements engineering that apply to goal and scenario models. For a comparison of these approaches to AoURN or an introduction to aspect concepts, see [11, 12, 13, 14].

In *Aspect-Oriented Software Development (AOSD) with Use Cases* [5], Jacobson and Ng consider a well-written use case a concern. Extension points identify a step in a use case where an extension may occur. Pointcuts in other use cases reference such extension points. Aspects allow use cases to be encapsulated throughout the software development lifecycle.

In *Scenario Modeling with Aspects* [5], Whittle and Araújo model aspectual scenarios with sequence-diagram-like *interaction pattern specifications* (IPS) and *state machine pattern specifications* (SMPS). IPS and SMPS define roles which can be bound to elements in other sequence diagrams and state machines.

In the *Aspectual Use Case Driven Approach* [5], Araújo and Moreira visualize how crosscutting non-functional requirements captured with templates are linked to functional requirements (use case diagrams or sequence diagrams). *Activity pattern specifications* (APS) similar to the aforementioned IPS and SMPS are used. In addition, new use-case relationships allow the impact of one use case on another to be described (restricting or contributing positively/negatively).

Barros and Gomes [3] apply aspect-orientation to activity diagrams (AD) by describing ways to merge stereotyped nodes in one AD with nodes in another. Whittle *et al.* [18] propose a metamodel-based aspect composition technique that uses graph transformation formalisms. This approach can be applied to any model for which a metamodel has been defined. In the UCM community, de Bruin and van Vliet [7] allow behaviour to be added before and after a UCM by explicitly adding "Pre" and "Post" stubs to the UCM. Yu *et al.* [20] identify aspects in goal models based on relationships between functional and non-functional goals. Goal aspects are proposed to address scalability issues but it is pointed out that the goal aspects' syntax still requires further research. Alencar *et al.* [1] identify aspects in i* models. Their extensions to aspect-oriented concepts, however, do not fully separate concerns from other concerns. Kaiya and Saeki [9] propose a pattern-based technique to compose viewpoints. The approach lacks formalization and limits its composition to a simple combinatorial approach instead of more powerful pointcut expressions.

3   Aspect-Oriented User Requirements Notation

The Aspect-oriented User Requirements Notation (AoURN) [11, 12, 13, 14] extends the User Requirements Notation (URN) by defining a *joinpoint model* for the Goal-oriented Requirements Language (GRL) and Use Case Maps (UCMs). All nodes of GRL graphs or UCMs optionally residing within the boundary of an actor or component are deemed to be joinpoints (except for purely visual elements such as direction arrows). Joinpoints can be matched by pointcut expressions. Therefore, pointcut expressions for AoURN models can identify any URN node which in turn can be transformed by the aspect. Joinpoints matched by a pointcut expression are indicated with small, filled diamonds called *aspect markers*, identifying the insertion points for aspectual behavior in the base model.

Pointcut expressions are defined on *pointcut diagrams (graphs and maps)* that are matched against the rest of the model. Pointcut diagrams are standard URN diagrams, allowing the requirements engineer to continue working with familiar models. Pointcut diagrams can also be parameterized for increased matching power by allowing names of modeling elements to contain wildcards ("*") and logical expressions (containing "and", "or", and "not"). The goals, behavior, and structure of aspects are defined on *advice diagrams (graphs and maps)* which are loosely coupled to pointcut diagrams, allowing advice diagrams and pointcut diagrams to be reused independently from each other. Again, advice diagrams are standard URN diagrams. Flexible composition rules are defined with URN itself and are therefore as expressive as URN and not restricted by the capabilities of any particular pointcut language (which for example could only allow standard before/after/around rules).

A *concern* is simply an organizational construct that contains all URN diagrams required to describe a concern. In the case of an *aspect* (i.e., a crosscutting concern), it contains (a) any number of advice diagrams and (b) any number of pointcut diagrams required to describe the aspect. Note that the order aspects are applied to an AoURN model can be specified (not discussed here due to space constraints; see [13]).

Note that in Fig. 3, Fig. 4, and Fig. 5 the aspect markers on the pointcut map, the long-dash-dot-dotted lines without arrowheads, and the dashed arrows are not part of the AoURN notation but have been added to the figures to clearly indicate the connection between the pointcut expression and the base model, the mapping of the pointcut expression to the base model, and the plug-in bindings for the UCM model, respectively. Any AoURN tool must retain the mappings and aspect markers in order to navigate and reason about the AoURN model in an aspect-oriented way. For example, double-clicking on an aspect marker presents a list of all matched pointcut expression to the requirements engineer. Selecting one of them then takes the requirements engineer to the advice diagram where the relevant portion of the diagram is highlighted.

3.1   Aspect-Oriented and Goal-Oriented Requirement Language

Aspect-oriented GRL (AoGRL) [13] adds support for aspect-oriented modeling to GRL. Advice graphs are very similar to the notion of GRL catalogues if the catalogue describes the goal model of only one concern. AoGRL adds the ability to easily include GRL catalogues multiple times into a GRL model by visually specifying a pointcut expression on a pointcut graph. All nodes and links in a pointcut expression are identified by *pointcut markers* (Fig. 3). Actors are implicitly included in the pointcut expression when an element of a pointcut

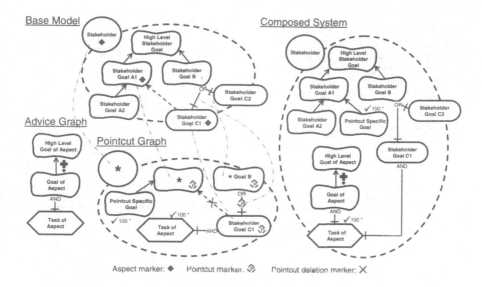

Fig. 3. Basic Elements of AoGRL Notation

expression resides within the boundary of the actor. For example, the pointcut graph in Fig. 3 matches against all goal graphs that contain a softgoal Stakeholder Goal C1 which is an OR decomposition of a softgoal ending with Goal B and has a correlation with another softgoal, all of which have to reside within an actor.

Pointcut graphs contain not just the pointcut expression, but also other elements not identified with a pointcut marker. These elements either reference elements in the aspect's advice graph or are new pointcut-specific elements introduced by the aspect. Connecting these elements with elements of the pointcut expression defines the *composition rule* for the aspect. The composition rule is applied to each joinpoint matched by the pointcut expression. The composition rule may also state that matched elements should be removed with the help of the *pointcut deletion marker* (Fig. 3). Note that the ability to mark elements in a pointcut expression is the only extension required for the jUCMNav tool in order to specify AoGRL models. The composition rule in Fig. 3 stipulates that Task of Aspect and Pointcut Specific Goal are to be connected to Stakeholder Goal C1 and the matched softgoal, respectively. Furthermore, the correlation between Stakeholder Goal C1 and the matched softgoal is to be removed. The composed system is shown on the right side of Fig. 3 as a traditional GRL graph.

3.2 Aspect-Oriented Use Case Maps

Aspect-oriented Use Case Maps (AoUCM) [11, 12, 14] extend UCMs with the ability to specify *pointcut stubs*, thus enabling aspect-oriented modeling. Pointcut stubs (Fig. 4) are structurally the same as dynamic stubs but have a slightly different semantic meaning (indicated by the P in the dynamic stub symbol). While dynamic stubs contain plug-in maps that further describe the structure

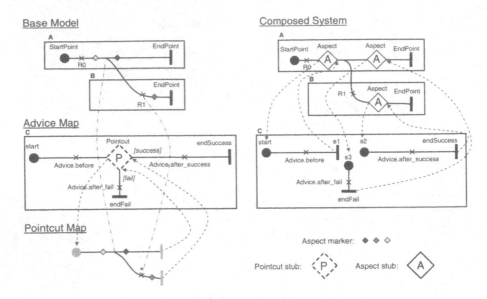

Fig. 4. Basic Elements of AoUCM Notation

and behavior of a system, pointcut stubs contain zero or more pointcut maps that visually describe pointcut expressions. This is the only semantic change to traditional UCMs required in order to model aspects with AoUCM. Note that the ability to mark stubs as a pointcut stub is also the only extension required for the jUCMNav tool in order to specify AoUCM models.

An advice map (Advice Map in Fig. 4) describes the behavior and structure of an aspect and differs from a traditional map (Base Model in Fig. 4) only in that it contains one or more pointcut stubs. For example, the pointcut stub in Fig. 4 contains a pointcut map that matches against all maps that contain an OR-fork followed by a responsibility on at least one branch. Start and end points without labels on a pointcut map are not included in the match but only denote the beginning and end of the pointcut expression to be matched (therefore they are shown in gray in Fig. 4). Although not shown here, a pointcut map may contain UCM components. In fact, any behavioral or structural UCM modeling element can be used on a pointcut map, allowing a wide array of partial maps to be matched.

The way a pointcut stub is connected to the rest of the advice map visually defines the *composition rule* for the aspect. Pointcut expressions and composition rules are therefore clearly separated. Figure 4 shows that Advice.before must be inserted before the joinpoint identified by the expression in the pointcut stub. Advice.after_returning and Advice.after_throwing are inserted after the identified joinpoint in the success case and fail case, respectively. In addition to the simple before and after composition rules, AoUCM can also easily model around, loop, concurrency, and interleaving composition rules [14]. The composed system is shown in a traditional UCM model on the right side of Fig. 4 with the help of *aspect stubs* (regular stubs that are used to insert aspect behavior). For more details on the visualization of the composed system and the techniques used to carry out composition in AoUCM see [12].

4 On the Relationship of Goal and Scenario Aspects

AoURN's ability to encapsulate NFRs as well as use cases in both model types helps bridge the gap between goal and scenario models. This gap is further narrowed by URN traceability links between modeling elements of goal and scenario aspects. Fig. 5 shows a simplified version of the YKeyK model. YKeyK stands for Your Key Knows, a system that allows drivers to find their car in a car park by following directions shown on a small display of the car key.

The AoURN model contains three concerns, one each for the Driver, YKeyK, and Car Park stakeholders, and two aspects, one for the use case UC002 and one for the Performance NFR. A stakeholder's concerns (i.e., the goals and alternatives related to a stakeholder) are modeled separately for each stakeholder on a goal graph (Fig. 5.a to c). The use case aspect contains the UC002 Pointcut Graph and the UC002 UCMs (Fig. 5.d, f, and h). The NFR aspect contains the Performance Pointcut Graph and the Performance Catalogue (Fig. 5.e and g).

The use case aspect in the goal model directly crosscuts the three stakeholder concerns while the performance aspect crosscuts the stakeholder concerns via the shown use case (as well as other use cases in the complete model). In the goal model, the use case pointcut expresssion matches the three intentional elements in Fig. 5.a to c as indicated by the aspect markers, thus adding the use case aspect to the stakeholder concerns. The performance pointcut expression matches the two dependencies in Fig. 5.d, thus adding the Handle Response Time task to the target of the dependency (the goals with the aspect markers in the YKeyK and Car Park actors of Fig. 5.d). In addition, the Performance Pointcut Graph stipulates that Performance goals have to be added to the actors in which the source and target of the dependency reside. Finally, URN links trace the Driver and YKeyK actors to their UCM components and the three tasks in Fig. 5.d to elements in their UCMs in Fig. 5.f and h.

The use case aspect in the scenario model contains three UCMs. Search for Car describes the main purpose of this aspect. The search, however, requires topology information about the car park which is transmitted when the car enters the car park. As this information is only required by the search capability but must take place during the execution of the Enter Car Park use case (not shown due to space constraints), the required responsibilities are added with the help of an aspect (Fig. 5.f) to the setup stage after the prepare price list responsibility in the Enter Car Park use case.

The use case in the YKeyK example shows that an aspect in AoGRL can be traced to an aspect in AoUCM. Often, use cases are not crosscutting in a scenario model but rather peers to each other. When modeled in AoGRL, however, use cases are usually crosscutting. With AoURN, the crosscutting use cases can be properly encapsulated even in goal models.

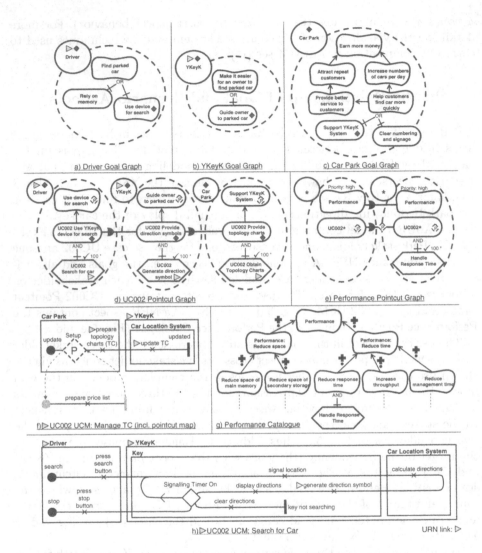

Fig. 5. AoURN Model of YKeyK System

Though not shown in the simplified YKeyK model, the performance aspect can also be traced to the scenario model. In this case, however, there are many ways of achieving performance improvements (e.g. caching, concurrency, ...). Each should be modeled as a separate concern in AoUCM. Clearly, there is a one-to-many relationship between crosscutting concerns in AoGRL and AoUCM. Cases, however, exist where aspects in AoGRL are not traced to any aspects in AoUCM and vice versa. AoUCM can model non-functional requirements that can be expressed as scenarios. AoGRL, however, can model a much larger class of non-functional requirements. For example, the quality of a software product may be modeled in an AoGRL graph and it may be decided that inspections are the solution for this goal. This solution cannot be modeled in AoUCM (or UCM for that matter). Similarly, new aspects may appear in AoUCM models since there is a difference in the abstraction levels of goal models and scenario models. Whatever the relationship between aspects in goal and scenario models may be, AoURN aspects can encapsulate crosscutting concerns across the two model types and URN links allow keeping track of these relationships.

5   Conclusion and Future Work

The Aspect-oriented User Requirements Notation (AoURN) extends the abstract syntax, the concrete syntax, and the semantics of URN with aspect-oriented concepts, hence unifying goal, scenario, and aspect concepts in one framework. AoURN helps clarify the relationship between aspects in goal and scenario models, allowing clearer management of major concerns in goal models that crosscut scenario models and vice versa (e.g. non-functional requirements and use cases). AoURN uses flexible composition rules that are only limited by the expressiveness of URN itself (as opposed to a particular composition language). While some support for aspect-oriented modeling is available in the jUCMNav tool as a proof of concept, further support for matching and composition is currently at the prototyping stage and has yet to be officially released in jUCMNav. Such support will ensure that aspect markers are added to AoURN models and that AoURN models can be navigated with the help of aspect and pointcut markers. Furthermore, additional qualitative assessments of AoURN with respect to desirable properties of aspect-oriented requirements models and quantitative assessments of AoURN based on metrics for aspect-oriented requirements models adapted for URN and AoURN are required. Finally, the relationship of aspects, GRL strategies, and UCM scenarios should be clarified and the applicability of advanced URN research to AoURN should be investigated (e.g. feature interaction, business process modelling, performance analysis, product lines, or modeling support for inherently existing communication aspects in UCM).

Acknowledgments. This research was supported by NSERC, through its programs of Discovery Grants and Postgraduate Scholarships, and by ORNEC.

References

1. Alencar, F., Moreira, A., Araújo, J., Castro, J., Silva, C., Mylopoulos, J.: Towards an Approach to Integrate i* with Aspects. In: 8th Intl. Bi-Conf. Wksh. on Agent-Oriented Inf. Systems (AOIS 2006) at CAiSE 2006, Luxembourg (June 2006)
2. Amyot, D.: Introduction to the User Requirements Notation: Learning by Example. Computer Networks 42(3), 285–301 (June 21, 2003)
3. Barros, J.-P., Gomes, L.: Toward the Support for Crosscutting Concerns in Activity Diagrams: a Graphical Approach. In: Workshop on Aspect-Oriented Modelling (held with UML 2003), San Francisco, California, USA (October 2003)
4. Buhr, R.J.A., Casselman, R.S.: Use Case Maps for Object-Oriented Systems. Prentice-Hall, Englewood Cliffs (1996)

5. Chitchyan, R., et al.: Survey of Analysis and Design Approaches. AOSD-Europe Report ULANC-9 (May 2005) (accessed November 2007), http://www.aosd-europe.net/deliverables/d11.pdf

6. Chung, L., Nixon, B.A., Yu, E., Mylopoulos, J.: Non-Functional Requirements in Software Engineering. Kluwer Academic Publishers, Dordrecht (2000)

7. de Bruin, H., van Vliet, H.: Quality-Driven Software Architecture Composition. Journal of Systems and Software 66(3), 269–284 (June 15, 2003)

8. Early Aspects website (accessed November 2007), http://www.early-aspects.net/

9. Kaiya, H., Saeki, M.: Weaving Multiple Viewpoint Specifications in Goal-Oriented Requirements Analysis. In: 11th Asia-Pacific Software Eng. Conf. (APSEC 2004), Busan, Korea, pp. 418–427. IEEE Computer Society Press, Los Alamitos (November 2004)

10. Kiczales, G., Lamping, J., Mendhekar, A., Maeda, C., Lopes, C., Loingtier, J.-M., Irwin, J.: Aspect-Oriented Programming. In: Aksit, M., Matsuoka, S. (eds.) ECOOP 1997. LNCS, vol. 1241, pp. 220–242. Springer, Heidelberg (1997)

11. Mussbacher, G., Amyot, D., Weiss, M.: Visualizing Aspect-Oriented Requirements Scenarios with Use Case Maps. In: International Workshop on Requirements Engineering Visualization (REV 2006), Minneapolis, USA (September 2006)

12. Mussbacher, G., Amyot, D., Weiss, M.: Visualizing Early Aspects with Use Case Maps. In: Rashid, A., Aksit, M. (eds.) Transactions on Aspect-Oriented Software Development III. LNCS, vol. 4620, pp. 105–143. Springer, Heidelberg (2007)

13. Mussbacher, G., Amyot, D., Araújo, J., Moreira, A., Weiss, M.: Visualizing Aspect-Oriented Goal Models with AoGRL. In: 2nd International Workshop on Requirements Engineering Visualization (REV 2007), New Delhi, India (October 2007)

14. Mussbacher, G., Amyot, D., Whittle, J., Weiss, M.: Flexible and Expressive Composition Rules with Aspect-oriented Use Case Maps (AoUCM). In: 10th International Wksh. on Early Aspects (EA 2007), Vancouver, Canada (March 13, 2007)

15. Roy, J.-F.: Requirements Engineering with URN: Integrating Goals and Scenarios. MSc. thesis, OCICS, University of Ottawa, Canada (2007) (accessed November 2007), http://www.softwareengineering.ca/jucmnav

16. URN Virtual Library (accessed November 2007), http://www.usecasemaps.org/pub

17. User Requirements Notation (URN) - Language Requirements and Framework, ITU-T Recommendation Z.150. Geneva, Switzerland (February 2003) (accessed November 2007), http://www.itu.int/ITU-T/publications/recs.html, (accessed November 2007), http://www.UseCaseMaps.org/urn

18. Whittle, J., Moreira, A., Araújo, J., Jayaraman, P., Elkhodary, A., Rabbi, R.: An Expressive Aspect Composition Language for UML State Diagrams. In: Engels, G., Opdyke, B., Schmidt, D.C., Weil, F. (eds.) MODELS 2007. LNCS, vol. 4735, pp. 514–528. Springer, Heidelberg (2007)

19. Yu, E.: Modeling Strategic Relationships for Process Reengineering. Ph.D. thesis, Department of Computer Science, University of Toronto, Canada (1995)

20. Yu, Y., Leite, J.C.S.d.P., Mylopoulos, J.: From Goals to Aspects: Discovering Aspects from Requirements Goal Models. In: 12th International Requirements Engineering Conference (RE 2004), Kyoto, Japan (September 2004)

Educators' Symposium

Miroslaw Staron

Software Engineering and Management
Department of Applied IT,
IT University of Göteborg,
Sweden
miroslaw.staron@ituniv.se

Abstract. Models are an integral part of every engineering discipline, as they become in software engineering. Modeling can be done in many ways and with different levels of formality. Teaching modeling is as important as the modeling itself since it educates the future engineers in good modeling practices. Without proper education in modeling software engineering cannot evolve into mature engineering discipline. This year's symposium was devoted to invited talks by practitioners and researchers who teach modeling and cooperate with industry. This document summarizes the symposium and the main discussion points. It also outlines the main future research directions in education in modeling.

1 Introduction

Model-driven development approaches and technologies for software-based systems, in which development is centered round the manipulation of models, raise the level of abstraction and thus improve our abilities to develop complex systems. A number of approaches and tools have been proposed for the model-driven development (MDD) of software-based systems, for example UML, model-driven architecture (MDA), and model-integrated computing (MIC). Using models as the primary artifacts in software engineering shifts the focus of the existing software engineering methods from code to models. As the code is the secondary artifact, techniques for estimations, verification and validation techniques, etc. need to be adjusted to take models as inputs. In parallel to transitioning from code centric to model driven development, a transition can be observed from programming oriented, computer science education, to model based software engineering education. Together, these transitions pose new requirements on knowledge goals for students, namely placing more focus on the learning abstract thinking, designing, and creating modeling languages rather than algorithms.

The educators' symposium at the MoDELS conference, the premier conference devoted to the topic of model-driven engineering of software-based systems, is intended as a forum where educators, researchers, practitioners, and trainers can meet to discuss model-driven development education from three perspectives:

- modeling-related content of courses and curricula: describing what should be taught to students

H. Giese (Ed.): MoDELS 2007 Workshops, LNCS 5002, pp. 317–319, 2008.

- pedagogical approaches, theories, and practices: describing how the material should be taught to increase students' learning process
- use of course materials and technology in the classroom: describing how textbooks, modeling tools, and other technology can be used to increase the students' learning process

Industrial training courses are of particular importance for the community as they provide the possibility to interact between academic and industrial teaching methods and practices. This kind of contributions is particularly encouraged.

The leading topic for the symposium in 2007 is transitioning from the traditional, programming oriented, curricula/courses to modern, model based, software engineering curricula/courses. An important aspect is how modeling courses integrate with students' career paths (e.g. how useful are modeling skills for the students' careers).

2 Summary

The main part of the symposium comprised of invited talks and the surrounding discussions.

The first talk was given by Lars Pareto from the IT University of Göteborg in Sweden on teaching domain specific modeling to undergraduate students. The speaker has an extensive experience in teaching and working closely with industry. In his talk he described experiences from teaching Microsoft's Domains Specific Language Toolkit in a software architecture course. The results showed that thanks to their background in modeling, the students were able to learn and use in practice domain specific modeling much faster than expected (1 week instead of 4).

The second talk was given by Thomas Kuehne from Darmstadt University of Technology in Germany on teaching formal modeling with Alloy. The speaker has an extensive experience with meta-modeling and teaching at both graduate and post-graduate levels. The talk communicated the author's experiences with teaching formal methods using graphical notations and Alloy as a modeling language.

The third talk was given by Robert France from Colorado State University in Colorado, USA on using a common repository of models in education. The talk described the initiative undertaken by the Colorado State University to build such a common repository – ReMODD.

The invited talks were complemented with position papers and short papers. The papers discussed issues in teaching various levels of formalities to undergraduate students. One of the papers was elected as a best paper, which is under publication in Information and Software Technology journal. The paper, titled "Students can get excited about Formal Methods: a model-driven course on Petri-Nets, Metamodels and Graph Grammars", describes experiences in teaching formalities to students in the software engineering curriculum. It is a representative contribution for this year's symposium topic.

In addition to paper presentations, the symposium contained discussions after each talk and a joint panel with the doctoral symposium at the end of the day. The goal of the panel was to gather teachers, students, researchers, and industry professionals to address the issues important when teaching modeling. Different roles of the participants provided a unique forum to discuss issues important in preparing future professionals for effective and efficient use of models. The outcome of the panel discussions included such conclusions as:

- modeling skills are more important than modeling notations,
- industry-like modeling in education should be essential part of courses and curricula, or
- tools are equally important as modeling processes in education as it is the tools that "dictate" the processes in practice.

It seems that the idea of a joint panel was well-received by the participants of both symposia.

3 Future Directions

Software engineering is a relatively new field with methods different than in other engineering disciplines. The use of models, however, is as important as in other disciplines to enforce the required degree of formality in describing software; the formality which, to a large extent, can help increase the quality of resulting software products.

Using models in education is a prevailing trend in all modern software engineering and computer science curricula. The plethora of methods and tools indicates, though, that modeling in software engineering is still in its maturing phase. Therefore it is important that the dialogue between researchers, teachers, students, and industry professionals is maintained to ensure the proper evolution of the field and bridging the gap between academia and industry. Educators' symposium provides such a discussion forum, which in the coming years should evolve into a forum of exchanging experiences through invited talks rather than paper presentations. The discussions and dialogues contribute to changes in course contents and industry expectations from modeling education. The industry also becomes more aware of the problems related to sharing industry models with academia in exchange for optimal education.

The goal of the symposium in 2008 will be to find ways for showing benefits of modelling in a way that is pedagogically effective and attractive to the students. It shall also try to result in recommendations for placing the modelling courses in the overall software development educational path, this not being limited to UML fundamentals but also focused on showing the importance and place of modelling in the overall path from business/environment to code.

Author Index

Lecture Notes in Computer Science

Sublibrary 2: Programming and Software Engineering

For information about Vols. 1– 4470
please contact your bookseller or Springer

Vol. 4821: J. Bennedsen, M.E. Caspersen, M. Kölling (Eds.), Reflections on the Teaching of Programming. X, 261 pages. 2008.

Vol. 4807: Z. Shao (Ed.), Programming Languages and Systems. XI, 431 pages. 2007.

Vol. 4799: A. Holzinger (Ed.), HCI and Usability for Medicine and Health Care. XVI, 458 pages. 2007.

Vol. 4789: M. Butler, M.G. Hinchey, M.M. Larrondo-Petrie (Eds.), Formal Methods and Software Engineering. VIII, 387 pages. 2007.

Vol. 4767: F. Arbab, M. Sirjani (Eds.), International Symposium on Fundamentals of Software Engineering. XIII, 450 pages. 2007.

Vol. 4765: A. Moreira, J. Grundy (Eds.), Early Aspects: Current Challenges and Future Directions. X, 199 pages. 2007.

Vol. 4764: P. Abrahamsson, N. Baddoo, T. Margaria, R. Messnarz (Eds.), Software Process Improvement. XI, 225 pages. 2007.

Vol. 4762: K.S. Namjoshi, T. Yoneda, T. Higashino, Y. Okamura (Eds.), Automated Technology for Verification and Analysis. XIV, 566 pages. 2007.

Vol. 4758: F. Oquendo (Ed.), Software Architecture. XVI, 340 pages. 2007.

Vol. 4757: F. Cappello, T. Herault, J. Dongarra (Eds.), Recent Advances in Parallel Virtual Machine and Message Passing Interface. XVI, 396 pages. 2007.

Vol. 4753: E. Duval, R. Klamma, M. Wolpers (Eds.), Creating New Learning Experiences on a Global Scale. XII, 518 pages. 2007.

Vol. 4749: B.J. Krämer, K.-J. Lin, P. Narasimhan (Eds.), Service-Oriented Computing – ICSOC 2007. XIX, 629 pages. 2007.

Vol. 4748: K. Wolter (Ed.), Formal Methods and Stochastic Models for Performance Evaluation. X, 301 pages. 2007.

Vol. 4741: C. Bessière (Ed.), Principles and Practice of Constraint Programming – CP 2007. XV, 890 pages. 2007.

Vol. 4735: G. Engels, B. Opdyke, D.C. Schmidt, F. Weil (Eds.), Model Driven Engineering Languages and Systems. XV, 698 pages. 2007.

Vol. 4716: B. Meyer, M. Joseph (Eds.), Software Engineering Approaches for Offshore and Outsourced Development. X, 201 pages. 2007.

Vol. 4709: F.S. de Boer, M.M. Bonsangue, S. Graf, W.-P. de Roever (Eds.), Formal Methods for Components and Objects. VIII, 297 pages. 2007.

Vol. 4680: F. Saglietti, N. Oster (Eds.), Computer Safety, Reliability, and Security. XV, 548 pages. 2007.

Vol. 4670: V. Dahl, I. Niemelä (Eds.), Logic Programming. XII, 470 pages. 2007.

Vol. 4652: D. Georgakopoulos, N. Ritter, B. Benatallah, C. Zirpins, G. Feuerlicht, M. Schoenherr, H.R. Motahari-Nezhad (Eds.), Service-Oriented Computing ICSOC 2006. XVI, 201 pages. 2007.

Vol. 4640: A. Rashid, M. Aksit (Eds.), Transactions on Aspect-Oriented Software Development IV. IX, 191 pages. 2007.

Vol. 4634: H. Riis Nielson, G. Filé (Eds.), Static Analysis. XI, 469 pages. 2007.

Vol. 4620: A. Rashid, M. Aksit (Eds.), Transactions on Aspect-Oriented Software Development III. IX, 201 pages. 2007.

Vol. 4615: R. de Lemos, C. Gacek, A. Romanovsky (Eds.), Architecting Dependable Systems IV. XIV, 435 pages. 2007.

Vol. 4610: B. Xiao, L.T. Yang, J. Ma, C. Muller-Schloer, Y. Hua (Eds.), Autonomic and Trusted Computing. XVIII, 571 pages. 2007.

Vol. 4609: E. Ernst (Ed.), ECOOP 2007 – Object-Oriented Programming. XIII, 625 pages. 2007.

Vol. 4608: H.W. Schmidt, I. Crnković, G.T. Heineman, J.A. Stafford (Eds.), Component-Based Software Engineering. XII, 283 pages. 2007.

Vol. 4591: J. Davies, J. Gibbons (Eds.), Integrated Formal Methods. IX, 660 pages. 2007.

Vol. 4589: J. Münch, P. Abrahamsson (Eds.), Product-Focused Software Process Improvement. XII, 414 pages. 2007.

Vol. 4574: J. Derrick, J. Vain (Eds.), Formal Techniques for Networked and Distributed Systems – FORTE 2007. XI, 375 pages. 2007.

Vol. 4556: C. Stephanidis (Ed.), Universal Access in Human-Computer Interaction, Part III. XXII, 1020 pages. 2007.

Vol. 4555: C. Stephanidis (Ed.), Universal Access in Human-Computer Interaction, Part II. XXII, 1066 pages. 2007.

Vol. 4554: C. Stephanidis (Ed.), Universal Acess in Human Computer Interaction, Part I. XXII, 1054 pages. 2007.

Vol. 4553: J.A. Jacko (Ed.), Human-Computer Interaction, Part IV. XXIV, 1225 pages. 2007.

Vol. 4552: J.A. Jacko (Ed.), Human-Computer Interaction, Part III. XXI, 1038 pages. 2007.

Vol. 4551: J.A. Jacko (Ed.), Human-Computer Interaction, Part II. XXIII, 1253 pages. 2007.

Vol. 4550: J.A. Jacko (Ed.), Human-Computer Interaction, Part I. XXIII, 1240 pages. 2007.

Vol. 4542: P. Sawyer, B. Paech, P. Heymans (Eds.), Requirements Engineering: Foundation for Software Quality. IX, 384 pages. 2007.

Vol. 4536: G. Concas, E. Damiani, M. Scotto, G. Succi (Eds.), Agile Processes in Software Engineering and Extreme Programming. XV, 276 pages. 2007.

Vol. 4530: D.H. Akehurst, R. Vogel, R.F. Paige (Eds.), Model Driven Architecture - Foundations and Applications. X, 219 pages. 2007.

Vol. 4523: Y.-H. Lee, H.-N. Kim, J. Kim, Y.W. Park, L.T. Yang, S.W. Kim (Eds.), Embedded Software and Systems. XIX, 829 pages. 2007.

Vol. 4498: N. Abdennahder, F. Kordon (Eds.), Reliable Software Technologies - Ada-Europe 2007. XII, 247 pages. 2007.

Vol. 4486: M. Bernardo, J. Hillston (Eds.), Formal Methods for Performance Evaluation. VII, 469 pages. 2007.